SLAVERY IN INDIAN COUNTRY

SLAVERY
—— IN ——
INDIAN
COUNTRY

The Changing Face of Captivity
in Early America

CHRISTINA SNYDER

HARVARD UNIVERSITY PRESS
Cambridge, Massachusetts, and London, England

First Harvard University Press paperback edition, 2012

Library of Congress Cataloging-in-Publication Data

Snyder, Christina.
Slavery in Indian country : the changing face of captivity in early America /
Christina Snyder.
p. cm.
Includes bibliographical references and index.
ISBN 978-0-674-04890-4 (cloth: alk. paper)
ISBN 978-0-674-06423-2 (pbk.)
1. Indian captivities—Southern States—History. 2. Indian slaves—Southern States—
History. 3. Slavery—Southern States—History. 4. Indians of North America—Southern
States—History. I. Title.

E85.S69 2010
970.004'97—dc22 2009038803

For Mike, Theda, and my family

CONTENTS

FIGURES

SLAVERY IN INDIAN COUNTRY

INTRODUCTION

A lready the Great Sun had wailed the death cry, which reverberated across the Grand Village of the Natchez as inhabitants joined their chief in mourning the death of his brother. The head servant had heard the cry clearly from where he worked within the house of Tattooed Serpent, just across the public square from the raised mound where the Great Sun lived. The servant glanced down at the litter that held the body of his master. Dressed in regalia befitting his high station, Tattooed Serpent looked as though he were about to depart on some diplomatic mission. The servant had painted his master's face red with vermilion, placed his best moccasins on his feet, and adorned his head with a crown of swan feathers. Though partially obscured by his clothing, Tattooed Serpent's skin graphically told of his great deeds in war and of the spiritual power he held by virtue of his noble birth. On the litter, the head servant placed Tattooed Serpent's arms, calumets, and a red cane pole marked with forty-six rings—the number of enemies his master had dispatched in war before his death.

According to custom, the head servant continued to prepare food for his master. Seeing that Tattooed Serpent did not eat, the servant asked him whether the meal was not to his liking. Still, his master did not move or draw breath. Aloud, the servant concluded that his master's days in This World—the realm of human beings—had come to an end; his soul would soon depart for the spirit country. The servant released his own doleful cry, which came back to him in a thousand voices.

Funeral arrangements consumed the next few days. Twice a day, retainers of Tattooed Serpent proceeded out onto the public square, where they performed the death dance before all the people. Among this group were those who had served Tattooed Serpent, including his adviser, doctor, pipe bearer, and the head servant; they were joined by his two wives, both necessarily of low birth; a noblewoman who had been a great friend of

Tattooed Serpent; and, finally, a few of the community's older women, who rejoiced in the opportunity to bring such honor upon their kin.

On the fourth and final day of ceremonies, the master of ceremonies asked the Great Sun for permission to begin the funeral. Although greatly saddened by the death of his brother, the Great Sun found comfort in the fact that so many subjects would serve his spirit. Having received permission from the Great Sun, the master of ceremonies crossed the public square, paused before Tattooed Serpent's house, and saluted him with an honorary shout. He then wailed the death cry, which was repeated by all the Natchez gathered for the ceremony. Those who had participated in the previous days' death dances filed out of Tattooed Serpent's house and took their places in the funeral procession. Holding the body of his dead infant, a man joined their ranks; this child, sacrificed to serve Tattooed Serpent in the spirit world, would raise his father up into the ranks of noblemen. Led by the master of ceremonies, the most senior warrior, and the six temple guardians who carried the litter holding the body, the retainers circled Tattooed Serpent's house three times before solemnly marching out into the square and assuming their prescribed positions. Among the retainers, the noblewoman and Tattooed Serpent's wives enjoyed the highest rank, and they placed their cane mats closest to the temple. The others, including the head servant, fanned out around the path leading to that sacred space. Just as he had practiced during the days of the death dance, the head servant knelt upon his mat. He and all the other retainers released a final death cry. Aided by eight attendants on this honored day, he accepted pills of compacted tobacco and a draught of water. Numbness now spread throughout the head servant's body, and he became enveloped in darkness as the attendants slipped a deerskin sack over his head; soon a cord girdled his neck. In an instant, he knew, it would be over. Three warriors who stood on either side of him would draw the cord, and the servant's days in This World would come to an end. His soul would travel to another realm, yet would remain eternally bound to serve Tattooed Serpent, kinsman of the Sun.[1]

In a nation passionate about freedom, the standard historical narrative tells us that bondage was an American aberration. Restricted in time and space, slavery characterized the antebellum South, and its victims were African Americans. Captivity, not slavery, was the practice of Indian tribes, and they targeted white women. But bondage cannot be so neatly

Sketch of Tattooed Serpent's funeral, by Antoine Simon le Page du Pratz, *Histoire de la Louisiane* (Paris, 1758), vol. 3, plate opposite p. 55. Courtesy of Rare Book and Manuscript Library, University of Pennsylvania Libraries.

confined. In 1725, near what is now Natchez, Mississippi, Tattooed Serpent's nameless Indian servant died not merely because he was loyal, but because he was a slave. In life, the head servant contributed labor and prestige to his master's household; in death, he confirmed the social order that privileged elites like Tattooed Serpent. Captivity and its most exploitive form—slavery—was indigenous to North America, it was widespread, and it took many forms. From Tattooed Serpent's slave to indentured servants in colonial Philadelphia to Apache women sold in the mission of San Antonio, the unfree were everywhere.

The American South, a familiar setting for bondage, reveals a new story. Pushing beyond the tobacco fields of Virginia and the rice plantations of the Carolina Lowcountry, this story moves into the heart of Indian country and explores how the region's Native Americans practiced and understood captivity. Among Native Americans, captivity was a normal accompaniment to warfare, and the practice forced people to define themselves and others during crucial historical moments. Those bound by kin ties, whether established at birth or forged through ceremony, maintained peace. In contrast, groups that lacked kin ties often waged war, and for Native Americans, warfare was not an exceptional state. Among enemies, conflict constantly simmered and regularly boiled over into war. Even before Europeans arrived, enemies darkened and bloodied the ground.

From the pre-Columbian era to the end of the Second Seminole War in 1842, Southern Indians adapted their wartime strategies, technologies, and targets to meet changing needs. Throughout this period, Indians went to war for complex reasons: men attempted to enhance their status; clans sought revenge; polities struggled for land, resources, and broader political goals. One constant, however, endured: captive-taking.

Captivity was not a static institution for Indians, but rather a practice that they adapted over time to meet changing needs and circumstances. This history of Southern Indians and their captives begins during the pre-Columbian era, when rival chiefs vying for power went to war and took prisoners, exploiting these conquered enemies to enhance the power of their own ruling lineages. Following the European invasion of America, Native people experienced demographic collapse owing to epidemic diseases and subsequent incorporation into a global economy that valued Indian slaves. Both factors encouraged them to capture and sell unprecedented numbers of captives. Even when the Indian slave trade declined in the aftermath of a devastating colonial war, captives remained flexible mediums of power. Throughout the eighteenth century, violent conflict often erupted as Indian nations labored to maintain their territorial integrity and political autonomy, Euro-Americans strove to control Indian land and African labor, and Africans sought freedom. During violent encounters, Native groups took enemies—white, black, and Indian—as captives. The crises surrounding U.S. expansion and, later, Indian removal prompted Native people to redefine their communities, change their economies, and develop a form of racial slavery. To deal with each challenge, Native people revised their notions of who captives should be and what role those captives should play in their communities.

Captivity encompassed a wide continuum of experiences, ranging from death to adoption to slavery. Thus, in this context "captive" can be defined broadly as a detained outsider. Among Southern Indians, captivity was never a fate suffered by insiders, not even by the worst transgressors of social rules. Captives usually arrived in Native communities as prisoners of war or as chattel via trade. Still others came voluntarily: among these captives were strangers who sought refuge in Indian communities, including runaways, criminals, and military deserters. Desperate to escape terrible fates in the colonies, these volunteers took their chances in Indian country, hoping that their captors would choose to adopt them. A slave was a particular sort of captive, one whose labor served to enrich a captor socially or materially. Unlike the situation in European colonies, among Indians slavery and race did not develop in tandem. Deeply rooted in Native history, slavery was already present when the first Europeans and Africans arrived in the sixteenth century. During the colonial era, slaves in Indian communities included individuals of Native, European, and African descent. Not until the late eighteenth century did Southern Indians begin to graft ideas about race onto their preexisting captivity practices.

Nor did modern Western ideas about freedom resonate with Native people. In the Native view, as in many African societies, the opposite of slavery was not freedom: the opposite of slavery was kinship. Throughout most of Southern Indian history, the most important affiliation in life was one's clan. Members of a clan reckoned that they were related, all having descended from an ancient, mythic ancestor, such as Wind, Bear, Panther, or Wolf. Clans were ranked relative to one another, and clan rank as well as one's position within his or her clan figured into status. High-status clans were said to be society's oldest, and, over time, lineages branched off to form more junior clans. The clan system could also incorporate groups of foreign people by assigning them to a new clan. Indians believed that kinship ties conferred power. Those who belonged to the oldest clans possessed the greatest power because they had the most kin. Members of junior clans had fewer kin and less power, but remained connected to an expansive web of relatives who collectively provided safety, food, shelter, and other kinds of support that sustain life. Captives, by contrast, had no place in the kinship system; they lacked the rights, obligations, and status that came with clan membership. No fictive kinship, such as that which characterized relations between masters and slaves in white households, existed between captors and captives in Indian societies. Among Native Americans, the powerful were well connected; the absolutely independent were absolutely vulnerable.[2]

Binaries have long shaped our understanding of history, but such categories often obscure more than they illuminate. A diametrical opposition between slavery and freedom, for example, would have made little sense to Native people or other early Americans. Colonial-era bondage was diverse and contested; it was a far cry from the nineteenth-century plantation slavery that dominates the American imagination. Slavery existed across early America, and it was marked by "fluidity and ambiguity."[3] Captivity, which both colonizers and Native people practiced, included a broad range of forms extending from temporary bondage to hereditary slavery. Through sexual relationships, adoption, hard work, military service, or escape, captives could enhance their status or even assume new identities. Some people, including African Americans who lived among the Seminoles, were neither slave nor free but lived perpetually in between. Indians, like other people in early America, found themselves locked in a web of hierarchy and interdependence and saw no stark divide between slavery and freedom.

This fluidity was not unique to early America. Societies throughout time and space, from ancient Romans to the medieval Norse to colonial African societies, have practiced flexible forms of captivity. The Aztecs, Carthaginians, and Greeks sacrificed captives; peoples from Iceland, Tanzania, and Margi held prisoners of war for ransom; many Asian and Middle Eastern groups adopted captured enemies. Slavery has existed in some form in nearly every society from hunter-gatherers to farmers to industrialized nations. It is still alive today, even in the United States, where immigrants are sometimes deceived or forced into bondage, laboring as prostitutes or as servants. Slavery is not peculiar, nor is the fact that Native Americans practiced it. What is peculiar is the form that slavery took in the antebellum South and elsewhere in the colonial Americas. American slavery, the most rigid form of captivity the world has ever known, was remarkable for targeting people of African descent almost exclusively and for freeing so few of them. Plantation slavery in the antebellum South rightfully looms large in history, but ignoring other forms of bondage in the American past narrows our scope of understanding and makes it difficult to engage in broader global debates about diverse—and ongoing—practices of slavery, servitude, and other forms of captivity.[4]

American understandings of slavery and freedom are a legacy of the Revolutionary era. Although nearly all societies have practiced captivity, they have not agreed on what it means to be free. Those unruly British colonists of the Revolutionary era thought that freedom meant independence from "direct economic control by a master." For them, the inverse of freedom was, of course, slavery, by which they meant forced dependence. Revolutionary-era Americans applied the term *slavery* more liberally than do contemporary Americans and found no shortage of examples, including their own bondage to Britain. As the nation grew and the industrial revolution created a large market for American staple crops, the United States became more invested in slavery. Slavery came to have a very specific meaning, one embodied by the lived experiences of the millions of African-descended people held in bondage across the nation.[5]

Initially, Native people did not share the American ideology of freedom. In a world where captivity operated on a continuum and the truly independent were slaves, the concept did not translate. As non-Western people, Native Americans had not participated directly in the European Enlightenment, and, before the nineteenth century, very few Southern Indians were Christians.[6] Native people doubted that outsiders were fully human, and they certainly did not believe that all people were endowed with natural rights. Native people's accounts of their origins typically focus on their own group, not on the origins of all Indians or all of humanity. Indian tribal names often translate as the "real people." *Cherokee*, for example, comes down to us from their neighbors and sometimes enemies, the Muskogees, for whom *chilokee* derisively means "people of a different language." Cherokees called themselves *Ani-Yun Wiya*, the Real People.[7] Oral traditions suggest that Native people did not believe that every being appearing in the form of a person was actually human. An evil spirit called Spearfinger, for example, prowled the forests near the Nantahala River. Under her robes, Spearfinger concealed a long, stone finger that she used to kill victims, but otherwise she appeared to be much like other elderly women.[8]

Also revealing are the epithets Native Americans hurled at their enemies. They reviled outsiders as "accursed nothings" or associated them with less esteemed members of the animal world, labeling enemies "wood rats" or "dunghill fowl." Kin were real people; others were something less.[9]

Americans have long regarded the South as an exotic realm of contradictions: a culture of hospitality and politeness undergirded by brutal racism; opulent, magnolia-lined plantations maintained by a scarred and stressed underclass; hoop skirts, juleps, and grand balls but also pellagra, illiteracy, and grinding poverty. But most central to our understanding of Southern history is the opposition of white versus black. And, more often than not, popular culture represents the antebellum South much as the dominant class, planter elites, might have experienced it: an implicitly white construction of the region and its way of life. But the South is more than the Confederacy. Native Americans and African Americans were just as southern as their white contemporaries, and their connections and memory and history run as deep and as true.[10] The South is not the exclusive physical and mental territory of elite whites and their progeny. Rather, it is a place where disparate racial, ethnic, and religious groups have offered competing visions for the region's future. Too narrow a focus on the region as the inevitable cotton kingdom obscures the complexity of the region's past and the diversity of its people.

Native Americans were the first people. Major players in the South's early history, Native groups dominated the region's core until most of them were forcibly removed in the 1830s. Much of Jefferson Davis's home state of Mississippi, for example, was only lately wrested from the Choctaws and Chickasaws and in the hands of white planters for a single generation before the Civil War. The Old South, as it turns out, was not so old after all. In dialogue with whites and blacks, Indians eventually named themselves as one of North America's three races. Instead of reifying the ideology of whites, Indians stressed their aboriginal possession of the continent, using racial discourse to critique colonialism and bolster their own claims to sovereignty. However, after the removal policy expelled most of them from the region, Indians were largely erased from historical memory. In works of history and fiction produced in the 180 years since removal, Native people most often emerge as bit actors in the teleological tale of a biracial South. The reality is much more complicated, for Native Americans were not just villains or victims or foils, but leading players. Participating in captivity as both victims and masters, Indians were among the first slaves owned by

Virginia and Carolina planters, and, a century later, Native slaveholders brought the plantation economy and black slavery to the interior South.

Before Europeans and Africans arrived, Southern Indians capitalized on the region's mild climate and fertile riverine soils, shaping their environment and creating a distinctive regional culture. Three thousand years before the birth of Christ, Native American farmers, who were almost certainly women, developed indigenous domesticated plants, including gourds, squash, and sunflowers, and they later discovered that their climate could support tropical cultigens such as corn and beans. By A.D. 950, corn became (and would remain) the American staff of life, used to support populations that were larger and more settled than ever before. Simultaneously, a new cultural tradition, called "Mississippian" by archaeologists, flourished throughout most of region. During this period, chiefs rose to the top of the social order, probably by gaining control over corn stores and long-distance trade. These chiefs, who ruled over subordinates and enforced hereditary succession, ushered in an era of unprecedented social inequality. Surviving artifacts and sites from this period, which are among the continent's most spectacular, suggest that chiefs used spiritually charged ideology to legitimize and support these revolutionary changes in lifestyle. Mississippian culture was a regional phenomenon that distinguished Southern Indians from other indigenous people of North America.[11]

Native people created a trail system that connected communities and probably facilitated the spread of Mississippian culture. They used both water and land routes to exchange goods and information across the region. Among these ancient highways was the Natchez Trace, which connected the Chickasaw towns near Natchez Bluffs in what is now northern Mississippi to the rich hunting territory of the central Cumberland valley in present-day Tennessee. The Natchez Trace remained an important road into the nineteenth century, when American settlers poured into Mississippi Territory, crowding and eventually displacing the land's first people. Native people marked the land by regularly burning forests, which created edge-environments that attracted game and opened fields for crops. By the time Europeans and Africans came to the interior South in the sixteenth century, they landed not in a pristine world, but in one that had been profoundly shaped by Native actors for the past 10,000 years.[12]

Edmond Atkin, a Carolina politician and longtime Indian trader, popularized the term *Southern Indians* in the Atlantic world when he argued that the British Empire should split Indian affairs into two North American districts: the Northern and the Southern. Although Atkin was not the first to suggest the idea, he articulated it most thoroughly in his *Plan of 1755*. Atkin's *Plan* demonstrates that this line of division was not arbitrary, but rather based on his own understanding of Indian cultures and histories. According to Atkin, the major Northern Indian nations included the Iroquois (or Six Nations), the Susquehannocks, the Delawares, the Shawnees, and the Miamis. Major Southern nations included the Cherokees, Creeks, Chickasaws, and Choctaws. Atkin observed that three characteristics distinguished Southern Indians: they were independent of the Iroquois sphere of influence; they were "by far the most numerous Nations"; and they had no British forts within their territories and thus lived largely outside the realm of imperial control.[13]

Long before Atkin submitted his report, however, Native people had constructed a regional identity. These groups had all experienced the Mississippian transformation, and, as Atkin suggested, they defined themselves *against* the Iroquois and their subordinates. This powerful confederacy of five (later six) nations was forged in the fifteenth century and dominated the Native Northeast and Ohio valley until the late eighteenth century. Although Iroquois rarely ranged south of the Ohio, warriors sometimes launched raids and took captives among Southern Indians. Considering the Iroquois menacing foreigners, Southern Indians counted themselves lucky that they lay largely beyond the oppressive grasp of the Five Nations. The *"Northern Indians,"* a Catawba chief explained in 1746, "are our Enemies." Two decades later, Thomas Gage reported that Southern Indians "call them all *Northwards* without distinguishing any particular Nation." This lack of specificity suggests that Southern Indians thought of the "Northern" or "Northward" people as outsiders, different from themselves in important ways. ("Northern Indians" reciprocated: The Iroquois, mocking the manner in which some groups modified their skull shapes, called all Southern Indians "flatheads.")[14] In the late eighteenth century, prompted by a popular nativist movement, Native Americans began to develop a racial consciousness as "red people." Highlighting their shared identity, Native leaders used the term *Southern Nations* to refer collectively to the region's major Indian polities.[15] Southern Indians were a group of people of varying political affiliations who nonetheless shared historical experiences as well as a similar culture dating back to the Mississippian era.

The interior South, the region bound by the Cumberland River to the north and the Mississippi valley to the west, was home to the five major southern nations—the Cherokees, Creeks, Chickasaws, Choctaws, and Seminoles—as well as their ancestors. These five nations represent the labored creation of Native people, and captivity, which provided a framework for the incorporation of new people, was central to their development. In contrast to more familiar settings for early American stories such as Virginia and New England, where English populations quickly overwhelmed Native people, Indian nations of the Southern interior remained formidable and autonomous much longer. As late as 1798, the governor of Mississippi

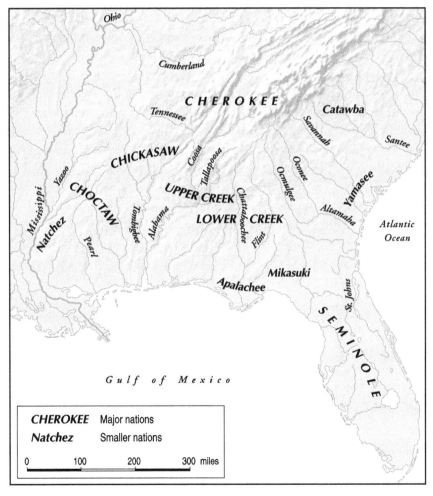

Native Americans of the South. Map by Philip Schwartzberg.

Territory, referring to the populous nations of his Indian neighbors, fearfully admitted, "We live *here* only upon sufferance and *their* good will."[16]

Captivity provides a revealing new look at early American history because it touched Europeans, Africans, and Indians and profoundly affected captor and captive alike. The violence that permeated the early South produced captives of many colors. Whites even became slaves. An apocryphal narrative printed at the outset of the Second Seminole War reveals the racial anxieties that captivity produced. In the too vehemently titled *An Authentic Narrative of the Seminole War*, Seminoles attacked the Godfrey family's frontier cabin. Mary Godfrey and her children managed to escape to a nearby forest, where they hid for three days. On the fourth day, a Seminole of African American descent discovered the family when the youngest, an infant, began to cry from hunger. Implicit in the text are Godfrey's sexual vulnerability and the possibility of cross-racial contamination through rape. The black warrior, however, "appeared much affected, and broke silence by assuring Mrs. G. that she had nothing to fear, that neither herself or her children should be hurt—that he had two children who were held in bondage by the whites." Though imagined, this episode suggests that captivity was an experience shared by many disparate people. Adding to this complexity was the very real possibility that those reared to understand themselves primarily as French, white, Kongolese, Negro, or Christian could and did transform into Choctaws and Seminoles.[17]

The Native bondage that had preceded the European invasion endured alongside, intersected with, and, at times, challenged the more familiar form of American slavery. By exploring the long history of captivity among Native people, this story offers a new perspective on race, slavery, and freedom. From ancient times through the colonial era, when Indians relied on localized modes of self-understanding such as kinship and political affiliation, they captured a wide range of enemies including Africans, Europeans, and other Indians. By the late eighteenth century, however, race eclipsed other markers of identity, and captors began to target African Americans almost exclusively. Native Americans' captivity practices, however, remained fluid long after their white neighbors hardened racial lines. Only the conclusion of the Second Seminole War could tear apart the complex communities that Native people had created through centuries of captivity.

1

INEQUALITY, WAR, AND CAPTIVITY

To understand Native Americans' long history of captivity, we must begin in the Mississippian era. The 1725 burial of Tattooed Serpent, the great Natchez war leader and brother of the chief, offers a glimpse of a much older tradition of funerary rites among Native Americans, one that had previously been widespread in the region. The Natchez lived on the banks of St. Catherine's Creek near the Mississippi town that now bears their name, and they are remarkable because they preserved their ancestors' Mississippian culture longer than other Native groups. Although many Native polities experienced dramatic population losses and dislocation during the seventeenth and early eighteenth centuries, the Natchez successfully maintained their society and remained in their traditional homeland.[1]

As the funerary rites of Tattooed Serpent suggest, bondage and inequality were deeply ingrained in Native societies. By virtue of his membership in the ruling lineage, Tattooed Serpent enjoyed a life and death of privilege. Made for finer things than cooking hominy, hewing wood, or hauling water, Tattooed Serpent needed servants for This World and, naturally, the afterlife as well. Usually acquired through war or trade, slaves endured a liminal existence unless, through adoption or marriage, they managed to join the kinship system that structured Native societies. When Pedro Menéndez de Aviles traveled across peninsular Florida in the sixteenth century, he reported that chiefs and other elites frequently killed slaves in ritual contexts "because they consider it the pious and natural order of things."[2] The Mississippian culture that dominated the pre-Columbian South was one of inherent inequality, engineered by the elite and naturalized through tradition. Rooted in notions of hierarchy and power, captivity would remain an integral part of Native culture until the nineteenth century.

Natchez culture was conservative but not static. Like other Native Americans, Southern Indians had a long and dynamic history. Around 10,000 years ago, Native people moved into the southeastern corner of North America. The region they discovered looked nothing like the landscape of today: during that last ice age, mammoths, mastodons, and giant bison roamed dense boreal forests. The people hunted these megafauna along with smaller game and supplemented their diet with gathered nuts, berries, and roots. Thereafter, the climate warmed and the biggest game died, but people adapted by hunting smaller game, fishing, and gathering plants. By 3000 B.C., Southern Indians independently developed agriculture and, in what archaeologists have dubbed "the container revolution," they began to make stone bowls and North America's first pottery. Both the adoption of agriculture and the manufacture of food containers point to an important change in lifestyle: Native people became more settled and more dependent on agriculture. Seeking to exchange valuable goods such as marine shell, copper, and workable stone with foreigners, they traded with people across Native North America. Some individuals, perhaps those with leading roles in long-distance exchange, began to receive elaborate burial in artificially constructed mounds. For most of the era before contact with Europeans, Southern Indians lived in tribally organized societies, wherein leaders earned their positions by achievement rather than ascription.

Around A.D. 750–950, however, the lifestyle of Southern Indians changed dramatically. Looking to feed a rapidly expanding population, Native farmers began to cultivate maize on a massive scale. In a relatively short period of time, they made the transition from consuming little or no corn to relying on the crop for 50 percent (and sometimes much more) of their total diet. To fit the demands of their new lifestyle, the people reorganized their societies. Chiefdoms—hierarchically structured, regional polities—appeared throughout much of the coastal plain, piedmont, and Appalachian highlands of the Southeast and along the Mississippi River valley. Highly centralized, chiefdoms vested great power in a single individual, usually a man, whose rank was ascribed at birth. From his mound at the chiefdom's capital, the chief ruled over his own town, subordinate villages, small farmsteads, and resource extraction sites, including hunting grounds, fishing spots, mines, and salt licks. Chiefdoms varied greatly in terms of size, but most probably had a population in the low thousands. The most powerful sort of leader was a paramount—a chief of chiefs—who controlled other polities and forced them to pay him tribute. Levied upon subjects and subordinate chiefdoms, tribute included surplus crops that supported a group of elites, including chiefs and their families, who maintained control over communal granaries.[3] This Mississippian culture dominated the South from about A.D. 950 to 1600. It was marked by a material culture that included high-quality shell- and limestone-tempered ceramics and ceremonial goods decorated with distinctive iconographic symbols and themes. The culture's most impressive physical manifestations were the broad, flat-topped earthen mounds that ranged in height from low rises elevated a few feet above the ground to man-made mountains that towered 100 feet. Whether mounds were short or tall, the tops of these monumental earthworks were large enough to accommodate one or more sizable structures, usually the houses or temples of chiefs. Mississippian society reached its apogee at sites such as Cahokia in southern Illinois, Etowah in Georgia, Moundville in Alabama, and Spiro in eastern Oklahoma.[4]

Central to the Mississippian transformation was a shared regional ideology, including belief in a three-tiered cosmos and rituals aimed at world

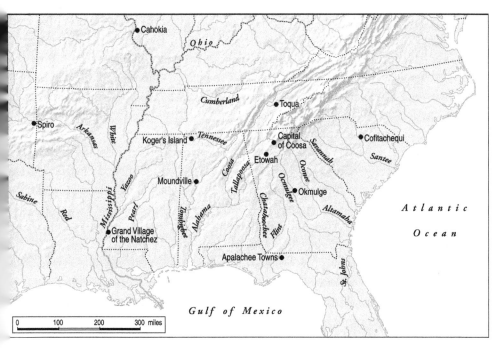

Mississippian sites. Map by Philip Schwartzberg.

renewal, which connected disparate people and legitimized chiefly rule. Each of the three worlds—the Upper World, the Lower World, and This World—had a distinctive nature. The Upper World was a place of perfect order and purity. It was the home of legendary birds, especially raptors, as well as the Sun, Moon, and Thunderers—all spiritually potent beings. The Lower World, populated by reptiles, amphibians, and fish, was a realm of disorder and fertility. Legendary monsters, including the Great Serpent and the Underwater Panther, prowled the Lower World. Striking a balance between the Upper and Lower, This World was the home of human beings, plants, and animals. The Upper and Lower realms, however, were not inaccessible; legendary heroes were known to have traveled between realms through portals, and otherworldly monsters might pass through those same gates to plague This World's inhabitants. Ordinary people lacked the spiritual power necessary to intervene in the Upper and Lower Worlds, but Mississippian chiefs claimed the ability to transcend the bounds of This World and keep the cosmos in order.

Long before European surveyors hauled their compasses and chains across the region, North America was a bordered land, where independent Native polities demarcated their territory and fought one another for control over people and resources.[5] In 1539, when Hernando de Soto entered the southern interior, he met people he called *indios*. This term, however, was unknown to the land's Native people, who instead referred to themselves as Apalachees, Cofitachequis, Chicazas, Coosas—as members of the dozens of chiefdoms that dotted the American South. De Soto and his army regularly captured Native people and attempted to force them into serving as guides or informants. During one such episode, the Spaniards' interpreter asked a man where he was from, whereupon he answered proudly that he was from the chiefdom of Apalachee "like one who gave to understand that he took offense from whoever might think that he was of another people but Apalache." Rather than give his clan or village, this warrior unhesitatingly identified with his chiefdom.[6]

Indians tailored their appearances to reflect their ethnicity and status. Communicating identity through bodily adornments was especially important for men. As society's warriors, traders, and diplomats, men left their chiefdoms more frequently than did women. Travels outside of their home polity exposed them to potential dangers from the outside world, including enemy warriors, potentially hostile strangers, and the myriad spirits that occupied This World. For Native Americans, the fastest and most effective way to identify a strange man was by the cut of his hair. According to an eighteenth-century French observer, men styled their hair "according to difference in nationality": "Some cut it entirely, leaving only a tuft on the top of the head in the Turkish fashion. Others cut it on one side only, on the right or the left, and keep the other side very long. Many also have the head completely shaved and have only a braided tress which hangs on each side, and others are clipped like our monks, having only a crown of short hairs."[7] The focal point of a man's hairstyle was his scalp-lock, a tuft of hair drawn up from the crown and decorated in a distinctive fashion, usually with feathers, ochre, and jewelry. Communicating ethnicity via hairstyle dated back at least to Mississippian times, when artists sketched hair and scalplocks in exquisite detail. One shell cup dating from the fourteenth century depicts eight warriors' heads, seven of which possess saw-toothed necks indicating that the heads have been severed. No two hairstyles are alike, suggesting that they represent conquered warriors from a variety of chiefdoms.[8]

In 1564, the South's first French settlers observed that Native Floridians declared war by going to the outskirts of enemy villages and planting arrows topped with their own scalplocks in order to assert their identity as the aggressors. In the seventeenth century, Savannahs took English trader Gabriel Arthur prisoner. The Savannahs' first clue that Arthur was not a member of any neighboring Indian group was not his complexion but the strange cut of his hair. Because hair was a key identity marker among Indians, scalps emerged as North America's preeminent war trophy. A warrior's hairstyle reflected not personal taste, but political affiliation.[9]

Some groups modified the shape of their skulls to distinguish themselves from other people. When infants from these groups lay on their cradle boards, families placed wooden boards covered with deerskin on their foreheads, making the cranial vault rounded and long.[10] The Catawbas, Chickasaws, Choctaws, and Natchez, who retained the practice into the eighteenth century, believed such skull-shaping enhanced beauty and intelligence. Groups that did not share this practice called the others "flatheads."[11] Cranial modification may also have been an indicator of status. At a Mississippian site in northern Georgia, elites were more likely than commoners to have modified craniums. However, the reverse is true at nearby Etowah, where commoners may have imitated the more privileged class. Into the twentieth century, oral traditions recalled that cranial modification

Detail of an engraved shell cup recovered at Spiro. Philip Phillips and James A. Brown, *Pre-Columbian Shell Engravings from the Craig Mound at Spiro, Oklahoma*, Paperback Edition Part 1. Peabody Museum Press. Copyright 1978 by the President and Fellows of Harvard College.

"was a sign of high social rank." Regardless of whether the practice was related to rank, it remained an ethnic marker; in societies where cranial modification existed, most people—elite and commoner—followed suit.[12]

Clothing, jewelry, paint, and tattooing also communicated identity. Some chiefdoms claimed particular connections with the spirit world, and inhabitants adorned themselves with symbols that connected them to that sacred power. At Moundville, both elites and commoners wore jewelry depicting the Lower World. Among these symbols was the eye-in-hand or ogee—in Native oral traditions the portal connecting This World to the Lower World—as well as animals and monsters, including snakes and feline water beings, which prowled the underworld. Because Moundville served as a regional necropolis in the fourteenth and fifteenth centuries, inhabitants may have believed themselves especially close to the Lower World and its guardian, the Great Serpent. Conversely, Etowah's inhabitants consistently wore clothing and jewelry that included images of raptors, inhabitants of the Upper World, which suggests that they shared a special relationship with that realm. The human body is a remarkably adaptable canvas, and Native Americans modified their appearances to reflect actual ethnic differences.[13]

One's political affiliation figured prominently in Mississippian notions of identity, but matrilineal clans were the blocks on which people built

Warriors planting arrows topped with pieces of their own hair outside an enemy village. Theodor de Bry, *Brevis narratio eorum quae in Florida Americae provi[n] cia Gallis acciderunt* (Frankfort, 1591), vol. 2, plate 33. Courtesy of the North Carolina Collection, Louis Round Wilson Library, The University of North Carolina at Chapel Hill.

their societies. Around the world, matriclans occur where groups of female kin communally farm a plot of land, manage agricultural resources, and pass inheritance through the maternal line. In the Native South, women controlled the world of plants; they likely domesticated the first plants, initiated the making of pottery, and oversaw the shift to more intense, maize-dominated agriculture. Mississippian art linked women with farming and fertility. An eleventh-century sculpture from Cahokia depicts a skirted, kneeling woman holding a hoe, tilling the back of a mythic water panther from the Lower World. Vines with gourds originating on the beast wrap around the woman's body, connecting the reproductive power of the Lower World with this female farmer, who may represent a female fertility deity. Although it is impossible to pinpoint when the matrilineal clans first appeared, they were intimately connected to female-controlled agricultural production, and the clan system became fundamental to Indians' economic, political, social, and spiritual lives. An individual's clan affiliation and position within that clan dictated privileges and obligations. Over the centuries, clans waxed and waned in importance, but they were an ever-present feature of Native life.[14]

Chiefdoms were kin-based societies, wherein all clans recognized that they were related in some way, if only through an ancient ancestor or by virtue of the rituals that created ceremonial kin ties. The matrilineal clan system, however, also allowed for great disparities in power and wealth. During the Mississippian period, some descent groups gained control over foreign trade and stores of communal staples, and thus ascended to the top of the social order. To retain power, the ruling clan perpetuated an ideology that supported its high position. Rank became a natural component of the kinship order: just as some individuals had more power than others within clans, so too did some clans outrank others.[15]

Moundville, a spectacular Mississippian site that spans 185 acres and includes 29 earthen mounds, was deliberately constructed to emphasize social rank. The site's focal point is the plaza, which is surrounded on its four sides by a total of fifteen mounds that alternate between large and small. Each of Moundville's clans controlled a pair of mounds, using the small one as a burial mound for elites and the other as a residence for its highest ranking members. Breaking this neat pattern is Mound B on the plaza's north-central axis. Towering over the rest, Mound B was probably home to that great chiefdom's ruler. In this ritual context, the constituent components of society—the clans—came together, but those in power used public space and ceremony to legitimize social hierarchy. Revising the more egalitarian, achievement-based social order that had been in place for most of the pre-Columbian era, Moundville elites inscribed their superior rank on sacred ground.[16]

Chiefs could still promote social cohesion because they could emphasize or deemphasize rank, depending on the situation. Just before the construction of the first mound at Etowah, soon to become the seat of a major chiefdom, a large group of people gathered to enjoy a feast. In later times, feasts were friendly celebrations, where groups of kin or allies ate and danced, sometimes for days on end. Archaeological excavations from the site of Etowah's pre-mound-building feast have not turned up the fancy jewelry or elaborate weaponry typically associated with Mississippian elites. This suggests that this feast was a noncompetitive gathering designed to bring people together. The Natchez temple keeper, a religious specialist, claimed that the first Great Sun had instituted such feasting among his people. A Mississippian chief sometimes found it convenient to mask social differences and remind his people of the ties that bound them together, but he retained a superordinate position among the kin groups.[17]

Mississippians assumed that people were born unequal. Although these chiefdoms lacked true classes, they contained three social groups: elites, commoners, and slaves.[18] At the top were members of the highest ranking kin group, the chief and his family. At the height of Moundville's existence, only about 5 percent of the chiefdom's population received high-status burial at the capital. Like other Mississippians, the Natchez practiced exogamous marriage: Suns married commoners, women carried the bloodline, and so male descendants gradually degraded in rank. This approach to descent-reckoning ensured that the Suns would remain a small group. In the early eighteenth century, French sources identify between eleven and seventeen Suns out of about 2,000 to 3,500 Natchez, or also about 5 percent of the total population. Below elites were the commoners who comprised the majority of a chiefdom's population. Belonging to nonruling lineages, commoners owed chiefs a portion of their annual harvest, occasional labor, and, in the case of men, military service. At the very bottom of society were slaves—captives taken in warfare and retained by or given to chiefs. In this hierarchical world, elites exploited commoners to secure their privileged lifestyle, but both social groups recognized that a kinship bound them. In this context, what distinguished slaves from even the lowest ranking commoners was the enslaved people's lack of kin ties to other members of society. Kinless people had no rights, not even "the right to live."[19]

At the top of the social order, chiefs drew their power primarily from close association with the sacred. It was spiritual power that legitimized their social and political authority. Such power came from harnessing the spiritual forces present in the mundane—animals, plants, and geographic features—as well as in the esoteric. Focusing on the esoteric, Mississippian chiefs sought out connections and experiences with lands beyond their polity, even with the Upper and Lower Worlds. Through ritual and ceremony, those who claimed the requisite knowledge could gain access to powerful sacred forces, which they could then use to control events and beings. French planter Antoine Simon Le Page du Pratz observed that the Natchez chief, or Great Sun, "is at the same time chief priest and sovereign of the nation." The Great Sun, like other Mississippian chiefs, claimed descent from the Sun, a celestial deity of great importance for these agricultural people. According to the Natchez, the first Great Sun descended from the sky, but on earth he was so powerful that he could kill men merely by looking at them. The first Sun ordered the people to build him a temple in which to reside so that his power might be better contained. Upon his death, this Sun transformed into a stone statue and remained within the temple as a symbol of the ruling lineage's divine ancestry. Apalachee chiefs claimed a divine right to rule that derived from their ancestor Nicoguadca, the Lightning deity and a son of the Sun who came to This World in the form of a man. After killing False Lightning, a pretender to the chieftaincy, Nicoguadca assumed leadership. Both the Natchez and the Apalachees recounted how these first theocratic chiefs reordered their societies and taught them the proper way to live.[20]

Using knowledge gleaned from religious specialists, a chief kept the three worlds in balance, ensuring his people's agricultural success. After announcing his impending death, Nicoguadca told his Apalachee subjects: "What I charge you today is that as soon as I die you should throw my body into some large pots with squashes, melons and watermelons and fill them with water. And put them on the fire until they boil very thoroughly so that I may leave with that steam, having converted into mist. This is for when you have your fields sown, I will remember you and give you water. And, accordingly, when you hear it thunder, it is a sign that I am coming."[21] In a world where agriculture sustained life, Mississippians depended on spiritually powerful chiefs like Nicoguadca to bring the rain, nourish the corn, and feed the people. Among the Natchez, the Great Sun attempted to use ritual to summon the power necessary to control the weather. Each morning, the Great Sun arose early to honor his kinsman the Sun as he rose from the east, all the while saluting him and offering him puffs of tobacco. A French friend of the Great Sun recounted how, in an attempt to bring rain during a drought, the chief had fasted for nine days, eating only a little corn and drinking water, and had abstained from sex. Like their Mississippian neighbors to the north, the Calusa of southern Florida believed that the rituals their chief performed behind the closed doors of the temple "afforded them the necessaries of life."[22]

Throughout the Mississippian world, chiefs donned regalia that they believed connected them with the Upper and Lower Worlds. As evidence of his intimate relationship with sacred birds of the Upper World, the Natchez Great Sun wore a crown of feathers. At Etowah, several elite men and boys were buried wearing an elaborate uniform that included bird wings, rattles in the shape of talons, forelock beads, and clothing and jewelry with avian representations. Almost certainly, these elites had been dressed as falcons—invincible warriors who (according to later oral traditions) could transform into the thunder deity and travel between This World and the Upper World.[23]

Elevated literally above the rest, chiefs lived in houses atop platform mounds. A Jesuit missionary visiting the Natchez reported that the raised earthen mound brought the chief closer to the Sun so that the two could more easily communicate. Across the plaza from the chief's residence was the village temple, which only elites and religious specialists could access. The Natchez oral tradition about the transformation of the first Great Sun into stone suggests that the temple contained powerful—and dangerous— sacred objects. Only those with the requisite knowledge and training could enter. Founders of Mississippian villages and cities laid their settlements out in formulaic fashion: the chief's residence and the temple bordered a central plaza, other important officials and elites lived nearby, and commoners resided in less prestigious space at a distance from the plaza.[24] Even when commoners came into close contact with elites, a body of sumptuary rules separated the groups. In the early eighteenth century, Father Charlevoix, a Jesuit missionary, described the deference other Natchez showed the Suns: "Their subjects, and even the chiefs of their villages, never come into their presence without saluting them thrice, and raising a cry, or rather a sort of howling. They do the same thing when they withdraw, and always retire going backwards. When they meet them they are obliged to stop, range themselves in order on the road, and howl in the manner above mentioned till they are passed. . . . In fine, no one, not even their nearest relations, and those who compose their nobility, when they have the honour to eat with them, have a right to drink out of the same cup, or put their hands in the same dish."[25] In his diary, another Jesuit, Paul du Ru, expressed doubt that Native Americans were sophisticated enough to maintain such a strictly ranked society. His first meeting with the Great Sun, however, banished such an illusion: "The chief's manner impresses me; he has the air of an ancient emperor. . . . The respect with which the other Savages approach and serve him is astonishing."[26]

It was the labor of subordinates that supported the elites' lifestyles. Among the Natchez, the Great Sun commanded a cabinet of officials who tended to matters of war, ceremony, diplomacy, public works, and public feasts.[27] He also contracted laborers to the French and then received their wages for himself. As Father Mathurin le Petit observed, "These people blindly obey the least wish of their great Chief. They look upon him as absolute master, not only of their property but also of their lives, and not one of them would dare to refuse him his head, if he should demand it; for whatever labors he commands them to execute, they are forbidden to exact any wages."[28] During the de Soto expedition, chiefs routinely provided the conquistador with porters—sometimes hundreds of them at a time. The ability to provide so many burden-bearers for the Spanish testifies to the chiefs' power to draw laborers from subordinate towns. So, too, do the hundreds of mound sites that dot the region. The mounds and their plazas bear mute witness to the ability of chiefs to direct subjects in the construction of public architecture. Such projects had the effect of exalting chiefs' ancestors and reaffirming the legitimacy of their rule. Laid out neatly around central plazas, Mississippian towns were *planned* communities made possible by centralized authority.[29]

Belief systems alone could not support Mississippian chiefs. To retain power, a chief also needed to provide for himself and his people by controlling staple foods and prestige goods. According to French chroniclers, the Natchez were obliged to give their Suns "the best of their harvest, and of their hunting and fishing." Evidence from a Mississippian site in eastern

Tennessee corroborates this observation. Excavated refuse pits revealed that the chief and his retinue ate not only a great quantity of corn, but also larger and higher quality cobs than did commoners. Corn was by far the most important Mississippian staple, and subjects gave some percentage of their crop to a communal granary, which the chief then controlled as he saw fit. Chiefs also used these stores to feed visiting dignitaries or allies. Control over communal granaries had a practical dimension as well, for it allowed chiefs to redistribute stores during lean times.[30]

Central to the rise of Mississippian civilization, maize agriculture fed larger, more densely packed populations, but it also created several health risks. Corn lacks the essential amino acid lysine, which helps the body absorb iron. Those who did not vary their diet and supplement corn with sufficient protein would experience nutritional stress. In addition, Mississippians living in close quarters (especially those with nutrient-poor diets) were more vulnerable to diseases that preceded contact with Europeans, including tuberculosis and treponematosis, a nonvenereal malady related to syphilis and endemic during the Mississippian period. Heavy reliance on corn could also presage famine if crop failure due to drought, pests, natural disasters, or the destruction of fields by invaders occurred. Sometimes, cycles of warfare, disease, and malnutrition combined in synergistic fashion to create very poor living conditions.[31] In west-central Illinois, the health of Mississippians lagged well behind that of their ancestors. Life expectancy plummeted for residents, who, by the Mississippian era, lived an average of only nineteen years. Puzzled by the people's failure to take advantage of the area's nutrient-rich resources like game, fish, and nuts, archaeologists have speculated that inhabitants may have traded the best of their foodstuffs to their chiefdom's capital city, Cahokia, in exchange for status-conferring luxury items, and thus deprived themselves of life-giving foods.[32]

Stressed and scarred by poor diets, Mississippian bodies generally suffered from overreliance on corn, but not everyone suffered equally. Non-elites disproportionately bore the health risks associated with the Mississippian lifestyle. Elites had constant access to communal granaries, and their subjects' tribute often came in the form of game, which enabled them to consume more protein than common people. At the Toqua site in eastern Tennessee, the choicest cuts of deer and bear meat—the front and hind quarters—appeared in trash pits near the mound and elite houses. At the Grand Village of the Natchez, excavations at the residential mound of the Great Sun revealed that he, too, enjoyed the best fruits of the hunt. Compared to commoners, elites in Mississippian-era Tennessee (especially elite children) consumed more protein-rich foods containing zinc and copper, trace elements found, respectively, in nuts and meat. Consumption of more protein afforded elites protection from iron-deficiency anemia, which raged wildly among virtually every Mississippian population. Elites' superior diet had another important physical benefit—chiefs were taller than the people they ruled. Hernando de Soto's secretary Rodrigo Rangel expressed astonishment upon meeting Chief Tascaluza, whom he described as a gigantic, powerfully built nobleman. The Spaniards estimated that Tascaluza was half a yard taller than any of them. Casting about for a comparison, Rangel declared that Tascaluza measured up to Antonico, a colossal bodyguard of Emperor Charles V. Tellingly, Rangel reported that Tascaluza "had a young son as tall as he." A combination of good genes and a protein-rich diet afforded Tascaluza's son stature equal to that of his father. As in other ranked societies, unequal access to resources afforded the privileged better health.[33]

Elite management of food stores gave chiefs control over their subjects' everyday lives, but prestige goods may have been more essential to retaining power. These were rare, exotic items available only to chiefs through trade with other chiefdoms, and common people lacked access to them. This restricted access, however, was not what made prestige goods valuable; rather, prestige goods served as evidence of a chief's "success in contacting or dealing with the distant realms whence such goods originated."[34] Elemental to chiefly power was control of the world outside one's polity. It is likely that few commoners had occasion to travel more than a day's journey outside their chiefdom. Chiefs, through direct or indirect participation in foreign trade, obtained columella shell beads from the Gulf Coast; conch drinking shells from the South Atlantic coast; shell-tempered ceramics made by specialists at Moundville or Cahokia and etched with images from the Upper and Lower Worlds; ornamental war clubs made of copper from Lake Superior; the skins of symbolically potent mammals, including rare albino deer and bison, and birds like cranes, hawks, and owls; and jewelry fashioned from shells, mica, copper, and shark teeth. In addition to these material objects, captives served as prestige goods. As foreigners, captives were object-like people whom chiefs used to evidence their mastery—even conquest—of the outside world. Prestige goods, including captives, made spiritual power concrete by providing physical proof of a chief's connection with sacred distance. Chiefs displayed prestige goods, especially in ritual and ceremony, to emphasize their knowledge of the world beyond their chiefdom and their ability to harness the supernatural in order to ensure success in agriculture, diplomacy, and war. Although chiefs controlled distribution of prestige goods, they did not hoard them. Instead, chiefs rewarded subordinates, including important warriors, religious figures, and members of their families with these goods.[35]

The use of prestige goods, including captives, was a means of preserving the social order that privileged elites. This is quite apparent at Cahokia, just across the Mississippi River from modern-day St. Louis, the largest pre-Columbian city north of Mexico, with a population in the low tens of thousands. The city once boasted over 120 mounds, the largest of which, Monks' Mound, had a base the size of twelve football fields. Just south of Monks' Mound is a much smaller earthwork whose lackluster name—Mound 72—comes from the numerical designation an early twentieth-century archaeologist gave it when he mapped this city of mounds. Barely noticeable amid Cahokia's more spectacular earthworks, this low rise, which has yielded the remains of 272 individuals, was once the scene of a mortuary ritual far more elaborate than that which accompanied the death of Tattooed Serpent. Mound 72, which Cahokians used between A.D. 1050 and 1150, contained several different groups of burials but had a clear overall pattern: a few richly adorned, elite individuals were accompanied into the afterlife by scores of ritually executed people of low status. The elite burials, containing grave goods commonly associated with Mississippian chiefs, had a decidedly martial theme. One elite man lay atop 20,000 shell beads from the Gulf Coast arranged in the form of a raptor, probably a falcon or eagle, birds closely associated with the sacred power of the Upper World. Among the most spectacular goods were projectile points—arrowheads—of exquisite craftsmanship and constructed from raw materials from throughout the region and as far away as Wisconsin. To complete the elite man's burial, Cahokians ceremonially executed fifty-three women between the ages of 20 and 25 and buried them alongside him. Another grave in the mound yielded the remains of four men whose heads and hands had been severed.[36]

The retainers of this burial mound were almost certainly captives, enemies obtained through war or trade whose deaths were engineered to enhance the prestige of Cahokia's ruling lineage. Through analysis of the retainers' dental and skeletal remains, physical anthropologists have found trace elements indicating that many of the executed women came from outside the region. Moreover, the women's bodies exhibited signs of severe nutritional stress, suggesting that their diet consisted almost entirely of corn. The malnourished state of these foreign women's bodies betrays their status as society's most marginal members.[37] Cahokians' willingness to sacrifice women of this child-bearing age suggests conspicuous consumption on a grand scale. In a world where female-dominated agriculture sustained life, these women were at the height of their productive and reproductive abilities. Perhaps only Cahokia, the leviathan among Mississippian chiefdoms, could afford to destroy so many at once.

Farther south, in the Black Warrior River valley of present-day Alabama, mortuary rituals at Moundville display a similar pattern. Over the past 100 years archaeologists have uncovered over 3,000 burials at Moundville. Like those of Cahokia, Moundville elite burials contained a rich array of trade and ceremonial goods, including copper axes, pearl and shell beads, copper necklaces and ear spools, and mineral paints. Perhaps more significant than the grave goods are the location of the burials; the plaza's mounds contain the most elaborate burials, while others of high-rank were interred in cemeteries flanking the mounds. Commoners' burials occurred at a greater distance from the plaza, and they typically contained a few shells or ceramic pots or nothing at all. The final type of burials were skeletons or isolated body parts that had been used in ceremonies. Included in this category were the bodies of infants, who were probably ritually killed like the child at Tattooed Serpent's funeral. These human remains usually accompanied elite burials in the mounds surrounding the plaza. The fact that many were either isolated skulls or decapitated bodies strongly suggests that these people were executed to accompany an elite burial. Furthermore, the placement of these mutilated bodies alongside grave goods with martial iconographic themes indicates that they belonged to captured enemies.[38] Even in the absence of written records, the physical remains of Mississippians document a strictly ranked hierarchy; privileged elites dominated a large body of commoners and ruled absolutely over a small group of slaves.

Warfare between Native groups reached back to at least 3000 B.C., but the dawn of the Mississippian era brought unprecedented violence to the region as ambitious chiefs sought to enhance their power by gaining access to greater food stores and more prestige goods. Throughout history, other chiefdoms achieved such growth by further intensifying agricultural production or, in patrilineal societies, by practicing polygamy. In the Native South, however, an expansionist chief waged war against his neighbors and, if victorious, incorporated them as his chiefdom's lowest-ranking members.[39] Thus, large Mississippian chiefdoms were not ethnically homogeneous. When Cahokia elites began to consolidate regional power around A.D. 1050, the city and its suburbs held 10,000–15,000 inhabitants, including various ethnic groups who possessed distinctive burial practices and architectural traditions. These ethnic outsiders were likely conquered people absorbed into Cahokian society. Over time, the outsiders' cultural practices became muted; their houses and burials looked more like those of other Cahokians. Around the mid-thirteenth century, however, when Cahokian elites began to lose power and the chiefdom disintegrated, the outsiders reclaimed their old cultural practices, reasserting themselves as separate peoples once more.[40] The cycle continued as, through war, a Mississippian chief would gain control over formerly autonomous groups, and, even if that control was fragile, it afforded him increased power through access to greater stores of food, more artisans, and new trade routes.

Far from an innocuous ritual, Mississippian warfare served essential political and material needs. The South's landscape bears mute witness to that violent age. To maximize agricultural production and minimize the spread of disease, Mississippian populations *should* have fanned out in small settlements along river valleys; more often, constant warfare drove them to huddle into nucleated, fortified villages. This settlement pattern is most apparent in the central Mississippi valley, where the densely packed capitals of rival chiefdoms straddled either side of the great river. Mississippian bodies betray the marks of this age of violent warfare. Men in particular suffered death from traumatic injuries at far higher rates than did their ancestors. At Koger's Island, a Mississippian mortuary site in Alabama, physical anthropologists have concluded that warfare-related violence resulted in the death of over one-third of adult men and nearly one-quarter of adult women. Compared to people living in the same area during the Archaic era (circa 7000–1000 B.C.), Mississippians were three times more likely to die violently. Several other individuals at Koger's Island had healed fractures, including one woman who had survived a violent blow to the face only to later perish of other traumatic wounds, including a scalped cranium. While Koger's Island is probably an extreme case, it is also emblematic of the escalating level of violence wrought by emerging chiefdoms.[41]

A chronicler of the Hernando de Soto expedition declared that a chief "did not carry on this warfare with only one of his neighbors, but with all those whose boundaries touched his, there being two, three, four, or more, all of whom were at war among themselves." Spanish explorers and missionaries noted that the Apalachees were always at war with one or more neighboring chiefdoms. In the mid-sixteenth century, a French settler reported how one chief purposely fueled the cycle of warfare: whenever the chief's kinsmen returned from a battle against the enemy without having taken a captive or scalp, he struck "the best loved" of them with "the same weapon by which his ancestors had been killed." As the chief explained, "This was done to renew the wounds of their death so that they would be lamented afresh."[42]

Chiefs engaged in hegemonic warfare, in which they competed not for territory but for control over the resources and labor of other chiefdoms. Invading warriors sought to destroy or steal an enemy's food stores and to seize prestige goods, including captives. In the 1560s, Chief Potavou explained to visiting Frenchmen why he began a war against the nearby chiefdom of Outina: "[H]e feared that Outina and his companions would take the hard stone from his lands to arm their arrows and that they would not be able to get any at a closer place." Because Mississippians did not practice metallurgy, they relied instead on workable stone to make arrow points and, perhaps more importantly, ornamental weapons carried by elites. Because high-quality stone was difficult to find, Potavou was willing to launch a preemptive strike against Outina in order to preserve his access to such an essential resource. Into the early eighteenth century, the Natchez declared war on neighbors who poached their game. As agriculturalists with relatively dense populations, each Native group fought to maintain its right to rich soil, game, salt, and minerals. If conquered by a more powerful chiefdom, a group might be forced to become tributaries, giving the best of their land's products to a foreign chief. To retain power, Mississippian chiefs needed to preserve their access to the trade routes from which prestige goods flowed.[43]

Warfare often came in the form of quick, deadly assaults on enemy chiefdoms and ranged in scale from small ambushes to mass invasions. One de Soto chronicler described smaller scale warfare as "surprise attacks on the fisheries, hunting grounds, cultivated fields, and roads, wherever they could find their adversaries off guard."[44] The Apalachees, who resided near modern Tallahassee, Florida, proved to be particularly adept at this sort of warfare; they harried the invading Spaniards throughout the winter of 1539–1540. During the winter, the Spaniards occupied Anhayca, the chiefdom's principal town. Apparently, the strategy of the Apalachee chief, Capafi, was constant irritation rather than direct confrontation. Warriors sometimes attacked in small groups at night, and they twice set Anhayca on fire. Whenever the Spaniards strayed from the village to hunt or collect firewood, Apalachees assaulted them. According to soldier Alonso de Carmona, Apalachees succeeded in killing twenty members of the expedition in this way. Chiefs may have encouraged chronic small-scale warfare in part because it directed aggression outside the chiefdom and provided an avenue for male commoners to enhance their status in an increasingly unequal society.[45]

Chiefs also engaged in large-scale assaults, including siege warfare and pitched battles. During an interchiefdom conflict in northern Florida, Frenchmen observed organized Native troops marching in formation against one another. The French noted that during sieges, attacking warriors lighted arrows topped with pitch-doused moss and rained fire upon enemy villages. Villages were often heavily fortified, surrounded by tall wooden palisades punctuated by watchtowers. At the palisaded village of Mabila in present-day central Alabama, Chief Tascaluza hatched a plot to destroy de Soto and his army. Luring de Soto and key members of his retinue into the town with a promise to give them additional slaves, Tascaluza then closed the gates, trapping the expedition's leaders inside and leaving the Spanish army outside. From within the town, roughly 5,000 warriors emerged from their hiding places and attacked de Soto and his men; from the palisade's bastions, archers shot at the exposed army. In preparation for the battle, warriors had burned houses and cleared trees to give them a better view of their enemies. Had the Spaniards not breached the palisade wall with their steel axes, Tascaluza and his people would have brought the de Soto expedition to a bloody conclusion.[46]

Once enemies accepted defeat, they entered into a tributary relationship with the victorious chief, giving him a share of their resources. In 1560, warriors from the Coosa chiefdom set out against the recalcitrant Napochies. Twenty years earlier, the de Soto expedition had encountered the Coosa chiefdom at its height. Over 200 miles long, the chiefdom stretched from Chiaha in eastern Tennessee to Talisi in central Alabama,

Warriors shooting flaming arrows into enemy villages, igniting thatched roofs.
Note the wooden palisade surrounding the village. Theodor de Bry engraving
after an original drawing by Jacques LeMoyne de Morgues, in *Brevis narratio
eorum quae in Florida Americae provi[n]cia Gallis acciderunt*, vol. 2, plate 31.
Courtesy of the North Carolina Collection, Louis Round Wilson Library, The
University of North Carolina at Chapel Hill.

controlling between seven and ten subordinate chiefdoms. Perhaps because of epidemic disease, Coosa's control over its subordinates had weakened, and some now refused to pay the chief tribute. The Napochies, who
lived to the northwest, had cut ties with their former overlords by killing
a number of Coosas. Arriving amid this turmoil in 1560, as a member of
Tristàn de Luna's expedition that tried—and failed—to found a Spanish
colony at Pensacola Bay, Major Sergeant Mateo del Sauz came to Coosa
seeking an alliance. Recalling that the earlier de Soto expedition had described Coosa as a bountiful chiefdom, Sauz hoped to secure provisions

from the Coosas, though the latter had plans of their own. The chief of Coosa enlisted the captain as well as twenty-five Spanish cavalry and an equal number of infantrymen to punish the Napochies. On the way to Napochie, the Coosa warriors marched in an equal-arms cross formation as directed by their war captains. Upon reaching the Napochie village, the Coosas and Spaniards found it deserted, but finally caught up to the warriors, who had barricaded themselves in a fortified village across the Tennessee River. Initially, the Napochies ridiculed the Coosas, but when a Spaniard fired his gun and killed a Napochie, the Napochies were surprised and intimidated. Perhaps believing the shooting a bad omen, the rebels surrendered. They agreed to resume their tribute to Coosa in the form of game, fruits, and nuts, paid three times annually.[47]

The Mississippian world was a dangerous one, and nonelites submitted to chiefly authority, at least in part, because they needed protection. Chiefdoms maintained a hierarchical settlement pattern, wherein outlying villages and farmsteads flanked the chief's central town. The chief negotiated peace between neighboring towns and commanded a coalition of warriors to fight outside threats. Physical evidence painfully bears out this dangerous reality. Small and medium-sized Mississippian settlements in what is today Alabama had much greater rates of mortality than palisaded capitals such as Moundville. About 10 percent of those at outlying sites suffered violent death due to scalping, cranial fractures, severed limbs, and embedded arrows; they were sometimes interred in mass graves. In contrast, researchers found no evidence of death due to violent trauma among elites and commoners at the capital city of Moundville, though two individuals had survived earlier scalpings. Living under the shadow of theocratic chiefs may have been oppressive at times, but Mississippian rulers controlled real military power that enabled them to protect their people and inflict damage on weaker neighbors.[48]

Drawing on their spiritual power, chiefs used ritual to control warfare. In 1564, Frenchman Rene Laudonniere witnessed Chief Saturiba's preparations for war against his enemy, Chief Outina. Laudonniere reported that Saturiba walked down to the St. Johns River, where subordinate chiefs brought him water. "This being done, he looked up to heaven and began to discuss many things by gestures, showing a great heat in his emotions and shaking his head first one way and then another. Then with a wrath such as I have never seen before, he turned his face toward the

direction of his enemies to threaten them with death. He also looked toward the sun, praying for glorious victory over his enemies." Demonstrating his control over cosmic forces, Saturiba threw drops of water, a substance from the Lower World, into a fire, an earthly representation of the
sun. Claiming power over life and death, the chief explained that he
would scatter the blood of his enemies. Through such ritual observances,
Saturiba invoked his intimate connection with the spirit world to fortify
himself and his warriors, and promised to use that sacred power to defeat
the chiefdom's enemies.[49]

Chief Saturiba's preparation for battle. Note the drops of water, signifying the
blood of Saturiba's enemies. The chief's elaborate tattooing signifies his high
rank, and his feathered crown invokes his connection to the Upper World. This
engraving also richly illustrates the regalia of Mississippian warriors. Theodor de
Bry engraving after an original drawing by Jacques LeMoyne de Morgues, in
Brevis narratio eorum quae in Florida Americae provi[n]cia Gallis acciderunt,
vol. 2, plate 11. Courtesy of the North Carolina Collection, Louis Round Wilson
Library, The University of North Carolina at Chapel Hill.

Much as chiefs controlled the preparations and execution of war, they laid claim to its spoils, both material and human. Through capture and domination of enemy people, a chief demonstrated his mastery of the outside world—not only of neighboring chiefdoms, but also of the sacred power of the Upper and Lower Worlds that had provided the requisite knowledge for victory. Chief Saturiba attributed his warriors' success against Outina to the efficacy of his ritual. The chief hung the enemies' scalps outside his house, "thus showing by this spectacle the triumph of the victory he had achieved." Saturiba chose thirteen Outina captives for himself and then divided the rest among his subordinate chiefs.[50]

Because captives were vanquished enemies, torn from their own chiefdoms and clans, chiefs used them to demonstrate their mastery over foreign places and external forces. Chiefs might ritually kill captives, retain them as personal servants or laborers, or give them away to supporters.[51] On occasion, chiefs might have extended kin ties to lucky captives, perhaps to those with valuable skills or to elites from other chiefdoms. The experiences of Juan Ortiz, a young Andalusian nobleman taken captive, illustrate chiefly prerogatives and goals in dealing with conquered enemies.

In 1528, Juan Ortiz traveled to La Florida with conquistador Pánfilo de Narváez. Charged with establishing the first European settlements north of central Mexico, Narváez hoped to emulate the success of Hernan Cortes by finding—and conquering—an Indian empire in North America as rich as that of the Aztecs. After the expedition's pilot lost his way and landed at Sarasota Bay, Narváez split his forces in two, putting himself ahead of a group that would travel overland and ordering the rest, including Juan Ortiz, to travel by sea to rejoin them at the Rio de las Palmas. Although the Spaniards believed their destination lay nearby, their scanty knowledge of North American geography made for a deadly miscalculation; the trip to Rio de las Palmas would have been roughly 1,500 miles, a journey that the overland group never completed. For months, those on the ships searched in vain for the land contingent, and they grew hopeful when they entered Tampa Bay and saw a letter sticking atop a split cane. Thinking Narváez had placed it there, Ortiz and a companion went to fetch it. The letter, however, was a trap set by Chief Ucita, who sought revenge against the Spaniards. Months earlier, Narváez had thrown Ucita's mother to hungry mastiffs and cut off the chief's nose for refusing to cooperate. When the Spaniards came ashore, Ucita's warriors seized them. The warriors killed Ortiz's unnamed companion as he tried to resist capture, and they brought Ortiz back to their chief. As his frightened companions sailed away, Ortiz, the nobleman from Seville, was forced to accept his new status as the slave of an Indian.[52]

By killing Chief Ucita's mother and maiming the chief, Narváez and his expedition insulted the chiefdom's ruling family and perhaps revealed to commoners the vulnerability of Ucita's semidivine lineage. Such an assault demanded retribution. The chief's warriors brought Juan Ortiz directly to him, for only Ucita could mete out punishment to such an offender. Ucita ordered that Ortiz be placed atop a grill made of cane poles. After the flames had roasted half of the Spaniard's flesh, Ucita relented and decided to allow Ortiz to live, perhaps persuaded by his daughter that "it would be more to his honor to hold him captive."[53] Having purged his sorrow and exacted revenge on Ortiz's companions, Ucita decided that Ortiz, now degraded and physically impaired, would serve as a living symbol of Ucita's domination. According to one chronicler, Ucita sometimes forced Ortiz to run back and forth across the town plaza, as villagers ridiculed and shot arrows at him. By ritually killing Ortiz's companions and displaying absolute control over the captured Spaniard's life, Ucita reasserted his own power, demonstrating to villagers that he retained the authority to rule.[54]

Chiefs used the capture and control of enemies like Ortiz to intimidate neighboring groups and broadcast martial feats throughout the region. Pedro Menéndez de Avilés, founder of St. Augustine, ransomed dozens of shipwrecked Spaniards from chiefs in southern Florida and the Keys. He reported that these chiefs "consider [captive-holding] a great glory and victory for them and the other caciques [chiefs] of the interior may hold a high opinion of them and they may triumph, saying that they live on the seashore and are the masters of the Christians and hold them as slaves." Because they lived in a more marginal environment where agriculture was not sustainable, chiefs of southern Florida had traditionally commanded fewer resources and less power than their counterparts farther north. However, these chiefs felt empowered by controlling Spanish captives—the "Christians"—who washed up on their shores.[55]

Tellingly, captives did not share the hairstyles of their masters' societies. Enslaved women among the Natchez, for example, were forced to cut their hair "extremely short," while female members of that society wore long hair with bangs in front. The Calusas directed male slaves to leave their hair long, rather than assume the style and cut of warriors. When reading another's identity, the Native eye went not to skin, but to hair, and the heads of these captives immediately communicated their degraded status. Native Americans were not alone in using hairstyle as a mark of identity. In fact, human societies across time and space have manipulated hair to mark social and cultural transitions, especially the transition from free to slave. As in many other cultures, masters muted the gendered identities of their captives: the alteration of a man's hairstyle was emasculating, and the shearing of a woman's head compromised her beauty. In addition to denoting slave status, such manipulation of hair distanced captives from the culture and aesthetics of their former people.[56]

Because captives were conquered enemies devoid of kin ties, captors were not bound to respect them as full human beings. Thus, they could employ captives' bodies to enhance their own economic or political fortunes. On several occasions during the de Soto expedition, chiefs willingly gave the Spaniards women to serve as sex slaves and laborers. Misconstruing this practice, the Spaniards believed that these chiefs readily gifted their own women, even their relatives, and deduced that Native societies placed little value on women. However, when de Soto and his men attempted to take women by force, chiefdoms responded violently. Because Southern Indians lived in matrilineal societies heavily dependent on female-controlled agricultural production, they esteemed women as creators and sustainers of life. Thus, chiefs surely did not offer up kin or female subjects; rather, they most likely gave the Spaniards women who were *already enslaved*—war captives from previous campaigns against enemies. Early Spanish accounts report that chiefs eager to make alliances invariably offered gifts as a way to initiate peaceful diplomacy. Along with valuable animal skins, jewelry, ornamental weapons, and minerals, generous chiefs offered their would-be allies captive women.[57] The gifting of captives—of bringing life rather than death—was a powerful overture of peace in a violent world.[58]

Similarly, chiefs probably gave captives to valued subordinates in return for loyalty or favors. During the de Soto expedition, following Chief Tascaluza's failed attempt to defeat the Spaniards within Mabila's fortified walls, de Soto and his men learned from Native survivors that Tascaluza had promised his collaborators human spoils: the Spaniards and all the captive Indians obtained earlier in the expedition. By using captives to reward subordinates and forge alliances, chiefs converted conquered people into political capital.

In addition to their symbolic and trade value, captives served as laborers. Juan Ortiz and several other Spanish men who became captives in the sixteenth century reported that they were forced to haul wood and water for their masters and other villagers. Traditionally, this burden fell on women, children, and slaves—but never on adult men. In the case of Ortiz and other Spanish men, their captors probably wished to emasculate them and reinforce their degraded status as nonwarriors.[59]

Ortiz also became a guardian of the town's charnel house. Widespread throughout the Native South, charnel houses held the decaying bodies of deceased elite men, women, and children, whose bones were thereafter placed inside special chests stored in temples. Ortiz had to remain awake every night to protect the bodies from scavenging animals. One night, as Ortiz dozed, a wolf entered the temple and dragged off the body of an elite boy. Waking with a start, Ortiz pursued the wolf into the dark forest. Somehow the Spaniard managed to strike the wolf with a spear and recover the boy's body. Thereafter, Ucita relented a bit in his harsh treatment of Ortiz. After Ortiz's extraordinary feat, Ucita may have feared that the Spaniard possessed spiritual power of his own.[60]

Chief Ucita's anxieties over Juan Ortiz point to a contradiction inherent in slavery. Because they lived outside the kinship system, slaves were liminal, even liminally human; at the same time, they were central to society because of their status-conferring power. Prestige goods drove Mississippian political economies, and, due to their versatility, captives may have been the most valuable of all goods. Treating people as objects could effectively broadcast a chief's mastery of the outside world, but such a strategy could backfire if a slave acted in a surprising way, as humans often do. By performing a spectacular act near a sacred place, Juan Ortiz demonstrated that he was more than an object in the shape of a human.

Despite slaves' unpredictability, their value as both status symbols and laborers was undeniable. Seeking to publicly display captives, chiefs throughout the region used them as personal servants. When the de Soto expedition captured the Lady of Cofitachequi, a powerful female chief who resided near modern Camden in South Carolina, she brought several "slave women" who attended her and carried her possessions.[61] In the sixteenth century, Spanish chroniclers reported that Calusa chiefs of southern Florida commanded a number of captives, many of whom were shipwrecked Spaniards. Thirteen-year-old Hernando de Escalante Fontaneda, born in Cartagena, was on his way to be educated in Spain when his ship sank off the coast of Florida around 1550. The Calusa chief, called "Carlos" by the Spanish, dispatched forty-two of the ship's crew, killing some immediately and reserving the deaths of others for special ceremonial occasions. He spared Fontaneda, perhaps because of the captive's youth. Fontaneda learned the Calusa language as well as three other Native Floridian tongues. The young linguist became very useful to Chief Carlos, who had grown frustrated with Spanish captives who could not understand his commands. He retained Fontaneda as a translator, and the Spaniard remained among the Calusas until ransomed at the age of 30.[62]

In Cofitachequi's chiefdom and in another near the Mississippi River, de Soto and his Spaniards saw maimed war captives engaged in agricultural labor, cultivating the fields of their masters. To prevent escape, captors sometimes severed their captives' Achilles tendons or cut off their toes.[63] Álvar Núñez Cabeza de Vaca learned that captive life among hunter-gatherers required almost unbearably difficult labor. Like Ortiz, Cabeza de Vaca was a member of the Narváez expedition who survived many years of captivity. A member of the overland group that failed in its attempt to walk to the Rio de las Palmas, Cabeza de Vaca and his compatriots constructed rafts and attempted to sail there. Predictably, the men were not successful, and they washed ashore on the Gulf Coast of modern Texas, nearly dead from thirst, hunger, and exposure. There, Cabeza de Vaca became the servant of a local family: "[A]mong many other tasks, I had to dig the roots to eat out from under the water and among the rushes where they grew in the ground. And because of this, my fingers were so worn that when a reed touched them it caused them to bleed, and the reeds cut me in many places because many of them were broken, and I had to enter into the thick of them with the [few] clothes I have said I was wearing." Frequently beaten and otherwise abused, Cabeza de Vaca, who reported that some fellow Spanish slaves were killed for minor infractions, lived in constant fear of death. Even in the absence of a capitalist economy, slavery was physically demanding and dehumanizing.[64]

After several years of harsh captivity under Ucita, Juan Ortiz was fortunate enough to gain a new master who made his life far more bearable. Mocozo, a neighboring chief, made war upon Ucita and succeeded in destroying his enemy's principal town. While Ucita and his subordinates fled to a tributary village, Juan Ortiz took advantage of the upheaval and presented himself to Mocozo. Throughout history, enslaved people have chosen to seek better circumstances during wartime, which created both chaos and opportunity. Luckily for Ortiz, Mocozo welcomed him but stipulated that Ortiz must never run away to another chief. Mocozo even adopted Ortiz as a kinsman and "he treated him like a well-beloved brother."[65] Prior to his adoption, Ortiz's existence had been precarious, dependent on the whims of an angry and vengeful master. After becoming kin to Mocozo, however, Ortiz became a member of a prestigious clan, which guaranteed him the right to live and protected him from physical abuse or degrading labor. Though free, Ortiz had to remain within the bounds of Mocozo's realm because the chief could only guarantee the Spaniard's safety therein. Elsewhere, Ortiz had no kin ties to protect him, and warriors from rival chiefdoms, especially Ucita, could easily enslave or kill him.[66]

In adopting Ortiz, Mocozo employed a far different strategy to enhance his power than did Ucita. Unlike Ucita, Mocozo probably did not endure personal tragedy at the hands of the Narváez expedition, but he had doubtlessly heard of the Spaniards' arrival so near his homeland. Like most chiefs, Mocozo did not regard Spaniards as godlike beings from another world; rather, Mocozo thought of them as foreigners who seemed to possess considerable military might and potentially dangerous powers of destruction. While Ucita chose to confirm his spiritual power and political dominance by humiliating Ortiz, Mocozo sought to tame the foreigner through incorporation. Employing the Spaniard as an informant and adviser, Mocozo probably hoped to use Ortiz's knowledge to understand Spanish motivations and ambitions in peninsular Florida. Mocozo suspected Ortiz would not be the last Spaniard to enter his territory. The chief was correct, for eight years after he adopted Ortiz, the de Soto expedition arrived. Mocozo heard of the expedition before they actually reached his territory, and he informed Ortiz that his countrymen had returned. Ortiz, however, thought that the chief was only testing his loyalty and replied that he wished to remain with Mocozo. The chief persisted and organized a small group of warriors to accompany Ortiz back to his people, but bade the Spaniard to remember his generosity and kindness. Just as Ortiz's adoption by Mocozo had saved the Spaniard's life during perilous times, so too did bonds of kinship protect Mocozo and his people from the unpredictably violent de Soto expedition.[67]

When Europeans invaded the South, Native people responded according to preexisting political and social mores. Initially, chiefs received Spanish conquistadores as powerful, if rude, visiting dignitaries. Unsure of the invaders' intentions, Native chiefs responded in a variety of ways: Tascaluza attempted to defeat and enslave the foreigners; Ucita wished to make a pathetic spectacle of Juan Ortiz to reinforce his own chiefly power; Mocozo's adoption of Ortiz indicates his interest in forming alliances with the Spaniards. In dealing with the invading Europeans, Native chiefs continued the diplomatic legacies of their ancestors. Chiefs even managed to use new materials brought by Europeans to reinforce their established social order. In the mid-sixteenth century, Chief Carlos of the Calusa counted among his prestige goods great stores of gold and silver from Spanish shipwrecks that had washed upon Florida's shores. He supplemented these treasures with prestige goods obtained from other chiefs and kept the lot in secret storage pits.[68]

Just as chiefs fit European goods into their old worldview, they did not create new categories for non-Native captives. A Spanish sergeant who served with Juan Pardo's expeditions in the 1560s observed "that the Indians were as cruel to other Indians they killed or captured in war as they were to the Spaniards."[69] Native people applied the same treatment to these newcomers as they imposed on other conquered enemies. At the bottom of a hierarchical society, Juan Ortiz and Hernando de Escalante Fontaneda, like other slaves, served the chiefs who held them.

Uncowed by European technology, unimpressed with Spanish religious overtures, and little fazed by the physical appearance of the newcomers, Indians probably did not afford their "first encounter" the monumental significance that many have bestowed on that event. In fact, early European efforts at settlement and exploration in the region were all spectacular failures. Chiefs of the Mississippi River valley successfully expelled the de Soto expedition from the continent, pushing the starving, miserable army into the Gulf of Mexico in a handful of makeshift rafts. Narváez fared even worse. A combination of bad weather, poor planning, and bellicose Native warriors destroyed his expedition. Out of an original army of 300, only four men, including Cabeza de Vaca, survived the overland trek to Mexico, though some, like Juan Ortiz, may have survived as slaves under Native masters. Within a few decades, however, the European and African newcomers did succeed in severely disrupting Native life, not with lances and horses, but with silent, terrible killers. Although the pre-Columbian world was not free of disease, Europeans and Africans introduced a host of deadly pathogens including smallpox, malaria, measles, influenza, cholera, typhus, and bubonic plague. Because Native Americans had never been exposed to these Old World diseases, they lacked the immunity that most Europeans and Africans had already acquired. Thus, in the Americas, "virgin soil epidemics" took life in devastating proportions, killing the young, old, and even those in the prime of life. Waves of disease, sometimes several at once, struck Native villages. Because virgin soil epidemics affected entire populations, the diseases created further destruction by disabling society's farmers and hunters. Although it is not certain when the first round of epidemics struck the American South, such diseases certainly accompanied the 1565 foundation of St. Augustine, a small outpost that nonetheless harbored people from throughout the Atlantic world.[70]

Demographic devastation severely compromised chiefly political economies. Because killers like smallpox and influenza struck the young and able-bodied, societies' most productive members were no longer able to produce the staple surpluses on which Mississippian elites depended. Disease also claimed the lives of artisans and disrupted trade networks that had brought prestige goods into Mississippian communities. Chiefs themselves may have died at higher rates than nonelites because as heads of foreign relations, they met with Europeans, other Native leaders, and perhaps even refugees fleeing disease-ridden communities. They thereby exposed themselves more frequently and more intensely to potentially deadly pathogens. Thus, 100 years after the de Soto expedition, most areas lacked the population and economic productivity needed to support chiefdoms.

As chiefdoms fell, so too did the social system that legitimized and supported privileged leaders. In their oral tradition, Cherokees commemorated the fall of Mississippian elites, whom they called the Aní-Kutání. The Aní-Kutání claimed to have visited the Upper World and conversed with the Master of Breath, who instructed them to institute new dances and ceremonies. Thereafter, "their persons became sacred in the opinion of the people." While demanding strict obedience from nonelite Cherokees, the Aní-Kutání "indulged their evil passions, without the least regard to the rights of others." Eventually, such hypocrisy and tyranny became so oppressive that the people rose up, killing the Aní-Kutání "where ever they were found."[71] In this early-nineteenth-century telling of the story, the Cherokee people, rather than disease and dislocation, assume a central role in dismantling Mississippian culture and destroying its rulers.

In the absence of chiefs, the people depended on what were probably traditional institutions—the matrilineal kinship system and the village—to guide their societies. As chiefdoms splintered, the hierarchical settlement pattern once mandated by chiefs collapsed, and those formerly living in outlying villages and farms moved into central towns. In the seventeenth century, the communal granaries controlled by chiefs disappeared; in their place appeared household corn cribs presumably controlled by extended families. Formerly, chiefs' burials were the only ones that yielded exotic prestige goods, but in the seventeenth century nonelites carried their valuable trade goods into the afterlife. Mound construction ceased and temples fell into disrepair. Many even abandoned their old chiefdoms, leaving behind the cosmically charged landscapes that had linked elites with esoteric power. In doing so the survivors opened themselves up to the possibility of assuming new identities in new places.[72]

Gradually, remaining towns forged alliances with one another, and new Native nations emerged. These nations often contained the remnants of several different chiefdoms, and their inhabitants had diverse ethnic and linguistic backgrounds. But they were not egalitarian; descendants of the Mississippians retained hierarchical societies composed of disparate kin groups of unequal status. Although often loosely integrated, postcontact Native nations maintained peace within and fought outside enemies. Autonomous towns came together in times of war and crisis. The largest nations, which endure to the present, include the Cherokee, Chickasaw, Choctaw, Creek, and Seminole. Throughout the eighteenth century, these nations continued to absorb smaller groups.

The fall of chiefdoms necessarily tolled the end of chiefly warfare, and clans began to take charge of their own disputes. Formerly, as in the case of the Coosas' campaign against the Napochies, chiefs had organized pitched battles in open fields. In the seventeenth century, however, clans and towns staged smaller forays into the lands of their enemies. The function of war rituals likely shifted from demonstrating chiefly sacred power to preserving the lives of individual warriors, and spoils were distributed more equitably. In the mid-eighteenth century, Choctaw war chiefs divided booty "among the warriors, and the relatives of those who have been killed in combat." As their populations fell, Indians also became more concerned with preserving the lives of their captives, who might become incorporated into their communities as servants or kin.[73]

The Native South that Juan Ortiz and other Europeans entered was not an egalitarian Eden, nor did it display the perfect order of the Upper World that Mississippian chiefs attempted to emulate. Rather, Mississippians lived in hierarchical societies where warfare, disease, and inequality were everyday realities. Slaves like Tattooed Serpent's head servant populated the lowest tier of this stratified world, with their lives, their bodies, and even their deaths controlled by the elites who held them. By the colonial era, the great Southern chiefdoms had fallen, but the descendants of Mississippian people survived. The transition to this new historical epoch was traumatic, but Native people managed to maintain many key elements of their culture. Chief among these were ideas about captivity.

Indians considered captivity a normal accompaniment to warfare. Over the course of centuries, Native warfare changed a great deal: leaders modified goals and tactics to meet contemporary needs; warriors acquired new technology, including firearms beginning in the seventeenth century. And as Native polities transformed from chiefdoms to nations, notions of "us and them"—of self and outsider—shifted. Captive-taking, however, remained constant. From the eleventh-century conflicts that produced retainers for Cahokian elites to the Seminoles' nineteenth-century wars against American imperialism, victors continued to claim human spoils of war.

After the Mississippian period, Native people continued to inhabit a kinship-ordered world in which captivity was characterized by the absence of kin ties. As the political superstructure of chiefdoms crumbled following demographic collapse, the kinship system underlying it persisted. Kinship, the central organizing feature of Native life, became more important in the post-Mississippian era. Clans rather than chiefs began to direct war, procure captives, and determine their fates. They targeted outsiders—those unconnected to them through kinship or ceremony. As enemies forcibly extracted from their own kinship groups, captives became tractable mediums of power.

Captivity would remain a flexible institution, affording the captors many options for retaining or disposing of prisoners. Colonial-era Indians, like the Mississippian chiefs who preceded them, used captives to advance their own economic, spiritual, and social prospects, and they did so in a variety of ways. Captivity operated on a continuum that ranged from adoption on one end to slavery on the other, and the practice's adaptability explains its longevity. Over the course of centuries, Native Southerners' economies transformed several times, shifting from maize-based agriculture to farming supplemented by commercial hunting and slave trading to a more diversified economy that included large-scale planting and ranching. The nature of Native polities changed as well—from theocratic Mississippian chiefdoms to towns connected by kinship to centralized nations. Whether they died in ritual, labored in the fields and forests, replaced lost kin, or fetched a decent price on the market, captives proved beneficial every step of the way.

Following the European invasion of America, as Native people attempted to combat the chaos that threatened to consume their world, successful groups altered their martial practices to fit the new demands of life in the colonial South, but they were the descendants of Mississippians, and they did not construct their "new world" out of wholly new cloth.

2

THE INDIAN SLAVE TRADE

In 1673, the Chickasaws met a group of explorers led by Father Jacques Marquette and Louis Joliet. These newcomers, who had set out from New France to traverse the Mississippi River, were busy piloting their canoes when they spotted armed warriors tracking them. The warriors signaled that they should come ashore, and, though fearful, the French complied. At Chickasaw Bluffs, the site of modern Memphis, Chickasaws and Frenchmen met for the first time. The Chickasaws eased French anxiety by offering the travelers a meal of grilled buffalo and bear meat as well as fresh plums. More impressive to Father Marquette was the array of European-manufactured trade goods that the Chickasaws carried, including "guns, knives, axes, shovels, glass beads, and bottles in which they put their powder." Throughout their journey, Marquette and Joliet noted that Indians possessed many items of European make. The Chickasaws were exceptionally rich in that regard, but others were less lucky. Neighboring Shawnees, for example, had acquired some European goods, but, to their consternation, they did not own firearms. For that reason, Marquette recorded, "The *Iroquois* are constantly making war upon them, without any provocation . . . and carrying them into captivity." When the Frenchmen asked the Chickasaws about trade, they told Marquette "that they bought their goods from the Europeans, who live towards the east. . . . That they were clothed as I was, and were very kind to them." The Chickasaws' European friends were not the Spanish, the earliest colonial presence in the South, because Spaniards did not give guns to their Native allies in the seventeenth century. Moreover, as Marquette noted, "I did not see anything about them that could persuade me that they had received any instructions about our holy religion." Franciscan fathers of the Florida mission system were not the Europeans of whom the Chickasaws spoke. The most likely candidates were British traders from Virginia, who ranged far into the interior. In exchange for all manner of European goods, the Chickasaws traded Indian slaves.

The French, encouraged by Chickasaw reports that the sea was close at hand, departed peacefully but did not get far. At the convergence of the Arkansas and Mississippi Rivers, the expedition met the Quapaws, who rowed out in canoes to greet them and bade them come into their village. By smoking the calumet, the Quapaws and French sealed an alliance, but Quapaw leaders informed Marquette and Joliet that they could not guide the expedition any farther down the river. Like the Shawnees, the Quapaws, at that point, had limited success in European trade; they owned some steel tools and jewelry but lacked guns. Their enemies the Chickasaws used superior firepower to prevent the Quapaws from trading with Europeans and even from visiting southerly Indian nations. Afraid to travel without guides, Marquette and Joliet, having persuaded themselves that the Mississippi's muddy mouth surely lay nearby, never completed their goal.[1]

Like many others who crossed the Chickasaws' path during this era, Marquette and Joliet bent to their will. Hamstrung by their ignorance of the land's geography and reliant on Native people to guide them, the French were probably not fully aware of the limitations that Chickasaw hegemony imposed on their expedition, but they experienced its effects just the same. Unlikely conquerors, the small Chickasaw nation descended from perhaps a single Mississippian chiefdom to become a major power player in the late seventeenth and early eighteenth centuries. The Chickasaws' rise, not incidentally, corresponded to that of Carolina. Founded in 1670 by ex-Barbadians and other ambitious planters and traders, Carolina's need for labor and a valuable export led to a voracious demand for Indian slaves. This demand, coupled with Native people's desire for British manufactured goods, led to a booming slave trade that affected every Native nation in the region. This deadly commerce resulted in widespread warfare and dislocation in which many lost their ethnic identities, if not their lives. It was against this tumultuous background that several Native groups adapted indigenous captivity practices to the demands of the Euro-American market. Especially successful were the Chickasaws, who used the slave trade to augment their economic and political power.

Before Europeans and Africans arrived on American soil, the land's Native people had taken one another as captives, and captors had long claimed the prerogative to exchange their spoils. During the Mississippian era, chiefs used captives, along with other prestige goods, to seal alliances with other chiefs and reward supporters. Native people continued to exchange slaves with their allies, who, by the colonial era, included Europeans. The capture and trade of enemy people was nothing new for Indians, but as they began to participate in a trans-Atlantic economy that placed a high value on slaves, warriors began to take unprecedented numbers of captives.

Although large-scale slave trading arose because of European demand, the heralds of change came to Southern villages in the form of gun-toting Iroquois warriors. In 1610, Dutch traders out of New York and Iroquois warriors began a mutually lucrative trade. In exchange for beaver pelts, the Dutch provided the Iroquois with clothing, tools, and—most importantly—firearms. In order to monopolize Dutch trade, the Iroquois used force and intimidation to cut off their neighbors' trading routes. Iroquois tactics were successful, and their military strength filled neighboring groups with terror. To satisfy increased Dutch demand for furs and to compensate for their own dwindling beaver population, the Iroquois engaged in a series of wars of expansion against nearby tribes. They nearly destroyed the formerly numerous Huron and Petun nations and successfully expelled the Eries, Susquehannocks, and Shawnees from the region. Though effective, these wars also cost the Iroquois thousands of lives. Consequently, Iroquois warriors engaged in additional raids, called mourning wars, in which they took captives from foreign groups to replace fallen kinsmen. These mourning wars demographically devastated already ailing northern tribes. By the mid-seventeenth century, the Iroquois ranged south of the Ohio River in their quest for captives; there, they found populous Native nations without access to guns. When Marquette descended the Mississippi in 1673, he encountered groups who lived under constant threat of Iroquois attacks. These mourning wars exacted a terrible toll on Natives throughout eastern North America, further aggravating populations destabilized by Old World epidemic diseases. Iroquoian militancy convinced other Native groups of the necessity of securing firepower through trade with Europeans.[2]

The nation that initiated a slave trade with Southern colonists had themselves been victims of Iroquois expansion. In 1654, the Iroquois attacked the Eries, competitors in the fur trade and obstacles to the beaver pelts of the Ohio valley. Shortly thereafter, the Eries moved south, settling near the falls of the James River in Virginia. In the South, these Eries became known as Westos. After some initial conflict, the Westos began a trading relationship with their English neighbors, providing beaver and deer skins in exchange for firearms and tools. In addition, the Westos sold their war captives to the Virginians, who put them to work as slaves on early tobacco plantations. Seasoned by their harsh education in the Northeast, the Westos brought Iroquois trade tactics to the South. They cut off other Indian groups from trade with Virginia and monopolized access to firearms. British colonists found that other Indians were "Afraid of ye very foot step of a Westoe . . . (which these say eat people and are great warriors)." Even the Virginians began to fear their trade allies, who were known to kill colonists who wandered into their territory, and so their relationship soured.[3]

In 1674, Carolina settlers, who would soon dominate the slave trade, sent linguist and diplomat Henry Woodward to negotiate an alliance with the Westos. The Westos showed Woodward drawings on trees, including "ye effigies of a bever, a man, on horseback & guns, Intimating thereby as I suppose, their desire for friendship, & comerse wth us." In the Westos' village along the Savannah River, Woodward reportedly saw Iroquoian-style longhouses festooned with the scalps of slain enemies. The Englishman found the tribe "well provided with arms, amunition, tradeing cloath & other trade," which they had procured from the Virginians through exchanging "drest deare skins furrs & young Indian Slaves." Formalizing their new alliance with Carolina, the Westos offered Woodward a young Indian slave as a gift. Captured near the falls of the Ashley River, this nameless boy was the first of thousands of slaves who would be traded to the Carolinians over the next forty years. Newcomers to the region who lacked allies, the Westos slaved indiscriminately among the Southern tribes. They warred throughout the Carolinas from mountains to coast and ventured farther south into the Native towns of the Florida mission system. The Westos and Carolinians maintained this trade for only a short while, for British traders and planters began to fear the rising power of their well-armed Indian allies. From 1680 to 1682, the Carolinians pursued a war of extermination against the Westos; they killed the men and sold women and children as slaves in the Caribbean. Although about fifty managed to escape to the Spanish Floridians or the Lower Creeks, the Westos ceased to exist as a political and ethnic group.[4]

Just as the Westos had borrowed martial practices from the Iroquois, so too did Southern Indians learn from the Westos. Those who lacked ties to

British colonies found themselves at a disadvantage in warfare and often became the slave trade's victims. Even before the Westos' defeat, Native groups began to ally with the British and sell slaves to their new trade partners. Among their earliest targets were the Native people of Spanish Florida's mission system, whose settled lifestyle and lack of firearms made them vulnerable. Strung along a chain that reached from the coast of modern Georgia to the Florida panhandle, these missions held about 10,000 Indians. In 1680, Lower Creeks and Cherokees joined the Westos on a raid against the Guale missions along the coast of what is now Georgia. Five years later, Scottish traders out of Carolina's Port Royal settlement allied with their Yamasee neighbors to attack northern Florida's Timucuans. Carolina's Indian allies conducted intermittent raids against the missions throughout the next several years, but the coup de grâce came in 1704 when Lower Creeks, in two major raids, conquered the Apalachees, by far the most numerous mission group with a population of 7,000. Over the next two years, British-allied warriors razed most of the remaining missions. By 1708, Florida's governor declared the mission system broken; nearly the entire mission population (as well as untold numbers of nonmissionized Indians) had been killed or captured. Slave raiders drove remaining Native Floridians southward to the Keys, where they begged Spanish mariners to take them to Cuba. Following the destruction of Florida's missions, the focal point of slaving shifted westward, where the Chickasaws were Carolina's key ally.[5]

Before the advent of the Anglo-Indian slave trade, no resident of the lower Mississippi valley could have predicted that the Chickasaws would rise to dominate the region. When Hernando de Soto and his army encountered the Chickasaws' ancestral chiefdom of Chicaza in 1540, they found a "well peopled" land abounding in maize. Despite the fact that two towns, Alibamo and Miculasas, were tributaries to Chicaza, the chiefdom seems to have been rather weakly centralized, with the population dispersed along the Tombigbee River in what is now northeastern Mississippi. Ironically, the decentralized nature of Chicaza society, perhaps a liability during the Mississippian period, became an asset in the decades that followed the de Soto expedition, providing the Chicazas with greater flexibility and self-sufficiency compared to those who lived under stronger chiefs. While other chiefdoms splintered, leaving survivors to construct new polyglot communities, the Chicazas had managed to maintain their homeland and ethnic identity. This feat, however, ensured low population levels— much lower than the other Indian nations taking shape during this period. During the late seventeenth century, the Cherokees, living to the northeast, numbered 32,000; toward the east were 15,000 Muskogees; on the Chickasaws' southern border dwelled 28,000 Choctaws. The Chickasaws, meanwhile, were only about 7,000 strong.[6]

The Chickasaws lived near the crossroads of several of North America's busiest trade routes: the Tennessee and Mississippi Rivers, the north-south Natchez Trace, and the east-west Creek Path, which led to the Creek Nation and the Atlantic seaboard. Native people enthusiastically engaged in trade long before Europeans arrived, and valuable items such as copper, seashells, chert, and sandstone circulated throughout the continent. The Chickasaws' advantageous locale afforded them access to these exotic, status-conferring items. By the seventeenth century, however, living at the crossroads of North America had become dangerous for the Chickasaws. Disease spread rapidly along trade routes, exposing the Chickasaws to waves of epidemics. And by the mid-seventeenth century, rifle-bearing Iroquoian raiders seeking captives ventured down Southern waterways to catch easy prey among bow-and-arrow tribes. Though small, vulnerable, and exposed, the Chickasaws soon developed a strategy for surviving and even thriving despite the grim realities of the early colonial period.[7]

Although it is unclear when Chickasaws began to trade with the British, Marquette and other French contemporaries indicate that the relationship was underway by the 1670s. The first British traders among the Chickasaws must have come from Virginia, but the Carolinians quickly made inroads. In 1685, when Henry Woodward set out to make an alliance with the Upper Creeks, he also sent emissaries to the more westerly Chickasaw Nation. By the 1690s, Carolina had eclipsed its neighboring colony to become the Chickasaws' premiere trading partner.[8]

Chickasaws showed an early interest in European trade. Such an interest was logical for Native Americans, who had exchanged goods with their allies for thousands of years. Gift exchange had been an essential component of foreign relations for chiefs, who needed prestige goods to confirm their elite status. When chiefs began to meet Spanish soldiers and missionaries in the sixteenth century, they received glass beads as well as hatchets and knives made of iron. These were novel items put to traditional use as prestige goods. By the early 1600s, when the Spaniards expanded their mission system, greater quantities of European jewelry and tools trickled into Native communities, but this commerce was nothing compared to the flood of consumer goods British traders introduced later that century. The British brought more metal tools, including hatchets, needles, knives, hoes, axes, and scissors, all of which served the same functions as similar tools of Native manufacture but proved more durable than those made of bone, wood, or stone. Indians particularly esteemed bronze kettles, sometimes using them for boiling water, sometimes cutting them up into gorgets and placing them about their necks in imitation of the shell and copper necklaces Mississippian chiefs had once worn. Among the most popular trade items were clothing, especially white linen shirts, petticoats, jackets, and woolen blankets called duffels that served as outer layers. According to Chickasaw war chief Oboystabee, "the beauties and fine women who are the warriors wives and mistresses . . . are so pleased to look sparkling in the dances, with the Cloaths bought from the English, that they would be very loath any difference should happen, least they again be reduced to their old wear of painted Buffeloe Calf skins." Native men and women admired their new clothes in looking glasses, which also aided them as they applied trade-acquired vermilion for purposes of war or ceremony. Native people smoked West Indian tobacco, which was milder than their native variety and thus suited for everyday use as well as special occasions. For the first time, alcohol flowed into Native communities, and warriors, in particular, favored Caribbean rum for the bold recklessness it seemed to impart.[9]

Southern Indians were discerning—they requested specific items, specific colors—but they were also eager consumers. British traders brought tools that made work easier and more efficient, ready-made clothes in new varieties and hues, and drugs that enhanced pleasure as well as bravery. Like their Anglo-American counterparts, Southern Indians experienced a consumer revolution that irrevocably altered their lifestyle. Moreover, they did so a bit earlier than the colonists, beginning around 1680 when British traders began to fan out across the region's interior. Native participation in the trans-Atlantic economy resulted not just from this new supply, but also from changes within their own societies. In the Mississippian period, chiefs controlled foreign exchange, acquiring headdresses made of Great Lakes copper and shell jewelry from the Gulf Coast as symbols of their spiritual power. As the chiefs' power declined, they lost the ability to regulate trade, and nonelite Indians began to seek access to outside markets. Although foreign goods may have lost some of their spiritual connotations, they retained the power to confer status upon their owners. By the early seventeenth century, through contact with the Spanish or down-the-line exchange with other Native people, commoners gained access to European-made wares such as brass bangles, copper bells, Venetian glass beads, and iron axes. In the past, only elites buried their dead with foreign trade goods, but after the breakdown of chiefdoms, such goods accompanied a significant portion of all Native burials. When the British market opened, traders sought animal pelts and Indian slaves, items that any skilled hunter or warrior could procure. The downfall of Mississippian societies upset traditional hierarchies, but in their place emerged a new order in which goods and trade connections became power in and of themselves.[10]

Native people prized their new clothing and tools, but, as Marquette discovered during his journey down the Mississippi, they desired rifles above all other trade goods. Seventeenth-century technological advances had made firearms increasingly practical weapons. A century earlier, Hernando de Soto's army had carried arquebuses, a type of matchlock. Cumbersome, inaccurate, and useless in damp conditions, the arquebus was poorly suited to the woodlands of eastern North America. In many ways, Native bows were superior weapons: experienced archers shot with ease and precision up to 70 yards and could launch arrows well beyond 100 yards. De Soto and his army employed the loud, smoking arquebuses primarily in attempts to impress or intimidate Native people. By the early seventeenth century, however, Flemish smiths had perfected the flintlock rifle, a lighter, more efficient weapon. To a greater degree than contemporary Europeans, American Indians adopted the flintlock, and by the mid-seventeenth century, English and Dutch merchants engaged in a booming gun trade with their Indian allies. The flintlock did have some clear advantages over Native bows: rifles shot an invisible projectile in a straight path (as opposed to the parabolic trajectory of the arrow, which skilled warriors dodged), and the guns had a range of up to 300 yards. Among Southern Indians, the most popular flintlock was the fusil, a simple smoothbore that weighed about 5 pounds. Still, when discharged, these firearms emitted loud blasts that scared away game and took longer than bows to reload; thus, they were not the best hunting weapons. Flintlocks were, however, ideal for making war.[11]

The arrival of flintlocks inaugurated a new era in Native warfare. Native warriors used these firearms to complement the martial skills they had cultivated for centuries: marksmanship, tracking, and stealth. The flintlock's flash and loud discharge served as an asset in warfare, inspiring panic and fear in victims, especially those without guns. In the colonial era, many Southern Indians proclaimed that firearms were related to the Thunderers, martial deities with great destructive potential. For unarmed groups, flintlocks remained a terrifying novelty. When war parties attacked enemy villages, the long range of flintlocks—as well as the psychological terror they inspired—gave them real advantages over bow-and-arrow nations. The Chickasaws explained to South Carolina Indian agent Thomas Nairne that firearms had changed their wartime fortunes: "Formerly when the Iroquois troubled these parts, they Drove the Chicasaws out of their Towns and made great Havock of them, but having attempted the like since they were furnished with Gunes found so warm a reception, that they thought fitt never to return since." Although Iroquois occasionally did return to the lower Mississippi valley, they found that the Chickasaws no longer made easy captives.[12]

Indians paid for these goods with pelts and slaves, drawing on traditional masculine pursuits to supply commodities for a new trans-Atlantic market. Initially, British traders purchased a diverse array of pelts including fox, beaver, raccoon, and otter. Due to decreasing European demand and colonial overproduction, this diverse trade declined sharply after 1700. British traders, however, did seem to have an insatiable demand for one product of the hunt—deerskins. Beginning in the early eighteenth century, a European cattle plague threatened the British leather industry, but American deerhides provided an acceptable substitute used by manufacturers in bookbinding, in saddles and saddlebags, and in deerskin breeches favored by American colonists. From 1700 to 1715, Indians supplied Charles Town merchants with 54,000 deerskins each year. The trade reached its peak in the mid-eighteenth century, when Native hunters provided upwards of 150,000 deerskins annually.[13]

The Indian slave trade, however, proved far more profitable for Native warriors. Traders paid captors the equivalent of up to 160 deerskins—about twice as much as a hunter could expect to take in a given year—for a single Indian slave. For the Chickasaws, the great distance to Charles Town often made the cost of transporting animal pelts higher than their value, so slaves became their major export to Carolina.[14] Speaking to a French soldier in 1700, a Muklasa Indian assured him that Carolina traders who lived among the Chickasaws traded "clothing, guns, gunpowder, shot, and a quantity of other goods. . . . But the greatest traffic between the English and the savages is the trade of slaves which the nations take from their neighbors whom they war with continuously, such that the men take the women and children away and sell them to the English, each person being traded for a gun."[15] Thomas Nairne, who had more intimate knowledge of the Chickasaw trade, claimed that his fellow Carolina traders offered Chickasaw warriors even more: "A lucky hitt at that besides the Honor procures them a whole Estate at once, one slave brings a Gun, ammunition, horse, hatchet, and a suit of Cloathes, which would not be procured without much tedious toil a hunting." Nairne concluded that "The good prices The English Traders give them for slaves Encourages them to this trade Extreamly."[16]

Why did the Chickasaws and other Native groups make war on enemy people and sell their human spoils to Euro-Americans? Because they did not yet think of themselves as a coherent group of people called "Indians." Native people maintained a very different view of themselves and their neighbors during the early colonial period, one that did not involve the idea of race. Broadly speaking, they divided people into three categories: kin, allies, and enemies. Kin were members of one's clan. Clans guaranteed their members rights to land and sustenance, redress for wrongs, and protection from aggressors. Clan affiliation was the most salient component of identity, dictating relative status and providing a framework for all social relations. Foreigners could be adopted into clans, and these initiates enjoyed the same rights as those born into the clan. Allies were fictive kin, transformed through ceremony from strangers to friends. Allied groups joined together as partners in trade and war. Forging fictive kin ties with multiple groups enabled Southern Indians to create vast networks across the region and beyond, but these alliances required maintenance, including gift exchange and ceremonial renewal, in order to remain strong.

As the Carolinians already knew, trade with Indians entailed more than an economic transaction—it was more akin to an exchange of gifts between

allies. Chickasaws, like other Native people, did not trade with their enemies or with strangers. Before Indians could trade with Europeans, they
first had to establish a formal social relationship. Marriage between British traders and Native women provided a solution. One trader found that
Chickasaw women scorned uncommitted sexual relationships: "what (say
they) you're among the Ochesses [Creeks] now, how brutall a
proposal you make, a night[.] [T]hats the way that beasts couple[;] it belongs
to mankind to be more particulare." Instead the women demanded, "He
that has me shall take incumbrances and all, and cohabit after that sociall
manner, which love and Freindship require and if you incline to that you
just aplay your selfe to my Unckle and Mother, and they'le tell you farther."
As the Chickasaw women told Nairne, a white trader who married into their
society gained far more than a wife. Through marriage, he became bound
to scores of her clan relatives throughout the Chickasaw Nation. Enveloped
in a Native world, British traders had to play by the rules of their hosts. Although traders sometimes believed their new Indian families to be a financial burden, they ultimately found the relationship beneficial. As Thomas
Nairne explained, the trader "has at once relations in each Village, from
Charles Town to the Missisipi, and if in traveling he acquants them with
what fameily he is incorporated into, those of that name treat, and wait on
him as their kinsman." Although traders were usually not adopted, their
wives' clan members provided them with food, lodging, protection, and
other aid. Once their place in Native kin structures was established, British
traders and Indians initiated proper gift exchange.[17]

Anyone not related through actual or fictive kinship was a potential
enemy, and enemies had no rights that Native people were bound to respect. Dualism pervaded Southern Indian culture, and such was the case
with categorizing others. Kin were loved, respected, and protected at all
costs; enemies were hated, denigrated, and attacked. While allies worked
to maintain peace, enemies frequently waged war. Native people considered torture, enslavement, and death appropriate fates for conquered enemies. Inside the kinship system, peace, security, and order dominated;
outside, danger, violence, and disorder reigned. In 1717, Louisiana's com-
missary general observed this dualism: "The Indians are savages only in
name. . . . They have a regular government among themselves after their
own fashion, no injustice, no quarrels, a very exact subordination and
great respect for their chiefs, whom they obey spiritedly." On the other
hand, he pointed out their martial prowess and hatred for enemies: "They

love war. They are brave. They despise those who show no indications of being brave. They suffer resolutely hardship, hunger, and even death. They lack generosity for the conquered, to whom they show no mercy."[18]

Native nations harbored animosity toward enemy groups close to home and far afield. When Marquette announced his plans to descend the Mississippi, his Menominee friends vehemently objected: "They told me I would meet with Indians who spare no strangers, and whom they kill without any provocation or mercy. . . . That the Great River was exceedingly dangerous, and full of frightful monsters who devoured men and canoes together and that the heat was so great that it would positively cause our death."[19] Enemies, monsters, and searing heat, the Menominees feared, threatened to destroy the black-robed Jesuit—especially now that he had become their ally. Native people so zealously demonized their enemies that they sometimes called them cannibals. Indian groups living along the Carolina coast told their British neighbors that the Westos, who slaved against them, ate children. From what planter Stephen Bull understood, the Westos "doe strike a great feare in these Indians havinge gunns & powder & shott & doe come upon these Indians heere in the tyme of their cropp & destroye all by killinge Caryinge away their Corne & Children & eat them."[20] The Choctaws called several tribes living to their southwest *Attacapa,* meaning "cannibal." (Defending themselves to a late-eighteenth-century visitor, the Atakapas said that formerly they had burned their prisoners to death but did not eat them.)[21] Cannibals have long populated the oral traditions of the Chitimachas. One Chitimacha story tells of how the Karankawas, a group living on the Gulf Coast of what is now Texas, used to steal into the bayous of southern Louisiana, hiding in the tall grass "naked" and "crouched down" like animals. If any children happened by, the cannibals struck: "The Karankawa would steal them, take them home and eat the children. Indian children or white children or any other—if they stole (any) of the children they ate them."[22] Significantly, groups accused of this practice were cultural outsiders among Southern Indians; the Westos were recent immigrants, while the Atakapas and Karankawas lived on the region's margins. To highlight just how different these groups were, other Indians accused them of cannibalism, an unspeakable act in their own societies.

In the early colonial period, Native groups feared one another much more than they did Europeans. After all, Indians had watched several early colonial ventures dissolve into oblivion, ruined by disease, starvation, and internecine fights. For example, the 1682 expedition of René-Robert Cave-lier, Sieur de La Salle, failed to make much of an impression on the Chickasaws, even though some members stayed in the area for a few years and built a fort. A generation later, Chickasaws described the Frenchmen as "poor ramblers" and recalled that they offered the vagrants a few empty fields to plant. In 1687, several years after he visited the Chickasaws, La Salle, like de Soto and Narváez before him, suffered an inglorious death when the mutinous survivors of his failed east Texas colony murdered him. By 1700, European settlement in the region was restricted to a few thinly settled outposts: English settlements at Charles Town and Port Royal Sound hugged the Atlantic seaboard; the Spanish had managed to establish a string of missions from the Georgia coast to Florida's panhan-dle, but those settlements were overwhelmingly populated by Native peo-ple; French settlers and soldiers had just built their first fort in Louisiana the previous year. The climate of fear among Native enemies prompted many to seek alliances with Europeans, who seemed weak in number but possessed a startling array of consumer goods. The Sewees, Native Caro-linians of the Port Royal Sound, rushed to embrace the colony's first En-glish settlers as they landed in 1670. Mustering a bit of Spanish, along with gestures and drawings, the Indians communicated their wish to ally with the English. Proving their peaceful intentions through trade, the Sewees offered the newcomers deerskins, and they received knives, beads, and to-bacco in return. According to one observer, "they hoped by our Arrivall to be protected from ye Westoes, often making signes they would ingage them with their bowes & arrows, & wee should with our guns." These coastal people had suffered from armed Westo slave raiders and now hoped to gain a European trade alliance of their own.[23]

The willingness of the Chickasaws and other Native people to engage in the Indian slave trade stemmed from their own needs and worldview. For at least several hundred years, the Chickasaws and their ancestors had captured their enemies, whom they felt they could kill, adopt, or sell ac-cording to Chickasaw needs. After all, war captives lacked kin ties in Chickasaw communities, and thus they had no rights. The exploitation and commodification of conquered enemies was nothing new in Native North America.

In 1682, La Salle and the members of his expedition caught bloody glimpses of a massacre. As they canoed the Pearl River, they saw an abandoned village belonging to the Acolapissas: "First we noticed something like many people; when we had landed, we saw that the crowds were crows, eagles, and other beasts that seek out carrion. . . . On approaching, we saw only carcasses of men and women, ruined huts, and others full of dead bodies, a coating of blood on the ground, and all their canoes broken and cut up with axes." Later, they found four women who had escaped, probably having fled in a canoe. When the Frenchmen asked "who had committed this destruction," the women replied "Auma, Auma"—the Houmas—and "Chiquilousa," the name of a Chickasaw town. The ghastly scene La Salle and his men found at the Acolapissa village was one that would play out again and again throughout the era of the Indian slave trade: well-armed Native groups made war against weaker people, killing some, capturing as many as possible, and selling thousands to European traders.[24]

Thomas Nairne, the Indian agent who once accompanied a Chickasaw war party, described how Chickasaws captured enemies. A hierarchy of officers, so elevated due to their achievements in war, commanded rank-and-file warriors. Officers carried medicine bags, pouches containing curative roots, bones, feathers of predatory mammals and birds, and locks of hair taken from their former captives. Through ritual, officers transferred the spiritual power contained in these items to their subordinates to ensure success. On the day of the battle, officers, employing a tactic traditionally used to drive game, ordered warriors to surround a portion of the enemy village in a half-moon formation. Then, according to Nairne, the war chief gave a whistle and "every man Clapes his hand to his mouth, gives the War Whoop, and then catch as catch can." After their initial assault, the warriors closed their half-moon formation into a complete circle around the village. As the battle progressed, a troop of ten to twelve young Chickasaw women sang to encourage the warriors: "If their own men succeed, they praise them highly and Degrade the Enimy, but if [the enemy] give Back the singers alter their praises into reproaches, Thus changing notes according as their party advance or give way." As the Chickasaws gained advantage over their enemies, warriors killed some of the men, but attempted to take a "good store of prissoners." Successful warriors bound their captives and hung their medicine bags about the prisoners' necks, demonstrating the reality of their spiritual power and its efficacy in defeating their enemies.[25]

In 1698, when the French began to explore the lower Mississippi valley, they found that the Chickasaws were the only group that possessed firearms amidst a sea of bow-and-arrow tribes. That year, Chickasaws warred as far north as Illinois country, where, along with Shawnee allies, they killed ten warriors and took captive 100 men as well as an unknown number of women and children. When Jean-Baptiste Le Moyne de Bienville visited the Acolapissas in May 1699, he found the small nation in an uproar. Shortly before, 200 Chickasaws and two Englishmen had launched a surprise attack "and had taken prisoner many of their people." A year later, Chickasaw warriors revisited the Acolapissas, whose great village now contained only about twenty houses. Their newly constructed palisade failed to repel the invaders, and fifty Acolapissas became Chickasaw captives.[26] An English trader claimed that the Chickasaws most frequently warred against groups to their southwest, against smaller nations like the Acolapissas, "wher they can with the Greatest Ease, get a Booty," but, he continued, they "have the most bickering with the Chactaws who live 60 Miles south of them." Three times as populous as the Chickasaws, the Choctaw Nation offered slavers great risk but also the potential for great reward.[27]

At this time, four divisions of Choctaws inhabited some fifty villages along the Pearl and Chickasawhay rivers and tributary streams. Survivors of collapsed chiefdoms, these Choctaws numbered roughly 21,000 in 1700. The Choctaws' ancestors had lived in chiefdoms strewn across the modern states of Mississippi and Alabama. After their chiefdoms splintered, these disparate groups decided to leave their old towns and move to a new place, perhaps to escape the taint of disease and death. They chose east-central Mississippi, an area that had been unoccupied for some time, having served as a buffer zone between chiefdoms. The region did not possess rich soil, but it abounded in game. In this new place, the Choctaws sought to overcome their divisions and forge a multiethnic confederacy. This impetus toward centralization resulted in part from the aggression of their newly armed Indian neighbors—especially the Chickasaws.[28]

Taking advantage of the nascent Choctaw confederacy's political and military weakness, the Chickasaws drew on their own group cohesion and British trade alliance to bully their southerly neighbors. Seeking to preserve their exclusive access to firearms, the Chickasaws cut off the Choctaws from potential English trading partners. By 1702, according to the estimate of Chickasaw and Choctaw chiefs, at least 40 percent of Chickasaw men owned guns, while firepower among the Choctaws was negligible. The Chickasaws also managed to restrict Choctaw access to hunting territory by hemming them in geographically. When Frenchman Henri de Tonti traveled with Choctaw warriors in 1702, he complained that they took him dozens of leagues out of his way to avoid trouble at the hands of roaming Chickasaw war parties. As a consequence of Chickasaw regional dominance, the early-eighteenth-century Choctaws controlled less territory despite their much larger population. When Chickasaw hunting parties made their camps near Choctaw settlements, they fearlessly heralded their presence through bonfire-lighted feasting, smoking, and dancing to the beat of drums. Such ostentation, the Chickasaws explained, was designed "to show the Chactaws how little we vallued them."[29]

During the early years of the Indian slave trade, Chickasaw attacks plagued the Choctaws. By 1702, Pierre Le Moyne d'Iberville claimed that during the past decade Chickasaw warriors had captured more than 500 Choctaws and killed an additional 1,800. Though only estimates, Iberville's numbers reveal the devastation the slave trade wrought. Chickasaws managed to take an average of fifty Choctaw captives each year, but they had to kill a staggering number—three for every captive—to do so. Though poorly armed, the Choctaws resisted fiercely, killing about 800 Chickasaws during that ten-year period.[30]

As the French sought to plant their own colony in the lower Mississippi valley, they forged alliances with many Indian groups reeling from Chickasaw warfare. Louisianans especially prized their relationship with the Choctaws, formalized in 1700. Like other residents of the region, the French harbored a great fear of the Chickasaws' military strength, and they sought out Native neighbors who might aid them in warfare. They realized that the Chickasaws controlled a portion of the Mississippi River and thus had the power to cut off Louisiana's lifeline to New France.[31] Louisiana's leaders also saw the Chickasaws as an extension of English imperial power. Bienville claimed, "the Chickasaws have no commerce except that in slaves which they carry on with the English for what they give them they induce by presents to take them from our allies in order to weaken us."[32] In a bid to protect French Louisiana as well as the Choctaw Nation, Iberville called a conference at Mobile in March 1702. With his brother Bienville interpreting, Iberville persuaded the Chickasaws to make peace with the Choctaws, to ally with the French, and to cease trading in Indian slaves. He explained "skins of buffalo, deer, bear . . . those are the slaves I want."[33] The Chickasaws, proving that they were not merely English pawns, agreed to Iberville's terms. Although Chickasaw headmen did not record their reasons for doing so, they, too, may have grown weary of incessant warfare, or perhaps French promises of favorable trading terms persuaded them to join the alliance.

The peace settlement was short-lived, for the Chickasaws quickly realized that the French were unable to provide them with the manufactured goods they desired. French officials privately admitted that British traders offered much better prices, owing to the lower cost and higher quality of English manufactured goods. To make matters worse, French Louisiana was poorly supplied by its mother country, especially in terms of all-important firearms and ammunition. A French officer addressing Louisiana's Naval Council speculated with only slight exaggeration, "If [hostile warriors] come to Louisiana they will find it easy prey since it has not enough [munitions] to defend itself for one day."[34] The Chickasaws had come to rely on firearms to support their newly won dominance; they certainly could not depend on such an unreliable trading partner as the floundering colony of Louisiana. In fact, the Chickasaws came to regard the Frenchmen of Louisiana as "women," using this label as a derisive epithet suggesting "military incapacity or fear."[35] Chickasaw war chief Oboystabee complained of the French trade agreement, "They b[u]oyed us up with a mighty expectation, of what vast profite we should reap by Freindship and commerce with them. . . . But after suficent Tryall made, our people are now undeceived." Speaking to a British trader, Oboystabee insisted that the Chickasaw warriors *chose* to traffic with Carolinians, "for they dispose of their slaves to your Traders much to their advantage." Acting in their own self-interest, the Chickasaws treated with whom they pleased.[36]

In 1704, English traders, sensing the Chickasaws' dissatisfaction with their French alliance, reentered Chickasaw towns to repair the breach. Like true allies, they came bearing gifts: twelve Taensa slaves. Having learned Native protocol, these Englishmen understood that, as a social relationship, trade was always a two-way street. In this significant exchange, the English gifted slaves in an unusual direction—back to Native people.[37] By 1705, Chickasaw war parties were active once again. Initially feigning friendship, the Chickasaws entered a Choctaw town and attacked, capturing several Choctaw families and rekindling warfare between the two groups. The following spring Chickasaw warriors launched a rare night raid on a Choctaw village, taking more than 150 captives. Although European sources recorded few details of the violence that plagued the lower Mississippi valley, warfare between the Choctaws and Chickasaws continued throughout the early eighteenth century and intermittently thereafter. The most devastating raid on the Choctaws came in 1711. The Carolinians, motivated by a Spanish succession crisis that initiated a global imperial conflict and spurred Queen Anne's War in North America, sought to bolster their own fortunes and enrich themselves in the process by attacking the most valuable allies of French Louisiana, the Choctaws. Enlisting the aid of their allies the Creeks and the Chickasaws, the English sponsored an attack that resulted in about 260 captives, at least 160 Choctaw deaths, and the burning of hundreds of houses and fields.[38]

English and French accounts dating from 1682 to 1713, which marked the height of Chickasaw participation in the Indian slave trade, suggest that the Chickasaws, sometimes acting in concert with their allies, captured a minimum of 1,200 captives. The actual number is probably much higher, perhaps 2,000 or more.[39] While an accurate count is impossible, available records elucidate the massive scale of the trade and undeniable devastation it visited on victims. If Iberville's estimate of three Choctaws killed for every captive taken is even close to accurate, then Chickasaw warriors killed more enemies than they captured. Along with other slaving societies during this period, they exacerbated Native demographic woes by further destabilizing ailing groups.

For the Chickasaws and other Native groups, the colonial slave trade retained important aspects of Mississippian captive exchange but also ushered in a new era. As their ancestors had, the Chickasaws made war upon enemy groups, captured prisoners, and exchanged them with one another or their allies, who, by the late seventeenth century, included the British. However, the disintegration of chiefdoms had brought changes to captivity practices. Disease and dislocation toppled chiefs who had wielded so much power over the lives of Mississippian people. Native societies became less stratified, governed instead by representatives from each clan. Indeed, clans fulfilled many of the responsibilities formerly belonging to chiefs. Clans now chose how to control and distribute their surplus crops and prestige goods, maintained social order, and took on more prominent roles in ritual and ceremony. The downfall of chiefdoms also changed the way Indians waged war. No longer did armed conflict serve elite goals of further concentrating resources and power in the hands of a few. As a group, Chickasaws now used captives to ensure their survival and preserve their autonomy.

Although the Chickasaws found the slave trade lucrative, constant war took the lives of many. French planter Antoine Simon Le Page du Pratz asserted that the Chickasaws "cut off a great many nations who were adjoining to them," but "could not succeed against their enemies without considerable loss to themselves, and that they have therefore greatly lessened their own numbers by their many warlike expeditions." During the late seventeenth century, when many of the Chickasaws' enemies lacked firearms, they usually attempted to evade attacks by fleeing their homes and hiding out in swamps or canebreaks, but these victims might also retaliate violently. John Stewart, a Carolina slave trader who accompanied Chickasaw war parties in 1692, depicted the Choctaws not as pathetic victims of Chickasaw warfare, but as dangerous, calculating guerrillas. According to Stewart, Choctaws trailed homeward-bound Chickasaw warriors: at night, the Choctaws circled Chickasaw camps and launched showers of arrows; during the day, they hid behind trees, bows drawn, and fired furtive shots; they tracked Chickasaws charged with providing the rest of their party with game, picking off hunters who strayed too far. Small parties of Quapaws and Illinois also stole into Chickasaw territory, surprising and capturing isolated Chickasaws on the outskirts of towns. After the Choctaws allied with French Louisiana, they also gained firearms: not so many as the Chickasaws, but enough to mount a more effective offense. In the fall of 1705, for example, when Chickasaw warriors invaded, Choctaws initially hid in the woods, biding their time as Chickasaws destroyed their homes and fields. At an opportune moment, Choctaws carrying French rifles emerged to attack the Chickasaws' rear guard, killing many. By the early eighteenth century, many Native nations of the Mississippi valley gained access to firearms by allying with the French, and increasingly well-armed foes made for heavier Chickasaw casualties.[40]

Such warfare created a destructive cycle in which warriors, animated by the deaths of their countrymen, sought revenge. When a Chickasaw man died, his relatives erected a wooden post beside his former house. They painted the post red and adorned it with his broken bow as well as his arrows, other military regalia, and white and red feathers. Normally, they would mourn him there for four months, but when men died in war the post would remain until a captive from the offending nation was tortured

and killed there. The Choctaws, too, avenged the death of their kin by
torturing enemy warriors. According to trader John Stewart, straggling
Chickasaw warriors whom Choctaws managed to capture were "burned
alive with Lingering torments." Stewart claimed that Lower Creeks regularly tortured war captives; while trekking back to Creek country after one
successful raid, the victors killed two or three prisoners every night. In
1712, a Carolina missionary reported that the Yamasees also burned male
captives. Wrongful deaths, so plentiful during the slave trade era, demanded vengeance and contributed to the overall death toll.[41]

In addition to losses due to warfare, Native people continued to suffer
from European-introduced diseases. French settlement of Louisiana and
the extension of British trade networks into the interior South facilitated the
spread of deadly pathogens. Warfare and epidemics worked in tandem to
cut the Chickasaw population nearly in half during the era of the Indian
slave trade, from about 7,000 in 1685 to 4,000 by 1715. Already a compara-
tively small nation, the Chickasaws steadily lost population until the mid-
eighteenth century.[42]

In an effort to slow population loss, the Chickasaws adopted captives.
This response to demographic crisis represented a shift away from Mississippian captivity practices. Mississippians did adopt some captives: Chief Mocozo made Juan Ortiz his kinsman; the Calusas almost certainly adopted
the Spanish women who married and had children among them; in the
1560s, Frenchman Rene Laudonniere reported that chiefs killed enemy
warriors but spared many of the women and children "and retain[ed] them
permanently." Adoption, like captivity itself, was probably an ancient cultural practice, but Mississippians used it more sparingly and for different
reasons. The earliest recorded instances of captive adoption, which date to
the sixteenth century, indicate that the decision fell to chiefs.[43] Just as they
did with other prestige goods, chiefs may have purposely rarified adoptions.
Mississippian remains bearing signs of death consistent with warfare include a relatively high percentage of women; this evidence suggests that invading warriors killed men as well as noncombatants. One archaeologist
has gone so far as to label warfare during that period "a relatively indiscrimi-
nate slaughter." This may be an exaggeration, but it is clear that Mississippian warfare came in the form of quick assaults designed to cower enemies
and force them into a tributary relationship. During the Mississippian period, captives were a by-product of warfare, not its object.[44]

As the Indian slave trade developed, the desire to take captives heavily influenced and sometimes drove warfare. Captors became more selective, sparing more women and children as well as some men. But not all captives became fodder for the Indian slave trade. Captors, even major slavers like the Chickasaws, adopted many in an effort to offset their own population losses. During his 1708 visit to the Chickasaw Nation, Thomas Nairne saw this strategy in action. He noted that if a Chickasaw killed a fellow tribesman, the deceased person's clan was obligated to either kill the murderer or replace the deceased with a captive. If the murderer's clan opted for the latter, "they must likewise put the first slave they take in his place, to make up the number of the fameily." Nairne also explained that whenever a Chickasaw was taken captive by an enemy group, he became socially dead; "as soon as any person is taken, they Account him dead, and call killing and being taken prisoner by the same name." Adopted captives replaced these fallen warriors and perhaps those killed by disease as well.[45]

Similar ceremonies occurred throughout the region, as nations stressed by war and disease struggled to survive. In 1700, when Jesuit missionary Jacques Gravier visited the Houmas, he noted, "They are not cruel and very far from putting to death any of the slaves they make; as soon as they enter the village the women weep over them, compassionating their being taken, and then treat them better than their children." Pushed out of their homeland by Chickasaw warfare, this small tribe moved farther south only to meet greater violence and instability. To endure as a separate people, they had to convert captives into kin. Although their situation was less dire than that of the Houmas, the Yamasees and Lower Creeks must have adopted some of their war captives, for they complained to Carolina's Commissioners of the Indian Trade that certain traders tried to pressure them to sell captives too quickly. Responding to these complaints, the commissioners ordered traders not to buy any Indian slaves unless they had lived in their captors' towns for three days, and they declared all captives adopted by their masters to be free.[46]

Because Native nations strove to sustain population levels, they often chose women and children over male captives. The demography of victim groups bears out this grim reality. In 1703, half the men of the Taensas, a lower Mississippi valley group, had no wives or children. Captors' preferences resulted in severely imbalanced sex ratios for victims and victors alike. Groups like the Taensa lost many or most members of the next generation.

Meanwhile, groups like the Chickasaws augmented their own numbers and enhanced their prospects for long-term survival. The adoption of sexually mature women was central to the Chickasaws' strategy for social reproduction. Nairne noted that polygamy was "in fashion among the Chicasaws." In this case, Nairne's diction is quite apt, for the popularity of this practice at the height of the Indian slave trade was no accident: polygamous families could create many more children than could a monogamous couple.[47]

By 1771, a Chickasaw man named North West claimed that he was one of only two "real original" Chickasaws left—all the rest were "of a slave race." By this statement, North West meant that nearly everyone in his nation had descended from former captives and thus were only naturalized Chickasaws. Although he surely exaggerated, North West did reveal the extent to which Chickasaws relied on captivity to ensure their continued existence as a people.[48]

Beyond sale, death, or adoption, Native people found still other uses for their war captives. The experiences of Lamhatty, a Tawasa Indian from the Mobile Bay area, illustrate the myriad roles Native captors assigned to their slaves. Lamhatty's remarkable story, which he related in 1707 via a Tuscarora interpreter to two Virginia colonists, represents a Native victim's perspective on Indian slavery. Lamhatty came from a multiethnic confederacy composed largely of former mission Indians who left Florida following the Creek raids of 1702–1704. According to Lamhatty, the Creeks came back in 1706 and again the following spring, when they took him captive and marched him to Tallapoosa. For three or four months, Lamhatty toiled in Creek fields, engaging in the same kinds of work that Hernando de Soto had seen slaves perform 150 years earlier at Cofitachequi. Because Lamhatty arrived among the Creeks in the spring and stayed through much of the summer, he probably helped the women tend to, and later harvest, the year's first corn crop. It was likely after the harvest that his Creek captors again moved Lamhatty, this time to the southern reaches of the Appalachians, where they sold him to a group of Savannahs, ethnic Shawnees who lived on the upper Savannah River. This group of six men, two women, and three children was headed north for a hunting expedition. His hands bound, Lamhatty traveled with them for six weeks, but when the group reached the Rappahannock River he managed to escape. Running southeastward, Lamhatty finally reached the colonial settlement of Mattapony, Virginia. Naked, exhausted, and desperate, Lamhatty arrived at the house of Andrew Clark, presenting himself as passively as possible in order not to alarm. During his nightmarish journey from Mobile Bay to Virginia, Lamhatty had played the role of captive, laborer, and chattel. When his captors finally sold him, it was not to the Carolina slave trader or planter one might expect, but rather to a Shawnee family. Lamhatty's story, recorded during the height of the Indian slave trade, demonstrates that Native cultural imperatives endured and Native trade networks still functioned.[49]

If Indians perpetuated some of the diversity that had characterized Mississippian captivity, they also departed from older practices in significant ways. Encouraging participants to take ever more captives, the slave trade escalated the scale of violence to unprecedented levels. The Chickasaws and several other slavers—the Creeks, Yamasees, Westos, and Savannahs—virtually destroyed dozens of tribes, especially smaller groups or those hit hard by epidemic diseases. Unfortunately, the Indian slave trade has left a sparse paper trail, making it difficult to provide even a rough estimate for the total number of victims. Scattered references exist in the letters and journals of colonial officials, traders, and missionaries, but those with the most extensive knowledge of the slave trade—Carolina traders who spent most of the year residing among their Indian partners—have left behind precious few documents. Carolina's Commissioners of the Indian Trade, a regulatory body that governed the trade beginning in 1710, heard the complaints of traders and Indians, but their records detail the conflicts that punctuated the trade rather than its everyday workings.[50] A rough Carolina census for 1708 indicates that about 1,400 Indian slaves lived in the colony, comprising about 15 percent of its overall population. By 1715, that number had risen to about 1,850 Indian slaves.[51] The total numbers, however, are much higher than the Carolina records might lead us to expect. Estimates based on current research suggest that between 1670 and 1715 British traders and their Southern Indian allies took between 24,000 and 51,000 war captives, most of whom were exported to New England or the Caribbean. The lower end of this estimate, perhaps 25,000 captives taken during this period, is most likely. Captors, however, did not sell all of their prisoners to the English; they killed some and kept others for their own purposes. Still, 25,000 captives sold, killed, or displaced is staggering. To this number, we must add the untold thousands who must have died resisting capture.[52]

Beyond the scale of captive exchange, the Indian slave trade warped Native diplomacy, encouraging nations to make war rather than peace. Resident traders doubtlessly played a role in this process, sowing unrest among the people and stirring up bile against enemies. Some longtime traders, such as Alexander Longe who lived among the Cherokees, even sat on war councils. Traders also accompanied their allies into battle and, if French sources on this account can be trusted, sometimes assumed leadership positions. Euro-American critics, mortified at the havoc the slave trade visited on their Native allies, blamed self-serving traders for the perpetual warfare they witnessed. Francis Le Jau, a missionary who served the Goose Creek parish near Charles Town, asked, "It is certain the Indians are very cruel to one another, but is it not to be feared some white men living or trading among them do foment and increase that Bloody Inclination in order to get Slaves?" The very presence of resident British traders, most of them incorporated into Native kin networks through marriage, changed the nature of captive-taking, for they doubtlessly encouraged their kin and allies to pursue bloody paths.[53]

The trade's enticements—as well as the upheaval it created—made for fickle alliances, even outright deception. After Chickasaw raiding pushed several smaller nations farther south, the Taensas came to a Bayagoula village seeking refuge. Shortly afterward, however, the Taensas, wishing to become sole masters of the village, surprised the Bayagoulas and massacred almost the entire tribe. The Taensas, in turn, invited Chitimachas and Yagenechitos (a small group whose recorded name means "Big Country" people) to come to their village "and eat wheat." Instead of sharing bread, the Taensas captured several of their guests and sold them into slavery. Reportedly, the Chickasaws also engaged in such treachery. In 1713, along with some Natchez and Yazoos, Chickasaws visited the Chawashas, a small nation in the lower Mississippi valley, under pretense of peace-making with the calumet. Instead, they killed the chief and several others and took captive ten Chawashas, including the chief's wife.[54]

From the Mississippian period to the early eighteenth century, Native societies changed dramatically, and the Indian slave trade played a major transformative role. A political map of the Mississippian South would display dozens of chiefdoms strung along waterways across the region. Because they shared similar resources and engaged in constant competition for political and economic power, chiefdoms in any given area tended toward parity in population, structure, and size. During the seventeenth century, when epidemic diseases forced the collapse of most chiefdoms, that same map would become nearly unrecognizable. But the effects of disease were uneven, taking a heavier toll in areas near the Atlantic and Gulf coasts where Europeans tended to visit or settle. Interior polities still suffered, but their distance from European settlement provided some protection. By the early eighteenth century, the South's interior would become the locus of Native power, drawing in survivors from defunct chiefdoms. The Indian slave trade accelerated this process, fostering a gross imbalance of power. Slavers, who could use captives to enhance their political and economic prospects as well as replace fallen kinsmen, dominated their neighbors. They drew captives from the small, the weak, and the unarmed, crippling and frequently destroying ailing groups. Those seeking refuge reinforced this trend by turning to stronger people, sometimes to European colonies, but more often to the emerging Native nations of the interior, the Cherokee, Creek, Chickasaw, and Choctaw. Over time, the South lost much of its ethnic diversity, as Indians created larger, more flexible polities better suited to overcoming the challenges of colonialism.[55]

The four major Southern Indian nations of the early eighteenth century experienced birth pangs as they struggled to achieve political solidarity, but the Chickasaws were the most cohesive group. Unlike the Choctaws and Creeks, motley groups composed of the descendants of disparate chiefdoms, the early-eighteenth-century Chickasaws shared a relatively homogeneous culture and remained in their ancestral homeland. In 1708, Thomas Nairne remarked that among the Indians whom he had met, the Chickasaws remembered the most about the de Soto expedition and could even point to the spot where the Spaniards had camped. Nairne's story highlights how continuity of people and place helped the Chickasaws forge a strong group identity.[56]

To meet the challenges of living in the colonial South, all Native groups restructured their societies. During the era of the Indian slave trade, the Chickasaws, among others, made the decision to militarize. Mississippian chiefs had relied on warriors to protect and enhance their political power, but for slavers warfare became all-consuming during this period, eclipsing even the civil functions of their government. A Chickasaw oral tradition recorded in the early nineteenth century surely harkens back to the old days of the slave trade: "They say that as far back as they can learn by their ancesters, verbally handed down, & extended from family to family that there was nothing but war all nations were at war. The Chickasaws were at war with all nations—this scene of war they remembered to continue for a long time."[57] At some point prior to the slave trade era, the Chickasaws developed a dual system of government, in which one chief served as their civil leader, managing internal matters and peaceful diplomacy, and another acted as a war chief, leading the people during times of conflict. By the first decade of the eighteenth century, the civil chief's power had eroded significantly. In fact, the acting civil chief, Fattalamee, decided that the post was no longer worth his efforts: "finding that the warriors had the best time of it, that slave Catching was much more profitable than formall haranguing, he then turned Warrior too, and proved as good a man hunter as the best of them." The economic and political benefits of the slave trade encouraged the Chickasaws to make war, and they reorganized their society accordingly.[58]

Decades of continual warfare cemented the bonds that held the Chickasaw Nation together. The rituals that accompanied warfare cut across clan lines, binding men of diverse rank and age groups together. Women also contributed by accompanying men into battle and providing both critiques and encouragements through song. In combat, Chickasaws carefully retrieved the bodies of those who fell. They usually interred the dead underneath their former houses, but when a Chickasaw died abroad, his countrymen gathered and bundled his bones, carrying his remains back so that they could be buried in the Chickasaw homeland. Returning to their nation after a victory, Chickasaw warriors redistributed their spoils, thereby allowing all members of society to benefit from their success. Although high-ranking warriors retained their captives for use by their own clans, more junior members of the party presented their prisoners to their "patrons." These patrons were important members of other clans, who accepted the captives as gifts. In return, patrons gave young men new war titles as well as "2 small white Arrows" to wear in their hair as marks of honor. Because Mississippian iconography abounds with warriors sporting such decorative arrows as hairpins, this ancient symbol must have had deep resonance in Native societies. It connected warriors to an unbroken military tradition and called to mind the legendary heroes who came before them. Redistribution of war spoils—including captives—and confirmation of the bonds that united all the Chickasaw clans prevented jealousy and material accumulation from tearing at the fabric of society. Simultaneously, this ritual exchange ensured that honor-seeking warriors would continue to replenish Chickasaw society with captives. At a time when some Native polities ceased to exist, the Chickasaws simultaneously maintained peace within their own nation and contributed to the chaotic violence that plagued the broader colonial South.[59]

Despite their small numbers, the Chickasaws managed to use their military might to project resounding power throughout the region, intimidating both Indian and European neighbors. Through trade in slaves, the Chickasaws "made themselves terrible" to Native groups "who wanted that advantage, so they have now the reputation of the most military people of any about the great river [the Mississippi]."[60] While traveling down the Mississippi in 1698, Jesuit missionary Jean Francois Buisson de St. Cosme listened to accounts of the Chickasaws from the Indians he met. St. Cosme, too, learned to fear the Chickasaws. When one of the enslaved Indian boys accompanying St. Cosme's mission failed to turn up after going to gather fruit in Quapaw country, the Jesuit fretted that "he might have been taken by some Chicacha warriors." St. Cosme's worries were well founded, but, luckily for the boy, he had merely lost his way and turned up the next morning.[61] Decades later, in his memoir of Louisiana, Bienville asserted that the Chickasaws "breathe nothing but war and are unquestionably the bravest of the continent."[62] Chickasaw warriors achieved legendary status among their British allies: "The Chickasaws are of all Indians the most Manly in their Persons, Sentiments, and Actions . . . by much the best Hunters; and without Exception (by the acknowledgement of all Europeans as well as Indians that know them, who respect them as such) the best Warriours. Even their Women handle Armes, and face an Enemy like Men."[63] Even today, Chickasaws highlight their martial reputation as one of the hallmarks of their identity: they are "unconquered and unconquerable."[64]

The Chickasaws also used peaceful means to enhance their power. Throughout the early eighteenth century, they allied with neighbors, including the Natchez, Yazoo, Mobiliens, and Chitimachas. To ensure strong relationships with other tribes, a number of *fanemingos*, "squirrel chiefs," acted as Chickasaw diplomats. Allied nations chose a fanemingo—usually a high-ranking warrior—to represent their interests; the Chickasaws also selected fanemingos to speak for them abroad. A fanemingo's job, according to Thomas Nairne, was "to make up all Breaches between the 2 nations, to keep the pipes of peace by which at first they contracted

Freindship, to devert the Warriors from any designe against the people they protect, and Pacifie them by carrying them the Eagle pipe to smoak out of, and if after all, ar unable to oppose the stream, are to send the people private intelligence to provide for their own safty." Nairne believed that European nations could take a cue from the Chickasaw fanemingos, who preserved open communication and promoted peace between allies. The French, in fact, participated in the Chickasaw fanemingo tradition during their short-lived peace. Following their 1702 conference with Louisiana officials, the Chickasaws requested that a French boy be placed among them to be groomed as a fanemingo. They received 14-year-old St. Michel, who, within a year, learned to speak fluent Chickasaw. While the Creeks and Choctaws absorbed large groups of refugee groups, the smaller Chickasaws showed less enthusiasm for ethnic pluralism within their own nation, relying instead on their fanemingos to maintain alliances.[65]

Success in the slave trade and concomitant military power translated into broader regional power for the Chickasaw people. Although many small groups became absorbed by larger nations or were consumed by the slave trade, the Chickasaws retained the power to rule themselves and even extended hegemonic power over others. Their ability to secure trade goods and their success in warfare convinced other groups that the Chickasaws made either powerful allies or terrible enemies.

The devastation suffered by the slave trade's victims highlights just how successfully the Chickasaws adapted to the demands and constraints of the early colonial period. The Apalachees, who hailed from the region of modern-day Tallahassee, Florida, had deep roots in the region but suffered a terrible downfall during the era of the slave trade. In Mississippian times, the Apalachee chiefdom controlled rich, arable lands between the Aucilla and Ochlocknee rivers and dominated at least one tributary chiefdom. Throughout most of the period, Apalachee chiefs ruled from the Lake Jackson site, which produced some of the Mississippian period's most sophisticated art. When Hernando de Soto arrived in Florida in 1539, the Apalachees, numbering 20,000 to 30,000, were one of the region's larger groups. As the Spaniards approached their territory, other Native Floridians informed the Spaniards that the Apalachees were a powerful chiefdom of fierce warriors. Indeed, the Apalachees harassed de Soto's army throughout the winter of 1539 and succeeded in killing a number of Spaniards.[66] A century later, another group of Spaniards—Franciscan missionaries—visited the Apalachees, who had been ravaged by epidemic diseases. The Apalachee chiefs elected to join the Spanish mission system and converted to Christianity. Despite the Apalachees' dissatisfaction with inadequate Spanish military protection and the *repartimiento* system that compelled many to labor without pay, they remained in the mission system until January 1704, when fifty Englishmen and a thousand-man army of Creeks and Yamasees marched against them. The Creeks, who launched an additional raid six months later, had particular grievances against the Apalachees, whom they counted among their "bitter enemies" since "time immemorial."[67] Altogether, the invaders destroyed fourteen mission towns and dozens of other Apalachee villages and farmsteads. Out of an Apalachee population of about 7,000, several hundred died and at least 2,000 became captives. Most captives wound up as English slaves, while some remained in Creek country. About 1,300 Apalachees surrendered, and the Carolinians forced these survivors into quasi-captivity by resettling them at the Westos' old haunt, Savannah Town, in order to protect the colony's southern border.[68]

Four hundred Apalachee refugees escaped to Mobile to ask for French protection. Many other small Indian groups, including the Chatots, Tawasas, Pascagoulas, Biloxis, and Houmas, also called at Mobile. The alacrity with which these refugees sought French friendship surprised officials in Louisiana. Bienville related, "I asked them why it is that they were leaving the Spaniards. They told me that they did not give them any guns at all, but that the French gave them to all their allies." Although this statement reveals more wishful thinking than truth, it does expose the depth of terror and vulnerability that unarmed groups felt. As English-allied Indians became increasingly well-armed and predatory, those friendly to the Spanish or lacking imperial ties altogether found themselves isolated in an increasingly dangerous world. After the French began to settle Louisiana, groups like the Apalachees quickly gravitated toward this new colonial power. Louisiana, too, needed allies, and officials eagerly embraced nations seeking protection. With Bienville's assistance, the Apalachees settled along the Tombigbee, just upriver from Mobile.[69]

After generations of mission life, the Apalachees were quite comfortable living under French protection. In fact, those who visited Bienville at Mobile told him that they would not resettle in Louisiana unless the French provided a Catholic priest to tend to their spiritual needs. (Those forced to resettle at Savannah Town also asked for a minister, telling South Carolina's governor that they formerly "had a Priest in every Town.")[70] The

Apalachees celebrated Mass every Sunday, sang Psalms in Latin, and buried their dead in the church graveyard. Catholicism united the Apalachees and French colonists, who especially enjoyed celebrating the feast day of St. Louis—the Apalachees' patron saint—with their Indian neighbors. French colonist André Pénicaut found very little to distinguish the Apalachees from the European residents of Louisiana: "They love the French very much, and it must be confessed that the only thing savage about them is their language, which is a mixture of Spanish and Alibamon."[71] Other Indian groups in the region concurred with Penicaut's assessment. Larger non-Christian groups told one French missionary that they would not convert because "if they should become Christians, they would become slaves of the French like the Apalachees."[72] The Apalachees who chose protection under the French probably believed that they shared more cultural ground with these fellow Catholics than they did with Native confederacies like the Creeks or Choctaws. After all, it had been the Creeks who burned Apalachee villages, razed their crops, and enslaved their kin. Tumultuous times created difficult choices for Native people.

The contrast between the Apalachees' and Chickasaws' experiences in the early colonial era could hardly be sharper. As victims of the Indian slave trade, the once mighty Apalachees suffered dramatic losses due to epidemic diseases, military defeat, enslavement, and dislocation. The destruction of their polity forced an Apalachee diaspora: British traders sold them as slaves to colonies ranging from New England to the Caribbean; Creek captors incorporated others, in capacities ranging from adoptee to slave, into their growing confederacy; and the colonies of Louisiana and South Carolina absorbed some as subjects. The Chickasaws, on the other hand, made a virtue of their small population, using their success as slavers to project power far in excess of their numbers. They managed to retain and even augment their territorial homeland as well as their autonomy. Because of their success in capturing enemies, the Chickasaws became the most feared warriors in the South. Indeed, in the colonial era, no European army marched successfully against the Chickasaws, though the French made three concerted attempts.[73]

Predating the arrival of Europeans, Native captivity practices fostered the development of a commercial slave trade in the late seventeenth century and aided the development of the South's first plantation societies in Virginia and Carolina. But even as groups like the Chickasaws participated in the emerging trans-Atlantic economy, they did not simply discard their older notions about captivity. Resisting traders' entreaties, they adopted many, killed some, and retained others as laborers or gifts for Native allies. The slave trade significantly enhanced the scale of captive exchange, altered Native diplomacy, and changed the structure of Indian polities, but older notions about captivity did not simply vanish as a new slave market arose.

The Yamasee War of 1715–1718 brought the violence that the Indian slave trade had wrought throughout the region into the heart of South Carolina, and its dénouement severely curtailed the Anglo-Indian slave trade. The war's namesake, the Yamasees, had lived along the Savannah River until Westo raiding led them to seek refuge in the Spanish mission system. After Carolina's annihilation of the Westos, the Yamasees returned to the Savannah and began to engage in the slave trade with Scottish traders who lived at nearby Port Royal. Within a few decades, however, the Yamasees came to believe that the Carolinians had not lived up to their responsibilities as allies. Traders beat and abused Yamasees whom they should have treated as brothers and sisters, and they captured and sold their Indian allies, leading the Yamasees themselves to fear enslavement. Economic factors, including Carolina's depreciating currency and the decline of a diversified pelt market in favor of one based only on deerskins, as well as Charles Town's inept diplomacy, exacerbated the situation. From the Yamasee perspective, their Carolina allies had become greedy, irresponsible, and violent, thereby destroying the chains of obligation that once bound them as allies. The first Carolinian to pay for his people's transgressions was none other than Thomas Nairne, South Carolina's Indian agent and chronicler of the Chickasaws. Aware of the Yamasees' grievances, Nairne traveled to their village at Pocataligo. On April 14, 1715, Nairne and other officials including former agent John Wright met with Yamasee chiefs. They feasted, drank rum, and discussed trouble in the trade. While the Carolinians probably went to bed believing they had mended relations with the Yamasees, they awoke to a far different reality. That morning, Good Friday, Yamasees dragged Nairne to Pocataligo's central square, where they bound the trader to a post and pierced him with scores of lighted splinters, which slowly burned him to death.[74]

Similarly discontented neighboring nations, including the Lower Creeks, Savannahs, and the captive Apalachees of Savannah Town, applauded the Yamasees' declaration of war and followed suit. Farther from Carolina, the Upper Creeks, Choctaws, Cherokees, and Catawbas killed most of their resident traders, though few of them participated in battles against the Carolinians. Within the Chickasaw Nation, fifteen Carolina traders were murdered, though the Chickasaws placed the blame on visiting Lower Creeks, claiming that the Creeks had killed the traders in an effort to force them into the war. It is unclear whether or not the Chickasaws participated in the murders, but this incident represents the extent of their possible involvement in the Yamasee War. The Chickasaws protected remaining traders and reassured Carolina of their friendship the following year.[75] Rather than a premeditated conspiracy, the Yamasee War represented a chain reaction of events, and many of the South's disparate Native nations took part. Although each group did so for its own reasons, nearly all expressed some dissatisfaction with British trade, which they directed at the colony of South Carolina. Indian warriors succeeded in killing 400 colonists, about 7 percent of the white population. Those who escaped the attacks fled in terror toward the colony's capital. Soon, Charles Town and its immediate environs held all of South Carolina's settlers and slaves. Fearing complete destruction of their colony, South Carolinians cobbled an army drawn from their own militia, enslaved African Americans, friendly Indian nations, and volunteers from Virginia and North Carolina. This motley force pursued a brutal campaign against the war's instigators. They enslaved most Yamasee survivors, and those who escaped sought Spanish protection at St. Augustine. The war effectively concluded in 1718, when South Carolina made peace with remaining militant nations and gained an important ally in the Cherokees.[76]

Although the Yamasees suffered defeat, they succeeded in their goal of punishing the British and reforming trade. Those who declared war killed nearly all the Carolinians who resided among them, wiping out a whole generation of traders. This blow crippled the Anglo-Indian commerce in skins and slaves for years thereafter. The deerskin trade rebounded by 1722, but the Yamasee War led many colonists to question the wisdom of enslaving Indians. In the mid-Atlantic colonies and New England, where Southern Indian slaves had already acquired a reputation as troublemakers and runaways, traders found that the market for "Carolina" or "Spanish Indian" slaves had evaporated. Even within South Carolina, planters feared another war with Indians. After the Yamasee War, they increasingly turned to African labor, despite the fact that Africans cost more and were taxed at higher rates than Indian slaves. Planters believed that

Africans' lack of familiarity with the landscape prevented them from escaping as easily as Indians. They also thought that Africans, especially compared to Indian men, were hardier and more capable of intense agricultural labor. Indeed, many Africans had acquired immunity to the Old World diseases—smallpox, yellow fever, influenza, malaria—that killed Indians in such great numbers.[77]

Significant as the Yamasee War was, it did not destroy the Indian slave trade. South Carolina's enslaved Indian population did not peak until 1724, when 2,000 toiled under white masters. Carolina was hardly an exception; throughout North America, from New England to New Mexico to the Caribbean, colonists enslaved and traded Native people. Within the South, Virginia was the only colony to ban Indian slavery outright, but the recurring confirmation of the law, originally passed in 1691 and reenacted in 1705 and again in 1777, suggests that it was not effective.[78] As late as 1760, Seminole chief Cowkeeper, who reportedly preferred warfare to hunting because the former was "more beneficial," suggested to Georgia's governor Henry Ellis that he intended to come to the slave market in Savannah and sell some *"Florida Indians"*—probably Yamasees. Cowkeeper did maintain a coterie of Yamasee slaves at his plantation, and since the chief claimed to have "taken so many of them prisoners" he may have sold others to British colonists. As Cowkeeper suggested, a small market for Indian slaves continued.[79] Outside of Anglo-America, captors seeking to sell their prisoners of war traded them to Native allies or to French voyageurs, who canoed down the Ohio and Tennessee rivers in search of skins and slaves. And even as the Indian slave trade declined after the 1720s, a new market in captured humans opened as colonies asked their Native allies to recover runaway slaves, military deserters, and convicts in exchange for guns, clothing, tools, and cash. In diminished form, the economic aspect of captive trade endured.[80]

From the 1670s through 1715, Native captivity practices fed Carolina's burgeoning economy, creating an explosive trade in Indian slaves. Native people had long captured and even exchanged enemy groups, but during the slave trade era, this trade escalated exponentially. Once a by-product of chiefly competition, captive-taking became a major object of warfare. Seizing the political and economic opportunities that alliance with Carolina offered, nations such as the Chickasaws used the slave trade to enhance their power. Even as the slave trade destroyed many Native ethnic groups, paradoxically it generated new nations. The slave trade's violence pushed survivors out of coastal regions and pulled them to the interior toward emerging Native nations. In the decades that followed the Yamasee War, as Indians sought to build multiethnic nations out of the ashes of chiefdoms, they placed more emphasis on retaining captured enemies in their own communities. There, the seemingly disparate practices of captive execution, adoption, and enslavement preserved social order, an increasingly important goal for Indian nations in the colonial South.

3

CRYING BLOOD AND CAPTIVE DEATH

For residents of colonial America, death was a familiar, if unwanted, specter. Smallpox, yellow fever, and other epidemic horrors took life with little discrimination, imperial warfare threatened every inhabitant, and the brutality of slavery and the slave trade killed untold thousands of Indians and Africans. Little wonder, then, that the eighteenth-century South was a haunted place. Native people believed it to be so: they felt the souls of the dead hovering about their former homes, and they heard voices crying out for vengeance. Indians attributed few deaths to what we might call "natural causes." They blamed most of them on the evil machinations of enemies, whether warriors or witches. The dead continued to act in the world of the living, needling their kinsmen to remember them, to avenge them, to help them enter the spirit country.

Bad deaths often led to war. In recounting their motivations, Southern Indians of the eighteenth century most often cited "crying blood," meaning that the blood of their deceased relatives cried out for vengeance. Like all people, however, Indians went to war for complicated reasons: politics, imperial alliances, and territorial encroachments compelled them to fight at times. On an individual level, a desire for prestige and social advancement enticed warriors to battle. Every eighteenth-century conflict, however, was connected to righting wrongful deaths in one way or another, and crying blood could only be quieted through captive-taking. After the Yamasee War, Indians continued to capture their enemies, using those captives, whether killed, adopted, or enslaved, to placate the dead and control the disorder that threatened to consume their world.

In Native societies, a simple law protected the lives of the people. As the Red Coat King of Oakfuskee told Governor Glen of South Carolina, "we must have Blood for Blood." In this practice, known as blood vengeance, clans avenged a relative's death—even if accidental—by taking the life of the one responsible, or a relative of the one responsible. To Native people, the murder of kin represented a dangerous loss of clan power. Eighteenth-century trader James Adair reported that warriors went to almost unimaginable lengths to redress that imbalance: "I have known the Indians to go a thousand miles, for the purpose of revenge, in pathless woods; over hills and mountains; through large cane swamps, full of grape-vines and briars; over broad lakes, rapid rivers, and deep creeks; and all the way endangered by poisonous snakes, if not with the rambling and lurking enemy, while at the same time they were exposed to the extremes of heat and cold, the vicissitude of the seasons; to hunger and thirst . . . to fatigues, and other difficulties." All of these efforts warriors considered "imaginary trifles" if they succeeded in their object: the capture of the enemy. Only this could satisfy the "craving ghosts of their deceased relations."[1]

When the murderer came from within a nation, the law of blood was easy enough to enforce. If both clans agreed, the offender and his relatives could give the victim's family a payment in goods or a captive.[2] The murderer's clan could also satisfy the demands of blood vengeance by surrendering one of its members—either the offender or a volunteer who paid the blood price. Around the time of the American Revolution, a trader named Nathaniel Folsom saw the execution of blood vengeance among the Choctaws. Along with the help of a friend, a Choctaw woman lured her husband into the woods, and, as he stooped to investigate a fallen yellow jacket nest, she knocked him on the back of the head with a wooden stick and threw his body into a nearby creek. When townspeople later discovered his body and questioned the woman, she confessed, saying, "I am willing to dye to pay it." Her relatives carried out the execution as a stunned Folsom sat on his horse watching. The woman accepted her fate stoically, "her eys like a ball of fire, no cry in her."[3]

In the colonial era, Euro-Americans understood the law of blood, and though they preferred to prosecute the person who had committed the crime, officials often accommodated Native standards of justice when dealing with Indian nations. On October 6, 1752, William Mackrachun, an employee of trader John Pettygrove, was shot and killed by a Chickasaw man whose war name, Noabbey, meant "one who kills a rambling enemy."[4] Frustrated when Noabbey would not give himself up, Governor Glen of South Carolina asked trader and diplomat Thomas Bosomworth to seek justice. Meanwhile, Noabbey remained in hiding, but his uncle stepped forth to pay the blood price. Noabbey's uncle reported to his chief that "if his Nephew was affraid to dye for the Good of his People and for Satisfaction to the English he [the uncle] would sacrifice his own Life for him." When Bosomworth pressed the Chickasaw chief to produce the actual murderer, the headman demurred, saying "by the Laws of [our] Nation one of the same Blood was equally satisfactory." Noabbey's uncle then "repaired to his own House to seek for his Gun which his Wife had hid from him, but finding a long French Knife, with that in one Hand and Paint in the other with which he besmeared himself, came out into the open Street and made a publick Declaration that as one of his Family had spilt the Blood of a white Man and was affrayd to dye for it, he was now going to pay the Debt for him . . . and with the greatest Undaunted-ness struck the Knife into the Gullet and immediately dyed with the Wound." Bosomworth, who had missed the excitement, sent a British trader to confirm that the debt had been paid. After some initial hesita-tion, the Chickasaw chief "ordered his Brother to go and open the Grave over which two Woman [sic] his Relations, were making doleful Cries and the Body was seen fresh in its Gore."[5]

Noabbey's magnanimous uncle paid William Mackrachun's blood price, and the British, in this case, were willing to accept Chickasaw justice. However, the satisfaction of blood vengeance by an outside party was rarely so straightforward. By the mid-eighteenth century, Chickasaws and British traders had forged both fictive and real kin ties in their already decades-long trading relationship. But what if the murder occurred between groups that were sworn enemies? Or by those who lived much farther afield? In reality, finding a murderer or his clan relatives was often an impossible task. Blood vengeance became much more complicated when the mur-derer belonged to an outside nation. Grieving clans focused on appeasing the spirits of the deceased rather than punishing murderers, and they fre-quently were undiscerning in their retaliation. Blood vengeance could be dangerously open-ended and lead to an ongoing cycle of warfare.[6]

Despite the difficulties of satisfying the law of blood vengeance, the victim's clan had to do so because otherwise the souls of unavenged clan members could not enter the spirit country and would remain in This World to torment the living. When they killed enemies, warriors typically scalped or otherwise dismembered corpses. Although compatriots strove to retrieve the bodies of the fallen in order to prevent such corporeal abuse, they were not always successful, and their relatives and friends sometimes remained unburied. By inflicting violent trauma on enemy bodies, victorious warriors captured a portion of the dead individual's spirit or soul. That circumstance—combined with improper burial or no burial at all—inhibited the spirit's journey to the afterlife. The balance of a murdered soul usually lingered near its former home, and the living, who shared their lands with myriad supernatural forces, harbored a general fear of these spirits. In 1791, traveler John Pope observed, "The *Creeks* in approaching the Frontiers of *Georgia*, always encamp on the right hand side of the Road or Path, assigning the left, as ominous, to the *Larvae* or Ghosts of their departed Heroes who have either unfortunately lost their scalps, or remain unburied. The Ghost of an Hero in either Predicament, is refused Admittance into the Mansions of Bliss, and sentenced to take up its invisible and darksome Abode, in the dreary Caverns of the Wilderness; until the Indignity shall be retaliated on the Enemy, by some of his surviving Friends."[7]

Creeks considered Okmulge, in what is now central Georgia, one of the most haunted sites in the region. By the mid-eighteenth century, Okmulge was already an ancient settlement with a storied history. Around A.D. 900, inhabitants began to construct what would become one of the largest Mississippian sites. Okmulge's most impressive monument was and still is the Great Temple Mound: Built atop a natural plateau, the 50-foot high earthwork seemed much larger—about 90 feet tall when viewed from the floodplain—and could be seen for miles around. Although Okmulge was abandoned for several hundred years, Creeks began to re-occupy it in the late seventeenth century in order to facilitate trade with Carolina. When relations soured during the Yamasee War, however, South Carolinians and their allies destroyed the town and massacred its inhabitants. To the Creeks, Okmulge, part Mississippian grandeur, part charnel house, must have seemed a particularly terrible, awe-inspiring mausoleum. Creeks tried to avoid Okmulge, but those engaged in trade could not, for it lay alongside the path linking the Lower Towns to Charles Town. While there, "they always hear[d], at the dawn of the morning, the usual noise of Indians singing their joyful religious notes, and dancing, as if going down to the river to purify themselves, and then returning to the old town-house." To Creek ears, these seemingly melodious voices cried out for blood.[8]

The unavenged death of a relative upset the balance between earth and cosmos, and a clan had to go to war to redress that balance. Among the Chickasaws, female relatives of a murdered warrior mourned his loss every morning and night until their kinsmen avenged his death. Elsewhere, mourning women cried, grieved, and cursed enemies, spurring on their kinsmen to fulfill the demands of blood vengeance. Restless spirits and social order demanded that clan kin shed "equal blood . . . to quench the crying blood of their relations, and give rest to their ghosts." The deaths of even the lowliest members of nations required retaliation. In the words of one contemporary, Indians must "take revenge of blood before they can rest, cost what it will."[9]

In addition to silencing crying blood, men went to war to achieve glory. Hereditary chiefs had ruled their ancestors, and although most chiefdoms had collapsed by the seventeenth century, social and spiritual inequalities persisted. While some men benefited from high status that came from being born into prestigious clans, war represented a unique opportunity for young men of all clans to enhance their social and material capital.[10] The desire for war honors was a cultural imperative that drove Native men to fight their enemies. A Creek warrior once told British officer David Taitt that he had initiated a war with the Choctaws that lasted from 1765 to 1777: "He says that he made war on purpose to keep his Young people from falling out with the English . . . as he knows they must be at war with some body." As this warrior explained, the Creeks had to focus their martial energy somewhere: better against the Choctaws than their British trading allies. Native culture demanded a *continuous* state of war.[11]

Almost from birth, boys trained for war. Their older clan kin sought to inure them to pain and hardship. At dawn every morning, they took icy baths in nearby lakes and streams. Regular ceremonial scratching with rows of gar fish teeth imbued boys with strength and stamina. Native Americans of the lower Mississippi valley celebrated a festival each September during which leading warriors and politicians whipped the boys, "telling them that they have been flogged to teach them to have no fear of the evils their enemies can do to them and to teach them to be good warriors that would never cry out or shed tears even in the middle of fire, supposing that their enemies should cast them into it." Beyond physical conditioning, elders doubtlessly prepared youths by telling them stories of the great heroes who came before them. Oral traditions are replete with brave young men who travel abroad and even into the cosmos to battle enemies and monsters, bringing back trophies and gifts with which to honor their communities. After careful physical, mental, and spiritual training, a boy went to war, and when he spilled blood, he became a man.[12]

Communities reproached unaccomplished warriors, while successful men expected such social accolades as the affection of local women and increased stature within the community. According to one early eighteenth-century trader, "The Beautys are so engrossed by the men of Action, by great Warriors and expert hunters that ordinary Fellows who are sloathfull and unfortunate, are obliged to take up with very mean stuff."[13] The society of warriors was a strictly ranked hierarchy, wherein a man achieved status through accumulation of plunder, scalps, and captives. In 1791, a visitor to the Creeks observed, "Every individual is at liberty to choose whether or not he shall engage in any warlike enterprise. But the rage of the young men to acquire war-names, and the thirst of plunder in the elder ones and leaders, are motives sufficient to raise gangs of volunteers to go in quest of *hair* [scalps] and horses at any time when they are disengaged from hunting."[14] When men presented captives or scalps to their communities, they received new honorific titles and tattoos commemorating their feats. In the words of one Chickasaw, such booty proved that a warrior was a "true man." For Native men, rank was constantly on display. Those who wanted a better seat in the council house or a more honored position during ceremonies depended on their accomplishments in war for social advancement.[15]

By the second decade of the eighteenth century, Native people developed a raiding style of warfare, which contemporary Euro-Americans called "cutting off" the enemy. War leaders had long since abandoned the large battles of their Mississippian ancestors and even scaled back the raids of the slave trade era. In cutoff warfare, the goal was to isolate a segment of the enemy group (ideally by surprise), kill or capture them, take war spoils, and withdraw with minimal losses. Though generally small in scale and limited in material and human costs, this warfare still remained deadly. Indeed, in a tactic that has been styled "conquest by harassment," Native nations did sometimes endeavor to cut off an entire region, a feat that required constant pressure over a number of years.[16] In 1723, during French Louisiana's ongoing war with the Chickasaws, the Superior Council suggested a peace overture. Bienville demurred, however, saying that their Choctaw allies would never brook such a settlement. According to Bienville, the Choctaws asserted "that we should listen to no sort of proposal of peace and [they have promised] that they would continue the war until the entire destruction of [the Chickasaw] nation."[17] Perhaps because the smaller Chickasaw Nation, quicker to procure and employ firearms, had bullied their more numerous neighbors for decades, the Choctaws wished to use their alliance with the French to crush them. A few decades later, as warfare raged between the Iroquois and several Southern Indian nations, a Catawba woman who escaped her captivity among the Mohawks returned home with a terrible story to tell. On a few occasions, she overheard her captors plotting against her countrymen, saying "that they intend to cut off every Soul of the Catawbas."[18] Successful warriors were given to hyperbole, but their words should not be regarded as mere boasting. Traditional enemies constantly fueled the cycle of vengeance and made the ground very bloody indeed.

As heads of matrilineages, clan matrons initiated warfare, instructing their young men: "Go to war! Avenge the death of our relatives, our allies, and our friends."[19] Trader James Adair, who lived among Native people for over thirty years, had plenty of opportunity to witness their cutting-off style of war. First, a war captain announced his intention to attack the enemy and invited others to join him. According to Adair, "On this, a sufficient number of warriors and others, commonly of the family of the murdered person, immediately arm themselves, and each gets a small bag of parched corn-flour, for his war-stores." Typically, twenty to forty warriors volunteered. Because success in warfare required considerable spiritual power, a warrior needed to prepare himself. Accordingly, those who volunteered went to the war captain's house where they sat in order of rank and drank black drink, a sacred tea made from yaupon holly leaves, which "inspire[d] them with an invincible prowess in war." After three days of purification, war parties set out against their enemies. To evade detection by the enemy, and thus employ the element of surprise, they traveled alongside swamps and canebrakes that provided ready cover. Upon reaching enemy territory, war parties attempted to catch isolated individuals or parties unawares, preferably outside of town.[20]

War parties tried to capture rather than kill their enemies. In the heat of combat, however, this was not always a practical goal. Warriors often killed enemy men because they were dangerous and difficult to transport. Women and children, however, also died during attacks. As Creek George

Stiggins reported, "It is a praiseworthy action for a man or a party to kill the women and children of their enemy, more so than to kill a man who is frequently in the forest. To kill a woman shows that he was not afraid to go into enemy country, but achieved the manly deed in the enemy's very house door and escaped."[21] Whenever war parties did kill enemies, they scalped the dead because scalps served as an acceptable substitute for live captives in ceremony. Before leaving enemy territory, warriors would "strip the bark off several large trees in conspicuous places, and paint them with red and black hieroglyphics." These "hieroglyphics" communicated how many the war party had killed and captured. The avenging clan signed the pictograph with a symbol of its totem.[22]

In addition to their weapons, parched corn, and spiritual safeguards, war parties brought along restraints with which they planned to bind captives. Such restraints took diverse forms. A group of Savannah Indians caught skulking in the South Carolina backcountry had on them "a Ligamen[t] of a black Colour made up of Buffalo's Wool." Upon interrogation by Governor Glen, a warrior explained, "It is to tie my Prisoners with." Similarly, Charles Johnston's Shawnee captors bound him to a tree every night with "a strong rope of buffalo hide." When one of his fellow captives attempted to escape, the warriors took stronger measures, tying a cord with an attached bell from each prisoner's neck to a nearby tree; every time the prisoner moved, the bell rang. In another incident, a coalition of American and Cherokee forces confiscated from a Creek war party "slave strings," which they described as "Strings to bind prisoners, of whom the Creeks make slaves." In addition to cords and slave strings, some parties brought along more advanced tools of captivity. Cherokee masters had "slave collars" ready for their new captives, and Creek warriors carried "Stocks prep[ared] to secure prisoners."[23]

Although often restrained and occasionally forced to carry booty, captives who later recorded accounts of their ordeal generally attested to their good treatment en route to captors' nations. Warriors attempted to preserve captives' lives until justice could be meted out in their home villages. Antoine Bonnefoy, a voyageur captured along with fellow Frenchmen André Crespé and Jean Arlois and one unnamed black slave in 1740, remembered that after his Cherokee captors plundered his boat, they offered the prisoners breakfast "and gave us to understand by signs that no harm should come to us, and that we should be even as themselves." As a token of their generosity and good intentions, the Cherokee warriors measured out a cup of rum to each prisoner, then to themselves, after every meal. John Stephens, taken captive in 1760, reported that "the Indians were very liberal of their provisions to the prisoners, [and] gave them of the best."[24] Fanny Scott, in her 20s when a Cherokee war party captured her, later said that they "were quite civil and kind to her, and would assist her up the mountains." Scott's captors even had the foresight to retrieve her saddle from her house and bring it with them, for they had horses waiting to carry them across the Smoky Mountains and back to the Cherokee Nation.[25]

Charles Johnston, whose boat was attacked by a combined party of Shawnees, Delawares, Wyandots, and Cherokees, received the surprise of his life when the warriors did not immediately torture him: "Bred up with an instinctive horror of Indians and of Indian cruelties, it was a situation which, of all others, I had most deprecated . . . already my imagination placed me at the stake, and I saw the flames about to be kindled around me." When it became clear that the warriors would take the boat, Johnston resigned himself to his fate and began to help his captors aboard. However, "When they entered, they shook hands with me, crying out in broken English, 'How de do! How de do!' I returned their salutation by a hearty squeeze of the hand, as if glad to see them." One of Johnston's traveling companions, Peggy Fleming, was taken by Cherokees in the war party. Although Johnston expected her to plunge "into grief and despondency," Fleming initially "enjoyed a high flow of spirits." Johnston entered into his captivity with a deep bias against Indians, but immediately he found himself forced to revise these notions, even to admire some aspects of Native culture.[26]

Although conquering European armies had, for centuries, raped women whose lands they invaded, sexual violence did not play a similar role in Native martial culture. Although women captives often had other complaints—hard labor and beatings, for example—they rarely accused their captors of rape. On the contrary, a French woman among the Choctaws, like many other captives, reported that "they showed her . . . all sorts of kindness."[27] Contemporaries of these female captives as well as modern scholars have puzzled at why Indian captors refrained from sexual violence. Many have made the ethnocentric assumption that rape is a "natural" accompaniment to warfare, when, in reality, rape as a tool of war is a cultural construct.[28]

In the eighteenth century, Native societies had a high tolerance for violence, even for certain forms of sexual violence, but powerful taboos prohibited them from raping captives during wartime. Native cultures linked sexual abstinence to success in battle. A warrior who broke the taboo risked the capture and death of his entire party. As trader James Adair observed, "The Indians will not cohabit with women while they are out at war; they religiously abstain from every kind of intercourse even with their own wives, for the space of three days and nights before they go to war, and so after they return home, because they are to sanctify themselves." Adair noted that even the Choctaws, whom he considered especially "libidinous," observed this proscription.[29] From his experience with nations of the lower Mississippi valley, the Jesuit missionary Charlevoix reported that a warrior who took his first captive had to abstain from all forms of sex for a month thereafter.[30]

Incest taboos also contributed to Native sexual restraint during wartime.[31] Native kinship networks were far more expansive than those of Euro-Americans: Indians counted as clan members all who were descended from an ancient ancestor, and some groups extended the taboo to include members of the clan of one's father. Thus, the incest taboo prohibited sex with a significant portion of one's nation. Because women were sometimes adopted into the clans of their captors, warriors avoided sexual contact with women who might become their kin. As explorer John Lawson reported, a dishonorable death awaited those who broke the taboo: "For if an *Indian* lies with his Sister, or any very near Relation, his Body is burnt, and his Ashes thrown into the River, as unworthy to remain on Earth."[32] Alabamas, an ethnic group within the Creek Nation, believed that incest among its members might cause "the earth [to] burn up."[33] Taboos against wartime impurity and incest served as powerful deterrents against captive rape, but both had an expiration date, meaning that captives could become vulnerable to sexual violence after a period of weeks or months.

Euro-American men indulged in sexual violence against captives with much greater frequency than Native men. In the Western world, rape had long been a prerogative of invading warriors, a devastating means of asserting domination over conquered people. Despite the biased nature of the historical record, evidence of rape or attempted rape committed by white men against Indian women has survived. Old Hop, a prominent Cherokee chief, cited rape as a leading cause of the Cherokee War, which began in 1759. According to Old Hop, three young officers from Fort Prince George broke into homes in the nearby Cherokee town of Keowee and raped women whose husbands were gone on the winter hunt. John Moultrie, who served as a major during the war that resulted, wrote that during his participation in retaliatory strikes he was "making free with the Cherokee squaws." Moultrie detailed how he "dr[o]ve them naked out of their beds to hide in the woods and mountains." Dispassionately, Moultrie concluded, "But this among others I did without much concern, besides burning of houses destroying fine fields gardens orchards &c." Two years into the conflict, acting South Carolina governor William Bull II expressed anxiety about housing female Cherokees as prisoners of war in the barracks at Charles Town. Bull feared that they might be "insult[ed]" by the "sailors who are now very numerous in Town." Three decades later, when Tennessee militiamen took another Cherokee woman prisoner at the militant Chickamauga town of Nickajack, General Robertson ordered her to deliver a letter to her people. She set out from Tennessee on her way back to the Cherokee Nation, but as she made camp that first night, the woman found that some white men had pursued her. As the men threatened her, she abandoned all her possessions, including her horse, to hide in a canebreak. Luckily, she managed to evade the men and complete the journey back to her homeland, letter in hand.[34]

Native warriors, on the other hand, treated most captives kindly, although that kindness could end abruptly once the war party reached its home village. Some captives met an unpleasant end even sooner. When a wounded or an ill prisoner faltered, captors unceremoniously dispatched him. Bonnefoy reported that after the initial ambush Cherokee warriors put slave collars on him and his three companions. During the battle, one man had been hurt, and his wounds steadily worsened. Seeing his condition, the Cherokees released him and told him to return to the French, "but not knowing where to go, he followed the pirogues for two days. On the third . . . the savages, tired of seeing him, gave him over to the young people, who killed him and took his scalp."[35]

Very young children also burdened war parties, as Anne Calhoun (cousin of future statesman John C. Calhoun) learned early on in her captivity during the Cherokee War. The abuses of British soldiers, including the rape of Cherokee women and the imprisonment of twenty-two headmen at Fort Prince George, provoked the conflict. In retaliation, on February 1, 1760, Cherokee warriors destroyed the Long Cane settlement in backcountry South Carolina, killing about fifty white and black inhabitants and taking a number of captives, including Anne and her sister Mary. A few months shy of her fifth birthday, Anne was only a small child. As the party made its way back to the Cherokee Nation on foot, Anne had a difficult time keeping up, but her captors "gave her to understand she must keep up, or they would kill her, by waiting for her they might be killed themselves." Young, sick, or disabled captives who slowed down war parties jeopardized the lives of all its members and compromised one of the key objectives of raids—returning home before the enemy could mount a counterattack.[36]

Upon reaching its village, the war party, in a series of shouts, communicated how many prisoners and scalps it had taken.[37] The party sang war songs, and every member related his accomplishments in battle. Those who had managed to take prisoners or scalps looked forward with pride to the war honors the community would bestow in a forthcoming ceremony. According to one observer, "One of the young Fellows, that has been at the Wars, and has had the Fortune to take a Captive, returns the proudest Creature on Earth, and sets such a Value on himself, that he knows not how to contain himself in his Senses."[38]

Up to this point, each captive remained the property of an individual warrior. While it is generally true that eighteenth-century Indian societies fostered a communal ethic, warriors needed to laud their individual accomplishments in order to advance socially. Over a warrior's career, his community tallied his war spoils, commemorating these deeds in song and ceremony. Captives, being the most prestigious war prizes, figured disproportionately in this equation.

An infamous episode from the Cherokee War illustrates how the desire for individual recognition drove warriors to take captives. In the spring of 1760, warriors laid siege to Fort Loudoun, now in eastern Tennessee but at that time the westernmost outpost of colonial South Carolina. In June of 1760, Loudoun fell and the British surrendered. Initially, the Cherokees agreed to allow the garrison to march eastward peacefully. After the column had marched about ten miles, however, hundreds of Cherokee warriors emerged from the woods around Ball Play Creek, surprising the garrison. In the fighting that ensued, the Cherokees won a complete victory, killing commanding officer Paul Demere and twenty-eight others and taking the rest—about 120—captive. Controversy has long surrounded this episode, in which the Cherokees seem to have reneged on the peace settlement negotiated just one day earlier. The answer seems to lie in the report of Tom, a man of mixed Cherokee and British ancestry, who claimed that after the fall of Loudoun, the warriors of two major Cherokee towns, Settico and Chota, disagreed over how to divide the plunder. Residents of other Cherokee villages believed that Chota had taken the lion's share of spoils from the fort (and perhaps from raids earlier in the war). Without such tokens of martial success, the other warriors would not be formally acknowledged in their village square grounds and thus could not advance in rank. Feeling shortchanged, warriors from Settico and other towns followed the garrison to Ball Play Creek and "fell on the Whites, intending to make slaves of them." According to several different accounts, each warrior tried to seize as many captives as possible. By taking additional captives, these warriors sought to even out the distribution of war spoils; their object was not the massacre of the retreating garrison, as some British colonists later claimed. According to Cherokee headman Mankiller, the warriors only killed those who ran away or otherwise resisted capture. After the attack, war spoils—including captives—seem to have been more equitably "distributed amongst the different towns."[39]

A warrior claimed a captive by being the first to lay hands on him. During the attack at Ball Play Creek, Oconostota claimed Fort Loudoun's junior commanding officer, Captain John Stuart, when he grasped Stuart by the hand. In 1776, when Cherokees went to war against American colonists, warriors Terrapin and The Glass paid an early-morning visit to the house of David Shettroe. Shettroe lived in Keowee, an old Cherokee town only recently occupied by Anglo-Americans, and he knew the warriors by name. When they called out, Shettroe opened his door, offered them some water, and began to kindle a fire. Shettroe was surprised when "the Glass laid hold of him, and told him he was his slave." The Glass claimed Shettroe but did so almost apologetically, saying "it was very bad times." Shettroe's houseguest William McTeer, still asleep on the floor, became Terrapin's captive when the warrior clapped a hand down on McTeer's unprotesting body. This episode may safely be counted among the least violent of captive-takings; without struggle, without blood, Terrapin and The Glass laid hands upon their white neighbors and so transformed them into captives.[40]

After successful warriors returned home and greeted their community, they transferred control of their spoils, saying something to the effect of "Here is the slave of our enemies that I present to you in token of my valor at war." Thereafter, warriors set off to the council house, where they observed a post-battle ritual during which they took emetics and other purifying medicines, washed their bodies and clothes, and briefly passed their weapons through fire. Exposure to blood, a spiritually powerful substance, was a dangerous experience, and warriors had to cleanse themselves before they could safely reenter society.[41]

High-ranking women, often called "beloved women," of the grieving clan received the prisoners. In a significant departure from Mississippian martial practices, eighteenth-century warfare was primarily a clan affair, and, as heads of lineages, beloved women had the power to determine how captives' fates would best fulfill the demands of justice. In their oral traditions, the Senecas, an Iroquois group with a long history of warring with Southern nations, remembered, "It was the custom among the Cherokee to let two women say what should be done with captives." According to the Senecas, "Each of these women had two snakes tattooed on her lips, with their heads opposite each other, in such a way that when she opened her mouth the two snakes opened their mouths also." At the center of descent reckoning, women conferred kin ties through blood, but also through their words and actions. Meting out justice was perhaps the most important function of the clans and afforded women a great deal of power.[42] As a visitor to the Cherokees reported, beloved women could "by the wave of a swan's wing, deliver a wretch condemned by the council, and already tied to the stake."[43]

Beloved women sorted through the captives, deciding whose fiery deaths would atone for past murders, who would take the place of deceased clan members, and whose labor would enrich the clan's wealth and prestige. Most cutoff battles were quick strikes in which warriors attempted to grab accessible captives, but, back at the village, beloved women could afford to be more discerning. Stripping the captives and beating men with canes or switches, women attempted to divine their overall health and strength. They also closely examined male captives' chests and arms for tell-tale blue pictographs—the tattoos that graphically told the stories of their exploits against enemy people. Very accomplished warriors could expect to "atone for the blood they spilt, by the tortures of fire." Those selected for the fiery torture were painted black, given a rattling gourd, and forced to dance; lucky adoptees were embraced by their new relatives; slaves were retained by their captors or sold to others.[44]

Native people believed that youths and women could transcend cultural and ethnic borders more easily and more completely than men. During the Yamasee War, Yamasee chief Huspah King dictated to a captive Carolina boy a remarkable letter in which the chief explained to South Carolina governor Charles Craven that the Yamasees would kill the men who fought against them but "as for the Women and Children them they will save alive." Euro-American traveler William Bartram also noted that Indians executed warriors, but he claimed, "they do not kill the females or children of either sex." Yet, sex and age were not the only variables at work. During the Cherokee War, Catawba allies of the British captured, tortured, and killed at least two older women. Captors also spared and adopted adult men, perhaps those they deemed exceptionally talented or likeable. Indeed, non-Indian men have left behind captivity accounts out of proportion to their numbers because they were more literate and had greater access to print media than other captives in the eighteenth century. Unfortunately, although women and children made up the majority of captives, their accounts are more fragmentary in nature, often related by kinsmen or government officials. In determining captives' fates, sex and age seem to have been important but not all-encompassing. What is clear is that, until the late eighteenth century, a captive's race did not determine her fate.[45]

Native Americans considered most warriors dangerous and unfit for adoption. Oral tradition tells of a young Creek boy taken captive by his people's longtime enemies, the Choctaws. Raised among them, he grew to become a great warrior and took many of his former people as captives. One day as a battle raged between the two groups, the former captive became separated from his fellow Choctaw warriors. The Creeks, by calling out to him in Choctaw, deceived him into coming out of a hollow tree, where he had been hiding. Although the warriors knew that the man was born a Creek, they killed him and took his scalp as a war trophy. They likely reasoned that such a man, trained in the arts of war, would violently protest his captivity, attempt to escape, and perhaps even kill his captor or other villagers. Such a price was often too high to consider.[46]

After the beloved women determined captives' fates, clans bound those slated for torture and tied them to the village's "blood pole."[47] There, through torture, clans quieted the crying blood of their deceased kin. According to William Bartram, "[A]bout twelve feet high . . . these pillars are usually decorated with the scalps of their slain enemies;—the scalp, with the hair on them, are stretched or strained on a little hoop . . . round about the top of the pole, where they remain as long as they last. . . . [T]he pole is usually crownd with the white dry skin of an enemy. In some of their towns, I have counted 6 or 8 scalps fluttering on one pole in these yards." Into the twentieth century, elderly Creeks still recalled the blood poles of the square grounds, remembering that the poles were shaped like war clubs, ancient and symbolically potent weapons.[48]

To preserve a captive's scalp, villagers either removed it or placed clay atop the prisoner's crown to protect the flesh underneath. Beneath the blood pole, the women lit and fueled the fire, and participants encircled the captive. If the victim attempted to run outward, the people burned him with torches or lit pipes. A trader who witnessed such an event observed, "Not a soul, of whatever age or sex, manifests the least pity during the prisoner's tortures: the women sing with religious joy, all the while they are torturing the devoted victim, and peals of laughter resound through the crowded theatre—especially if he fears to die."[49]

Fire seems to have been the universal means of torture among Southern Indians, but some groups, especially those on the fringes of the region, differed in the details. In the lower Mississippi valley, participants fashioned a frame out of three poles and tied the prisoner in the form of a St. Andrew's cross, stretching his arms and legs in an "X" shape. Native people of the Carolinas "split the Pitch-Pine into Splinters, and stick them into the Prisoners Body yet alive. Thus they light them, which burn like so many Torches; and in this manner, they make him dance round a great Fire, every one buffeting and deriding him, till he expires." John Lawson, who observed this form of torture around 1701, died in the very same manner ten years later as one of the first victims of the Tuscarora War.[50]

For his part, the tortured ideally endured this painful death with stoicism, behavior that amazed Euro-American spectators. In their continuous wars against enemies, eighteenth-century warriors often faced mortal peril. Pragmatically, they adopted a fatalistic attitude toward death, "for they affirm, that there is a fixt time, and place, when, and where, everyone must die, without any possibility of averting it."[51] The chorus of a Choctaw song advised, "All men must surely die / Tho' no one knows how soon."[52] Preferring death to the dishonor that came with slavery, warriors encouraged their torturers: "During all these torments the captive takes care to show a constant undaunted courage, to rebuke his enemies as cowardly and womanish people for inflicting on him such a womanish death, that he only laughs at all these torments, that nothing better has previously happened to him, that his death even in this manner will soon be found out."[53] Some captives went further: "They even taunt their executioners by saying that they are not suffering enough. If things were reversed, the victims would know how to make the executioners suffer even greater torment."[54] A victim commonly promised his tormentors that the cycle of vengeance would continue, saying he looked forward to the day when they, too, suffered a similar fate. While the Cherokees tortured one Northern Indian, he threatened, "there was 600 French Men and as many Indians coming in with an Intent to kill, take, and destroy."[55]

Beyond satisfying the demands of blood vengeance, torture served as an augur "to divine the physical and spiritual strength of the enemy." As participants doled out ever-increasing pain, the victim challenged them with threats and insults. Thus, torture became a test of the victim's mettle, a miniature contest of strength between two enemy people. A Frenchman in Louisiana reported that captives sometimes endured for three days and nights, singing all the while. When a captive finally expired, the clan gained access to the spiritual power he had managed to accumulate.[56]

Following a victim's death, members of the grieving clan took the warrior's preserved scalp and either tied it atop the blood pole or placed it on the roof of their dead relative's house. The victim's fiery death and the exposure of his scalp released a relative's wandering soul into the afterlife, where he or she could rest peacefully. As trader James Adair explained, "when that kindred duty of retaliation is justly executed, [the dead] immediately get ease and power to fly away."[57]

At times, war affected an entire Native nation, and in those cases torture became a national affair. During a mid-eighteenth-century conflict with the Cherokees, Choctaw warriors managed to ambush an invading Cherokee war party. All the party's thirteen members save one wounded man managed to escape. Choctaws scheduled his execution in four days time and in the interim paraded this Cherokee through several Choctaw towns, where inhabitants whipped and abused him.[58]

During the Cherokee War, warriors from throughout the nation participated in the conflict and, after the fall of Fort Loudoun, all were eager to enjoy its spoils. John Stephens, a soldier later ransomed from his captor for sixty pounds sterling, reported that after the garrison fell, the soldiers' new Indian masters immediately stripped their captives of their clothing and possessions and marched them to Chota, one of the mother towns of the

Cherokee Nation. As part of the victory celebration at Chota, masters forced their captives to dance before Mortar (a Creek chief with Cherokee kin ties) and other prominent warriors. The next evening "every Indian took his prisoner back to his town." At village square grounds throughout the nation, captors "there beat and abused them . . . and obliged them likewise to dance." Stephens himself went back with his master Tuskeegi-Tahee to Settico. There, Stephens claimed, he saw captive Luke Croft "gradually tortured, in the most shocking manner, to death; after which they cut him in pieces, set his head and right hand upon a stake in the [chunkey] yard, as a spectacle to the other prisoners, and gathered up and burnt his other members." During Croft's torture and death, all the villagers beat the British captives with sticks. Captives reported similar incidents at Estatoe and Sugartown. After captors burned a few of the soldiers, the rest suffered no more beatings; masters put their captives to work, fed and clothed them, and hinted that they might eventually ransom them. By forcing the captives to dance at Chota, warriors signaled that the victory over Loudoun belonged to the whole nation, not just a single clan or village. Though few of Loudoun's captured garrison suffered torture and death, ritualized, nonlethal beatings of the remainder enabled wronged Cherokees to vent their grief and satisfy the demands of blood vengeance.[59]

When warriors failed to bring captives back to village blood poles, scalps served as acceptable substitutes. In eastern North America, the earliest archaeological evidence for scalping comes from sites dating to roughly 2500–500 B.C. At a site in western Tennessee, the crowns of three men's craniums were found scored with a series of circular cut marks, evidence consistent with historical accounts of scalping.[60] Among later groups, warriors cut a circle around the top of a victim's head, lifted the skin, and cut or pulled off the scalp. Scalping usually, though not exclusively, occurred after a victim's death.[61] Afterward, warriors tied "with bark or deer's sinews, their . . . trophies of blood in a small hoop, to preserve it from putrefaction, and paint the interior part of the scalp, and the hoop, all round with red, their flourishing emblematical colour of blood."[62] Although Indians sometimes took other disarticulated body parts, the distinctiveness and portability of scalps made them the most popular war trophies. Because hairstyles reflected identity, warriors and their communities easily discerned to which enemy nation the former owner of the scalp had belonged.[63]

Scalps, believed to contain a portion of the conquered enemy's soul, could stand in for captives in ceremony. In February 1792, when Chickamauga warriors returned to their settlement at Lookout Mountain after a success-ful raid against their American foes, they celebrated their acquisition of scalps "with all the forms, gestures, exultations, and declarations, of a war-dance." Treating one scalp as though it were a captive, the warriors "tore it with their hands and teeth, with great ferocity." After such scalp dances, returning warriors presented the trophies to grieving relatives, who then exposed the scalps atop the houses of the deceased. Whether warriors killed enemies abroad or clans tortured them at village blood poles, the successful acquisition and exposure of enemy scalps satisfied blood ven-geance and released murdered relatives' souls. Captives and scalps alike enabled noncombatants to participate in quieting crying blood.[64]

When Europeans and Africans became embroiled in conflicts against or between Native Americans, they were necessarily subject to deeply rooted Native rules of engagement. During the Natchez War of 1729–1731, after the Natchez captured a French soldier whom they recognized from a pre-vious campaign against them, they attempted to break him emotionally during torture, "their intention being to make him shed tears, so as to call him a woman not a warrior."[65] The more culturally savvy newcomers, es-pecially educated Jesuit priests (who perhaps sought their own martyr-dom), knew what was expected of them and did not disappoint their Indian audiences. During the Franco-Chickasaw Wars, the Chickasaws captured a group of French settlers and soldiers, including Father Antoine Sénat. Mingo Ouma, a war chief among the Chickasaws, later recounted that during the torture "The Black Robe . . . had sung until his death."[66]

Euro-Americans, even as they recounted tales of torture in voyeuristic detail, quickly condemned the practice as "barbaric." In describing the exotic, alien nature of torture, however, chroniclers were a bit dishonest. In fact, for centuries, torture had played an important role in European justice, and, in the eighteenth century, Europeans still flocked to public quarterings. In 1757, after Robert-François Damiens attempted to kill King Louis XV, a French crowd watched executioners burn, pierce, and, finally, quarter the criminal. A contemporary newspaper reported, "This last op-eration was very long, because the horses used were not accustomed to drawing; consequently, instead of four, six were needed; and when that did not suffice, they were forced, in order to cut off the wretch's thighs, to sever the sinews and hack at the joints." In Europe, brutal torture and ex-ecution were prerogatives of the state; the public were only spectators.

Native Americans, in contrast, saw torture as a public right belonging above all to those most directly affected by the death of a loved one. Although Euro-Americans purported to see only chaotic mob violence, Native clans used torture to quiet crying blood, maintain social order, address cosmic balance, and augment group power.[67]

Throughout the eighteenth century, various Euro-American men tried to convince Native people to give up the fiery torture. Resident traders, for example, routinely offered money to ransom the condemned captives, especially if those captives happened to be white. The more honest chroniclers admitted that their attempts were usually unsuccessful. James Adair related that during the Franco-Chickasaw Wars, the Chickasaws put a number of Frenchmen to death in their fires: "The English traders solicited with the most earnest entreaties, in favour of the unfortunate captives; but they averred, that as it was not our business to intercede in behalf of a deceitful enemy who came to shed blood, unless we were resolved to share their deserved fate."[68] Similarly, Nathaniel Folsom, who lived among the Choctaws for decades, reported that a white trader once offered Choctaw captors a parcel of English textiles in exchange for a Creek captive. They refused, explaining, "the Creeks burns us and when we ketch them we will do so too," and then handed the man to beloved women who set him alight.[69]

Blood demanded blood, and outsiders had no business interfering in captive death. In 1774, William Bartram quoted an old trader as saying that the Creeks no longer practiced "burning or tormenting their male captives; though it is said they used to do it formerly." Later in his narrative, however, he contradicted this statement, claiming that at their public squares "modern and even present nations of Indians" practiced torture. Writing at about the same time, Bernard Romans asserted that Native people regularly tortured prisoners of war. In a revealing moment during Joseph Brown's captivity among the Chickamaugas, his captors threatened to take him to "Running water town"—more isolated than the other main village at Nickajack—where there were "no white people" to interfere. In accord with the law of blood, clans continued to kill captives because the practice fulfilled essential social and spiritual needs.[70]

This World was alive with spirits: monstrous serpents from the Lower World dwelled in deep pools; witches walked among ordinary villagers; mountain sprites aided travelers in need; deer, falcons, panthers, wolves, and other animals retained some of the spiritual power of their ancient, more perfect ancestors. So, too, was the land animated with the spirits of the dead who implored their kin to seek vengeance. Crying blood motivated eighteenth-century Indians to go to war and take captives, and these captives served as flexible mediums through which clans extracted power. To redress the imbalance that resulted from the loss of a loved one, however, captives need not die. Adopted or enslaved captives also enhanced clan strength by performing labor, producing children, and conferring status.

4

INCORPORATING OUTSIDERS

Choctaw statesman Peter Pitchlynn related the story of the Crawfish
People, a clan of crustaceans who became humans, to artist George
Catlin in the early 1830s. "They formerly, but at a very remote period,
lived under ground, and used to come up out of the mud—they were a
species of crawfish; and they went on their hands and feet, and lived in a
large cave deep under ground, where there was no light for several miles."
According to Pitchlynn, the Crawfish lacked hallmarks of humanity:
"They spoke no language at all, nor could they understand any." Nearby
Choctaws took an interest in the Crawfish, and they "used to lay and wait
for them to come out into the sun, where they would try to talk to them
and cultivate an acquaintance." Following many attempts at capturing
the Crawfish, the Choctaws finally succeeded when they smoked the
Crawfish out of their underground tunnels. After the Choctaws captured
the Crawfish, "they treated them kindly—taught them the Choctaw
language—taught them to walk on two legs—made them cut off their toe
nails, and pluck the hair from their bodies, after which they adopted them
into their nation." The only reminder of their former identity was their
clan name, the Crawfish People.[1]

The Crawfish People were not mythic figures, but an actual Indian
group absorbed by the Choctaws in the early eighteenth century. The
Choctaws called them *shåktci homma*, meaning "red crawfish." The Chakchiumas lived at the confluence of the Yazoo and Yalobusha rivers, near
the Choctaws. Like their neighbors, the Chakchiumas became French allies and joined the Louisianans in campaigns against the Yazoos, Koroas,
and Chickasaws. Already a small group, war and disease further weakened
the Chakchiumas. Around 1730, the Chakchiumas sought refuge in Choctaw communities. As is commemorated in the oral tradition, the Choctaws
incorporated the Chakchiumas. While the Choctaws normally assigned
individual captives to preexisting clans, in the case of the Chakchiumas,

who numbered at least several dozen, the Choctaws created a new clan designation for them—the Crawfish People.[2]

The Crawfish story serves as an allegory about captive adoption, capturing the spirit and purpose of naturalizing foreigners. Initially, the Crawfish were nothing like the Choctaws: the Crawfish lived below ground, the Choctaws above; the Crawfish walked on four legs, the Choctaws upright; the Crawfish lacked a spoken language, the Choctaw language was one of the most salient markers of their identity. Even so, the Choctaws determined to incorporate these foreigners. Displaying their good intentions, the captors "treated [the Crawfish] kindly." The foreigners' first step toward humanity was their mastery of the Choctaw language, which endowed them with a distinctly Choctaw worldview and the ability to communicate with their captors. Second, the Choctaws "taught them to walk on two legs"—a metaphor for instructing their captives in proper behavior. Finally, the Choctaws changed the Crawfish People's physical appearance, cutting off their long nails, removing their body hair, and generally tailoring their looks to Choctaw tastes. Mentally, behaviorally, and physically transformed, the Crawfish became fully Choctaw. The Crawfish allegory was a testament to Indians' ability to transform aliens into members of their own society. Through proper ritual, anyone—regardless of appearance or cultural background—could become a full member of society.

Oral tradition suggests that Native Americans believed that the appearance and behavior of humans, animals, and plants were mutable. In the Chakchiuma case, the Choctaws transformed crawfish into humans. Similarly, when humans rejected these cultural norms, they sometimes reverted to an animal or even monstrous state. According to Cherokees, bears originated when the *Ani-Tsaguhi* clan began to spend too much time outside of the village, preferring to make an easy living off of the bounty of the mountains instead of farming. After seven days of living in the wilderness, "they had not taken human food and their nature was changing." Members of the Ani-Tsaguhi clan became covered with fur, and soon they were no longer humans, but bears.[3] Creeks told the story of a hunter who ate a mixture of taboo foods, namely, "a black snake, a black squirrel, and a wild turkey." The man mutated into a black snake or, in some versions of the story, a tie-snake, a monster with the body of a snake, antlers like a deer, and wings of a raptor. For Native people, humans kept their form because of culture, not nature: those who practiced cultural norms, no matter what their original state, could be groomed into kin; those who did not were less than human.[4]

The Creek chief Malatchi once remarked that "it is in no Man's Power to bring our People that have been killed back to Life again." In adopting captives, Southern Indians took a different approach than the Iroquois, who used their prisoners to ritually requicken the dead, going so far as to assign deceased relatives' names to new bodies. Southern Indians did not believe that adoption could bring the dead back to life. When mourning, relatives felt so great a loss that they wailed and tore their hair and blackened their faces. In going to war and killing enemies, they attempted to ensure that every soul made it to the spirit country. Eighteenth-century Indian societies were foremost collections of kin groups, and their values stressed the corporate rather than the individual. Mourning relatives could not reanimate the dead, but they could adopt relatives whose labor and reproductive capabilities would compensate for that loss. By using ceremony to incorporate new people, clans regenerated themselves and survived.[5]

Coming from the outside world, foreigners were "wild"—physically different, uneducated in behavioral norms, and potentially dangerous. Indians transformed wild people into family members through ritual. According to an early eighteenth-century account, when a Chickasaw clan decided to adopt a captive, they first gathered about the adoptee and wept copiously, shedding tears not for the captive and her ordeal, but for the deceased relative she would replace. The clan then carried the adoptee around the town's central fire four times. All Southern Indians recognized four as a sacred number, associating it with the cardinal directions and, perhaps more significantly here, with the seasonal cycle, with death and rebirth. The clan then sprinkled water in her hair and carried the captive to the river, where they washed her. For four days thereafter, the captive took medicines prepared from cleansing herbs and bathed again. Ritually purged of her former life and character, the adoptee could now assume her new role within the clan and broader Chickasaw society.[6]

In 1742, when Frenchman Antoine Bonnefoy arrived at the Cherokee town of Tellico, he was stripped, given a white stick and rattle (white being the color of peace), and forced to sing for much of the next two days. Eager to please his captors and preserve his life, Bonnefoy later recalled that he sang every tune he knew, "singing both French and Indian songs." On the second day, the Cherokee clans buried a lock of Bonnefoy's hair, signifying the death of his old life. Afterward, the Cherokees and Bonnefoy sang again in the council house, a place of honor. Singing had a spiritual dimension, and the act of joining other Cherokees in song at the council house forged sacred bonds between the adoptee and his new people. Afterward, Bonnefoy's new brother led him to the cabin they would share, "washed me, then, after he had told me that the way was free before me, I ate with him, and there I remained two months, dressed and treated like himself." After being symbolically purged of his former identity, shorn and scrubbed, Bonnefoy was born anew as a Cherokee.[7]

Four decades later, the Chickamauga faction of the Cherokee Nation adopted Joseph Brown. Though bordering on adulthood, Brown was "very small" for his age and looked younger than his 15 years. Luckily for Brown, the Wolf clan decided to adopt him, and he became nephew to The Breath of Nickajack, one of the most respected chiefs among the Chickamauga. During Brown's adoption, The Breath "seemed very solomn" and told Brown to join hands with him. The Breath told the boy that he must discard his old identity. Brown recalled, "He . . . informed me that I would have to become an indian or I could not be saved. . . . [H]e would put me in his own family & I must call him uncle." Joseph's new kinfolk then tackled his appearance: "The same day [that I was adopted] they cut my hair all [off] except a patch on the top of my head to ty a bunch of feathers to & Shaved all the balance of my head & bored holes through my ears." Integral to Brown's "becom[ing] an indian" was not the alteration of his skin color, which was unimportant to the Cherokees, but rather the tailoring of his hairstyle, dress, and jewelry to Cherokee norms.[8]

Even Native captives who managed to escape from enemies and return to their natal societies had to go through adoption ceremonies. Native people considered those taken captives to be socially dead, for they "call[ed] killing and being taken prisoner by the same name."[9] When the niece of Cherokee headman Attakullakulla returned home after a long captivity among the Miami Indians, she, like Bonnefoy and Brown, had to undergo ritual rebirth. After a British deputy in the Illinois country ransomed her, she canoed down the Mississippi River, then sailed around the Florida peninsula and up the Atlantic coast to Charles Town, and finally traveled overland for a few weeks before she reached her hometown. But Attakullakulla and her relatives could not yet embrace their long-suffering kinswoman. Instead, she "was obliged to undergoe Eight days Confinement in the Town house . . . and after that to be strip'd, dip'd, well wash'd and [thereafter] Conducted home." Attakullakulla's niece was Cherokee-born, but her long captivity and subsequent travels had exposed her to the myriad pollutants of the outside world, possibly to evil forces that could endanger her village. Like adopted captives, this Cherokee woman needed to sing and pray at the council house, to cleanse herself, and to dress in the Cherokee style before she could reassume her old identity.[10]

Recorded throughout the eighteenth century, these adoption rites are remarkably similar. All involve the captive's social death and his or her rebirth into a new society. Captives achieved this monumental transformation through purification. Physical activities such as bathing, medicine-taking, and redressing served as outward manifestations of the captive's personal transformation. Central to this process was manipulation of the adoptee's appearance; captors gave their new relatives clothes and jewelry. Hairstyle remained a paramount signifier of identity, and captors paid particular attention to men's hair, cutting and styling it to conform to their own standards. All adoptions concluded with forms of public ceremony that demonstrated the new ties binding clans and their adoptees.

Because sex and age, not race, were a captive's most important characteristics throughout the colonial era, African American adoptees usually experienced the same ritual and treatment as their white and Indian counterparts. A young, free black man, John Marrant, produced one of America's most fascinating captivity narratives. Born in New York, Marrant moved to Florida and then Georgia before settling in Charles Town, South Carolina, where he became renowned as a musical prodigy. At age 14, Marrant heard George Whitefield and converted to Methodism. His fervor convinced his family that he was "insane." Shortly thereafter, in 1770, Marrant ran away from home, and a Cherokee hunter found him wandering in the Carolina piedmont. Brought before a chief, the captive cried and prayed, fearing an unpleasant end. The chief, according to Marrant, "expressed a concern for me, and said I was young." Like Joseph Brown, John Marrant was on the cusp of manhood but young enough to be spared from a warrior's death. After the chief's clan adopted him, Marrant "assumed the habit of the country" and dressed "purely in the Indian stile." Marrant passed his time learning the language, dressing skins, and sharing his religious beliefs with other Cherokees. More fortunate than many African Americans of his time, Marrant never experienced enslavement—not at the hands of whites, not among the Cherokees.[11]

With little or no memory of their former lives, child captives made the best new kin. Children readily learned Native languages, kin relations, gender roles, and belief systems. The Creeks seem to have thoroughly assimilated Tempest Ellice during her captivity. Ellice, taken from her family's home near present-day Athens, Georgia, in 1787, lived as a Creek for nine years. Prompted by the petition of Tempest's mother Esther, Georgia governor Edward Telfair called on federal Indian agent James Seagrove to retrieve the child. Upon locating Tempest Ellice, Seagrove reported, "she is 13 years of age, but does not remember anything of her [birth] family."[12]

As heads of households, women took charge of rearing captive children. Choctaw Greenwood LeFlore recounted, "The mother was always considered entitled to the possession and control of the children. It was her business to prepare their food and take care of them." Fathers, LeFlore explained, "paid very little attention to them." In accord with matrilineal kinship practices, the dominant male figure in these children's lives was their adoptive uncle. He took charge of educating boys in the masculine arts of war and hunting, but his sister remained the authority figure. According to LeFlore, he stepped in only if his sister treated the children badly.[13] Such instances were probably rare. Euro-Americans, who considered corporal punishment an essential tool in child-rearing, chided Indians for sparing the rod and spoiling youths "to a degree which often proves their ruin."[14] Ideally, kinship ties forged by adoption would be just as strong as bonds of blood, and a Native mother was expected to care for an adopted child "as if it was the child of [her] body." This control over adoptive children again demonstrates women's central roles in captivity: women urged their kinsmen to go to war, determined captives' fates, and reared adoptive members of their societies alongside their biological children.[15]

When birth families attempted to redeem children adopted by Indian families, the children often responded with horror. As part of his diplomatic mission following the Cherokee War, Lieutenant Henry Timberlake tried to round up Anglo-American children captured and adopted by the Cherokees. Timberlake found many unwilling to return to South Carolina: "Among them were above twenty boys who had become so habituated to the Indian manners that, after they were delivered up, they did nothing but cry, and would not eat."[16] When Joseph Brown came to "redeem" his 5-year-old sister Polly, captive for just one year with the Chickamaugas,

Polly "would not leave her Indian mother, who had ever treated her kindly, but wept and clung to her neck."[17] So successful were clans in "habituat[ing]" adopted children "to the Indian manners" that the children considered clan kin to be their authentic families and loathed returning to a life that they could not remember.

Although many birth families eventually redeemed their stolen children, other captives grew to adulthood in Native nations. During the American Revolution, a clan from Hilabi adopted 9-year-old captive Daniel Eades. Eades family lore suggests that Daniel's adoptive uncle was what the Creeks called a *hilis haya*, or medicine maker, "who raised him and taught him his craft in roots and herbs."[18] By 1793, Daniel Eades answered to the name "Sausey Jack" and sported "a remarkable scar on the inside of his left thigh above the Knee."[19] Eades likely acquired this "remarkable scar" while warring or hunting with his male kin, activities that defined masculinity in Creek culture. Like Daniel Eades, John Hague was taken captive as a young boy. Adopted by a Yuchi clan, Hague grew to adulthood among them, married a Yuchi woman, and had a number of children. By the early nineteenth century, one observer dubbed Hague "as great a savage as any of them."[20] During 1795 treaty negotiations, the Chickamaugas attempted to comply with the United States' demand that they release all former captives, giving up three young children recently taken. However, they reported, "There is also a man in the Nation captured at twelve years of age now married, has Children & unwilling to return to the white People."[21]

George Mayfield, captured in 1786 around the age of 10, adjusted well to his new life. After his adoption, Mayfield was reared as a Creek in the town of Pucantallahassee.[22] Like other Creek boys, Mayfield probably learned to shoot arrows and track game, skills befitting a hunter. Mayfield likely also participated in the most popular of Native sports—stickball, an intensely physical, lacrosse-like game whose Creek name, *hólli icósi*, meant "younger brother to war."[23] Alongside his peers, Mayfield doubtlessly listened to the oral traditions of his elders, who educated him about the history of his adoptive people, about This World, and about the cosmos. In the 1790s, friends of the Mayfield family began to lobby George to return home; some even visited the Creek Nation. George, however, was reluctant to return to Tennessee. He had forgotten English and "had contracted a fondness for [the Creek] mode of life."[24] Mayfield's Tennessee kin and friends also pestered Creek agent Benjamin Hawkins, and, in a

1798 meeting with the Upper Creek chiefs, Hawkins suggested that Mayfield should be released. The chiefs responded that "Mayfield had been long at liberty to go where he pleased." Finally, the chiefs, too, encouraged Mayfield to "go and see his friends."[25] In 1800, Mayfield finally complied, but, as he later said, he did so without "any intention, on his part, to abandon the Indians."[26] Thereafter, Mayfield resided mostly in Tennessee and regained control of his native tongue, but he never forgot his life as a Creek. Indeed, Mayfield had become so thoroughly Creek that he attempted to apply aspects of matrilineality to his new life in Tennessee; peers chided Mayfield for granting his mother and sisters virtually his entire estate. Mayfield also served as an interpreter and remained in touch with his old Creek kin. Even decades after his return to Tennessee, George Mayfield continued to straddle the Creek and Anglo-American worlds.[27]

Hannah Hale, taken captive during the Revolution at the age of 11 or 12, certainly fulfilled the expectations of her new kin. After coming of age in the town of Thlothlagalga, Hale married a headman called Hopoie (or Far-off) and reared their five children. As Creek women had done for centuries, Hale controlled her household's production, which by the late eighteenth century included spinning and weaving as well as farming. Other Creeks appreciated Hale's honesty, work ethic, and solid command of their language.[28] Beginning in the 1790s, the state of Georgia attempted to redeem Hale and several other captives. Hale, however, refused to leave the Creek Nation. In 1798, Hale's relatives from Georgia kidnapped her and tried to convince her to remain with them. Distraught, her husband Hopoie traveled to Georgia. Influenced by his own upbringing, which taught Hopoie that a husband should reside with his wife's family, he "intended to come and reside with her relatives who would build a house for him." Although he reported that he was "kindly treated" by Hale's relatives, Hopoie complained that he missed his hometown, Thlothlagalga, that "the chiefs of his town would not consent to his leaving of them," and that living in Georgia simply "would not suit him." Upon returning to the Creek Nation, Hale's husband proclaimed that Hannah "was a free woman" and that she must choose her own path.[29]

After so many years in the Creek Nation, life in Georgia did not suit Hannah either, and she returned to Thlothlagalga. Perhaps, as Hopoie suggested, she missed "her family and property." Reassuring Georgians that the Creeks had not compelled Hale to return to their nation, Agent Benjamin Hawkins asserted, "She possesses the rights of a Creek woman, and can throw away her husband whenever she chooses." A Creek woman's "rights" included the ability to divorce her husband and to accumulate wealth that she could then pass on to her children. These were liberties Hale could not have enjoyed in the state of Georgia. Mary Jemison, a captive who also chose her adoptive Indian community over the Anglo-American world of her birth, lauded many aspects of Native life, including the nature of women's work. Captured in 1758, Jemison was adopted by the Senecas, a nation of the Iroquois Confederacy that, like Southern nations, reckoned descent matrilineally and subsisted largely on female-produced corn, beans, and squash. Challenging the widely held white view that Indian men treated their women as drudges, Jemison claimed that while Indian women farmed, cooked, and managed households, "their task is probably not harder than that of white women." Jemison added that female clan kin farmed communally (as opposed to white frontier women who often labored in isolation), making the work easier and the time pass more pleasantly. Women like Hale and Jemison, when offered the rare opportunity to choose between societies, often elected to remain in Indian country. Native societies, especially those which placed women at the center of kinship reckoning, afforded women greater control over their economic and sexual lives than did contemporary colonial or European societies. When the Creek National Council convened in 1799, Hannah Hale stood before all the chiefs and headmen, affirming that she wished to remain Creek.[30]

A long view of Native history reveals that Indian groups had a great deal of practice in incorporating outsiders. Following the collapse of Mississippian chiefdoms, Native groups forged bonds of kinship with strangers, making new nations inhabited by diverse people. In 1763, Cherokee chief Judd's Friend claimed, "Our women are breeding Children night and Day to increase our People." Population loss due to war and disease continued to plague eighteenth-century Indians, and, as Judd's Friend suggested, social reproduction remained a major concern for clan leaders. Judd's Friend touted natural increase, but captive adoption achieved the same end. By the late eighteenth century, Native Americans had relied on the practice as a survival strategy for at least 300 years.[31]

Native villages were truly multiethnic, home to Indians of various nations as well as people of European and African descent. In an 1800 letter to Thomas Jefferson, Indian agent Benjamin Hawkins related how, from his desk at the Creek agency, he could "hear the languages of Scotch, French, Spanish, English, Africans, Creeks, and Uches [Yuchi]."[32] Centuries of captive-taking contributed significantly to the diverse composition of these communities. When Frenchman Antoine Bonnefoy and his companions arrived in Tellico, they met several European and African residents. One of Tellico's most famous inhabitants was Christian Priber, a German by birth who attempted to create a utopian society among the Cherokees. Priber envisioned Tellico as colonial America's "City of Refuge," a color-blind haven for debtors, runaway slaves, religious dissidents, and other oppressed people. Encouraged and perhaps influenced by the Cherokees' multiethnic society and their tradition of captive adoption, Priber believed that his dream could be realized within their nation. The British, however, fearing that Priber was a French spy, hampered his efforts. Cherokees rejected British bribes to give Priber up and continued to protect him because "he was adopted into the nation." (Unfortunately for Priber, Georgia colonists and their Creek allies did succeed in capturing him a few years later, in 1743. He died in prison at Fort Frederica that same year.)[33] When Priber met Bonnefoy and his captive companions, he told them, in French, "that he was very sorry for the misfortune which had come upon us, but that it would perhaps prove to be our happiness." Tellico was home to a number of captives, several of whom appear to have been content with their fortune. Bonnefoy and his companions were perhaps surprised to learn that they were not the only Frenchmen in town—the Cherokees held two other voyageurs, who had been captured on the Ohio River. Residents of Tellico also included "a negro and a negress who formerly belonged to the widow Saussier, and having been sold in 1739 to a Canadian, deserted when on the Ouabache, on their way to Canada, and were captured by a troop of Cheraquis who brought them to the same village."[34]

Native Americans enjoyed tremendous success at transforming strangers into kin, but they did not encourage complete cultural amnesia. In fact, captors valued the skills adoptees brought to their communities. Cherokee adoptee Christian Priber was, by all accounts, a man of exceptional intelligence. In addition to his native German, Priber spoke English, French, Latin, and Cherokee, and he reportedly compiled the first English-Cherokee dictionary (which, sadly, has not survived). According to one English trader, the Cherokees asserted that Priber "was made a great beloved man," a title of esteem and affection that enabled Priber to speak in Tellico's town councils.[35] The French voyageurs brought to Tellico their knowledge of the fur trade market, which would have been of great interest to eighteenth-century Indian men. The African couple, formerly belonging to the widow Saussier, had fled from the lower Mississippi valley, perhaps from New Orleans. Like most enslaved Africans in early Louisiana, they probably came from Senegambia and were experienced agriculturalists. Nearly all Africans in early Louisiana were multilingual, speaking one or more African languages as well as French or Creole. Cherokees, like other Indians, valued such individuals as translators, especially during the mid-eighteenth century as they dealt with three imperial powers—England, France, and Spain. Captives also brought new technologies into Indian communities. In the Creek Nation, Hannah Hale spun and wove cotton and churned butter, tasks that she had probably performed or observed as a girl in rural Georgia. By the late eighteenth century, when the Creeks sought to transform their subsistence-level economy into one based on commercial planting and ranching, such skills were in high demand. The selective adoption of outsiders into their communities allowed Indians to control the process of cultural change. They embraced certain individuals, technologies, and ideas and rejected those they did not value.[36]

Captivity was usually born of the violence of warfare, but captives themselves sometimes acted as diplomats between traditional enemies. Former captives became important kin, in part, because they came from the outside world and thus knew foreign languages and customs. That knowledge made them ideal cultural mediators. Just like the Chickasaw *fanemingos*, former captives served as messengers and peacekeepers. A Cherokee-born man called The Thigh, a longtime captive among the Shawnee, returned to his people in adulthood. The Thigh, however, retained an allegiance to the Shawnee, visiting his former captors, speaking to Cherokee headmen on their behalf, and carrying messages between the two nations. During the Seven Years' War, when the Shawnees fought alongside the French, The Thigh delivered a belt of black wampum to the Cherokee council as well as a talk urging his countrymen to abandon their long-standing alliance with the British. The Thigh's attachment to the Shawnees suggests that he had been adopted into a Shawnee clan. Birth to a Cherokee mother afforded The Thigh Cherokee clan membership, and his Shawnee adoption gave him another. Because the Shawnees were partrilineal, this new clan membership did not negate or compromise The Thigh's position in his natal, matrilineal clan. Thus, The Thigh benefited from a kind of dual citizenship, one that enabled him to move easily in two Native societies, but also obligated him to advocate for both.[37]

From the mid-seventeenth century through the 1760s, the Iroquois and Southern Indians engaged in continuous warfare. The Cherokees, living closer to Iroquoia than any other major Southern nation, suffered the loss of many kin to death and captivity. In April of 1767, British Indian agent John Stuart estimated that 350 Cherokees had fallen victim to Iroquois depredations in the past twelve months. At that time, the Cherokees, having recently endured a smallpox epidemic, numbered about 7,000; thus, this loss represented about 5 percent of their total population.[38] But they retaliated in kind. When Mohawk John Norton visited the Cherokees from 1809 to 1810, he noted that the nation was home to many of Iroquois descent. Norton was especially keen to explore the tangled history of the Cherokees and Iroquois because he claimed that his own father was a Cherokee by birth. Norton told the story of how his father was captured as a boy at Keowee when British forces destroyed it during the Cherokee War. Supposedly adopted by a British soldier who gave him the surname Norton, the boy moved to Scotland and later married a Scottish woman. John Norton, who maintained that he was the captive's son, was born in Scotland and later joined the British Army. However, John Norton's time line makes his autobiography suspect. It is more likely that his parents were both Scots and that he lacked Native ancestry, but during the 1780s, as a member of the British Army, Norton moved to Canada where he served as a Mohawk translator. Although Norton's Cherokee roots are doubtful, he was undeniably Mohawk, for a Mohawk clan adopted him. Eventually, Norton became a chief with the title of *Teyoninhokarawen* or "Open Door."

Norton zealously embraced his Native identity (whether newfound or ancient), and when he journeyed southward to seek out his supposed father's relations, Cherokees welcomed him as a long-lost kinsman. Norton was delighted to meet an aunt, a woman who had lost a brother during the Cherokee War and who, accepting Norton's story, greeted him as a nephew. Norton also became acquainted with several cousins, and he eagerly sought out other ties. Among the more prominent Cherokees Norton met was The Glass, a headman who had enjoyed great success in war as a youth. The Glass told Norton that his father was a Wyandot who had been adopted by the Cherokees. Perhaps motivated by an interest in his father's ancestry, The Glass "had been to the Northward" and "formed a friendship" with Joseph Brant, the prominent Mohawk chief who served as Norton's adoptive uncle. Oconostota, another Cherokee war chief, informed Norton that he had an Onondaga half-brother. The men shared the same father, but the Onondaga's mother was a natal Cherokee who was taken captive while she was pregnant. Likely adopted by an Onondaga clan, the woman gave birth in Iroquoia and passed her new clan affiliation along to her son. Oconostota first met his half-brother as a young man, when the Onondaga traveled south to visit their father "and thus the two Brothers became acquainted." As Norton discovered, decades of war between the Iroquois and Cherokees resulted in terrible bloodshed, but the legacy of captive-taking also pulled these traditional enemies in the opposite direction and, over time, encouraged recognition of the kinship ties that increasingly bound them together.[39]

Just like Native captives, white and black captives acted as translators, advisers, and go-betweens, bridging the gap between Native nations and American colonies. James Carey, taken by the Cherokees in his youth, became a translator for the Cherokee National Council as an adult. Carey's uncle, Little Turkey, introduced him to the council members, saying, "though a white man, I consider [Carey] as one of my own people, for I have raised him from a boy."[40] When Creek headman Hoboithle Miko negotiated with officials from Georgia during the American Revolution, among his consultants was a white woman (almost certainly a captive) who "much rejoiced him to see that his Plan of doing good had so far taken Place."[41] When Native diplomats made alliances with other nations, they typically brought along several women as a sign of their peaceful intentions. Hoboithle Miko's female companion possessed English language skills and knowledge of Anglo-American culture that heightened her importance. Similarly, Marianne Bienvenu, taken along with some French fur traders by the Chickasaws, attempted to broker a peace between the French of Louisiana and her captors. She wrote letters to Governor Vaudreuil on behalf of the Chickasaws, conveying their hopes for peace.[42]

Native Americans rarely sought the total destruction of an enemy people. Rather, through captivity, Native nations selected some former enemies and incorporated them into their societies. In addition to strengthening diplomatic ties with former enemies, captivity augmented population levels reduced by disease. Following American victory in the Revolution, Creek headman Fine Bones was incredulous that the British were deserting his people. He beseeched them to remember the bonds forged between the two groups through captivity: "[The Creeks] often took prisoners whom the English redeemed and had children by them who live among us. . . . Do the English mean to abandon their own children with their friends?" With this rebuke, Fine Bones attempted to call the British to task, reminding them how captivity had created indelible ties of kinship between the two.[43]

Beyond the adoption of prisoners of war, Indians used captivity as a framework for incorporating entire groups into their societies. As the Chakchiuma case demonstrates, nations absorbed formerly independent polities, just as lineages adopted formerly unrelated individuals. Wars, epidemics, and shifting alliances made the colonial South a dangerous homeland. As Native chiefdoms throughout the region declined and collapsed, survivors became vulnerable to the vicissitudes of everyday life as well as targets for Indian slavers. Groups weakened by war and disease sought protection from more powerful people. Sometimes, as in the Apalachee case, Indians allied with Europeans, but more often they looked toward emerging Native nations. Refugees sought the protection of other Native groups not because they shared a common language or ethnicity (often they did not), but because they shared a belief system, a way of seeing the world. Part of this shared culture was the notion that ceremony could transform foreigners into kin.[44]

No polity in the colonial South absorbed more refugees than the Creek Nation. Trader James Adair asserted, "The nation consists of a mixture of several broken tribes, whom the Muskohge artfully decoyed to incorporate with them, in order to strengthen themselves against hostile attempts."[45] Archaeological evidence indicates that in the late seventeenth and early eighteenth centuries refugees gathered around a number of populous towns with a recent history of stability. These strong towns—Tuckabatchee on the lower Tallapoosa River, Abihka on the middle Coosa, and Cusseta and Coweta on the lower Chattahoochee—became the Creek "mother towns," the birthplaces of the nation.[46] The history of Tuckabatchee, in particular, demonstrates how the Creek Nation became home to a remarkably diverse group of people. During the seventeenth century, when many Native towns and chiefdoms vanished, Tuckabatchee's population soared. Founded around 1400, Tuckabatchee became the most populous Upper Creek town of the colonial era, attracting Native immigrants from

throughout the South and as far away as the Ohio valley. Among the newcomers to Tuckabatchee were refugees who, according to a late-eighteenth-
century visitor, had been "almost destroyed by the Iroquois and the Hu-
rons." These refugees were probably Shawnees forced out of the Ohio
River valley by Iroquois warfare. Among Eastern Indians, Shawnees were
well known for their ability to move easily among disparate Native groups;
they bridged the cultural divide that often separated Native people from
different regions and acted as mediators and messengers.[47]

Wide travel and diplomatic success, abilities usually associated with
great spiritual power, afforded the Shawnees a certain cachet among
Southern Indians. Creek oral tradition recalls that these refugees came
bearing powerful medicine and gave local leaders sacred copper plates,
which the Tuckabatchees believed were from the Upper World. After the
Shawnees' arrival, the Raccoon, Fox, and Aktayatcalgi clans formed a
new phratry (a descent group composed of several clans) called the *Sawanogalga* meaning "Shawnee people." These may have been the clans that
the newcomers joined. Alternatively, native Muskogees may have forged
this phratry in an effort to attract some of the sacred power that the Shawnees seemed to possess. When they played other Creek towns in stickball
or met in national diplomatic contexts, the Tuckabatchees sometimes collectively referred to themselves as Sawanogalga. The influence of the
Shawnee refugees is also apparent in Tuckabatchee's ceremonial title—
Tuckabatchee spokogi. All four Creek mother towns had such titles: the
Lower Creek capitals were known as "Tall Coweta" and "Big Cusseta,"
while the meaning of Upper Town Abihka's designation—*nagi*—remains
obscure. For the Tuckabatchees, *spokogi* probably reflects a Muskogeean
corruption of the *Kispokoke* Shawnees, the band that settled among them.
The Tuckabatchees' decision to include the appellation in their ceremonial title reflects how integral the Shawnee refugees were to their group
identity.[48]

Seeking protection among the Creeks, other groups followed the Shawnees' lead. By the late seventeenth century, Alabamas and Koasatis settled
in or near Tuckabatchee. Over the next several decades, a panoply of Native ethnic groups, including Natchez, Yuchis, and Hitchitis, would join
the ethnic Muskogees who made up the core of the Creek Nation. A 1726
visitor to Creek country reported that a visiting Seneca delegation applauded this population-boosting technique, saying, "Take Care That you
oblidge all Such as you make a peace with That they Imediately Remove

and Setle near you. By that you will have all your Friends Ready to oppose your Enemies."[49] A contemporary exaggerated just slightly when he called the Creek Nation "the receptacle for all distressed Tribes."[50] Pushed away from their homelands by warfare and disease, refugees were also drawn to the Creeks' diplomatic and military successes. Along with the Chickasaws, the Creeks shared a reputation as the region's most warlike Indian nation. Native people "who were too weak to resist the attacks of an enemy, came immediately to beg them for help."[51] British Indian agent John Stuart dubbed the Creeks the most "insolent" Southern nation. He explained that the Creeks' success in engaging in play-off diplomacy with the region's three imperial powers had garnered them significant social and political capital. While many other Native polities languished and disappeared, the Creek Nation grew over the course of the eighteenth century as it absorbed other people. Reaching a nadir of perhaps 9,000 in 1700, the population rebounded thereafter, numbering between 15,000 and 20,000 by the late eighteenth century. In the words of one visitor, "Their numbers have increased faster by acquisition of foreign subjects, than by the increase of the original stock."[52]

Although the Tuckabatchees regarded Shawnee newcomers with a certain amount of reverence, most refugee groups did not enjoy that luxury, and they became incorporated into the nation as junior members. In addition to Shawnees, those seeking protection included large numbers of people from what is now central and southern Georgia, who spoke an unintelligible dialect of Muskogee called Hitchiti. The nation's dominant ethnic group, speakers of Muskogee proper, referred to the others as *istenko*. Englishmen, understanding that the term was derisive, misheard it as "stinkard" and probably reasoned that Muskogees believed that Hitchitis were dirty or tainted. The term actually meant "worthless hand," a definition that may allude to regional history. The formidable chiefdoms to which Hitchitis once belonged had crumbled, leaving only isolated villages behind. Such settlements, severed from their former body politic, joined the Creek Nation. The word "istenko" is similar to an Iroquois word for captive, *we-hait-wat-sha*, meaning "a body cut into parts and scattered around." As one Iroquois man explained, his people "figuratively scattered their prisoners, and sunk and destroyed their nationality and built up their own." The semblance between the two terms—worthless hand and disarticulated body—betrays similarities in how Creeks and Iroquois understood captivity. Multiethnic, aggressive, and politically savvy, both rose to become the most powerful Indian nations of the colonial era within their respective regions, and they did so by absorbing broken groups.[53]

The Yuchis, a group from what is now eastern Georgia, were even more linguistically distinct from Muskogees than were Hitchitis. Yuchis had warred against the Lower Creeks, yet they sought the protection of the Creek Nation in the 1730s. Muskogees later promulgated a legend that the Yuchis were a defeated people "long held in captivity by the victorious Creeks."[54] When George Stiggins, a Creek of Natchez descent, wrote a history of the Creeks in the early nineteenth century, he depicted the Yuchis as subversives who refused to learn Muskogee, calling them "savage," "indolent," "thievish," "dissipated," and "depraved."[55] Like other formerly independent groups, the Yuchis gave up a measure of their autonomy in exchange for security and became an ethnic minority within the Creek Nation, but they never forgot their heritage. The antipathy between Muskogees and Yuchis may well come from the fact that Yuchis had been loath to give up their distinct culture. Other groups assimilated more completely. By 1799, the Koasatis, as one observer noted, "lost their language, and speak Creek, and have adopted the customs and manners of the Creeks." Meanwhile, the Yuchis steadfastly retained their native tongue, and some in Oklahoma speak it today. Perhaps more disturbing to other Creeks were the Yuchis' subversive gender roles: men farmed in the cornfields alongside women.[56] Despite the cultural dissonance between Muskogees and Yuchis, they came together when it mattered. As William Bartram noted during a 1775 visit to the Yuchis, "They are in confederacy with the Creeks, but do not mix with them . . . and are usually at variance, yet are wise enough to unite against a common enemy, to support the interest and glory of the general Creek confederacy."[57]

Elsewhere, dominant groups extended ties to weaker ones. Continuing what was probably a Mississippian practice, they usually incorporated newcomers as society's lowest-ranking members. Around the turn of the eighteenth century, the Natchez absorbed several small nations from the lower Mississippi valley that had suffered significant casualties due to recent wars and the Indian slave trade. These groups included the Tioux and Grigra, whom the Natchez called *istenko*. After the Natchez War of 1729–1731, the Natchez themselves became refugees. Those who avoided death or capture fled their homeland and attempted to join other Indian groups. Unlike the Shawnees, however, the Natchez were largely unsuccessful in their bid to parlay their storied culture and history into a position of privilege in host societies. Shortly after the Natchez War, a Natchez captive told his Quapaw masters that "the Chickasaws had killed part of the Natchez who had withdrawn among them and kept their wives and children slaves, and that the rest had escaped."[58] Chickasaws reportedly put their Natchez slaves to work at "the most servile tasks."[59] By 1750, a Jesuit missionary reported that the Natchez lived among other Native nations "precariously and almost as slaves."[60] In addition to the Natchez, the Chickasaw Nation also adopted small groups of Chakchiumas, Yazoos, and Koroas. As the Creeks set about building a veritable empire of disparate Native people, they even attempted to absorb their Muskogee-speaking cousins the Chickasaws, who were then reeling from a series of wars against the French and Choctaws. The Chickasaws refused.[61]

Native groups were ethnocentric, and each tended to see itself as the one, true people. Nations of the colonial era saw strength in numbers and sought to incorporate smaller groups, but the strong did not want to meet the weak on a middle ground. Rather, dominant kin groups tried to set the terms of engagement, and they reserved positions of power for themselves.[62]

In the eighteenth century, each Southern Indian nation represented not a collection of individual citizens, but an alliance of groups with disproportionate access to power. The Choctaws, for example, were split into two moieties. The more senior moiety was called *Inholahta* or "chiefs." Inholahtas probably descended from the Moundville people as well as those who lived on the Tombigbee's western tributaries. When these eastern groups moved to central Mississippi, they were joined by people coming from the west: from Nanih Waiya (the Choctaw's "mother mound"), from settlements along the Pearl River, and from the southerly Sixtowns region. These western and southern groups formed the junior moiety, variously called *Imoklasha* ("their own people"), *Kashapa okla* ("divided people"), and *Yuka-tathlapi* ("the five slave people")." Yuka-tathlapi was a derogatory epithet that Inholahata probably used when members of the more junior moiety were out of earshot. They called themselves Imoklasha, as did a Sixtowns leader called Tomatly Mingo in 1765, when he explained, "I am of the Race of Imoklasha & in Consequence the Second in Rank in the Choctaw Nation, The Race of Inhulahta is before me."[63]

Similarly, the Chickasaws were divided into a superior *Imosaktca* moiety, whose leading clan always produced the nation's religious leader, and a lesser *Intcukwalipa* moiety. Among the Intcukwalipas, the four lowest-ranking clans had names indicating their lack of permanent housing or homelessness, labels that commemorated their entrance into the nation as refugees. Creeks were also divided into two moieties, *Hathagalgi*, the "white" or peaceful people, and *Tcilokogalgi*, "people of a different speech" or "foreigners." American diplomat Caleb Swan concluded that certain members of the Creek Nation "are called, of the slave race, and cannot arrive to much honorary distinction in the country on that account." These members of "the slave race," a label Swan probably heard from elite Creeks with whom he associated, were doubtlessly foreign groups integrated into the clan system as junior members.[64]

Within the Creek white moiety, the Wind clan was the most powerful group. In his early-nineteenth-century memoir, Creek George Stiggins called the Wind clan "the largest and most privileged." In Creek oral traditions concerning the origins of clans, the Wind holds a place of honor. Creeks recall that a fog once enveloped This World, but that one day it began to clear. As visibility improved, groups of people named themselves after what they saw: panther, deer, bear, and so forth. These became the groups' clan names. Finally, a gust blew all the fog away, and a group named themselves after that powerful Wind. In the eighteenth and nineteenth centuries, Creeks associated the Wind clan with pure Muskogee ethnicity. Wind members held the lion's share of political offices because, as Stiggins explained, "The strongest link in Creek political and social standing is their clanship or families."[65] As carriers of the bloodline, women of the Wind clan commanded tremendous prestige; all other Creeks respectfully referred to them as "grandmothers," extending this honorific title even to young adults. Wind members enjoyed certain legal privileges. Although most Creeks suffered beatings and corporal mutilations for committing adultery, members of elite clans often received little or no punishment for this transgression. While the victim's kinsmen usually meted out this punishment in a single, swift episode, if the cuckolded spouse was a Wind, the punishers could "take up the sticks a second time."[66] Such unequal punishments for adultery almost certainly originated in the Mississippian era. Natchez Suns had enjoyed similar privileges, and Cherokee oral tradition claimed that the Aní-Kutání "exempted themselves from the observance of the doctrine they taught." Mississippian societies fell, but Native notions of the connection between heredity and power remained. Outwardly, especially in ceremony, moieties and clans appeared to have equal, complementary roles; within each nation, however, certain kin groups enjoyed a disproportionate share of power.[67]

Given that their ancestors had lived in chiefdoms with institutionalized social rank, it is not surprising that colonial-era Natives entered into relationships of dominance and subordination as they formed new nations. Much like victorious chiefdoms of the Mississippian era, expanding Native nations incorporated foreign groups by assigning them a low-ranking position within their kinship systems. Indian nations born in the eighteenth century were multiethnic, composed of formerly independent Native groups as well as those of European and African descent. Adoption, with its ceremonies of conquest, submission, and incorporation, enabled ambitious nations to augment their populations. This sort of eighteenth-century nation-making resulted in the decrease of Native ethnic diversity in the region, as the major Southern nations absorbed formerly autonomous groups.

Although host nations might dub weaker groups "worthless," "homeless," or "slave people," Indians were remarkably successful in incorporating them and thereby strengthening their own nations. Native groups maintained strict exogamy rules, forcing members to marry outside of their clan and sometimes outside of their moiety as well. As one visitor reported, "Those of the same family or clan are not allowed to intermarry; although no relationship, however remote, can be traced between them."[68] Incest taboos encouraged Indians to develop inclusive societies. As trader Thomas Nairne observed, "Establishing a Custome of not marrying in the same name for family seems at first to have been a politick contirvance to encrease Freindship and keep peace."[69] Whatever the origin, exogamous marriages had the effect of integrating disparate and unequal groups, and made Native nations fluid, diverse societies. The social fabric that joined strangers and even former enemies together by ceremonies of incorporation became stronger through ties of affinity.

Because Native people had to marry outside of their clans, they chose partners among clans of different rank, even from other ethnic and racial groups. The Chickasaws, for example, used marriage to forge ties with the English, Cherokees, Choctaws, and Creeks. High-ranking clans encouraged their women to marry Euro-American traders. Through these ties, elites attempted to tame and incorporate outsiders and to control the flow of manufactured goods into their communities.[70] Marriage ties bound groups together and could even transcend national interest, as headmen discovered during the Cherokee War. In 1756, the British constructed Fort Loudoun within the Cherokee Nation near the towns of Chota and Tellico. Relations between the soldiers and Cherokees were initially peaceful. Because the soldiers did not grow their own food, they traded goods to the Cherokees in return for corn. The purveyors of this corn were, of course, women. During the course of their regular visits to the fort, some women developed relationships with British soldiers, and several couples married. When relations between the British and Cherokees deteriorated several years later, the Cherokee women did not abandon their husbands. Cherokee warriors besieged Fort Loudoun beginning in the spring of 1760. At that point, supplies were already low, and conditions quickly became desperate. By June, rations were down to one-third a pint of corn per day, and, by July, the soldiers resorted to eating their horses. Two men who managed to escape fled to Hiwassee where they found food, but at that point the pair, suffering from starvation, supposedly "burst themselves with eating" and died.[71] Those with Cherokee wives fared much better. During the siege, Cherokee women continued to visit their husbands, bringing food and information. Frustrated, Cherokee war chief Willenawa attempted to hide the corn stores and even threatened the women with death, "but they laughing at his threats, boldly told him, they would succour their husbands every day, and were sure, that, if he killed them, their relations would make his death atone for theirs."[72] Recognizing the marriage ties that bound them to certain British men, the warriors ultimately acquiesced to the women's wishes. Before the warriors stormed Fort Loudoun, they offered refuge to those who had Cherokee wives; "considerable numbers" accepted the offer and deserted Loudoun. Stubbornly strong, marriage ties bound disparate groups together and made Indian communities among colonial America's most diverse.[73]

Ceremonial life, including diplomacy, funerary rites, and annual harvest festivals, also had an integrating effect, as each moiety depended on the other to fulfill its complementary role. As explorer John Lawson trekked his way across the Carolina piedmont in 1701 among the coalescent Catawbas, he noted that when two nations entered into a peace someone appointed by the chiefs composed a song. Such songs, Lawson related, told of "how the bad Spirit made them go to War, and destroy one another; but it shall never be so again; but that their Sons and Daughters shall marry together, and the two Nations love one another, and become as one People."[74]

Burial practices among the Choctaws demonstrate how ceremony brought their diverse nation together. Composed of the survivors of disparate chiefdoms, those who became Choctaw had different ideas about how to bury the dead. Some interred full-length bodies under their former homes; others bent corpses into the fetal position and placed them in burial urns; most treated elites differently than commoners. Around 1700, when these groups formed a confederacy, they adopted a uniform mortuary practice, and, remarkably, they chose the most elaborate sort, the kind formerly reserved for society's elite. When any Choctaw died, members of the opposite moiety constructed a scaffold and placed the body on top. After the flesh decomposed, the bone-picker, a high-ranking member from the opposite moiety who specialized in mortuary processing, stripped all tissue from the bones, then cleaned the bones and placed them in a special chest inside the town's charnel house. This multistep process, requiring prolonged and intimate association with the dead, indebted the Inholahta and Imoklasha moieties to one another. When the charnel house became full, Choctaws reburied the bones of their ancestors together in an earthen mound. The importance of this final step of the mortuary process is suggested in the Choctaws' origin story. According to this story, sickness forced the Choctaws to flee from their former homes, making them wander the land for decades. Throughout this journey, relatives carried the bones of their dead kin: "a live nation packing on their backs an entire dead nation, our dead outnumbering the living." Finally, spiritual leaders pointed them to a new homeland. Once there, they deposited the bones of their dead in a mound called Nanih Waya, saying, "Our journey lasted many winters; it ends at Nunih Waya." This mound, whose name means "mother hill," still stands near the home of the Mississippi Band of Choctaws, serving then as now as a focal point for Choctaw identity.[75]

Throughout the colonial period, Native people divided their captives according to sex and age, no matter what their color. They continued to capture other Indians in their frequent wars: Creeks took Cherokees, Saponis took Senecas, Choctaws took Chickasaws, and so forth. As with other Indians, Native people categorized European and African newcomers as either kin or enemies. Even though enslaved Africans had no choice in joining their European masters, they, too, received the same treatment. Because Indians encountered Europeans *and* Africans through every step of colonization from initial explorations to a fully developed plantation economy, they placed Africans firmly in the category of invader.[76] In colonial-era wars, some black men experienced torture and death alongside their white masters. Tuscaroras, during their war against Carolina settlers, targeted white and black men, and Indians who attacked the Florida mission system killed—and sometimes tortured—black slaves. Other men, women, and children had the good fortune to become adopted, as did a "free Negro that lives among the Catawba and is received by them as a Catawba." Like South Carolina governor James Glen, this fellow's Catawba kin must have appreciated his ability to speak "both their Language and English, very well."[77]

During the colonial period, Europeans and Native Americans shared similar views on physical difference. Educated Europeans and colonial Americans believed that all humans shared the same ancestors—Adam and Eve—and that bodily differences resulted from environmental factors. In a 1781 speech to Cherokee beloved women, treaty commissioner William Christian clearly articulated this environmental view of race: "human Nature is the same in all People: Learning only makes the difference. When your Children & ours are born they are the same; and bring them up together, will still be the same. Let one of our sons be brought up amongst you & he will be like your selves; and let one of yours be brought up with us & he will be like ours. . . . We all descend from one Woman."[78] Explaining variations in skin color remained problematic, but Europeans thought, in their own ethnocentric manner, that all humans were born white. Traveler Jean-Bernard Bossu argued, "A combination of many causes must have been responsible for turning men from their original white color to black, red, and brown."[79] A German visitor asserted that the Yuchis' skin was "black-yellow, which is due not only to the sun but rather to their unusual manner of living." These hue-altering lifestyle choices included "color[ing] their faces with all sorts of colors, especially black shaded with red."[80]

Although eighteenth-century Europeans did not believe that they benefited from inherited racial characteristics, they did think that they were *culturally* superior to Native Americans. On the origin of Indians, Bossu speculated, "I believe that those who come the closest to the truth are the ones who believe that the Americans are of Tatar origin. You have no idea of the similarity between the customs of the Americans and those of the ancient Scythians. This is evident in religious ceremonies, habits, and diet."[81] Bossu likened Native Americans to the Scythians, the most "uncivilized" group of *barbaroi* (meaning non-Greeks) that the ancient historian Herodotus encountered. Herodotus described barbaroi as people who maintained customs contrary to those of the civilized Greeks, claiming "the Scythians are dead-set against foreign ways, especially against Greek ways." The Western inheritors of Greek thought used the term *barbarian* to describe people who were not European and were, therefore, culturally inferior. Classical discourse on barbarism profoundly influenced educated travelers in early America, including Bossu and Bernard Romans. In the eyes of Euro-Americans, Native people, just like the barbarians of antiquity, frequently warred, engaged in bloodthirsty acts like scalping, and inverted gender roles by having the women farm while men only hunted. According to these Europeans, nothing in Natives' bodies or blood made them inferior; they simply lacked cultural sophistication.[82]

Certainly, Indians noticed the physical differences that distinguished themselves from European and African newcomers. The Euro-Americans whom they most frequently encountered were men, who, in comparison to Indian men, had a profuse amount of body hair. As one Frenchman put it, "In that respect, they say we resemble animals." According to Creek Alexander McGillivray, Indians initially distinguished themselves from Spaniards because the latter had "hair over their bodies." The Euro-American propensity to consume raw salads did nothing to dispel Indians' observation that they were animalistic; humans, according to Southern Indians, generally cooked their greens.[83] An African American man who became a captive of the Creeks in the 1760s recounted how they anticipated his appearance even before they saw him: "They can tell the Black people's track from their own, because they are hollow in the midst of their feet and the Black's feet are flatter than theirs." Jean-Bernard Bossu's Indian guide could also "read" the footprints of Frenchmen, Indians, and Africans.[84]

Although Indians commented on the physical qualities of Europeans and Africans, they also fixated on these foreigners' behavior. Jesuit Pierre de Charlevoix's guide told him that when his people drew Frenchmen in their pictographs, "they were represented by their arms upon their haunches in order to distinguish them from Indians whose arms were left in a hanging posture. This distinction is not very arbitrary but proceeds from their having observed the French make use of this attitude frequently, which is never done amongst them."[85] A kind of symbolic shorthand, such pictographs communicated information, broadcasting declarations of war and detailing warriors' accomplishments in battle. Significantly, Indians of the lower Mississippi valley chose posture as the most salient characteristic of the French. In another revealing episode, a Natchez man told a French friend that conversational styles distinguished the two groups. When two or more Natchez spoke, each took his turn, never interrupting one another. Such interruption was seen as a breach of etiquette and the height of rudeness. In contrast, the Natchez man explained, "Our people say that when many Frenchmen are together they speak all at once, like a flock of geese."[86] Skin color was but one of a host of differences that separated Europeans and Africans from Native people, who, not surprisingly, reportedly found their own coppery hue most handsome.[87] Equally as remarkable as skin color were newcomers' hairy bodies, uncivilized diets, distinctive footprints, odd posture, and bad manners.

Southern Indians seem to have reserved the label "white people" exclusively for the British and Anglo-Americans, probably because they stressed this characteristic to a greater extent than other Europeans. Native people generally called the Spanish "Christians" and the French "French."[88] At a 1767 conference between the Seminoles and British, Governor James Grant related an illuminating story about the Seminoles' categorization of others. Recently, shipwrecked Frenchmen had washed up on the coast of East Florida. Newly arrived, the Frenchmen obviously lacked kin ties, and Seminole warriors who happened upon them decided, for whatever reason, to kill them. Shortly thereafter, "The Headmen took the alarm in order to give satisfaction, but upon enquiry finding that no *white men* (so they call the English) had been killed, they thought there was no harm done."[89] In Native eyes, these Frenchmen were French, not "white." Before the Choctaws adopted racial labels for people, they used terms completely independent of phenotype. According to longtime trader Nathaniel Folsom, in the old days, "they sade wite man was a now hallo," or "very beloved." Cyrus Byington's early-nineteenth-century dictionary offers a more nuanced and ambivalent translation of *na hollo* as "one that creates fear and reverence; an inhabitant of the invisible world." In ancient times, Choctaws had used the term to refer to supernatural beings, but later they applied it to Europeans, undoubtedly because of their odd behavior and sophisticated material culture rather than their light skin.[90] Throughout the colonial era and for thousands of years before, skin color was not an important component of identity in Native North America, and, in Native eyes, neither Indians nor Europeans constituted racial groups.

Throughout the colonial era, Euro-Americans and Indians thought that identity was mutable. After all, it was clear that both groups could swap languages, foods, medicines, clothing, hairstyles, jewelry, and even sexual partners. Both groups believed in the possibility of cultural conversion and downplayed the importance of phenotype. Among Native Americans, kinship determined identity. In diplomatic rituals of alliance, ties that bound communities could be made or remade. Thus, eighteenth-century Indian politicians who created alliances with Europeans spoke of having a "French heart" or becoming "Spanish."[91] In a conversation with John Stuart, Creek chief Mortar reminded the British Indian agent of the ties of fictive kinship that bonded the two despite physical differences: "both our Faces [are] Ugly; it's impossible, said he, we should ever fall in Love with each other by Looking on them but we now know each others' mind and I shall always consider you as my Brother."[92]

The fluidity of identity in early America is most evident in the context of captivity. Through adoption, total strangers, former enemies, even animalistic beings could and did become kin. After the fall of Mississippian societies, as Indians set about constructing new, more flexible societies, they incorporated ethnic outsiders, including Africans and Europeans. Remarkably successful, Native Americans reasoned that they would continue to adapt and survive in their beloved homeland, just as they had for the past 10,000 years.

5

OWNED PEOPLE

On the morning of January 21, 1802, shotguns and piercing cries alarmed the farming community at Mantanzas, near St. Augustine, Florida. Planter Jesse Dupont, who was outside working with his sons and slaves, "concluded that we Should Soon be landed into Etarnity." Mikasuki Indians captured ten of Dupont's slaves and his indentured servant, but most members of the household found cover in the nearby woods and marshes. After fleeing the Dupont plantation, two enslaved African American women went to check on their neighbors, the Bonnellis. Knowing that the Bonnelli patriarch, José, was away in St. Augustine, the women tried to warn the family of impending danger. Before reaching the Bonnelli house, "they heard three Guns fire and directly the crys of the family." In terror, the enslaved women fled back to their own plantation and alerted its inhabitants. As their master Jesse Dupont soon discovered, the Mikasukis had killed the eldest Bonnelli son, Tomas, and taken captive Mrs. Maria Bonnelli and her five other children—Antonia, José, Teresa Maria, Catarina, and Juan.[1]

The Mikasukis, who resided in north-central Florida, had been angry over the imprisonment of a leading warrior named Macloggy, accused by the Spanish of aiding the rebel William Augustus Bowles in his attempt to overthrow their government. East Florida governor Enrique White had asked Macloggy to deliver a letter to the fort at San Marcos de Apalache, where the warrior was captured and imprisoned. In retaliation, the Mikasukis began their war in the summer of 1800, taking captive a number of slaves from Francis Fatio's expansive New Switzerland plantation. "I think my friend thare is no sense in keeping Macloggy in the fort," Lower Creek headman Jack Kinnard warned Governor White. "I am afraid that they will do more Mischief if he is not turned out." Kinnard's message proved prophetic as Mikasuki attacks continued for another year and a half, culminating in the January 1802 raid.[2]

Antonia Bonnelli, then 15 years old, later recalled that she and her younger sister Teresa Maria had to take turns carrying newborn sibling Juan on the twenty-four day journey back to Mikasuki Town. Once there, the Bonellis were "turned over to some Indian women who came out to meet us." With horror, Antonia remembered how the Mikasukis had celebrated acquisition of her brother Tomas's scalp. In testimony over thirty years later, Antonia offered no more details of her captivity, saying only that she "experienced many hardships and cruelties, and her trials were very severe; and the circumstances and history of her captivity and that of her family were so peculiar and barbarous that . . . she does not think that anything but death can efface them from her memory." The unspeakable "hardship" that Antonia endured was slavery. Within her lifetime, Antonia's status changed from daughter of a poor farmer to the slave of an Indian master to a propertied white American woman. Antonia remembered, but she did not want to look back.[3]

The death of Tomas Bonnelli and the taking of his scalp served to quiet the crying blood of an unnamed, wandering Mikasuki soul, but captors had different goals in mind for the remainder of the Bonnellis. The capture of the Bonnellis and other East Floridians gave the Mikasukis the political leverage to force the release of Macloggy. Moreover, the Mikasukis benefited materially from the captives' labor and eventual ransom. Representing one extreme of the captivity spectrum, slaves served to enhance the social or material capital of their masters.

Native people called their slaves something akin to "owned people." Creeks dubbed them *este vpuekv*: "este" means person and "vpuekv" indicates an owned being, a term they also applied to livestock. The Cherokee term for "slave," *atsi nahsa'i*, similarly translates as "one who is owned." In his travels among Siouan-speaking Indians of the Carolinas, John Lawson noted that their term for "slave" referred to both enslaved humans and tame beasts: "So when an *Indian* tells us he has got a Slave for you, it may (in general Terms, as they use) be a young Eagle, a Dog, Otter, or any other thing of that Nature, which is obsequiously to depend on the Master for its Sustenance." A mid-eighteenth-century traveler among the Choctaws claimed that they treated slaves "as their dogs." This sort of terminology seems to have been fairly widespread across Native North America. In many Northeastern languages, Native terms for "slave" translate as "domesticated animal" or "tamed."[4]

In stark contrast, nonslave members of Native societies recognized that they were all related in some way and generally referred to one another in the language of kinship. Those who belonged were beloved brothers, sisters, uncles, grandmothers, and so forth. To highlight his own divine origins, the Natchez Great Sun went so far as to call the celestial Sun his "elder brother." Allied nations also used kin terms to describe the ties that bound them. When the Choctaws, for example, attempted to stage a peaceful parlay with their old foes the Chickasaws, they humbly referred to themselves as younger brothers. During the 1781 Treaty of Hopewell negotiations, members of the Cherokee Women's Council addressed the American men who served as treaty commissioners as "our sons." In so doing, these clan matrons invoked the power they held in Cherokee society and selected a more junior kinship label for the American men.[5] (In an attempt to emulate Native diplomatic protocol, Euro-American officials proclaimed themselves "fathers" to their Indian "children"—a faux pas because Southern Indians thought of their fathers as "kind, indulgent nonrelatives who had no authority over them."[6]) No fictive kinship, such as that which characterized relations between masters and slaves on white plantations, linked owned people to Native masters. It was the absence of kin ties, rather than a color barrier, that separated the two groups.

Recounting his trek throughout Creek and Seminole territory, William Bartram asserted that he saw slaves "in every town."[7] Because Indians warred indiscriminately among their white, black, and Native enemies, their slaves included people of different colors and ethnicities. Slaves were usually adult men and women, but they occasionally included youths. Although the individual warrior who caught the slave became his master, he could share that slave's labor with other clan members. A captor could also sell his slave. Antoine Bonnefoy, captive among the Cherokees, observed how a clan bought one warrior's slave: the "merchandise is collected from all the family of the one who makes the purchase, and is delivered in an assembly of all the relatives, each one of whom brings what he is to give and delivers it, piece by piece, to him who sold the slave." In another case, Tiger King, a Lower Creek, called African American captive Sambo "his famely Property." Since clans were the locus of property-holding during this period, most slaves probably belonged to an extended matrilineal household—a "family" in the words of Bonnefoy and Tiger King—rather than to an individual. Captors did not necessarily have to destroy an enemy to take his life. By enslaving that enemy, they could benefit from working or selling him and thus diminish the loss of a relative's labor. At the same time, they denied the captive kinship ties essential to membership in their community.[8]

Spared from the blood poles and denied adoption ceremonies, these captives endured liminal existences. While other residents of Native communities belonged to vast kin networks that stretched across the region, owned people, unmoored from the natal bonds that had once tied them to relatives, allies, and ancestors, found themselves most precariously attached to their captor and his family. As in most societies with slaves, the experiences of owned people depended largely on the objectives of their masters, and captors treated them as laborers and commodities.

Masters put their owned people to work. When trader John O'Reilly attempted to purchase white captives Elsey Thompson and Nancy Caffrey from a Creek man, the women's master educated him on the purpose of their captivity. O'Reilly learned that "they did not bring the prisoners there to let them go back to the Virginia people [Americans], but had brought them to punish and make victuals and work for them, the Indians."[9]

Because Indians did not yet work for wages or hire outsiders to help them, Native people could only depend on their own labor or that of their families when they decided to build houses, plant corn, or hunt game. However, those who owned slaves could use them to supplement the labor of their households. Moreover, owned people, unlike kin, could not ask for anything in return. Nancy Caffrey, for example, hoed corn and beat meal alongside other Creek women, while captors placed Elsey Thompson at work in the cornfields. Among the Natchez, enslaved French women prepared food, sewed, and mended clothing. In the early-eighteenth-century Carolina piedmont, John Lawson's guide Enoe Will brought along an Indian slave "who killed us Turkies, and other Game, on which we feasted." Lawson observed that Carolina Indians had few packhorses, so they employed male slaves as burden-bearers on long treks for hunting, trading, and diplomacy. In 1776, after Cherokee warrior The Glass enslaved his Keowee neighbor David Shettroe, the warrior gave Shettroe 100 deerskins, instructing his captive to make himself some decent shoes and carry the rest of the skins to a trading house to buy his master a new horse.[10]

Occasionally, masters directed male slaves to assist them in war. During the Cherokee War, a group of chiefs told John Stuart that, in return for his life, they expected the officer to assist them in defeating the English. Following their capture of Fort Loudoun, the war party seized its cannon and some firearms, and they discovered a hidden cache of power and shot. At a national meeting, Cherokee chiefs decided to use the weapons to seize Britain's other major redoubt on the Southern frontier, Fort Prince George. Who better to haul the cannon over the mountains, the chiefs reasoned, than "their white slaves"? As a disgusted superior officer later reported, some of the desperate captives—though not Stuart—agreed to tow the cannon and "lay waste the southern colonies."[11]

As their Mississippian ancestors had, elites such as chiefs and traders often used their slaves as personal servants. A visitor to early-eighteenth-century Creek country who called at Chief Brims's house in Coweta found, "He has a number of slaves who are busy night and day cooking food for those going and coming to visit him." Brims, according to this account, treated his guests to fresh cuts of beef served up on silver dishes. Deeply impressed, just as the chief had undoubtedly intended, the visitor concluded that Brims was a successful politician and "very rich" to boot. When William Bartram toured the region in the 1770s, a number of powerful Native leaders hosted him. Among the Seminoles, Chief Cowkeeper had as attendants "many Yamasee captives, taken by himself when young." According to Bartram, "They were dressed better than he [Cowkeeper], served and waited upon him with signs of the most abject fear." They brought in a feast of "venison, stewed with bear's oil, fresh corn cakes, milk and homony, and our drink honey and water." To the north and west, at Apalachicola, Bartram stayed at the house of Indian planter and merchant Boatswain, where young African American slaves brought "excellent Coffee served up in China Dishes."[12]

Chiefs, in particular, needed extra laborers to help them maintain political power and high status, and they frequently turned to slaves to avoid overburdening their own relatives with work. When slaves prepared and served feasts for guests, they enabled chiefs like Brims and Cowkeeper to bolster their reputations as generous hosts—essential qualities for Native politicians. Tuckabatchee Hadjo, for example, kept 500 head of cattle, mostly for the sake of visitors rather than himself. One observer estimated that Tuckabatchee Hadjo slaughtered about one cow each week so that he could offer beef to his guests, proof of the headman's "unbounded hospitality." These episodes call to mind the conspicuous consumption of Mississippian chiefs. Although the labor of owned people was important, their symbolic value was sometimes greater. As in many other slave-owning societies around the world, some owned people in Indian communities probably consumed more than they produced. Slaves, after all, were status-conferring commodities. When Cowkeeper entertained William Bartram, he provided his guest with a lavish meal, but he made an equal show of his Yamasee captives, demonstrating his mastery over foreign people and places and the wealth that enabled him to keep his slaves dressed in such fine style. Though diminished in scale, the mores of eighteenth-century elites, the inheritors of Mississippian cultural traditions, were not different in kind.[13]

At Mikasuki Town, the Bonnellis likely labored alongside their masters. Maria Bonnelli and her daughters Antonia, Maria Teresa, and Catarina probably worked in the fields and prepared food, just as Mikasuki women did. José, 14 when captured, almost certainly helped his masters in hunting and tending to the vast herds of Mikasuki cattle.

When Antonia beat cornmeal or José herded cattle, they engaged in labor appropriate for their respective genders, but such was not always the case for owned people. Masters also assigned slaves, especially male slaves, tasks that violated Native gender roles. In doing so, masters marked owned people as lesser beings to whom the rules did not apply. In Natchez society, for example, men hunted and women butchered meat and dressed skins, but Natchez women sometimes ordered their male slaves to assist in these feminine tasks. Elsewhere, masters allowed male slaves into the men's council house—the most masculine of village spaces—but then asked them to perform women's work, including serving food, tending to guests, and cleaning up after feasts.[14]

In most Native American societies, women controlled agriculture, while men hunted and warred. When societies adopted non-Indian men, they reeducated the newcomers about appropriate work roles. After adopting Anglo-American James Smith in 1755, the Mohawks, a matrilineal society whose gender roles mirrored those of Southern Indians, discovered that Smith desperately needed instruction in the masculine arts of hunting, tracking, and combat. Early on, Smith wandered into the cornfields, picked up a hoe, and began working alongside women. The women, amused, egged him on. Smith remembered that they "applauded me as a good hand at the business." Afterward, when his male kin learned what had happened, they "chid me, and said that I was adopted in the place of a great man, and must not hoe corn." Though ashamed, Smith was also secretly delighted, recalling "as I never was extremely fond of work, I readily complied with their orders."[15]

In sharp contrast, Indian masters did send male *slaves* to the cornfields. African American David George, for example, performed female labor during his captivity in the 1760s. George, who ran away from a cruel Virginia master, fled westward to Creek country. Near the Okmulgee River, in modern central Georgia, a hunting party captured George, and he became Chief Blue Salt's "prize." On the nature of his work, George recalled, "I made fences, dug the ground, planted corn, and worked hard." George had performed the same sort of labor under his former Virginia master, but in Creek country that work had a different meaning—digging the ground and planting corn was women's work that emasculated George.[16]

To ensure that male captives did not escape from their womanly agricultural labor, masters sometimes maimed their feet. Early-eighteenth-century traveler John Lawson described the procedure: "They first raise the Skin, then cut away half the Feet, and so wrap the Skin over the Stumps, and make a present Cure of the Wounds." In this case, Lawson clearly meant male slaves, for he wrote that captors "cut *his* Toes, and half *his* Feet away." This treatment, Lawson explained, "commonly disables them from making their Escape, they being not so good Travellers as before, and the Impression of their Half-Feet making it easy to trace them."[17] This practice dates back at least to the sixteenth century and probably much earlier. In the chiefdom of Cofitachequi near modern Camden, South Carolina, and in Pacaha on the Mississippi River, a de Soto chronicler reported that masters also compromised their slaves' mobility by "disabl[ing] them in one foot, cutting the nerves above the instep where the foot joins the leg, or just above the heel."[18] Because Indians feared keeping male captives as slaves, masters sapped their power by disabling them.

In a practice harkening back to the Mississippian era, captors forced male and female slaves to fetch wood and water, a task traditionally belonging to women and children. In December of 1794, Creeks attacked the Titsworth family farm in middle Tennessee. Warriors killed most of the men and spirited away two captives, 13-year-old Peggy and the family's 15- or 16-year-old slave Mingo. Although Peggy and Mingo had formerly possessed very different stations within the Titsworth household, they found that, as slaves of the Creeks, they shared the same lowly status and performed identical tasks. Both Peggy and Mingo, "cut wood, made fires, [and] brought water."[19] If they could help it, Native men avoided such tasks, which they "reckoned beneath a man." Indian masters barred slaves from participating in the activities that defined masculinity in Native societies—hunting and warfare—and, instead, forced them to engage in labor considered feminine or menial. In doing so, masters prevented these male slaves from acting like real men.[20]

All across Native North America, from the Northeast to the Northwest coast and as far away as Alaska, Native masters sent their slaves out to the forests and streams to hew wood and draw water. During the sixteenth century, the earliest European chroniclers witnessed this practice—Juan Ortiz and Cabeza de Vaca both performed these tasks during their captivities—but it probably predated European arrival by centuries or even millennia. The widespread nature of this phenomenon may be indicative of an ancient association between slavery and these tedious chores.[21]

Life without plumbing and electricity is the stuff of oral tradition in most American families, so understanding the burden of hauling wood and water requires some contextualization. Many Native communities deforested the area immediately surrounding their villages. Agriculturalists across eastern North America slashed and burned nearby woods to make fields for their crops. As communities grew or old fields became sterile, people cleared larger areas. They also needed wood to make houses, palisades, boats, and tools. Mostly, though, they used it for cooking and heating. When looking for firewood, Native people avoided girdling and killing old-growth hardwoods that they valued for their shade and nuts, and instead sought out fallen limbs and newer, smaller trees. Over time, people had to travel greater and greater distances to find the right wood. Creeks, for example, had continuously occupied Tuckabatchee since at least 1400; by 1799, one observer noted that "the wood for fuel is at a great and inconvenient distance." Communities often relocated after a few generations, and deforestation was a motivating factor. Retrieving wood would have been a time-consuming chore, and, since Southern Indians lacked indigenous beasts of burden and only slowly adopted them in the eighteenth century, it was a back-breaking one as well. Drawing water was no easier. Although Native people often lived on or near streams, rivers, or lakes, during periods of warfare or population growth they moved into the upcountry, farther away from water sources. In addition to their tediousness and difficulty, these chores were also dangerous. Traveling outside the village could expose one to attacks from enemy groups, who may have been loath to launch an assault on a fortified town but found isolated individuals a much easier target. During the Cherokee War, for example, some English slaves feared that leaving the Cherokee settlements would expose them to Iroquois attacks, a realistic possibility during that period. As society's most marginal people, slaves took on menial, demanding, even life-threatening labor.[22]

Native Americans were not the only masters who forced slaves to engage in gender-inappropriate labor. A few hundred miles away from the Creek fields where David George toiled at women's work, colonial Virginians attempted to defeminize black women by demanding that they do heavy field labor traditionally assigned to men. Native captors in the Northeast forced captive men to serve food and process skins like women. When Cherokee and Iroquois men taunted one another during wartime, they threatened to make captive warriors "beat Corn." On the other side of Native North America, Nootka masters on the Northwest coast directed male slaves to engage in the female task of processing and preserving fish. Among the Nyinba in Nepal, enslaved men served food, carried wood and water, and even sat in the women's section at village temples. In West Africa, male slaves farmed like other men, but they also carried wood and water like women. At slave markets in Africa, China, and the Middle East, eunuchs were among the most highly valued individuals, perhaps because they were already androgynous. These examples suggest that degendering may be a transhistorical aspect of slavery. Whether laboring as a craftsman in ancient Rome or as a sex slave in the modern-day borderlands between the United States and Mexico, slaves across space and time have shared two burdens: they are marginal, and they are, in some sense, property. The commodification of slaves, combined with their lack of power, compromises their humanity. By denying slaves one of the most fundamental components of identity in any culture, slaveholding societies reinforce the dehumanization of their captives.[23]

Captives, like other trade goods, traveled well-worn routes of exchange throughout the Indian nations of eastern North America. An exchange of captives commonly accompanied peace between former enemies. In 1753, when the Shawnees attempted to reconcile with the Chickasaws, they brought "a Chickesaw and a Creek Woman whom they had formerly taken Slaves." In return, as "a Present," the Chickasaws gave the Shawnees a young French girl enslaved five years earlier. In one episode during the epic Creek-Cherokee War, which lasted from 1716 to 1751, a Creek warrior brought a Cherokee slave woman back to her people, saying that if the Cherokee agreed to a peace "they would send all the Cherokees home which they had Amongst them as Slaves."[24]

Indian diplomats even extended the practice to their European allies. In an attempt to broker peace with Louisiana, Chickasaw chiefs offered up some captive Natchez who had warred against the French just a few years earlier. The chiefs reasoned that the Natchez "had shed French blood; that therefore it was just that they should be our slaves." In 1760, seeking French aid during the Cherokee War, a Cherokee envoy traveled to Fort Toulouse and presented French officials there with a gift of "two white men." Like other forms of trade in Native North America, captive exchange strengthened diplomatic ties between allies.[25]

Indians also traded captives for goods. Shortly after Antoine Bonnefoy's capture, his Cherokee masters met up with some Chickasaws, and the two parties "made several exchanges of merchandise and slaves, [and] smoked together." In 1789, Chickamaugas (and possibly Creeks) attacked the Johnston farm in east Tennessee, taking five Johnston children captive. The captors then traded the children to their Wyandot allies far to the north in what is now Ohio. Four years later, one of the children, Elizabeth, was back in the southern Appalachian region because the Chickamauga warrior Otter Lifter had "obtained her by purchase from the Northward Indians."[26]

Once former enemies had achieved peace, they could ransom kin taken in earlier wars. When the Chickasaws and Choctaws reached an accord in 1746, they agreed that the former could redeem captives among the latter: "to obtain their slaves they had only to bring fifty skins for the young ones and forty for the old ones, in return for which they would be delivered to them."[27] As Euro- and African Americans became tangled in conflicts with Indians, they, too, had to abide by Native mores of captive exchange. After hearing repeated American demands for captive repatriation after the Chickamauga Wars in early Tennessee, Chickamauga leaders wearily responded that exchange was possible, but captors commanded "a considerable Price."[28]

During the Cherokee War, the Cherokees captured several hundred English colonists, and during peace negotiations, they demanded payment for each captive. In addition to the capture of Loudoun's garrison, Cherokee war parties obtained captives in their raids on Carolina backcountry settlements. By the time the Cherokees sued for peace in the spring of 1761, commanding British officer Colonel James Grant estimated that they had taken 300 captives.[29] This diverse group included British soldiers, backcountry settlers and their black slaves, as well as free and enslaved African Americans in the service of the British, who carried letters and helped build and maintain military posts. Colonel Grant quickly discovered that Cherokees thought of their captives not merely as bargaining chips in the peace settlement, but as valuable commodities whom they would relinquish only in exchange for trade goods or cash. Grant lamented to South Carolina's governor William Bull that redeeming the captives would be expensive since the Cherokees "have been so long accustomed to receive from this province almost whatever they ask."[30] When the British proved stingy, Cherokee captors responded by claiming that their English slaves were "hunting . . . and could not be found." Others, they claimed, had been adopted and now refused to leave. Grant fumed, "They hint at Presents."[31] Cherokee chief Attakullakulla told British officials that captors would demand at least the equivalent of 150 pounds of deerskins for each captive. Ultimately, the British conceded to Cherokee demands, paying for captives in guns, clothing, and pounds sterling. Grant and other officials managed to ransom at least 120 captives. The rest endured a variety of fates: some died at the hands of their masters; others were sold to the French of Louisiana; the balance remained in Indian country as slaves, spouses, or adoptees.[32]

After the Yamasee War, Indian captors found their colonial neighbors eager to ransom black or white captives, but less enthusiastic about buying Indian slaves. Despite decreased Anglo-American demand for Indian bondspeople, Native people continued to capture other Indians because slaving served important social and economic needs. When the Catawbas agreed to join the English against the French in the Seven Years' War, they stated, "We want no Pay, only what we can take and plunder, what Slaves we take to be our own of Indians."[33] Certainly, Native American groups whose autonomy had been compromised through direct victimization or unfair trade wanted an end to slaving, but, as in Africa, "the people adversely affected were not the ones making the decisions about participation."[34]

Humans had long served as legitimate spoils of war and acceptable commodities, and throughout the eighteenth century, slaving endured on a diminished scale.

When Spanish Floridians attempted to recover the Bonnellis and other captives of the Mikasuki War, they discovered that they would have to pay the captors handsomely. In all, the Mikasukis had taken roughly seventy captives, and they were a diverse lot. Most of them were enslaved African Americans who belonged to East Florida planters. Other captives included a free black family, a Mrs. Persalls and her four children; Mikasukis had killed Antonio, the husband and father, during a June 1800 attack. The Persalls were members of East Florida's small but vibrant free black community. Taking advantage of the colony's liberal land-granting policy, they were homesteaders. Other captives included Euro-Americans of low rank in Spanish Floridian society. Among them were Jesse Dupont's indentured servant, a boy originally from England, as well as the Bonnellis. José and Maria Bonnelli had emigrated, respectively, from Italy and Minorca in 1768 to serve as indentured servants on Dr. Andrew Turnbull's plantation at New Smyrna. Within several years, most of the 1,255 indentures who arrived at New Smyrna had died of disease and malnutrition, but José and Maria were among the 600 who escaped bondage in 1777, when the survivors petitioned Governor Patrick Tonyn for asylum in St. Augustine. Twenty-five years later, Maria found her freedom revoked once again. The captive-taking that accompanied the Mikasuki War united the diverse population of East Florida in a panic. While José Bonnelli clamored to find the money and political support to redeem his family, planters complained that war had resulted in chaos among the enslaved population: "Fathers and mothers" deserted the plantations "in order to reunite with their stolen children."[35]

Under great pressure from subjects, Governor Enrique White leaned on Native chiefs, especially Kinache of the Mikasukis and Payne, leader of the Alachua Seminoles who lived near present-day Gainesville, Florida. Kinache was reticent to push for the return of his community's slaves—an understandable position, since the taking and holding of captives was a traditional prerogative of victorious warriors. Moreover, the prominent Mikasuki warrior Macloggy remained imprisoned at the fort at Apalache. Far more responsive was Chief Payne, a skilled politician who maintained strong ties with the Spanish government at St. Augustine.

When Payne agreed to negotiate for the return of the captives, Governor Enrique White was relieved, counting on "My friend Payne who has always kept his people in friendship with us." White also enlisted the help of trader Juan Forrester and translator Jamie Durouzseaux, an East Floridian of partial Native ancestry. Seminole chiefs, including Chief Payne, along with Spanish representative Juan Forrester, went to Lower Creek Chief Jack Kinnard's house on Kinchafoone Creek, where they asked several Creek chiefs to serve as mediators between the Spaniards and Mikasukis. The Creeks agreed, and the peace party, now including chiefs from the Seminole towns, Upper and Lower Creek headmen, and several hundred warriors, journeyed down to San Marcos de Apalache to negotiate for Macloggy's freedom.[36]

By mid-August 1802, the party had arrived at Apalache, and the commandant, eager to secure a peace with the Mikasukis, released Macloggy. The peace party returned to Mikasuki with Macloggy in tow, and the Mikasukis and Chief Kinache agreed to enter into negotiations to sell their East Florida slaves. With Kinnard and Payne presiding, Juan Forrester, who represented the governor and citizens of East Florida, offered to purchase the captives from the Mikasukis on behalf of their families or owners. Forrester found that the Mikasukis drove a hard bargain. As a medium of exchange, Forrester had brought only cattle—usually a favorite currency among the Seminoles—but he found that many captors preferred other goods. Even if masters were willing to accept cattle, Forrester did not bring enough. Recovering the Bonnellis was obviously a priority for Forrester and, for $300 worth of cattle, he succeeded in redeeming Maria along with only *three* of her *five* children. Not even the entreaties of Chiefs Payne and Kinnard could secure the release of the two eldest children, Antonia and José, who remained slaves. Perhaps Mikasukis kept these teenagers because their value as laborers was greater than that of the younger children. Whatever the case, their masters were unwilling to release them. In addition to the Bonnellis, Forrester bought "Seventeen Negros of Mr. Fatio's, four of Mr. Duponts, [and] four free Negroes"—the Persall family. As Forrester left town, a Mikasuki runner bearing a message caught up with him; the runner said that the Mikasukis would give up more captives if the Floridians paid for them properly.[37]

Chroniclers who witnessed slavery in Indian country disagreed on its severity. Even as William Bartram extolled slaves' relative material comfort, he also described them as meek, defeated people, "the tamest, the most abject creatures that we can possibly imagine . . . they seem to have no will or power to act but as directed by their masters." And John Lawson, while arguing that "Their Slaves are not over-burden'd with Work," also claimed that Indians placed their owned people firmly in the category of property.[38]

Those with intimate knowledge of Indian slavery, on the other hand, were quick to compare it to bondage as practiced by white Southerners. David George, who escaped his cruel Virginia master only to be reenslaved by a Creek chief, found the experiences similar. Although George preferred his life among the Creeks, in both situations he became the property of another and performed difficult agricultural labor. Peggy Titsworth, the white Tennessee teenager taken captive along with her family's black slave Mingo, claimed that she and Mingo received the same treatment. Put to hard labor, Peggy later told her father that she "was whiped & in other respects treated as a Slave." Nancy Caffrey, taken by the Creeks, similarly reported that she "was treated as a slave . . . and made to hoe corn, beat meal, and to perform other duties of slavery." A fellow Creek slave, Lillian Williams, also claimed that her masters physically abused her, saying they punished her "with much severity, having been often beat until she was black and blue." Anne Calhoun, enslaved from age 4 to 7, said that she never suffered a beating but was twice punished by her Cherokee master. Once, when Anne refused to fetch water, "She was shut up all day without anything to eat." On the second occasion, she had obeyed her master's command to fetch water, but in doing so she broke his drinking gourd "for which she was taken by the two hands and plunged into the river three times, without giving her time to breathe."[39]

Lacking clans to protect and sustain their lives, owned people were the most vulnerable residents of Indian country, especially in times of danger or dearth. Shortly after a 1760 Cherokee attack at Long Cane, Colonel Archibald Montgomery and his troops struck back at the Cherokees, burning several towns. Among their targets was Estatoe, the site of Anne Calhoun's captivity. Shortly before Montgomery's arrival, residents of Estatoe learned of the impending attack and fled their town. During the melee, Anne's captor showed little regard for the girl's safety as she struggled to keep up with the townspeople. Perhaps because he did not want Anne to fall back into British hands, a warrior struck her on the side of her head with a warclub and left her for dead. After lying in a semiconscious state for what she believed to be three days, Anne Calhoun was saved by a headman called the Raven, who reenslaved her. Another captive among the Cherokees also suffered as a result of Montgomery's invasion. After troops razed the cornfields of several major towns, food shortages plagued the Cherokees for a full year. Abraham, an African American man who risked his life during the war carrying messages between the frontier and Charles Town (for which he later earned his freedom), hinted that owned people may have suffered the worst privations during the famine. He reported that a white woman and her three children were among the first captives ransomed by the British, but the woman "had been so cruelly used, that she died soon after."[40]

Captivity resulted in individual trauma, but it also affected families. Although Anne survived the attack on Long Cane, a number of family members—including grandmother Catherine, uncle James, and sister Kitty—did not. Because Anne and her sister Mary had different masters and lived in different towns, they saw one another only once during their captivity. One summer, when many of the villages of the Cherokee Nation came together to celebrate the Green Corn Dance, Anne caught a glimpse of Mary "and made towards her." Their masters noted this and obstructed them. Anne never saw her sister again, noting in her memoir that she never found out whether Mary "died or was killed or taken to other parts, not known." During the captivity of the Caffrey family, Creek captors separated Nancy from her 3-month-old son John and gave him to another to suckle, a cruelty she later characterized as particular to slavery. Although a trader redeemed Nancy two years later, she had to travel to Nashville without John, fearful that she would never see him again. (In fact, John's captor did release him several weeks later.) The accounts of Caffrey, Williams, Calhoun, and others include the key elements that made all forms of slavery so deplorable: difficult and undesirable labor, physical abuse, and forced separation from loved ones.[41]

Unlike those held in bondage on large plantations, owned people could not develop a cultural and social life independent of their masters. When warriors conducted raids, they generally captured a group of people who already knew each other, whether they were family or fellow villagers. Upon returning to the warriors' village, however, the group broke up— some died, while others became adoptees or slaves in the households of individual captors. During the captivity of the Brown family, for example, members of the Wolf clan at Nickajack adopted Joseph, while sister Polly joined her new family at Running Water; Creek warriors carried Joseph's mother and two other siblings into their nation. Such separation resulted in part from individual warriors' claims on captives, but Native societies also discouraged contact between related captives. In Anne's case, for example, captors prevented her from speaking to or even seeing her sister Mary. Within captors' households, owned people probably had little time or space to themselves. Owned by a matron, these large households usually included her husband, her daughters and their husbands and children, her unmarried sons, and her elderly relatives. The family spent their winters in snug houses and their summers sleeping under detached, covered porches. No matter what the season, quarters were tight. If the matron owned another building, she usually devoted it to storing food and tools. Before the late eighteenth century, when wealthy Indian families like the McGillivrays and Vanns began to build big houses and separate slave cabins, it is likely that owned people lived cheek by jowl with their masters. They, like other slaves in Native American societies, probably slept in the least pleasant areas of the house—those with less protection from the elements and more exposure to vermin. Absorbed into their masters' households, owned people contributed labor and conferred prestige, but they received none of the benefits of kinship.[42]

Maria Bonnelli initially had opposed attempts to redeem a portion of her family because she wanted to keep everyone together. Finally, however, she relented and took the youngest children back to their East Florida home. Juan Forrester may have convinced Maria to do so because he later stated that they were in such a "miserable Situation" that they had to leave. Maria found comfort in the fact that José and Antonia would have each other, even though they remained enslaved in Mikasuki. Apparently, however, José's hatred of slavery proved stronger than his desire to protect his sister. Soon after Forrester redeemed most of his family, he ran away. From Mikasuki, he fled westward, finding his way to the fort at San Marcos de Apalache. There, Lieutenant Colonel Jacobo Dubreuil arranged José's passage on a ship, and the young man earned his keep as a sailor while the boat called at various ports on the Gulf. In the fall of 1803, roughly one year after his escape, José finally returned to St. Augustine. The Mikasukis, meanwhile, kept their accounts; they returned to San Marcos de Apalache in June 1805 and took thirty-five cattle, later explaining that the Spaniards owed it to them for José's release.[43]

Seven months after the Bonnellis' capture, Antonia was the only member of her family in Mikasuki. The Bonnelli family's relative poverty was not the only impediment to Antonia's freedom; her Indian master would not release her. The commanding officer at Apalache, Jacobo Dubreuil, offered him 100 pesos, and Chiefs Payne and Kinache presented him with ten cows, but these offers achieved nothing. Apparently, "her Indian master was a *hechicero* [sorcerer], and he had decided not to give her up." Perhaps more appropriately called "the Doctor of Mikasuki," this man used herbal medicine and supernatural knowledge to heal the sick. Given the careful manner in which chiefs and Spanish officials approached him, this captor may have been a member of a more elite group of doctors called "knowers" or "prophets." Men of extraordinary spiritual power, knowers, in addition to diagnosing disease, could also foretell the future and shape its course, and they could use their power to either help or harm others. Knowers generally inspired a mixture of fear and reverence in their communities. Because he had four grown sons, the Doctor was at least middle aged and perhaps older, having by that time accumulated prestige in his community. The Doctor enjoyed enough material comfort to find the Spaniards' offers unappealing. (Indeed, he may have bought Antonia from another Mikasuki.) Kinache and Payne advised Juan Forrester not to attempt to take Antonia by force for "it might end with very bad Consequence, for the villain with his four sons might follow [Forrester] on the road & murder the Girl."[44]

Those who attempted to buy Antonia from the Doctor reported that he had "taken her as a wife." Documents only hint at what transpired within the Doctor's household, and Antonia herself was silent on the details of her enslavement: Did she enter into this relationship to improve her station in Mikasuki society? Was she forced to do so? What is certain is that the Doctor was both master and sexual partner to Antonia.

During the eighteenth century, many Euro-Americans assumed that captive women need not fear sexual assault from Indians. From captivity narratives like that of Mary Rowlandson, they learned that Indian attackers committed many atrocities, but they did not rape. As Rowlandson recalled, "*I have been in the midst of those roaring Lyons and Salvage bears that feared neither God, nor Man, nor the Devil, by nights and day, alone and in company: sleeping all sorts together, and yet not one of them ever offered the least abuse of unchastity to me, in word or action.*"[45] Some even doubted that Native American men were masculine enough to sexually violate white women. In *A Narrative of the Capture of Certain Americans at Westmoreland*, an anonymous author wrote, "I don't remember to have heard an instance of these savages offering to violate the chastity of any of the fair sex who have fallen into their hands; this is principally owing to a natural inappetency in their constitution."[46] However, the reality is more complicated. No strangers to rape, Native people used sexual violence as a punitive measure against adulterers, foreigners, and enemies.[47]

Southern Indians considered adultery a dangerous form of spiritual pollution, which, if unchecked, invited disaster. In 1738, for example, the Cherokees suffered a catastrophic smallpox epidemic that struck half of the population and killed hundreds. Considering the disease a punishment for spiritual transgressions, religious leaders located fault in "the adulterous intercourses of their young married people, who the past year, had in a most notorious manner, violated their ancient laws of marriage in every thicket." Polluting intercourse required cleansing and deterrents against repetition of the crime. Indians' scarlet letter came in the form of cropped ears, a permanently visible mark of shame that immediately communicated an adulterer's crime to all whom he met. Clan members of the victimized spouse sought out both guilty lovers, beat them with sticks, and cut off the outer portions of their ears. Cherokee elders explained to a Carolina trader that "if wee doe nott put Dread [on] our Yownge people . . . they being naturally given to mischife and all sorts of debochery they will murder one and other and Comite all sorts of outreages." Women caught committing adultery on multiple occasions were subject to harsher punishments than ear cropping. The Cherokees and Choctaws (and perhaps others) sometimes used gang rape as a punishment for repeat offenders. Kinsmen of the cuckolded husband "revenged the injury committed by her, in her own way; for they said, as she loved a great many men, instead of a husband, justice told them to gratify her longing desire . . . they followed her into the woods a little way from the town, (as decency required) and then stretched her on the ground, with her hands tied to a stake, and her feet also extended, where upwards of fifty of them lay with her, having a blanket for a covering."[48]

Foreign women who passed through Indian nations also risked this form of sexual assault, what the Choctaws called "running through the meadow." According to one chronicler, women subject to this treatment lacked kin ties and came without invitation.[49] This motivation may have been what animated a group of Creek men to rape the wife of George Tillet in 1792. Tillet and other citizens of St. Marys alleged that William Kinnard, a prominent Lower Creek headman and trader, robbed Tillet's house and raped his wife. According to the governor of Spanish Florida, Juan Nepomuceno de Quesada, officials at Amelia Island "gave for certain that [William Kinnard] and five or six other Indians enjoyed [Mrs. Tillet] by force." One Alexander Steele, who claimed to have witnessed the assault, swore, "we found that they had Carried her and Dragd her a considerable Distance into the fields where we went to Rescue her and found her in the possession of about fourteen or fifteen Indians, and with one in such positon [sic] and others a holding her that we Doubted not but they had ravished her." These allegations of rape emerged during a border war between the Creek Nation and the state of Georgia, and the Tillets lived on disputed land. Like many other Lower Creeks, Kinnard considered Tillet a squatter who infringed on the territorial sovereignty of his nation. Some, including Spanish Floridians who called Tillet a thief and "a Rogue," doubted that the rape occurred, but if William Kinnard did commit the act, he may have done so because he considered the Tillets illegal and unwanted trespassers in his nation.[50]

Traveler Bernard Romans, who eagerly recorded Native sexual practices of all sorts, reported that victorious warriors sodomized "the dead bodies of their enemies, thereby (as they say) degrading them into women."[51] When Native men sodomized their enemies and labeled them "women," they did so not because they considered women degraded creatures (as Romans assumed), but to call attention to their enemies' failings as warriors. In Native societies, males who performed poorly in warfare could not be men in the fullest cultural sense. Sodomizing conquered bodies placed enemies in a submissive sexual role and demonstrated the dominance of the victor.[52]

Like enemies, outsiders, and adulterers, captives were also vulnerable to sexual violence. The need to remain pure during warfare and taboos against incest with potential kin lapsed once warriors' purification period ended and clans had denied captives adoption ceremonies. Female slaves were especially vulnerable to sexual assault by masters. Slaves like Antonia lived on the margins of society, without kin to protect their bodies or lives. In contrast, Native women generally enjoyed sexual freedom in their premarital lives, the ability to choose a marriage partner, and the right to divorce at will. On the matter of matrilineality and female power, one trader who lived among the Cherokees asserted, "I have this to say that the women Rules the Rostt and weres the brichess and Some times will beate their husbands within an Inch of thire life . . . the man will not Resesstt thire poure . . . if the woman was to beate his breans out."[53] These prerogatives, like other liberties within eighteenth-century Indian societies, stemmed from clan membership. Because an Indian's identity and property came from his or her mother's clan, Native people rejected Europeans' fixation on paternal certainty and patriarchy. Female slaves, however, lacked the clans that gave women such rights. Owned women became degendered in the sense that they lost control over their bodies.[54]

Antonia's case is emblematic of the hazy bounds that separated consensual from coerced sex in early America. White masters also confronted female servants and slaves with a combination of persuasion and threats, leading the victims of their aggression "to consent to the best of two unpleasant paths to sexual relations."[55] As Antonia Bonnelli's case demonstrates, an Indian master might call his female captive both "wife" and "slave." One of Chief Payne's slaves, who mediated between the Mikasukis and the Spaniards, reported to Governor Enrique White that Antonia "was taken as a wife against her will." After conversations with Payne and Kinache, Juan Forrester concluded, "the fellow that has her is a great villain." Although Antonia herself was silent on the details of her sexual relationship with the Doctor, it is reasonable to assume that she had little choice in the matter.[56]

Antonia entered into a relationship with the Doctor "against her will," but some owned people seem to have chosen marriage as a path to enhanced status. When naturalist William Bartram visited Creek headman Boatswain's plantation on the Apalachicola River in 1774, he noted that Boatswain had about fifteen black captives who waited on him and tended his crops. However, Bartram learned that when they married "they bec[a]me Indians." Based on his observations, Bartram believed that marriage was tantamount to citizenship, and, once wed, the former slaves enjoyed "equal privileges with the Indians." Similarly, Henry Timberlake argued that in Cherokee society former captives who married were "generally allowed all the privileges of the natives." Marriage did not bind captives to their host societies as tightly as did adoption. They did not become members of a clan, but they did gain some protection from their spouse's clan. In 1820, a visitor to the Chickasaw Nation observed, "By marriage, the husband is considered as, in some degree, adopted into the family of his

wife." Of course, without a clan of their own, slaves who married remained vulnerable to some forms of abuse. If, for example, Antonia had
discovered that the Doctor was engaging in an adulterous relationship
with another woman, she would have had no clan to punish him or otherwise curb his behavior. Nonetheless, marriage did serve as a sort of emancipation. No longer owned people, married captives assumed new roles as
spouses and parents. Kin ties enhanced their status, moving them from
society's bottom tier into the category of people who belonged.[57]

Some captives who married into Indian societies preferred their new
lives. In fact, Euro-American officials were disturbed by the frequency
with which white women who had married Indian men evaded attempts
to "redeem" them. In 1796, when Brigadier General James Wilkinson negotiated with the Shawnees for the return of white women captives, he felt
sure that friendly chief Blue Jacket would assist him, but Wilkinson also
expressed anxiety: "The great fear is, that being helpless, unprotected females, they may have lost their innocence, & formed attachments, which
spoiled their return." Sexual encounters with Native men may have, in
Wilkinson's view, "spoiled" these young women, but more worrisome
were the "attachments" they might have formed. As Wilkinson knew, although Native people cajoled and coached some into becoming kin,
others needed no such encouragement. When Lieutenant Henry Timberlake attempted to recover Mary Hughes, a captive taken during the Cherokee War, her new husband "though reluctant, was disposed to comply,
but she absolutely refused to return with her countrymen." In another example, when British official David Taitt and his companions tried to find
a white woman held captive in the Creek town of Tamatley, he discovered
that she had "run off with an Indian who is her husband, so that they
could not find her." These episodes highlight the transformational nature
of captivity: those who crossed cultural boundaries, when given the
choice, sometimes rejected their old lives and assumed new identities.[58]

Owned people who did not marry could still hope that their masters
would one day adopt them or ransom them back to their countrymen.
This seems to have been the case for a man the Cherokees called "French
John." Born in Canada, this John or Jean was probably a fur trader captured by the Cherokees while he traveled through the backcountry in the
early 1750s. French John became the slave of Old Hop, a leading Cherokee statesman who resided at Chota. As opposed to a fellow French slave
in Toqua who constantly begged English traders "to relieve him from

amongst the Infidals," French John seemed content, but always looked for opportunities to improve his station. In a short time, John learned to speak the language, accompanied war parties, and, in a bold move, counseled Cherokees on the potential merits of a French alliance. An "active, cunning Fellow," French John may have been angling for Old Hop to adopt him, for he cultivated the old man's favor. Some Cherokees whispered that the sycophant gave Old Hop "Ribbons and knives" or delivered to his master special messages from French officials. In any case, French John's efforts met with some success; in 1757, Attakullakulla reported that Old Hop looked on the Frenchman "as his own Child." French John still remained a slave, but Old Hop allowed him to travel along with a Cherokee delegation to Fort Toulouse, New Orleans, and Mobile. French John agreed to return thereafter because, in the words of one Cherokee, "he is a Slave to Old Hop, and he went upon those Conditions." According to Oxinaa, a Cherokee woman who accompanied the delegation as a translator, John sought presents to encourage the Cherokee Nation to ally with France as well as gifts "to purchase his Freedom of his Master, Old Hop." This plot did not quite work for French John, either—perhaps Old Hop accepted the gifts, but did he not release, adopt, or otherwise free his slave John. In August of 1757, the British, seeking to counter French influence among their longtime allies, offered Old Hop 500 pounds of deerskins for his slave French John. In the end, French John, fearful that a worse fate awaited him among the British, freed himself by running away.[59]

Twenty-one months into Antonia Bonnelli's captivity, in October 1803, the Doctor agreed to release her in exchange for $200. After refusing ransom offers for so long, the Doctor finally acquiesced, but stipulated that a male kinsman must redeem Antonia. Accompanied by Chief Payne and one of Payne's slaves, Antonia's brother-in-law Tomas Pacetti traveled to Mikasuki and redeemed her. Antonia was eight months pregnant. Although the Doctor's motives are unclear, he may have released Antonia at that point in her pregnancy because she could no longer engage in arduous labor. Or perhaps he did not want the child to burden his household. Whatever the reason, the Doctor gave Antonia up to Pacetti. Shortly after returning to St. Augustine, on December 19, 1803, Antonia gave birth to a girl. When the infant was christened three weeks later, she was called "Maria Antonia," daughter "of the Indian named Doctor of the Town of

Mequisucke and of Antonia Bonelly." Antonia's captivity, marriage, and *mestiza* child did not alienate her from Spanish Floridian society, which, like contemporary Southern Indian nations, was fluid and multiethnic. Four years later, Antonia married a fellow Floridian of Italian descent, Bartolome Leonardi. It is tempting to speculate about the life of Maria Antonia, the daughter of Antonia and the Doctor: How did she fit into colonial St. Augustine? How did she relate to her stepfather? How would she have related to the many half-brothers and -sisters that came after her? Unfortunately, Maria Antonia died at the age of 6, and these questions remain unanswered.[60]

Maria Antonia lived the entirety of her short life in and around St. Augustine, but had she remained in the village of her father, she would have been free. Among Southern Indians, slave status did not pass from parent to child. The case of Lillian Williams, a settler who lived along the Nolichucky River in eastern Tennessee, illustrates how Native societies absorbed the children of their slaves. On April 25, 1797, Williams visited Governor John Sevier of Tennessee and pleaded for his help. Nine years earlier, Williams explained, the Creek Indians had taken her captive while she was pregnant. Williams became a slave in the town of Okchai, where she gave birth to a girl, whom she called Molly. As Molly grew, her mother probably worked in the cornfields with other Creek women. Williams recounted her many trials in Creek country to Governor Sevier and others, claiming that her masters treated her badly, often beating her. Her daughter Molly, however, had quite a different experience. As Williams explained, the Creeks had renamed her daughter "Esnahatchee." The infant, unlike her mother, had been adopted into a Creek clan. Having benefited from Williams's labor all those months, her captors now incorporated her child to strengthen their own clan. Eventually, the Creeks released Lillian Williams, probably after her relatives ransomed her. Her joy at this news was short-lived; the Creeks informed her that Esnahatchee would remain with them "because [she] was born in their Nation." Bound and privileged by ties of kinship, Esnahatchee was now a Creek.[61]

After Choctaws killed an English merchant in 1726, Dog King of Oakfuskee suggested retaliation, telling British agent Tobias Fitch, "I have heard that the Chocktaws mades as good slaves as Negroes." Although Fitch and Dog King came from very different cultures, both men were quite familiar with slavery. Tobias Fitch had traded in Indian slaves, while the Oakfus-kee headman's war title as well as his proposal suggests that he, too, was no stranger to slaving. This exchange harkens back to the days of the Indian slave trade, when the intersection of Native and Euro-American captivity traditions was perhaps most apparent. Native slaving fed Carolina's economic needs and vice versa, but the captivity practices of the two groups diverged after the Yamasee War.[62]

During the early colonial period, Euro-Americans had relied on a broad range of bonded labor to sustain their economies. Bondspeople included black, white, and Indian indentured servants; convicts; prisoners of war; and African and Indian slaves. These early colonial societies were much messier and less biologically determined than the plantation South that succeeded them. Beginning in the late seventeenth century, however, Euro-American elites moved toward the racialization of captivity, focusing especially on the Africans whom they imported in ever-greater numbers. Beginning in 1662, Virginia's General Assembly moved toward codifying transgenerational slavery by decreeing that the children of enslaved women could be held in perpetual bondage. Over the next decade, the assembly declared that religious conversion could not free a slave, that masters should have life-and-death power over their bondspeople, and that they would deploy the power of the state to police the enslaved. In 1696, early South Carolina settlers, drawing on a code they had already established in Barbados, created their first slave statutes, which echoed those of Virginia. Other colonies followed the lead of Virginia and South Carolina, gradually strengthening the institution of black slavery through custom and law. By the time that the Oakfuskee headman made his offer to Tobias Fitch, only 7 to 8 percent of the enslaved in South Carolina were Native Americans. Already, African slaves overwhelmingly dominated the unfree labor force in the Southern colonies.[63]

When Dog King attempted to persuade Fitch that Choctaws made "as good slaves as Negroes," he demonstrated that Native people were well aware of the white South's turn toward black slavery. Indians, meanwhile, continued to enslave enemies of all colors and sorted them according to sex and age rather than race. Their notions of the proper duration of enslavement also differed from that of colonists. In Euro-American colonies, masters targeted African Americans almost exclusively, and slavery became a perpetual state, passing from mother to child, though manumission remained possible. Among Native people, slaves could shed their status when they forged kin ties through marriage or adoption. At most, slavery lasted a single lifetime, for the children of slaves became free in the sense that they joined the clans who had captured their parents. Native slavery could be dehumanizing—and even serve commercial ends—but it was also a mutable, transitory state without basis in phenotype.

6

VIOLENT INTIMACY

In the spring of 1788, Revolutionary War veteran James Brown, his family, and his slaves traveled down the Tennessee River en route to the Cumberland valley farm that he had purchased three miles outside of Nashville. On May 9, before the Browns had reached their destination, a group of Indian men flagged them down, and one of them who spoke English told the Browns that they wanted to trade. Soon, however, groups of warriors in canoes surrounded the boats and forced their way on board. Instead of a group of traders, this was an allied party of Creeks and a faction of Cherokees called Chickamaugas, who fought together in an effort to reverse the tide of American expansion. During the fight that ensued, the warriors killed James Brown and his eldest sons, and they captured several women, children, and African American slaves.

Fifteen-year-old Joseph Brown, who was "very small" for his age, became the property of Chickamauga warrior Kiachatala. Leading the boy back to Nickajack, Kiachatala was accompanied by his stepfather, an Irishman named Tom Turnbridge, who had deserted from the British Army and lived among the Cherokees for eighteen years. Although he may have received some initial comfort from speaking English with Turnbridge, Joseph soon perceived that he was in danger. The elderly mother of Cutteotoy, the chief of Tuskeegee Island, arrived at the house and began to shout at Turnbridge and Kiachatala. Although Joseph could not understand her harangue, he knew from her gestures and tone that the woman was speaking of him in anger. After some arguing, Kiachatala and Turnbridge handed Joseph over to Cutteotoy and his Chickamauga warriors. Cutteotoy and the warriors took Joseph to the nearby village of Running Water. There, Joseph recalled, "they began to pull my clothes off to keep from bloodying of them. As soon as they got them all of[f] I fell on my knees & began to pray." Joseph, certain of his impending death, anticipated torturous fire at any moment. Quite abruptly, however, the warriors handed a confused Joseph back to Kiachatala. Joseph had been spared not because of prayer (as he sometimes said in later years), nor because of his youth. He was saved because Kiachatala had threatened to kill the Browns' slave Sue, whom the warrior Cutteotoy had taken during the battle, if he did not spare Joseph. Cutteotoy relented, releasing Joseph. Joseph later recalled that other Chickamaugas teased Cutteotoy, saying "he loved me & would not kill me." Cutteotoy responded, "it was the negro he loved it was not me."

Thereafter, Joseph's fortunes improved. He became a member of the Wolf clan when The Breath, the powerful chief of Nickajack and Kiachatala's uncle, adopted Joseph as a nephew. Other Chickamaugas, however, resented The Breath's decision to adopt Joseph, which they demonstrated by abusing the boy and, on occasion, threatening to kill him. Cutteotoy's mother protested Joseph's adoption from the first. After Joseph was spared, she cut a chunk of hair from his crown, saying she "would have the virginians hair any how." Even a fellow member of the Wolf clan, a young man fresh from warring against Americans in the Ohio country and still mourning the deaths of three fellow warriors, beat Joseph the first time the two met. As Joseph recalled, the young man later said, "when he seen me . . . [he decided] he would whip me for satisfaction." Joseph was most frightened of the militant Creeks who dwelled among the Chickamaugas, and with good reason. One day, a Creek passing through town traded some bear oil to Joseph's kinsman. Upon seeing Joseph, "he enquired if I was a virginian." Upon receiving an affirmative answer, the man grabbed a switch from the boy's hand and whipped him with it. Joseph survived these trials with the help of his closest kin—Kiachatala, The Breath, Tom Turnbridge, and Polly Mallet, who was Turnbridge's wife and Kiachatala's mother. Mallet knew a great deal about Joseph's condition; born in French Mobile, she was taken captive as a young girl.[1] After living most of her life as a Cherokee, Mallet told Joseph that she had little desire to return: "if I went back, the white people would not think anything of me after being raised by the Indians; and if I stayed there [the Cherokee Nation], I would be thought as much of as my neighbors."[2]

After eleven months and fifteen days of captivity, Governor John Sevier redeemed Joseph in exchange for Chickamauga captives taken by the Tennesseans. Although Joseph's later correspondence revealed genuine affection for his Indian family, he remembered his captivity as a time of great peril and unease. Five years later, in September 1794, General James

Robertson chose Joseph Brown to guide an army against the Chickamauga towns, "the place of my Captivity thare being no other person that was aquainted with the situation of the place." In that campaign, known as the Burnt Corn Expedition, Tennessee militiamen destroyed the towns of Nickajack and Running Water, killing over fifty men, taking some twenty women and children captive, and effectively ending Chickamauga resistance on the Southern frontier. Here, Lieutenant Henry Timberlake's 1761 warning to the Cherokees seems prophetic: Adoption "has been a detriment to the nation; for many of these returning to their countrymen, have made them acquainted with the country-passes, weakness, and haunts of the Cherokees; beside that it gave the enemy greater courage to fight against them."[3]

Joseph Brown's revenge on his former captors continued when, in 1814 on his way home from fighting in the Red Stick War, he paid a visit to Cutteotoy, the warrior who had captured his father's slave Sue. The other enslaved people belonging to the Browns had long since been "sold by the Indians that had them to the french that lived on the other side of Missippy." Cutteotoy, however, retained Sue and the descendants she had produced during her captivity, which included daughters Lucy and Jenny as well as five grandchildren. Seeking to recover what he considered his family's rightful property, Joseph kidnapped Sue and Sue's children and grandchildren—a total of eight people. For years Cutteotoy tried to recover Sue and her family, but, in the end, he received only a paltry financial settlement.[4]

The Brown family's story contains familiar themes—violent conflict, the killing of adult men in battle, the capture of women and children— but, in many ways, it is emblematic of a new era. The anger of Cutteotoy's mother over Joseph's adoption, for example, points to an important change that was occurring within Indian societies: the erosion of clan power in favor of more centralized authority under male chiefs. An elderly clan matron, this woman resented the fact that a circle of warriors and chiefs had excluded her entirely from the decision-making process that once belonged to women alone. Her taking some of Joseph's hair served as a symbolic gesture toward reclaiming a traditional prerogative.[5] In addition, Joseph's adoption was not a successful one in the sense that he never came to identify with his captors. The sentiment seems to have been mutual. Following Joseph's adoption, his uncle The Breath told Joseph that he was now "an Indian . . . & he would caution all his people to consider

Joseph Brown late in life. Tennessee Historical Society, Picture Collection, box 2, folder 35. Courtesy of the Tennessee State Library and Archives.

him as such." However, many (perhaps most) Chickamaugas never embraced him as one of their own.[6] Even his closest kin probably doubted that he could become one of them. While most Chickamauga teenage boys were training for war, Joseph's family put him to work hoeing corn alongside Polly Mallet and fetching wood and water—the kind of menial tasks associated with slavery. At 15, Joseph may have been too old for adoption, but the evidence indicates that it was not Joseph's maturity that prevented his absorption into Chickamauga society: it was his race. By the time of Joseph's capture in 1788, the Chickamaugas and Tennesseans had fought for control of the land for over a decade. Chickamaugas, along with other Indians, grew increasingly pessimistic about the possibility of incorporating people of European and African descent into their societies. Like the combined Chickamauga-Creek war party that attacked the Browns, Native Americans largely ceased fighting one another and began to stress their identity as a separate people—the "red people." Meanwhile, they sought out African Americans, such as Sue and her family, as captives to be sold for profit or held in hereditary bondage. During the years of the early Republic, as Native people confronted the ambitious and rapidly expanding United States, they once again revised their captivity practices.

By the mid-eighteenth century, Euro-Americans dominated portions of North America, having wrested control of the land and its resources from Native groups in areas like New England and Virginia. But the interior South was still largely Native ground, and Euro-Americans could not yet seriously contest for control of the region. Until 1763, three empires had vied for the South, and each measured its power not by counting white inhabitants or land acreage, but by tallying the number of its Indian allies.[7] Chronically low on settlers, French Louisiana and Spanish Florida were particularly attentive to the Native nations who defended and even fed them. Indians followed the conclusion of the Seven Years' War with alarm: while they depended on British trading partners, they feared the hordes of Anglo-American settlers. In 1764, when British officials sought to increase the size of newly won Pensacola, they petitioned Creek headmen for a small land cession around the fort. Reflecting his nation's anxieties about British colonists, Wolf of Muccolossus "said that all the land Round, was their hunting ground, and hinted, that as soon as the English began to settle lands, they would declare War & begin to Scalp the Settlers."[8] The Creeks did grant some land but stipulated that the limits of the cession must be marked. The British confirmed that "if any white People settles beyond them we shall never enquire how they came to be Killed."[9]

Matters grew worse in the early 1770s, when unruly and increasingly numerous colonists pressed British officials for greater cessions. In 1770, John Stuart, British superintendent of Southern Indian affairs, fretted, "The Indians throughout the District are at present extremely attentive to our encroachments; the Virginians [Americans] are insatiable, and if gratified to the extent of their Wishes, a coalition of, and rupture with all the

Nations on the Continent must, I think, be the consequence."[10] Two years later, Georgia colonists pushed the Creeks to cede more land. When discussing the matter, headman Emisteseguo asked trader William Gregory whether he would wish Emisteseguo "to fetch him Wood & Water." In this revealing conversation, Emisteseguo implied that should Anglo-American designs on Creek land succeed, he and other Creeks would lose their autonomy and live in a state that Emisteseguo linked to Indian notions of slavery.[11]

A turning point in Native American history came on a spring day in 1775, when a Cherokee delegation comprised of chiefs, warriors, and women gathered at Sycamore Shoals in the rich ridge and valley country of the eastern Cherokee Nation. There they met Anglo-American representatives of the Transylvania Company, headed by Richard Henderson and his guide Daniel Boone. At the Treaty of Sycamore Shoals, the two groups negotiated over the sale of Cherokee land. The chief of Great Island, Dragging Canoe, agreed to a portion of the cession but argued that the Cherokees should not part with the Cumberland valley. Dragging Canoe reminded his fellow Cherokees that the Cumberland "was the bloody Ground" and told Henderson that the region "would be dark, and difficult to settle."[12] By calling the Cumberland "bloody ground," Dragging Canoe meant that it was hunting territory, one of the few that Cherokees had left. His allusions to the dark and difficult nature of the country served both as a warning and a threat: if the settlers came, violence would follow. Some other Cherokees echoed Dragging Canoe's concerns, saying to Henderson, "it was a bloody Country, and if he went to it they would not hold him by the hand any longer, and must do it at his own Risque, and must not blame them if any thing happened to him." Ultimately, however, the Cherokee delegation agreed to cede their claim to much of the modern state of Kentucky as well as north-central Tennessee in exchange for a houseful of trade goods valued at £10,000. Dragging Canoe, unwilling to support the sale of the Cumberland, refused to take part and withdrew from the conference. Although Britain deemed the treaty illegal, undeterred settlers piloted rafts down the Cumberland and drove their wagons westward on a Native American trail they called "the Wilderness Road."[13]

With his boycott of the treaty, Dragging Canoe heralded a new era. Beginning with Dragging Canoe's withdrawal from Sycamore Shoals and lasting to the conclusion of the Second Seminole War in 1842, whites and

Indians fought for control of the American South. Each group legitimized its claim to the land differently, and both Indians and settlers wanted *exclusive* control over that land. During this period, large numbers of Native and non-Native Southerners moved closer—geographically and culturally—than ever before. As contests over the land heated, however, Indians and settlers highlighted and exaggerated their differences.

Although their conceptions about private property may have differed from those of white settlers, Indian nations considered land sovereign territory. Frontier whites and politicians were fond of stating otherwise—a convenient fiction to justify the theft of Indian land. In reality, though, Native nations had long marked their territories with painted posts, scored trees, and rock piles. They maintained very clear understandings of their own boundaries as well as those of others. As trader James Adair reported, nations were "very jealous of encroachments from their christian neighbors."[14] A Creek chief claimed that Anglo-Americans "on our frontier" were "habitual violators of our rights."[15] In justifying their land claims, Indians stressed their original possession of the soil. Some groups maintained an oral tradition that they had come from under the earth to emerge into their homeland. Choctaws, for example, recall that they came out of the Nanih Waiya mound in what is now north-central Mississippi. Yuchis tell of how they came down from the sun, becoming the first people to settle the Savannah River valley. Other groups asserted that the Creator of all humans specifically selected Indians to occupy their own ground and that American settlers should not violate that divine sanction. As Cherokee Chief Old Tassel explained, "the great Being above that made us all *placed us on this Land and gave it to us and it is ours.*" Dependent on agriculture, Indian nations had long sought to maintain their own territorial bounds, but their need to mark and claim the land took on urgency in the late eighteenth century as Natives confronted a new and more pernicious colonial power in the United States.[16]

American settlers, meanwhile, used victory in the Revolution and their status as a "civilized people" to justify their claim to the interior South. The Revolution became America's creation story: "the winners constructed a national mythology that simplified what had been a complex contest in Indian country, blamed Indians for the bloodletting, and justified subsequent assaults on Indian lands and cultures." In the early Republic, the American dream was economic independence based on individual land ownership and settlers sought to realize that dream by moving westward to the land they believed they had won in the war.[17] Indeed, many Americans discounted all Indian claims. As one 1792 editorial in the *Knoxville Gazette* argued: *"the original right of these aborigines to the soil . . . is a right of which I have never thought with much respect. It is like the claim of the children; it is mine, for I first saw it; or what that of the Buffaloe might be, it is mine, for I first ran over it."* Disregarding Indian women's long history of farming, the editorial went on to explain that white settlers' cultivation of the soil gave them a legitimate claim to the land. Echoing John Locke, Americans argued that because Indians did not use land properly, "civilized" nations could justly claim it.[18]

Native people recognized a host of physical and behavioral dissimilarities that separated them from European and African newcomers. Although not of great importance until the late eighteenth century, phenotypical differences did not escape Indians' attention in the colonial era. As early as the 1720s, Native people began to read their neighbors' black and white bodies as a way to understand the cultural chasm that separated the groups. In 1725, the chief of the Taensas told a Jesuit that "he had learned from his ancestors that the whites were to show them the road." The chief told the missionary that "so long ago that the winters can no longer be counted . . . there were three men in a cave, one white, one red and one black." Independently, each man tried to find his way out of the cave. The white man was the first to succeed, "and he took the good road that led him into a fine hunting ground." The red man emerged second. Unfortunately, he could not find that good road, but he located another path that led to a "less abundant" land. Finally, the black man "got entirely lost in a very bad country in which he did not find anything on which to live." The Taensa chief concluded, "Since that time the red man and the black man have been looking for the white man to restore them to the good road."[19] This story, though crafted to flatter the Jesuit father who related it, contains important traces of race-thinking. The Taensa chief divided the colonial South's people into three categories based on skin color and suggested that these people were separate, each emerging out of the cave independently. The story also told of a hierarchy of material wealth: the white man went to an abundant hunting ground, while the red man's ground was less rich, and the black man's poorer still.

Roughly contemporaneous stories echo the themes of the Taensa chief's tale. In 1730, a Cherokee conjurer called the English the whitest people "under the sun." He said, "The grate king of heaven has given yow the knowledge of all things[.] Shurely he has a grater love for yow then us and for us then The negrows for . . . he has given a blessing by degrees to Everyone as itt pleased him some more some less."[20] Six years later, a German visitor asked the Yuchis about their beliefs on the hereafter. They told him that they believed in an afterlife. A good hunter went "above to the white man who bestows on him freedom to catch the best game without difficulty." However, a poor hunter traveled "below to the black man," who lived in a deserted country "where nothing but thorns, thickets and underbrush and no game are to be found."[21] From the Mississippi valley to the Atlantic seaboard, Native people engaged in conversations about African and European newcomers: How should we understand ourselves and the people around us? Why are some privileged and others poor? Are these differences divinely directed and thus immutable? By asking questions and telling stories, Native people began to categorize themselves and their neighbors.

By the eve of the Revolution, nativist spiritual leaders spread a gospel of pan-Indian identity and polygenesis. Crystallizing the race-thinking that had circulated in Indian communities across eastern North America for decades, nativists theorized that a Creator had made Africans, Europeans, and Indians separately and had given each people an innate, distinct nature. The Creator made white people knowledgeable and greedy; he favored red people and gave to them North America; black people were the least lucky, and their lot was toil and hardship. For Indians to remain spiritually pure, they had to maintain their distinctiveness and avoid the ways of Europeans and Africans.[22]

In the early nineteenth century, Mikasuki chief Neamathla told the governor of Florida a far more elaborate story of race than did his early eighteenth-century ancestors. According to Neamathla, the Creator had accidentally first made a white man but felt sorry for him because he was "pale and weak." The Creator tried again, "but in his endeavor to avoid making another white man, he went into the opposite extreme, and when the second being rose up . . . he was *black*!" According to Neamathla, the Creator "liked the black man less than the white, and he shoved him aside to make room for another trial." Finally, the Creator succeeded in making his favorite—the red man. Initially, these first men found themselves upon the earth with nothing, but the Creator sent down three boxes of presents to help them. Because he pitied the white man, the Creator let him choose first. The white man picked a box filled with implements of learning including "pens, and ink, and paper, and compasses." Then the Creator said, "Black man, I made you next, but I do not like you. You may stand aside. The red man is my favorite; he shall come forward and take the next choice: Red man, choose your portion of the things of this world." The red man, the most masculine of the three, "stepped boldly up and chose a box filled with tomahawks, knives, warclubs, traps, and such things as are useful in war and hunting." Neamathla recounted how the Creator applauded the decision of his red son. Finally, only one box remained for the black son—"That was filled with axes and hoes, with buckets to carry water in, and long whips for driving oxen." Neamathla explained that this "meant that the negro must work for both the red and white man, and it has been so ever since." Drawing upon the nativist thinking that had so deeply influenced his people, Neamathla provided a Native view of racial hierarchy, one in which the Creator pitied the clever but weak whites, maintained a special love for the red people, and assigned black people servile labor.[23]

Perhaps because of its great explanatory power, the nativist theory of separate creations circulated widely among Indians and transformed their notions of identity. Kinship and, to a lesser extent, political affiliation, culture, and language, had traditionally defined Native American communities, but nativists articulated a broader vision, one that had the power to unite Indians against colonialism. The movement was at its height from the late 1770s until the mid-1790s, when Indian politicians and prophets joined forces in an attempt to push back the tide of American expansion. Nativists envisioned their kinship networks becoming more extensive, embracing all Native people—allies, foes, and strangers alike. According to Cherokees Nutsawi and Pinelog, "All the Indians came from one father. The Delawares are the grand fathers of all the other tribes, while the Cherokees are uncles to the Creeks, Choctaws, and Chickasaws, and some other tribes are brothers to the Cherokees."[24] Although Nutsawi and Pinelog reserved a place of honor for their own people in this new family tree, they stressed unity among all Indians, and especially among Southern nations. As Native people's ideas about identity shifted, they changed their captivity practices. Those who believed in the nativists' message argued that red people should not make war on other red people, but that all Indians should be allies. In a talk sent by the Choctaw chiefs to "all their elder brothers the Creeks in general," they implored their fellow Indians to lay aside ancient differences, saying, "Brothers! . . . The same father made us all red people and desired us to live in peace. . . . [I]f we continue united they can never take [our lands] from us, but if we kill one another, who will be left to defend them?"[25] Many argued that American settlers and slaves who encroached on Indian land were the real enemies.

In May 1776, about a year after Dragging Canoe famously stormed away from treaty negotiations at Sycamore Shoals, he and other leaders met with a delegation of Northern Indians that included Iroquois, Ottawas, Delawares, and Shawnees. The Northern delegation vilified Anglo-American encroachers and gave the Cherokees belts of white wampum, which symbolized the peace they hoped would reign among all red people. The last speaker, a young Delaware man, produced an extraordinary emblem of war—a purplish-black belt of wampum nine feet long and six inches wide. He boldly declared "that the red people who were once Masters of the whole Country hardly possessed ground enough to stand on; that the Lands where but lately they hunted close to their Nations were thickly inhabited and covered with Forts & armed men; that wherever a Fort appeared in their neighbourhood, they might depend there would soon be Towns and Settlements; that it was plain, there was an intention to extirpate them, and that he thought it better to die like men than to diminish away by inches." A Cherokee headman who had been a captive of the Mohawks was the first to accept the belt. Many younger warriors followed his example and joined with the Northern delegation in singing a war song, but the older chiefs remained silent.[26]

That summer the militants went to war. Dragging Canoe rallied warriors to the cause, saying "that they were almost surrounded by the White People, that they had but a small spot of ground left for them to stand upon and that it seemed to be the Intention of the White People to destroy them from being a people."[27] By August, nativist warriors reversed the tide of expansion, having pushed most settlers out of what is now eastern Tennessee. The summer campaign, however, was a costly one. Virginia, North Carolina, South Carolina, and Georgia all sent retaliatory forces to Cherokee country, where they waged a relentless scorched earth campaign. A soldier from North Carolina reported that his company spent most of its time "cutting and destroying all things that might be of advantage to our enemies," including thousands of acres of crops as well as "curious buildings, great apple trees, and whiteman-like improvements."[28] American forces destroyed some thirty towns, bringing years of famine and death to the Cherokee Nation. Colonel William Christian of Virginia reported, "The miseries of those People, from what I see and hear seem to exceed Description; here are men, women and children almost naked. . . . I see very little to cover either sex, but some old Bear skins, and we are told the Bulk of the Nation, are in the same naked situation."[29]

By the spring of 1777, most Cherokee chiefs agreed to peace, but those who wished to continue militant resistance followed Dragging Canoe westward to the area near modern-day Chattanooga. Although this faction continued to call themselves *Ani-Yun Wiya*—"the Real People"— other Cherokees called them *Tsi-ka-ma-gi* or "Chickamauga" after the region in which they settled. Situating their five towns at the crossroads of eastern North America's most important trail systems, the Chickamaugas had ready access to the Upper and Lower Creeks, East and West Florida, the British at Detroit, and American settlements in Kentucky and the Ohio valley. Sending out diplomats to other Indian nations, the Chickamaugas enjoined all Natives of the east to join their campaign of resistance.[30]

Alexander McGillivray emerged as another important leader in the nativist movement. McGillivray, born to Sehoy II of the prestigious Wind clan and Scottish trader Lachlan McGillivray, rose to power during the Revolutionary War. Following the 1782 death of Chief Emisteseguo, a fellow villager from Little Tallasee, McGillivray became a prominent member of the Creek National Council. His Charleston education and bilingualism made McGillivray an invaluable diplomat despite his youth. Following American victory in the Revolution, McGillivray, like Indian leaders throughout the East, expressed shock at the British defeat and anger that he had not been invited to treaty negotiations at Paris. Well versed in the parlance of nativism and republicanism alike, McGillivray asserted that Britain had no authority to cede Indian land, explaining that sovereignty was one of the Indian nations' "natural rights . . . which belong[ed] to our ancestors and hath descended from them to us Since the beginning of time."[31]

Employing a deeply rooted Native diplomatic strategy, McGillivray forged a chain of alliances to counter American influence in the region. In Spanish Florida, McGillivray found friends eager to stem the tide of U.S. expansion. McGillivray gained their nominal support as well as more useful arms and ammunition.[32] Calling upon other Native nations of the

East, McGillivray attempted to forge a "Grand Indian Confederacy of the Northern & Southern Nations." According to McGillivray, this confederacy was to include the Choctaws, Chickasaws, Cherokees, Iroquois, Wyandots, and Shawnees. McGillivray asserted, "[W]e have agreed Jointly to attack the Americans in every place wherever they Shall pass over their own proper Limits, nor never to grant them Lands, nor Suffer Surveyors to roam about the Country."[33]

Chickamaugas and Creeks led the nativist movement in the region, but others also waved the standard of pan-Indianism on occasion. Their most consistent allies were the Shawnees, key mediators between Native nations of the North and South who widely circulated the nativist message. Shawnees resided among both the Chickamaugas and the Creeks, and Southern warriors returned the favor by sending delegations north of the Ohio River. Northern and Southern nations sometimes coordinated their attacks, forcing the Americans to fight on several fronts.[34]

Farther removed from encroaching settlers, the Choctaws and Chickasaws received the nativist message with less enthusiasm. Anglo-Americans had invaded Cherokee and Creek lands in the 1770s, but they did not attempt to settle the more westerly nations until later: the Choctaw Nation in the late 1780s and the Chickasaw Nation in 1804. Hesitant to embrace the radical implications of the nativist message, many Choctaws and Chickasaws remained skeptical, preferring to act as independent nations rather than as members of a pan-Indian confederacy. Creeks, however, attempted to push Choctaws into an alliance. Creek warriors killed some Americans who resided within the Choctaw Nation and took a white woman captive, whom the captors threatened to kill unless they received 300 deerskins. Creek ambassadors warned the Choctaws "to beware of being deceived by the Americans who are seeking only to seize their lands, and to enslave their women and children, as was the case with the Cherokees."[35] Many Choctaws resented the Creeks' aggressive tactics. Even in the Sixtowns district (supposedly the most anti-American), a principal chief, when intoxicated, "said it would be good to kill the Creeks."[36] A Chickasaw informant told Spanish officials that the nativist message was less popular among the Chickasaws than any other Southern Indian group; only about half the people favored joining a multinational Indian movement. An Abenaki chief who traveled as an ambassador to the Chickasaw Nation "hoping to induce them to preserve the peace between people of their color" found that "the Chickasaws paid little attention."[37]

Despite their reticence, other nations did offer Creek and Chickamauga militants some support: Seminoles helped Lower Creeks push back the Oconee settlers and raided Anglo-American plantations in East Florida; groups of Chickasaws, including the influential Colbert family, collaborated with the Chickamaugas in the Cumberland and Ohio valleys; parties of Cherokees continually flowed into Chickamauga towns, especially following clashes with American settlers. Creek militant John Galphin, rather hopefully, stated, "our Nation I beleve is now all one way a thinking . . . the Americans only want to rob us of our rights of this our hole nation is now convinced. The Chacktaws Chikesaws & Cherokies are now all one talk. To those people that has Settled over this side of the ocean, we are now Determined to go in a large Ba[ttle] against them."[38]

Although warriors attacked American encroachers throughout the region, they focused on two critical areas—the Oconee region between the Creek Nation and Georgia and the Cumberland valley in what is now Tennessee. In the late eighteenth century, most captives came from these two regions. Neha Miko and Hoboithle Miko, who represented a minority faction of pro-American Creeks, ceded the Oconee lands to Georgia in a series of treaties in the mid-1780s, but most Creeks considered those treaties illegitimate.[39] As for the Cumberland region, the British (and later U.S.) government disavowed the Treaty of Sycamore Shoals, but settlers moved there anyway. During the winter of 1779 flotillas of settlers began to arrive near present-day Nashville and founded settlements along the Cumberland River. Four of the five large Southern nations—the Cherokees, Creeks, Choctaws, and Chickasaws—responded to this intrusion with great alarm because all claimed portions of the Cumberland as their hunting ground. Territorial governor William Blount, whose aggressive quest for Indian land earned him unflattering sobriquets like "Dirt King" and "Dirt Captain" from Native people, was aware of the effects of American expansion: "Cherokees and Chickasaws Say the Creek Hunting Ground is bounded on the North, by the Ridge which divides the Waters of Mobille and the Tennessee, and that when General Oglethrope first landed in Georgia, they generally hunted down to the Sea Shore, and did not turn their attention toward Cumberland until they were driven from their Sea Shore Hunting Grounds." Population pressure from the eastern seaboard and lower Mississippi valley had forced Southern Indians to share what little hunting territory they still possessed.[40] By 1794, Cherokee chiefs complained that their hunting territory was nearly gone, a circumstance that obliged them "to apply to other nations of red people for liberty to hunt on their land." American invasion of the Cumberland was of concern to all Indians and had the effect of attracting more adherents to the nativist movement.[41]

Using raids, militant nativists attempted to dislodge American settlements in the Oconee and Cumberland country. As Alexander McGillivray boasted, he hoped to "Crush their hopes of possessing our Country" by constantly sending young men to make war in the disputed territory, charging them to destroy crops, houses, and livestock.[42] Chickamauga warrior Bloody Fellow explained to Spanish officials that nativists endeavored "to pay the whites in their own kin[d] . . . we mean to penetrate as fare over the white peoples line, as the whites have done over our line." With this strategy, nativist leaders attempted to push American settlers closer to the Atlantic seaboard and maintain Indian control of the interior South.[43]

Although these strikes were sometimes effective, many settlers refused to be intimidated by Indian violence. In attacking their Indian neighbors, they even incorporated Native practices into their own martial culture. White men of the frontier shared with their Indian counterparts a violent masculine ethos that celebrated individual honor, courage, and brutality. Like Indian men, they collected disarticulated human body parts, such as scalps, eyes, and ears, as trophies of war. These white warriors also reckoned honor and rank in their communities according to achievements in brawls and warfare. Significantly, white men concurred with Native traditions that dictated physical trauma, death, and enslavement as legitimate fates for defeated enemies. Border warfare, therefore, became a mutually understandable language through which Indian men and white American men violently negotiated possession of disputed territory. A pacific Cherokee headman, the Prince of Notoly, told South Carolina officials that his people had evacuated several of their towns to avoid warfare: "the Creeks and white people may fight it out themselves as I suppose *they both love fighting.*"[44]

Indians began to identify encroaching Americans—white and black—as their common enemy, and they called these enemies "Virginians." In Native eyes, Virginians were their foil: red people were natives of North America, Virginians were intruders; red people were original owners of the soil, Virginians relentlessly stole that land; the red people sought to protect what was rightfully theirs, the Virginians were a rootless, lawless people. The Virginian appellation seems to have originated in the mid-eighteenth century and extended to both Anglo-Americans and their African American slaves who encroached on Native territory. By the late eighteenth century, Creek Chief Alexander McGillivray explained that the term was "a name or an insulting expletive which they give to the Americans."[45] McGillivray characterized the relationship between his people and the Virginians as one of mutual "hate and rancor."[46]

As McGillivray pointed out, Indians usually reserved the term *Virginians* for citizens of the United States, but they also used it for others who *acted like Virginians.* For Southern Indians, Virginian was not an ethnic or a racial term; it was a political descriptor levied against those who violated Native sovereignty, especially territorial sovereignty. Virginians also included subjects of the Spanish crown, many of whom were planters of Anglo-American descent who took advantage of liberal land grants in Florida and Louisiana. Lower Creeks and Seminoles could not help but notice how East Florida's prewar population of some 5,500 settlers and slaves tripled during the Revolution, thanks to a massive influx of Loyalist refugees. After Lower Creeks raided Virginians residing south of the St. Marys River, East Florida governor Vincente Manuel de Zéspedes wrote to Chief Alexander McGillivray, asking him to tell warriors that these settlers were "not Americans." To Creek warriors, however, the distinction was largely meaningless. Indians also worried over the emigration of whites into the lower Mississippi valley, where towns like New Madrid, Natchez, and Nogales (later Vicksburg) grew dramatically in the 1780s and 1790s.[47] In 1784, a delegation that included Cherokees, Shawnees, Chickasaws, and Choctaws visited the Spanish governor at St. Louis, protesting, "The Americans, a great deal more ambitious and numerous than the English, put us out of our lands, forming therein great settlements, extending themselves like a plague of locusts."[48] In 1789, Creek warriors attacked plantations at the Spanish settlement of New Madrid because the settlers there were all "from Virginia."[49] Despite assurances from Spanish officials that newly arrived whites in Natchez were "naturalized Spaniards and subjects of our great Emperor," Choctaws suspected that they were "really Americans" who had come to "take possession of these lands."[50] In the eyes of nativists, even Indians could be Virginians. When Hanging Maw, a Cherokee chief who had urged peace and conciliation with the United States, moved to the Chickamauga village of Will's Town, he reported that "the Creeks called me Virginiane and stole my Horse."[51]

In their fight to push back the Americans, warriors killed and captured both black and white Virginians. It may seem unfair that enslaved African Americans who unwillingly accompanied their white masters to the frontier then suffered alongside them. Nativist militants, however, had little interest in guilt or innocence; they *were* interested in restoring a balance lost due to encroachment. And enslaved African Americans were equally guilty of trespass. Indeed, as Native observers doubtlessly noted, slaves did more than their fair share of work as they cleared forests, planted crops, herded cattle—all on Indian land. In 1788, eight warriors emerged from a swamp trail in Liberty County, Georgia, and slaves working in a nearby field spotted them. When the Creeks tried to capture them, the slaves "run and hollowed out to the Guard, which run immediately to their relief." As a warrior seized one enslaved man, he resisted capture and lashed out. This warrior, finding the plantation guard upon him, "shott a ball through him [the slave] and cut this throat and Scalped him and run off." Although the warriors might have preferred to capture the man, the threat posed by the guard forced them to flee with only a war trophy. That same year, on a plantation just miles away, a war party took captive a 7-year-old African American boy named Billy. Seeking to retrieve their lost boy, Billy's parents provided the Liberty County justice of the peace with information on the attack. Those seeking Billy met with no luck; he passed through several hands in the Creek Nation and then likely went to Pensacola before being sold at a slave auction in Havana. When warriors attacked the Oconee settlements in the fall of 1794, they surprised two young women, the white daughter of William Cessna and an enslaved African American woman owned by Bennitt Posey. Both were shot and scalped, though the black woman survived. Although white Southerners tried to cultivate in their slaves a fear of Indians, those who had lived at the frontiers had seen violence levied against master and slave alike, and they may not have needed convincing.[52]

In response to nativist warfare, white settlers adopted a sort of racialized blood vengeance. When a white settler was killed, they sought out an Indian—any Indian. Many frontier whites referred to Indians as "the common enemy," and some even called for their extermination. In contrast to contemporary American and European intellectuals, who were heavily influenced by Enlightenment theories of race, many Southern whites shared a belief that Indians and African Americans were inherently inferior, and they put this belief to practice in their everyday lives.[53] The 1776 retaliatory expedition against the Cherokees illustrates the increasingly racial tone of border warfare. At Burning Town, several militiamen seeking to plunder houses found a wounded Cherokee woman instead. According to one officer, "she was so sullen, that she would, as an old saying is, neither lead nor drive, and, by their account, she died in their hands; but I suppose they helped her to her end." At Tomassee, where General Williamson's troops surrounded a group of Cherokee warriors, some engaged in hand-to-hand combat. During one intense fight, as a North Carolina bruiser struggled with a Cherokee warrior, the North Carolinian placed his long thumbnails on either side of the Cherokee's eye, about to gouge it from the socket. According to a witness, the Cherokee man cried *"Canaly!"* which he took to mean "Enough!" (but which may actually have been *"Ga-na-li!"* meaning "Beast!"); "'Damn you,' says the white man, 'you can never have enough while you are alive." He threw the Cherokee down, scalped him alive, then beat him to death with the butt of a rifle.[54]

John Robertson, another militiaman serving under General Rutherford in 1776, was more explicit in his fulfillment of racist blood vengeance when he killed "an old Indian prisoner" under his guard. According to another soldier, the reason he gave for doing so was "that the Indians had killed his father, or some of his relatives." When General Rutherford placed Robertson under guard "for such a violent breach of orders and of the rules of war," the other soldiers "were so incensed against the Indians that the thought of seeing Rober[t]son punished seemed rather disgusting."[55] The old Cherokee man, as a member of the offending race, answered Robertson's desire for bloody justice, and the other militiamen upheld his course of action. "[T]he Crackers," noted one condescending contemporary, "think it very hard indeed that a *white person* should suffer for killing an Indian."[56]

The cycle of blood vengeance continued for decades. In September 1793, a group of Georgia volunteers seeking to avenge recent nativist attacks stormed into Little Oakfuskee, a Creek town unaffiliated with nativist militancy, where they scalped and killed six men and took eight women and children captive before looting the houses and burning the town. During May of that year near Knoxville, Tennessee, a small group of white men shot and killed three Indians. The murderers probably took the Indian men for Chickamaugas, but they were actually Chickasaws friendly to the United

States. One man had served with Arthur St. Clair against nativist militants in the Northwest Territory, and another, John Morris, was a regular guest at Tennessee governor William Blount's house. Morris was buried with full U.S. military honors, and Governor Blount served as a chief mourner at his funeral. Blount denounced the murders, but many Southern whites claimed that they could not tell one Indian from another. Federal Indian agent Silas Dinsmoor lamented, "I believe it would not be transgressing the bounds of Charity to say they do not wish to distinguish."[57]

Chief Alexander McGillivray sardonically accused Virginians of carrying out a "savage mode" of warfare. Drawing on tropes of anti-Indian propaganda found in American newspapers and fiction, McGillivray claimed that Virginians cut infants out of Native women's wombs and stuffed the mouths of dead women with severed male members.[58] Perhaps no guerrilla persecuted Indians with more lust than Benjamin Harrison, whose single eye—the other lost in a gouging competition—and disfigured visage testified to his violent past. Harrison organized an attack on the Creek town of Padjeeligau, near the Georgia border. There, his gang killed and dismembered sixteen men. He later bragged to another white man "that there S[h]ould Never be a peace with the Indians whilst his Nam was Ben Harrison for he was abel to raise men enough to kill half the Indians that might cum to aney Treaty and observed that he had began the Business."[59] Retaliating against Harrison's raid, Creeks struck the American settlement at Old Bush's Fort, taking livestock and killing white bystander Isaac Vansant. Vansant's widow Anne placed the blame squarely on Benjamin Harrison, but she seems to have been in the minority on that account. According to Anne, "The doctrine in her neighbourhood was, let us kill the Indians, bring on a war, and we shall get land."[60]

As Isaac Vansant's death demonstrates, Indians, too, adopted a racial form of blood vengeance wherein whites answered for the misdeeds of other whites. In 1784, after several attempts to kill white men, a young Coweta man murdered William Marshall, the younger brother of resident Creek trader Thomas Marshall. The Coweta said he did so because "his father had been killed by a white man, and a white man he would have." Thomas Marshall, whose wife was Creek, demanded justice, and the young Coweta's clan kin agreed to execute him. He was satisfied in death, saying "that his heart was straight and he was a man." Such scenarios became commonplace on the frontier: Choctaw Lewis Vaun, seeking vengeance for a brother killed in Mississippi Territory, wounded a Mr. Patterson; on the road to Nashville, Creeks killed one Mr. White, in revenge for a fellow Creek who was killed in Kentucky; Choctaws angry over the murder of an Indian in Natchez wounded a Mr. Hogan.[61]

In a petition to Congress, the Territorial Assembly of Tennessee claimed, "Scarcely . . . is there a man of this body, but can recount a dear wife or child, an aged parent or near relation, massacred by the hands of these blood-thirsty nations [Cherokees and Creeks], in their houses or fields."[62] Although the assembly exaggerated, frontier warfare scarred many families and shaped the political ideology of a generation of Southern politicians, most notably Davy Crockett, John C. Calhoun, and Andrew Jackson.

David ("Davy") Crockett was named after his grandfather, who was murdered by Chickamauga and Creek warriors nine years before his birth. The same warriors killed his grandmother, wounded his uncle Joseph, and captured another uncle, James, who remained with the Creeks for nearly eighteen years before being redeemed by a trader. South Carolina statesman John C. Calhoun hailed from Long Cane, a frontier community targeted by the Cherokees in 1760 and 1776. In 1760, warriors killed Calhoun's grandmother, aunt, and uncle and captured his cousins Anne and Mary; Mary was never redeemed. Like Calhoun, Andrew Jackson came from the Carolina backcountry. Born at Waxhaws, a district with a history of Anglo-Indian violence, Jackson began his military career at age 13, when he volunteered with a local company to avenge "Bloody" Banastre Tarleton's massacre. His service continued through the First Seminole War, in which he acted as the commanding general. Jackson lost his mother and two brothers during the Revolution, and though Native Americans were not to blame, Jackson conflated Tories and Indians. Crockett, Calhoun, and Jackson were profoundly influenced by what one contemporary called "a long continued course of aggression and sufferings," having experienced nativist warfare firsthand or learned of it at the knees of their parents. Crockett maintained mixed feelings about Indians. He believed that they were savage in character, but, as a Tennessee congressman, Crockett was one of the very few western politicians to vote against the Indian Removal Bill, calling it "a wicked, unjust measure." Jackson and Calhoun were less ambivalent. These men anticipated and shaped theories of scientific racism that emerged in the 1830s: they argued that Indians were racial inferiors who had no place in the new American empire they sought to build.[63]

Rather than a one-way monologue crafted by the white elites, the language of race was a dialogue shared by whites and Indians and shaped by the violent intimacy of the Southern border wars. New articulations of race blended with—and complicated—older notions of Native identity. Challenging colonialism, Indians drew on their experiences with "Virginians" to craft a racial ideology underpinned by nativism. This ideology encouraged them to extend their kinship horizons to all Indian groups and push whites and blacks into the category of other. In this shift toward pan-Indianism, Southern Indians significantly altered their captivity practices. Since the Mississippian era, they had maintained a broad captivity spectrum, one that included torture, adoption, and enslavement. By the turn of the nineteenth century, however, that spectrum had narrowed considerably.

In accord with new notions of identity, Southern Indians only rarely adopted whites and blacks into their families. In fact, an employee of Panton, Leslie & Company claimed that the only "white people" Indians tolerated "in their Land" were traders—useful men under the protection of their wives' clans. In a 1816 treaty, Chickasaw leaders prohibited unconnected whites from settling in their nation.[64] Even those with Indian wives were subject to scrutiny; in 1798, the Creek National Council voted to expel troublesome white residents of their nation, including Richard Bailey, John Shirley, Francis Lesley, Samuel Lyons, William Lyons, and Robert Killgore.[65] Cherokee chiefs also attempted to police their borders and, in 1802, prohibited whites from settling within their nation. Acknowledging that adoption and intermarriage had already made the Cherokee Nation racially complex, the chiefs made exceptions for those with Cherokee spouses, including white women (some of whom were doubtlessly former captives) married to Cherokee men, saying "The White Women may stay with their red Husbands as Men love Women and Women love Men."[66]

As tensions between whites and Indians mounted, even those who had been adopted into Native societies felt uneasy. Daniel Eades decided to turn his back on his adoptive people and return to the Anglo-American society of his birth. Eades, taken from Georgia during the American Revolution, was 9 years old when a Creek medicine maker adopted him as a nephew. Remaining with the Creeks for at least fifteen years, Eades learned his uncle's craft while living in the small town of Hilabi. In Creek country, Eades abandoned his natal name and assumed a new identity as "Sausey Jack." Sometime around the turn of the nineteenth century, Jack/Daniel left Hilabi and returned to Georgia. It is unclear why he did so. His father, John Eades, had petitioned the federal government for his return, so perhaps Eades, like George Mayfield before him, left the Creeks at the behest of his family. It is also plausible that rising nativism within the Creek Nation and the racism of the Southern frontier factored into Eades's decision. Many years later, in the spring of 1811, Daniel Eades came back to the Creek Nation, this time alongside several white family members and about 100 slaves. Like thousands of other Americans, Eades hoped to establish a plantation in Mississippi Territory, and he had to traverse Indian country to get there. Seeking to avoid paying tolls at ferries operated by Indian families, Eades ordered his slaves to cut down trees and build small bridges across waterways. Unsurprisingly, this angered Creek residents, who threatened the Eades family. Daniel returned their threats in Muskogee and retrieved his father's "long sword that he wore in the revolution, brandish[ing] the sword . . . tell[ing] them that they were fools, that they could never whip the whites and their nation would be destroyed." Although he retained command of the Muskogee of his youth, Eades, having chosen to take his place on the opposite side of the racial divide, was Creek no more.[67]

Although they still took white women and children captive, Indians usually ransomed these Virginians, selling them back to their families, traders, or Indian agents. As a visitor to the Creek Nation noted, "they set the price of ransom upon them according to the rank and estimation in which they may be held among their countrymen."[68] In September 1792, when Creeks raided a farm belonging to the Gillespie family, the warriors killed one boy and took another captive. The following month they agreed to deliver young Gillespie to Cherokee interpreter James Carey in exchange for 250 pounds of leather and a horse worth £15. At about the same time, Creek warriors who had taken a young white woman named Alice Thompson received a much greater ransom when they sold her to a white trader for 800 pounds of deerskin worth over $250. In 1793, Creeks broke into John Franklin's house in the disputed territory and took a great deal of valuable property as well as Franklin's wife, whom they valued at $150 in ransom.[69] When Lower Creek chief Thomas Perryman returned several white captives to Spanish Floridians, the commanding officer at San Marcos de Apalache gave him only fifty dollars for each captive. Perryman grumbled that "fifty dollars . . . is just about the sum I payd for them," plus he fed, housed, and provided guides for the captives. He thought sixty dollars per head more appropriate compensation.[70] In a pattern that occurred throughout the 1790s, all these captors kept their prisoners for only a short time and then sold them back to family members or government officials for cash, livestock, or deerskins—all valid forms of currency on the Southern frontier.

In a letter to a Spanish official, Thomas Perryman related another illuminating story regarding the changing nature of captivity. According to Perryman, Lower Creeks captured and enslaved a white woman from Georgia. Perryman claimed that she was "used so cruelly by the Indians that I bought her for upwards of seven hundred dollars." Together, Perryman and the white woman had three children. Over time, however, Perryman claimed that his wife was made to feel uncomfortable in Creek country, and he began to fear for her safety. So, Perryman sent her and the three children back to Georgia. This action aroused the ire of his fellow Creeks, who pointed out that they could have received a great deal of money for the white woman's ransom. According to Perryman, some Creeks on the Lower Chattahoochee who owed him 3,740 deerskins would not pay their debt, saying, "that the white pepoel I have sent back come to more then these debts." Increasingly ostracized from Creek families, "the white pepoel" became commodities.[71]

As race began to color the way Native people saw their world, they became less inclined to attack, kill, or capture other red people. A Choctaw woman, perhaps taken during the Creek-Choctaw Wars of 1765–1777, remained a slave into the early 1810s. Owned by Creek chief Bob Catalla, she married one of the chief's black slaves and had several children.[72] Another notable exception was Lydia Carter, also known as the "Little Osage Captive." Taken in 1817, when groups of Cherokees migrated west to what is now Arkansas and clashed with the resident Osages, the young girl became the captive of a Cherokee warrior who sold her to another Cherokee named Aaron Price. Price treated the girl as a slave, and, when approached by missionaries among the Cherokees, agreed to sell her for $100. Lydia Carter, a wealthy divorcee from Natchez, volunteered the ransom and became the Osage girl's patron and namesake. In 1818, when Osages sued the Cherokees for peace, the case of the "Little Osage Captive" became something of a cause célèbre. Osage leaders battled with missionaries and the Cherokee government for custody of the child, but her case was never resolved, for she became ill and died in March 1821. The Osage girl's captivity includes many older elements of captive-taking: A prisoner-of-war turned slave, she was poorly fed and clothed, then sold. At the same time, the enormous amount of press and patronage that whites and Cherokees alike lavished on the Little Osage Captive suggests that this captive-taking episode was extraordinary, a throwback to a different era. Although Cherokees considered Osages "uncivilized" outsiders who possessed a different culture and history than themselves—Cherokee chief Doublehead called people like the Osage "western wild Indians"—Osages were still Indians, and many Cherokees believed that Native people should not be slaves.[73]

Outside of the Cherokee-Osage War, the only other nineteenth-century conflict in which Southern Indians took and retained significant numbers of Native captives was the Red Stick War of 1813–1814. During that war, Cherokees captured at least 300 Creek women and children, most of whom they released. Some, however, were adopted and elected to remain in Cherokee country after the war. Choctaws also took Creek captives during the Red Stick War. John Pitchlynn, a white interpreter who grew up among the Choctaws, adopted a baby girl whom he named Onaheli, and Pitchlynn and his Choctaw wife reared Onaheli alongside their other children. Onaheli came to identify as Choctaw, and, when given the chance as an adult, refused to return to the Creek Nation.[74]

As warfare among Indians declined, most Native adoptees were orphans rather than prisoners of war. Horatio Cushman, who resided among the Chickasaws and Choctaws in the nineteenth century, observed that Indian families adopted many orphans and easily incorporated these new members into their households. Cushman argued that they did so "not through mercenary motives, but to be protected, cared for and loved, not to be enslaved for the few dollars and cents that anticipation whispered would be made out of them by adoption." Here, Cushman critiqued the contemporary white American practice of "binding out" orphans, in which families housed and boarded children until they reached adulthood. As Cushman implied, some white families overworked and abused these children, never embracing them as true kin. In contrast, Native people, drawing on their long tradition of captivity, readily incorporated Indian children into their families.[75]

In the late eighteenth century, as the nativist movement intensified and Indians became increasingly anxious over retaining their political autonomy and territorial integrity, chiefs began to assume powers formerly held by clans, including control of warfare and punishment of enemies. Clan and village affiliations, which had been of paramount significance during the colonial era, became less important to nativists who stressed their collective identity as red people.

Working through the Creek National Council, a congress of all the nation's headmen, Alexander McGillivray attempted to centralize his nation's government. Through his partnership in the Pensacola trading house Panton, Leslie, & Company, McGillivray strong-armed other Creek leaders using his control of trade and gifting. He also set up an armed, mounted police force composed of his Wind clan relatives, an unprecedented act in Southern Indian history. Formerly, clans had maintained social order and executed justice, but the national police force usurped that duty and enhanced the power of an emerging Creek state. In another breach of clan power, McGillivray himself directed Creek war parties on the Oconee and Cumberland, supplying them with the Spanish arms he had procured in Pensacola.[76]

McGillivray died at the age of 34 in 1793, but his successor, Efau Hadjo, attempted to continue his legacy. In a talk to the Seminoles, Efau Hadjo said that each Southern Nation should police its own warriors, especially along their borders with the United States and Spanish Florida. Most significantly, Efau Hadjo determined to put an end to the warfare that had raged intermittently between Creeks and Americans since the Revolution. To secure a peace, Efau Hadjo attempted to collect all the white and black captives taken by the Creeks. Although a logical political maneuver, Efau Hadjo's ploy angered those who believed that captive-taking was a prerogative of all successful warriors. In a conversation with the commanding officer at San Marcos de Apalache, Lower Creek Chief Jack Kinnard revealed how the issue divided the Creeks. When Efau Hadjo invited Kinnard to a council meeting regarding the return of captives, Kinnard "replied that being informed of what was to be discussed he did not find it convenient to attend." Kinnard explained, "it was useless to do so" since for each pacific headman "there were a hundred of the opposing party of mad youths . . . he was quite certain by the common voice that the result of the assembly would be to arm and to man the frontiers in order to oppose the operations of the Americans."[77]

Following the lead of McGillivray and Efau Hadjo, Native leaders who favored centralization tried to curb blood vengeance. Most significantly, chiefs sought an end to public torture. As they attempted to deal with an increasingly powerful American government and weave meaningful alliances with other Native nations, Indian leaders wrested the execution of justice away from the clans. Following the conclusion of the Chickamauga Wars, the Cherokee National Council, seeking to avoid another bloody conflict with Americans, voted to abolish the practice in 1797. Although the ban was not immediately successful, blood vengeance largely disappeared by 1810, when representatives of the seven clans authorized the National Council to absolve all blood debts. In 1798, the Creek National Council moved to outlaw blood vengeance and, the following year, revived McGillivray's lighthorse police force to enforce the decree. Choctaws and Chickasaws continued to avenge intratribal killings, but, beginning in the early nineteenth century, leaders prohibited their people from taking revenge on Americans. By 1812, in the Cherokee, Creek, Choctaw, and Chickasaw nations, those who murdered Americans were publicly executed. Police forces, established among the Creeks and Cherokees in 1799, the Choctaws in 1820, and the Chickasaws in 1829, meted out justice and dealt with other crimes ranging from theft to bootlegging to murder. Wielding a tremendous amount of power, the lighthorsemen, in the name of nation, acted as "sheriff, judge and jury." Unfortunately, the United States proved unwilling to police its citizens in a similar fashion. Most egregiously, Southern state courts would not convict white men who killed Indians. Native nations, however, demanded some sort of redress, and federal Indian agents worked with states to compensate an Indian victim's family with a cash payment.[78]

Like Jack Kinnard, many Indians resented their national governments' intrusion into clan life. Nonelites, in particular, still looked to their clans to maintain peace and order in a changing world.[79] Uneasy about the new justice system, clan kin worried about the spirits of murder victims. In the 1830s, a Cherokee informant told an interviewer that the unavenged "will never be permitted to rest." Some families, troubled by the wandering souls of their deceased kin, continued to prepare food for the dead and leave it in conspicuous places.[80]

To satisfy the spirits of the slain, some warriors perpetuated violent killing of enemy men and occasional torture, but they did so away from village blood poles and beyond the watchful eyes of their leaders. In 1789, Creek warriors took a Mr. Clark near the St. Marys River. Some African American slaves who witnessed the episode said that the Creeks "carried him about two miles," and then "they burnt his eyes out first and tortured him to death." According to the witnesses, "the reason as they give for doing so they said he was a Virginia man and it was good to kill him."[81] By the 1790s, however, torture was no longer a prominent component of Native Southern warfare. When A. W. Putnam, one of the first historians of Tennessee, conducted extensive research on the Chickamauga Wars, he found only two reports of torture by Indians. A few isolated cases were reported during the Patriot War (1812–1813) and the Second Seminole War (1835–1842), but, like the torture of Mr. Clark, they occurred outside of Native communities at or near the site of the victim's capture. During the Patriot War, Seminoles waylaid, tortured, and killed three postriders, including one Mr. Maxwell. According to those who recovered his body, they found Maxwell naked, "dreadfully tortured and murdered having his nose ears and privities cut off scalped and otherwise barbarously used." In nearly identical fashion, Seminoles killed and mutilated another postrider during the Second Seminole War. Jane Murray Sheldon, whose husband was a plantation overseer on Florida's east coast, also accused the Seminoles of capturing a Mr. Gould whom they tortured and killed on the spot. Once a public rite, torture became a rare, illicit activity perpetuated by wayward warriors.[82]

The militant phase of the nativist movement ended in the mid-1790s following the loss of important chiefs and the eruption of old tensions between Indian nations. The most capable and effective Southern nativist leaders, Dragging Canoe and Alexander McGillivray, died in 1792 and 1793, respectively. John Watts (also called New Tassel), Dragging Canoe's nephew, became the new leader of the Chickamaugas, but he lacked the military genius and leadership skills of his famous uncle. In September 1794, Major James Ore and his Tennessee volunteers (with the help of Joseph Brown) destroyed the main Chickamauga towns of Running Water and Nickajack. Thereafter, Cherokees developed nonviolent ways of resisting American expansion. Among the Creeks, Efau Hadjo urged reconciliation with the Americans, and he continued to champion cooperation and kinship among all Southern Indians. Unfortunately, he did not possess the education and broad political connections that made McGillivray such an effective cultural mediator, and the Spanish cut off their arms supply to the Creeks in 1795. Lacking a popular leader and unsure about how to deal with an increasingly powerful and intrusive American state, the Creeks were a deeply divided people.

Chickasaw leaders resisted Creek attempts to draw them into an anti-American alliance, and tensions between the two groups flared for a decade. After Dragging Canoe and Alexander McGillivray failed in their attempt to convince preeminent Chickasaw chief Piomingo to join them, the Creeks resorted to more forceful tactics: they killed American traders in Chickasaw country and burned their stores. An angry Piomingo secretly allied with Governor William Blount of Tennessee, promising to protect Cumberland settlers in exchange for arms. Creek and Chickasaw hunters who met one another in the borderland that separated the two nations exchanged insults and occasionally fought. In 1795, after discovering the dead body of one of their warriors, the Chickasaws assumed the Creeks were to blame, and they killed a Creek fanemingo who lived among them. Creek warriors invaded the Chickasaw Nation, but privy Chickasaws surprised and routed them.[83] The Chickasaws went so far as to take captives, and rumors circulated that they sold their fellow red people as slaves "to the white people of New Cumberland." Although the two sides came to an uneasy peace by early 1796, the spirit of nativism declined in the wake of such bloodshed.[84]

By the turn of the century, nationalist chiefs discouraged all violence against outsiders, leaving Native men with fewer opportunities to validate themselves as warriors. To prove their masculinity, they increasingly turned to stickball, an ancient game traditionally used to train men for battle. A field sport, stickball is loosely related to modern lacrosse, although players use two web-ended sticks rather than one and score points by hitting a slender pole (or sometimes an object atop the pole) rather than a netted goal. In Native languages, the sport's name means "younger brother to war" or "little war."[85] It was, by all accounts, a most appropriate surrogate for warfare. Stickball had always been dangerous. In 1676, a Franciscan missionary (who wished to ban it) reported that the sport resulted in "many lamed, broken legs, persons without the use of one or both hands, blinded in one eye, broken ribs, and other broken bones. . . . And not just a few, but many!"[86] On occasion, players died. Since games could last a day or longer, stickball certainly simulated the physicality of war as well as the "hunger, thirst and fatigue" that accompanied it.[87] Many of the same rituals accompanied both warfare and stickball. Before both, men abstained from sex, alcohol, sleep, and most foods: they consulted conjurers, danced, took medicine, painted themselves, and donned special regalia. Ball sticks served as symbolic war clubs, and blood poles doubled as goal posts. When a Choctaw player scored a point by striking the post, he shouted *illi tok!*—"dead!"[88]

Beyond keeping men masculine, stickball brought Native people together during a crucial moment in their history. During the Mississippian period and into the seventeenth century, opposing chiefdoms played one another in stickball, but by the late eighteenth century, two towns within the same nation usually challenged one another. Such rivalries proved wildly popular. During his tour of the South in 1809, John Norton reported, "Here they think nothing of going sixty or seventy miles to see a Ball-play."[89] Moravian missionaries among the Cherokees lamented, "It is indescribable how taken the nation is by this ball play, and from year to year it gets worse. No weather is too bad, no road too far! Old and young hurry there, and a ball play is hardly over in *one place* when preparations are made in another." At stickball games, people from many different towns and villages came together to watch, gamble, cheer, and gossip. Along with treaty talks and religious festivals, intertown stickball matches provided a forum for exercising national identity. Much more than sport, stickball provided a satisfyingly ancient and uniquely Indian touchstone on which to build new nations.[90]

Although the late-eighteenth-century nativist movement did not stop American expansion, it left important legacies among Indians. Most significantly, Native people increasingly began to think of themselves as "red people," as a distinct, inherently different people who owned their native ground by right of divine sanction. The Native South remained fractious, as the Chickasaw-Creek War of 1795 demonstrated, but those who believed in the nativists' message agreed that Indians should not fight, kill, or capture one another. In 1792, Southwest Territorial Governor William Blount recorded a marked change in Native martial behavior; he exaggerated only slightly when he claimed that "Indians no longer kill Indians."[91] As they faced the crises of the late eighteenth century, many Southern Indians must have believed, as Efau Hadjo did, that "[t]he four Nations of red people ought to be as one."[92]

As chiefs prevented villagers from torturing and clans grew pessimistic about incorporating non-Indians, the once-broad spectrum of captivity narrowed considerably. Indians embraced a collective identity as red people, and as they began to focus on black and white Americans as their common enemy, they largely ceased taking one another captive. Although torture was no longer common, white men still suffered beatings and, occasionally, death. Clans rejected white women and children as potential family members but sought ransom for them instead. As captive-taking became a largely economic pursuit, African Americans of both sexes and all ages became the prime targets, for they had the highest value.

7

RACIAL SLAVERY

One summer morning in 1787, a war party crossed the Oconee River into disputed territory claimed by both Georgia and the Creek Nation. The party approached the farmstead of John Lang and seized his 12-year-old African American slave, Lucy. She was Lang's most valuable possession, not only for domestic and agrarian labor but also for the children Lang expected her to bear in a few years. Lang immediately notified his nearest neighbors, the McMichaels, who agreed to help him search for Lucy. Ezekieh McMichael followed the trail near his home, which led to the Oconee River. Lang and Ezekieh's brother heard three gunshots ring out and then saw Ezekieh's horse approach without its master. Lang and McMichael followed the trail to the river where they found no trace of Lucy but saw Ezekieh's body. In their haste to escape, the Creek warriors had left behind three guns, five bags of shot, and two pieces of scalp. The latter, Lang and McMichael deduced, "were taken off the head of the Decest Ezekieth McMichael" because they matched two raw wounds atop Ezekieh's head. As for Lucy, her captors forced her across the Oconee and into Creek country, where she would live and labor, bear children and survive to see her grandchildren born, and remain enslaved under Indian masters.[1]

By the late eighteenth century, Native warriors began to single out people of African descent as preeminent captives. When they served as British allies during the American Revolution, Creeks recalled that they had been "told by the General [Prevost] before they went into Carolina that whatever plunder they got should be their own property and that they saw the King's Army Seize upon all the Negroes they could get upon which they did the same and intend to carry them into the Nation."[2] As the war drew to a close, American officials urged Creek headmen to restore slaves, but most masters proved unwilling to relinquish their spoils of war. Residents of Coweta "refused to give up the Negroes in that town because the[y] Said they were given to them as a present by the White people [the British] . . . wou'd not deliver the Negroes but drove them into the woods."[3] This shift in captive-taking grew more pronounced during the post-Revolutionary border wars. When Juan Forrester told Payne, chief of the Alachua Seminoles, about a livestock theft in East Florida, Payne replied that white vagabonds—not Mikasukis or Lower Creeks— were to blame. He explained, "had it of been Indians they would of taken negroes in preference to horses."[4]

Though difficult to come by, extant figures for the period bear out this trend. During a two-year period in the war over the Oconee, Creek warriors captured at least 140 Georgians, 80 percent of whom were African Americans. A 1794 tally featured in the *Knoxville Gazette* listed a total of ninety-six people recently killed or captured by combined Creek/Chickamauga war parties in middle Tennessee and southern Kentucky. Within a six-month period, the sixty-nine recorded casualties were all white, and women and children represented 35 percent of the dead. Meanwhile, African American men, women, and children accounted for 93 percent of all captives—twenty-five out of a total of twenty-seven. Included in this tally was a June 1794 strike in which a party of Chickamaugas led by White Man Killer attacked a boat of settlers and slaves on the Tennessee River. The Chickamaugas killed the thirteen whites on board and took all twenty-two African American slaves captive. In determining an enemy's fate, race had clearly eclipsed factors of sex and age.[5]

In contrast to white captives, whose only buyers were family members or government officials, black captives fetched much higher bids from a wider variety of buyers. In the waning years of the deerskin trade, these captives became the most valuable commodity on the southern frontier. In exchange for livestock, cash, deerskins, or dry goods, captors exchanged African American captives to Spanish subjects in the Floridas and Louisiana, Euro-American government agents or traders, and other Indians. Those unconcerned with legal titles found ready slave traders among Indians. In his testimony against fellow trader Charles Weatherford, John Fitzpatrick asserted that Weatherford's friends "publickly offer[ed] half price for Negroes and Horses which should be Stolen or brought to him from and out of the Limites of the United States." Among those who supplied Weatherford with captives was John Randon, a Creek warrior who had been active in Oconee raiding. In the Creek Nation, Randon met a man who had recently escaped from a cruel Pensacola master. Randon told the man he could find freedom among the Cherokees, and offered to arrange his travel. However, with Weatherford's help, Randon sold the runaway as a slave in the Cherokee Nation. Sixty years after the Yamasee War, some had chosen to revive their traffic in humans.[6]

Captors engaged in a bustling trade at Pensacola with the Spanish, who had captured the port city in 1781 from the British. According to Spanish governor Arturo O'Neill, Indians initiated this commerce. In March 1783, O'Neill explained, "some of the Talapuche [Upper Creek] Indians have brought here Negros for sale, [and] I have offered to continue this practice."[7] The Creeks told O'Neill that they had captured the African Americans, along with horses and cattle, from citizens of the United States. O'Neill deemed these black captives legitimate spoils of war, and proclaimed that they would be sold legally in Pensacola. That June, O'Neill reported, "The chiefs of the Talapuches have arrived with cattle, skins, and Negroes. I have exchanged them for dry-goods from the stores in this town, and I am left loaded with them."[8] In addition to trade goods, O'Neill and other Spanish officials heaped accolades upon Creek warriors who devastated the frontier plantations of Georgia and transferred capital into Florida. A deserter from the British Navy told Agent Patrick Carr that while in Pensacola he discovered "Indians and White Peple is Constantly Carying Droves of Negroes to that place & that the Spanish Govener buyes the Chief of them & Encourages them to fetch the Rest & tell them the[y] scall Receive the Cash for all the[y] fetch." Some Pensacola merchants turned a profit by reselling these captives on the more competitive Havana slave market. If Native warriors were willing to run their black captives to West Florida, they found welcome buyers.[9]

Those who sold African American captives engaged in shrewd bargaining. In the fall of 1788, an Upper Creek captured a free black soldier, Juan Gros, who was serving in a Louisiana Company near Pensacola. Shortly thereafter, the captor sold Gros to a white trader, who, in turn, resold Gros to the Mikasuki chief Kinache. While passing through Mikasuki, a Spanish trader spotted Gros and attempted to ransom him. Kinache demurred but said that having bought the man for eight cows, he was not interested in selling. Determined to redeem Gros, the commanding officer at San Marcos de Apalache, Captain Diego de Vegas, invited Kinache to discuss the matter. Kinache drove a hard bargain. Claiming that "on account of his being a rich Indian, and having a great deal of affection for the Negro," Kinache originally wanted 600 *libras*—the value of 600 deerskins at the Panton, Leslie & Company store—for Gros. Eventually, Vegas talked Kinache down to 400 libras, but Kinache grumbled "that he bought the Negro in wartime, when the cattle fetched a high price, and that he [Gros] was very expensive." When Kinache got around to delivering Juan Gros almost a year later, the chief claimed that he would need at least fifty more libras plus several kegs of brandy. The Spaniards agreed.[10]

Other warriors chose to sell black captives in their own nations. Buyers were usually chiefs or resident traders, both of Native and non-Native descent. Choctaw chief Franchimastabé took several black captives during the American Revolution and later sold two of them to white men living among the Choctaws, interpreter Robert Welsh and trader Benjamin James, who paid the chief one horse each for their slaves. This transaction entered the historical record years later, when Welsh hoodwinked James and stole his slave Batteas. Because of the frequent exchange and occasional theft of slaves, people like Batteas confronted unstable lives in Indian country. The fortunes of a party of five black captives taken in 1788 illustrate typical buyers and demonstrate how such captives became rapidly dispersed within Indian nations and beyond. After killing a 50-year-old enslaved man named Will, Chehaw warriors took the five slaves from John Whitehead's plantation in Liberty County, Georgia, and sold them to others living among the Lower Creeks. A white trader named Neah Harreal purchased Dido and Chole, two women in their 20s. By 1803, Dido and Chole had produced a total of five children, also retained by Harreal. A Creek headman named Humlathluchee or Big Eater bought Hector and Daffney, and later sold Daffney's two daughters to Lower Creek headman Jack Kinnard. Finally, a woman named Rose was resold more than once in the Creek Nation before eventually being traded to Panton, Leslie, & Company in Pensacola.[11]

Continuing an ancient practice, Indians also traded their captives to Native allies. As a missionary traversed Cherokee country during the latter years of the American Revolution, he saw Shawnees en route to buy black captives from the Creeks. In 1795, Chickamauga chief John Watts reported that some years earlier Shawnee warriors had taken an African American girl captive on the Cumberland, then traded her to a Chickamauga ally. Watts said the girl had "passed from the Shawaneese warriors" to a Chickamauga called Flea, then to another warrior, Five Killer. A young woman named Aggy came to the Creek Nation following a 1792 raid on her master's plantation. Soon after Aggy's capture, her captor sold her to Alexander McGillivray. When McGillivray died the following year, his heirs sold Aggie again, this time in the Cherokee Nation. In another case, when the governor of East Florida sought to recover African Americans taken from his province by the Mikasukis, he asked Lower Creek Chief Jack Kinnard for assistance. Kinnard told the governor to attend to the matter swiftly, for if he did not hurry "they [the slaves] will be Scattered so as they cannot be Collected." Once taken, captives traveled along well-worn routes of exchange between allies.[12]

It was not unusual for Indian masters to resell slaves casually and quickly when they needed to pay debts or obtain cash. Because residents of Indian nations did not bother with the legal deeds required by colonial or American law, they readily purchased slaves taken from settlers. When Euro-American officials pressed Indians to return slaves, they often responded like Jack Kinnard, "who refused to give [the slaves] up, alledging that the negroes had passed thru several hands, and finally now was his."[13] Virtually every pre-removal treaty demanded that Indians return African American captives and runaways, but, as Kinnard's comment reveals, this was often an impossible task. As Cherokee agent Silas Dinsmoore argued, "It is useless to expect the return of slaves captured by the Indians during the wars, as they have changed hands so many times in the Nation." Creek chiefs concurred, saying, "some are sold, and bartered, from one to another, and the property paid for them consumed by those who got it, which makes it a difficult matter for us to obtain negroes under those circumstances." Despite years of lobbying, James Smith, a planter from Liberty County, Georgia, only recovered six of the thirteen slaves Creek warriors took from him in May 1793. One captor sold Smith's slave Sarah to trader John Milligan, who, in turn, resold her to Smith for $64.25. Creek chiefs managed to recover three more of Smith's slaves, handing them over to officials in 1795, and Smith purchased another of his former slaves from trader Timothy Barnard. Twelve years after the raid on Smith's plantation, Agent Benjamin Hawkins redeemed the sixth captive, Mary, but Creeks refused to release the four children Mary had borne during her captivity. As the Smith case illustrates, federal agents and, later, state governments attempted to coax and cajole Indians into returning slaves, but they met with limited success. Even as their power within the region declined, Native Americans managed to retain many war captives (and the children and grandchildren of those captives) from the Revolutionary era.[14]

After the conclusion of the southern border wars in 1795, Southern Indians had fewer opportunities to take captives in warfare. During the 1813–1814 Red Stick conflict, a Creek civil war, militant Red Sticks captured African American slaves belonging to enemy Creeks and Americans. Fighting against the Red Sticks were Creeks and Cherokees, who, in turn, captured and retained Red Sticks' slaves. During the Cherokee-Osage Wars of the 1810s, Cherokees reportedly took dozens of Osage captives, including the "Little Osage Captive" Lydia Carter. Creeks also took captives during wars and slave raids against the Seminoles from the 1810s through 1839. While the ancient association between war and captive-taking remained, warfare itself became rarer and thus a less reliable source of captives.[15]

By the turn of the nineteenth century, Indians more often looked to purchase, rather than capture, slaves. Would-be masters acquired slaves from fellow countrymen and Indian allies, but they increasingly turned to trade with whites. In 1808, aspiring Cherokee planter James Vann journeyed to Virginia, where he purchased twenty enslaved men, women, and children. In the early 1820s, Choctaw Molly McDonald purchased an African American slave from white neighbors, paying for the man in eight cash installments. When the Cherokee Young Wolf died, his wife Janney (or Jane) Wolf turned their plantation "big house" into an inn. In the early 1820s, Janney Wolf used the inn's profits to buy more slaves, adding to the two Young Wolf had purchased before his death. In 1824, Choctaw Peter Pitchlynn's father, John, urged his son to seek out a white man named Morgan and trade the family's horses for slaves. A bill of sale from 1832, on the eve of Choctaw removal, records another of Peter Pitchlynn's purchases: $2,075 to Booth Malone for five slaves. After the closing of the trans-Atlantic slave trade in 1808 and the post-1812 cotton boom, Southern planters, especially Indian masters, ranked slaves among the best investments. Since Native nations held territory communally, land was not among the commodities owned by individuals. Private property included improvements such as houses and other buildings as well as chattels such as household possessions and slaves. As removal approached and elite Indian families liquidated their assets, many purchased African American slaves.[16]

For most of the eighteenth century, Indians had relied on the deerskin trade to supply them with European manufactured items including guns, clothing, and metal tools. By the 1790s, however, the trade was clearly in decline, and they would have to look elsewhere for the goods on which they had come to depend. Seeking to recover from the stress associated with the loss of land and game, some used their African American captives to launch new economic ventures such as planting and ranching. Those who pursued new economic strategies believed that they could best preserve their nation's autonomy by retaining their economic independence. In American popular imagination (as in most historical writing on the antebellum period), there is no room in the "Old South" for Indians who planted cotton or herded cattle. The gap between perception and reality comes not from Native Americans' inability to survive in a changing South, but rather from their expulsion from the region. When the removal policy relocated them to Indian Territory in the 1830s and 1840s, so too did the act remove Indians from Southern historical memory. Although most were ultimately forced from the region, Native Americans participated in the economic revolution that transformed the interior South.

A leader in the new economy, Lower Creek chief Jack Kinnard managed to accumulate wealth and power through working and selling his black captives. He led many raids against encroaching settlers, and by 1791, he had accumulated forty African American captives and 1,500 head of livestock. An index of his success as a warrior, Kinnard's spoils also enabled him to become a rancher, planter, and trader in the region. Selling his cattle for manufactured goods at Pensacola, he exchanged rum and cloth to other Creeks to turn a profit. Meanwhile, Kinnard carried on a trade in black captives with others in the region. He acquired most of his captives through raiding, taking them from white planters in frontier Georgia counties like Liberty and Camden. He purchased others from neighboring whites, including elites like Arturo O'Neill, governor of West Florida. Although Kinnard seems to have retained most captives to work on his plantation, he sold some to other Creeks. In a letter to Indian agent James Seagrove, Kinnard dispassionately described his role in human trafficking: "when the Negroes came the red people wanted to buy [them]." Kinnard also assisted East Floridians in recovering runaway and stolen slaves in the region—for a fee.[17] According to a contemporary, Kinnard's newfound wealth underwrote his status, raising him "to the dignity of a chief."[18]

As a planter, Kinnard helped supply the Spanish fort at San Marcos de Apalache with produce. He kept a jealous watch on the African American captives who worked his fields. Complaining to Spanish Floridians that Americans always attempted to steal his slaves, Kinnard said that he would have to remove to a more remote area "where his negroes might work usefully." For conspiring with revolutionary William Augustus Bowles, the Spanish imprisoned a black man named Billy who was owned jointly by Jack Kinnard and his brother William. When Kinnard wrote to the commanding officer holding Billy, he received word "that he was a bad Negro and he would not turn him out." Attempting to reason with Billy's guards, Kinnard pointed out that his slave's labor produced food, which he then traded to the men at Apalache: "I wish you would let him out and Send him to the plantation to his work for as Long as he is in the fort he is no use to you nor me." Eventually, Kinnard did secure Billy's release—a testament to the power he wielded on the Creek-Spanish frontier and the success of his appeal for his slave's labor.[19]

Jack Kinnard was not the only warrior who used plunder to transform his economic fortunes. Doublehead, a Cherokee headman turned warrior, probably joined the Chickamaugas in June 1788 after Tennessee militiamen killed his elder brother Old Tassel and captured some of his female kin. Out of all the Virginians' transgressions, the murder of Old Tassel was particularly odious to Cherokees since the senior statesman, attempting a peaceful parlay, had approached the militia while bearing a white flag. After Old Tassel's death, Doublehead engaged in extensive raiding in the Cumberland region. By the time hostilities ceased in November 1794, Doublehead had accumulated a number of captives as well as livestock. In his retirement from warfare, Doublehead became a businessman. He established a plantation, but rather than compromise his own masculinity through farming, Doublehead put his African American captives to work. More at ease with ranching, Doublehead once referred to this activity as "Hunting and Gathering my Beef Cattle." Seeking more slaves, Doublehead sometimes resorted to duplicitous means. For example, in 1802, Paul Smith, a free black man, accused Doublehead of kidnapping him and forcing him into bondage. To his agricultural investments, Doublehead added a trading post, which offered more competitive prices than American traders in the area and attracted crowds of Cherokees and Chickasaws. In 1804, after encouraging officials to plot a new federal highway through the Cherokee Nation, Doublehead opened a ferry on the Tennessee River at Muscle Shoals. From his ferry on the Tennessee, Doublehead hoped to enhance his wealth by shipping goods to market at New Orleans and even planned to trade manufactured goods to western Indians in exchange for furs. In August 1807, the old warrior was executed for participating in underhanded and privately lucrative land deals, bringing his entrepreneurial schemes to an abrupt close.[20]

Coming of age in the violent Revolutionary period, Jack Kinnard and Doublehead were part of a new generation of Native men. Taking active roles in the nativist movement, they fought to preserve Indian autonomy and enrich themselves with war spoils in the process. The upstart capital they gained through raiding eased the transition from warrior to planter. The Chickamaugas were especially successful in that regard. Their political activism in the 1780s and early 1790s, combined with an influx of wealth gained through raiding, shifted the balance of power in the Cherokee Nation to their region, and, following the wars, a vocal faction of Chickamauga leaders promoted a new economy based on planting, ranching, and other commercial enterprises. In less dramatic fashion, the same transformation took place across the region as retired warriors and anxious women, facing the aggressively expansionistic United States, took steps to preserve their families and their nations.[21]

This desire for economic change dovetailed with the U.S. government's "civilization" policy. Implemented in the 1790s, the policy sought to "civilize" Indians by introducing them to Anglo-American gender roles, commercial agriculture, private property, Western-style education, and Christianity. Underfunded and impossible to enforce, the policy met with mixed success. Native people, responding to their own needs, showed more interest in the policy's economic dimensions and largely ignored its social and religious aspects. Dominant in Native households and Native fields, women initially were more receptive to the policy. Perhaps eager to seize more economic power after decades of the male-dominated deerskin trade, women petitioned federal Indian agents for steel plows. Women also showed an early interest in cotton, asking agents for spinning wheels, looms, and cotton cards, and they began to grow the crop in the 1790s. They also sought out instruction from American women; perhaps adoptee Hannah Hale, who knew how to spin and weave, taught neighbors in Thlothlagalga. By the first decade of the nineteenth century, Native women across the South produced their own cloth. For the first time, an old trader reported, women no longer depended on products of the hunt and "now could cloth[e] themselves."[22] A Chickasaw agent noticed that women delighted in making fashionable clothing: "It is their constant practice to appear in their best apparel at their public meetings; also when they visit the country villages in the white settlements."[23] Cherokee women even fashioned their own petticoats, crafting the frames out of mulberry root bark, weaving strips of it "like basket work." What cloth their households could not consume Native women sold. In 1820, one incredulous visitor asserted that in a single year Choctaw women had produced over 10,000 yards.[24]

Doublehead's description of herding as "Hunting and Gathering my Beef Cattle" suggests his level of comfort with this aspect of the new economy. After millennia of intimacy with the animal world, Native men more readily engaged in herding than planting. The Apalachees, whose mission experience provided ample opportunity to learn Spanish ranching techniques, became the South's first cowboys in the late seventeenth century. Following the destruction of their missions in 1704, Apalachee captives introduced the Lower Creeks to cattle. Specifically, they practiced free-range ranching, allowing cattle to forage in the woods, a low-maintenance strategy that did not interfere with seasonal hunts. By the 1720s, Lower Creeks and Seminoles had incorporated stock-raising into their economies, but the practice did not spread to others until later that century, when the livestock rustling that accompanied the Revolution and subsequent border wars infused Indian nations with horses and cattle. As the deer population declined and the pelt trade became less profitable, many chose to diversify their economy through commercial ranching. They had little choice. As Choctaw chief Mushulatubbee explained, "We cannot expect to live any longer by hunting. Our game is gone." Born of necessity, ranching proved profitable for Native people, who supplied nearby Euro-American settlements and exported goods to larger markets, including Knoxville, St. Augustine, Pensacola, Natchez, and New Orleans. By the late eighteenth century, Native men, including Creek Jack Kinnard and Seminole chief Payne, owned some of the South's largest cattle herds.[25]

Native men showed less enthusiasm for farming. In the late 1790s, trader Nathaniel Folsom reported that Choctaw men had begun to work in the fields "a little."[26] Around the same time, some Cherokee men, including influential chief Little Turkey, became farmers. When Englishman Adam Hodgson visited Creek country in 1820, he saw some men farming but reported that many more engaged in ranching. According to subagent John Allen, few Chickasaw men took up farming until the early

1820s. As game declined and the fur market collapsed, a desire to contribute to their household and national economies probably motivated some to become farmers. In the pre-removal era, however, most Native men were loath to take up the hoe and engage in what they were conditioned to see as the work of women. When a Cherokee chief decided to send his son to the Brainerd mission school, which required agricultural training for male students, he "offered to find a slave who should work all day, if the missionaries would excuse his son from agricultural labour between school-hours."[27] This Cherokee chief and many other Native men who were averse to farming but eager to diversify their economies found a solution in slave labor. Like their Mississippian ancestors, Native masters sent slaves into the fields, but this time they demanded more intense, profit-oriented work. Agent Benjamin Hawkins noted that Creek residents of Eufala held stock and planted large corn and rice crops. He noted, "Several of the Indians have negroes, taken during the revolutionary war, *and where they are, there is more industry and better farms.*"[28] An unnamed Lower Creek headman boasted that his black captives were not only saleable commodities, but they also "Could Cut well and make Corn for him." Adam Hodgson's notes for his 1820 journey across the Creek, Chickasaw, and Choctaw nations suggest that labor in well-to-do Indian households conformed to a general pattern: men raised livestock, slaves and Native women farmed, and matriarchs managed the home.[29]

As Indians made this economic shift, they became more invested in slaveholding. Although compatible with a broad range of economies, slavery is most useful for large-scale agriculture. Under Native masters, slaves worked in the fields, where they planted, tended, and harvested staples like cotton and corn. Helping masters look after livestock, slaves herded, slaughtered, and butchered the animals. During the first three decades of the nineteenth century, the federal government opened a network of roads that crisscrossed the interior South, and Indians started businesses that catered to the increasing number of travelers. Native families opened stands, selling supplies and food, including what one American described as "the best cured & sweetest bacon." Some also operated ferries and taverns. One white traveler on the Natchez Trace asserted that Choctaw inns "actually excel many among whites." At these service-oriented businesses, slaves supplemented the labor of Native families. To cite just one of the capacities in which African Americans served, they often translated between English-speaking customers and Native entrepreneurs. For their masters, slaves also built new houses. By the early nineteenth century, many Indians had abandoned their traditional wattle-and-daub homes in favor of log cabins as well as brick and wood-frame houses. Wealthy Native families acquired what has been dubbed the "mark of success all over the South"—the two-story big house. Slaves worked to maintain and improve houses, barns, corn-cribs, and fences. Inside Native households, slaves waited on masters and served meals, chores reminiscent of the conspicuous consumption practiced by earlier Indian elites and contemporary white Southern planters alike. Indians' culture and the sovereignty of their nations distinguished them from other Southerners, but they were not impervious to the flow of ideas or to the larger economic forces unleashed by the industrial revolution and American encroachment. Some, on the backs of their slaves, managed to ride the crest of that wave, accumulating wealth that rivaled that of contemporary white planters.[30]

In constructing their ideas about racial slavery, Indians combined what they observed in Euro-American society with their own theories, new and old, about identity and belonging. Native people had long considered unadopted captives to be less than fully human. In the late eighteenth century, some Natives grafted notions of polygenesis and race onto older captivity practices. Those who listened to the prophets' story of separate creations used phenotypical differences between themselves and encroaching white and black settlers to explain the cultural chasm that separated the groups. By the turn of the century, Indians had developed racially descriptive terms to classify the South's people. Calling themselves "red people," they labeled Euro-Americans "white people" and distanced themselves from "black people," who were *luste* in Muskogee, *lusau* in Chickasaw, *lausau* in Choctaw, and *enecka* in Cherokee. As phenotypical traits eclipsed other modes of self-understanding, Indians developed a concomitant vocabulary.[31]

In 1799, Choctaw chiefs began to complain bitterly about an interpreter named Cezar, and the nature of their complaints illustrates the centrality of race to Native notions of power and identity. Cezar was an African American employed by the Mississippi territorial governor to translate Choctaw speeches. African Americans who lived in the southern borderlands often knew multiple languages, and, for decades, they had been among the most capable translators. However, by the late 1790s, Choctaw chiefs "complained of Cezar's acting as interpreter whose color they say

degraded them in the eyes of their own Nation." Beyond Cezar's objection-
able color, the chiefs felt he was "very insolent." To Indian agent John
McKee, the chiefs explained that they could not report the governor's talks to
their nation "having received them from the mouth of a Negro." After hearing "repeated murmurs . . . against [Cezar's] acting as interpreter," McKee
advised Governor Sargent to hire another translator. The Choctaws recom-
mended either Daniel McCurtin (the bilingual son of a Choctaw woman
and a Scot), longtime trader John Pitchlynn, or "another whiteman."[32]

As Native people adopted these attitudes, they also revised their notions
of captivity. Once a loose spectrum of practices, captivity became more
fixed and rigid. Formerly, owned people might have been slaves for life,
but their condition did not pass to their progeny. By the turn of the nineteenth century, however, Indians made slavery perpetual for those of African descent. During the border war with Georgia, Creek warrior Mopli-
gie took a 17-year-old black woman named Bette and later retained the
three sons that Bette bore over the next several years. From a fellow Lower
Creek, Jack Kinnard bought two African American sisters, daughters of an
enslaved woman taken from Georgia. Over the next few decades, the sisters had a total of six children, whom Kinnard also kept. The most radical
innovation in turn-of-the-century captivity practices, transgenerational
bondage grew out of and reinforced racism.[33]

Lucy, captured in the Oconee borderlands at the age of 12, was among
those forced to see her children and grandchildren inherit her condition.
Shortly after her 1787 capture, Lucy was sold to the Sullivan household.
Stephen Sullivan, a white trader, lived with his Creek wife and their children at Tuckabatchee. Lucy probably spent her days tending to the Sulli-
vans' fields and doing domestic chores. Within the Sullivan household,
she lived and worked alongside other African American captives including Dinah, who had been taken from the Oconee borderlands a decade
earlier than Lucy, and Sam, a middle-aged man captured while driving a
team of horses outside Nashville around 1789. By 1798, Stephen Sullivan
had died, but his Creek family kept Lucy and her children. For decades,
Lucy's former master John Lang tried repeatedly to retrieve his slave, her
five children, and sixteen grandchildren, but Sullivan's Creek wife refused
to give them up.[34]

The status of black runaways also points to changing notions of race.
Runaways who took their chances in Indian country had always faced an
uncertain future. There, Indians, resident Euro-Americans, and runaways

themselves negotiated over the status and position of these voluntary captives. African Americans had long attempted to persuade Indians to join them in fighting the threat they saw in the Anglo-American plantation economy. In 1751, some runaways from South Carolina told Cherokees that "the white People was coming up to destroy them all." One of the slaves added "that there was in all Plantations many Negroes more than white People, and that for the Sake of Liberty they would join them."[35] In 1759, free mulatto Philip Johns of Charles Town had "a vision in which it was revealed to him that in the month of September the white people be all underground[,] that the sod would . . . shine with their blood, that there should be no more white kings, Governors, or great men but that the Negroes should live happily and have laws of their own." Johns claimed to have the support of "the Indians," who, after their harvest, "would come and assist in killing all the Buckraas."[36] While there is no evidence of such Indian support, Johns probably hoped for an alliance with the Cherokees, who were then at war with South Carolina. Johns's hopes were not unfounded, for some slaves did realize their dream of freedom by fleeing to Indian nations. As late as 1788, three enslaved men, Isaac, Pearo, and Orange, found refuge in a Creek community and became warriors. Seven weeks after their initial escape, they returned to their old plantation with a Creek war party. Together, the party killed three enslaved African Americans and captured six more. Joining Creek society as free men, Isaac, Pearo, and Orange reversed their fortunes, transforming themselves from slaves to captors.[37] Even after Indians instituted racial slavery in their own nations, some African Americans continued to seek aid from them. When asking a Lower Creek headman for sanctuary in 1803, a group of black men tried to shed their former status as slaves, saying "they did not know how to work but give them guns and go to war they knowed how to do that."[38]

By the turn of the century, however, black runaways rarely found the freedom they sought. In 1803, East Floridian Wiley Thompson journeyed to the house of William Kinnard, brother of Jack Kinnard, who resided on the lower Chattahoochee River. There, Thompson sought to recover black captives on behalf of his government. At Kinnard's house, he unexpectedly met several Mikasukis as well as William Augustus Bowles, who was passing through on his way back from the Upper Creeks. Bowles was an Anglo-American radical who attempted to place himself at the head of a republic populated by Creeks, Seminoles, African American runaways, and loyalists. Expressing anger over Thompson's mission, Bowles "said that he had denied that any should go into the Indian Land, he assured me that I run the risque of losing my hair on presenting myself there on such business." Bowles had overestimated his influence among the Lower Creeks, for Jack Kinnard quickly called him down, saying "if he meddled with [Thompson] his hair should pay for it." Furthermore, Kinnard pointed out that "Bowles's waiting man," Jack Philips, had himself run away from the Pensacola trading firm that owned him. Kinnard ordered his kinsmen to seize Philips, and Bowles attempted to hold onto his companion even while the Kinnards beat him. When Bowles appealed to visiting Mikasuki warriors to help him, "they sat still and did not say a word and the Canards took the negro and put him in Irons."[39]

Many of those seeking freedom in Indian country would be sorely disappointed, for Native people usually reenslaved runaways. One absconded slave, Cooper, described by a former master as a "prime likely young negro boy, 19 or 20 years old, bread to Cooking, washing, and Ironing, of Clothes," ran away to Creek country in 1793. Doubtlessly, Cooper hoped to live as a free man among the Creeks, but he did not succeed. At some point during the next three years, a group of Creeks captured Cooper and attempted to return him over to officials in exchange for a ransom. Lashing out against his captors, Cooper stabbed one of them with a piece of wood; shortly thereafter, the Creeks "put him to death by beating or otherwise."[40] In 1823, a similar incident occurred in the Choctaw Nation. Around February 20, Choctaws captured an enslaved man who had run away from his Kentucky master. Although clapped in irons, the man managed to escape, and he hid in Choctaw country for two weeks. A chief finally spotted the man and sent two warriors after him. Initially, the warriors attempted to persuade the runaway to come with them, but he refused and brandished a stick. Unwilling to risk injury, one of the Choctaws pulled out a tomahawk and, with a sharp blow to the head, killed the runaway. By this time, runaways and other people of African descent faced dwindling possibilities for inclusion in Native societies. Like Cooper and the unnamed runaway in Choctaw country, most were captured and resold to residents of Indian nations or ransomed to federal Indian agents.[41]

Fear and uncertainty often accompanied encounters between Indians and African Americans in the borderlands. In 1795, a Yuchi man camped near Tensaw shot and killed a slave of that town owned by Miguel Melton.

A Tensaw boy asked the Yuchi "why he had he killed the Negro." The Yuchi responded "that he had killed him because he is the same as a dog."[42] After an African American couple fled Tomas Comir's Mobile plantation, they encountered a Creek man near Tensaw. For unknown reasons—perhaps because the couple feared capture—they killed him. In retaliation, the Creek man's wife managed to grab a long knife and decapitate the male runaway. She nearly succeeded in doing the same to the woman, but another resident of the town restrained her. Although this episode represents an extreme, this was a time and place of great instability and frequent violence; Indians and African Americans did not necessarily see themselves as natural allies against white Southerners.[43]

Edmond Flint, an African American enslaved for many years in the Choctaw Nation, asserted that bondage among Indians "was not different from slavery in the states": "There were humane and inhumane masters and occasionally some of the cruel and brutal type."[44] George Sanders, a former Cherokee slave, cast his experiences in a more positive light, saying, "While these old slave days were trying, and we went through many hardships, our Indian masters were very kind to us, and gave us plenty of good clothes to wear, and we always had plenty to eat."[45] In W.P.A. interviews conducted some sixty years after their emancipation, African Americans gave greatly varying accounts of their captivity under Indian masters: some praised their former masters and mistresses; others recalled cruelties; some, like Flint, found little to distinguish between white and Indian masters. There is no evidence to suggest that Indian masters sympathized with African American slaves as fellow people of color. Class, rather than race, may be a more useful prism through which to view masters of color. In addition to Indian masters, the antebellum South was also home to a small class of black slaveholders. Although some free people of color, like Denmark Vesey, worked to undermine slavery, most black and Indian masters did not. Their class and free status distinguished them from enslaved people.[46]

Although the narrowing of captivity clearly troubled some Indians, they were not conflicted about the institution in the same way as whites. To begin with, they lacked the paternalist culture that pervaded the non-Indian South. White men were absolute masters of their households, which included subordinate white relatives and slaves who fell into the category of fictive kin (though biological ties surely abounded). In addition to controlling his household's labor, an ideal patriarch also policed behavior and instructed his white and black family in morality and civility. Following the First Great Awakening, Christian fervor surged among whites and blacks, bringing them closer spiritually and leading many planters to provide increasingly elaborate justifications for slavery. In contrast to whites, Indians never maintained the fiction that slaves were part of the family. The status of individual slaves could change if captors adopted or married them, but owned people, as a whole, had always been defined by their lack of kin ties. Matrilineal power declined in the nineteenth century, and although some Indian planters favored paternalism, such an ideology was too foreign to be embraced with much enthusiasm. Christianity, too, divided Indians from other Southerners. Before removal, only a small minority of Southern Indians converted. When Moravian missionaries spoke to Anne Shorey McDonald, the elderly Cherokee woman explained that her reservations related mostly to her status as a slaveholder. McDonald feared that she could not become a true Christian because "she still might not be able to treat her Negroes in a friendly way all the time, which would after all be her duty. Indeed, it could even happen that she would err as much as punishing one or the other of them, because there were some of them who brought her much displeasure through their evil life."[47]

Christianity emerged as an important fault line separating Indians and African Americans. Most Indians preferred Native spiritual practices and remained indifferent to the missionaries' messages. When Moravian missionaries Johann Christian Burckhard and Karsten Petersen visited Creek country in the early nineteenth century, they found few interested in the good news. Impatient Indians were likely to roll their eyes, replying, "Oh, yes, yes, yes, I know it." Burckhard and Petersen were shocked to discover that whites living in Indian country showed a similar lack of enthusiasm. Timothy Barnard, a longtime trader who had a Yuchi family, "called Moses and David murderers and scoundrels and said that he was better than all of them had been." Another missionary described federal Indian agent Benjamin Hawkins, who lived among the Creeks, as "a religiously lost person." Phil, one of Hawkins's slaves, reported that he had prayed for his master but was doubtful his prayers had done any good.[48] Missionaries learned that slaves like Phil were often their only eager listeners in Indian country. When preachers began to arrive in the Cherokee, Creek, Choctaw, and Chickasaw nations at the turn of the century, African Americans flocked to hear them. In 1799, Reverend Joseph Bullen came to the Chick-asaw Nation, and one elderly enslaved woman told him that she had trav-eled thirty miles to hear his sermon, saying that she had long lived in a "heathen land" and was "very glad to hear the blessed gospel." As mission-aries established churches, African Americans often made up the majority of members and took on active roles, translating the gospel into Indian languages, heading prayer groups, and contributing to services by reading passages.[49]

Whereas African Americans embraced Christianity, many Indians saw it as a form of imperialism or as a tool of insurrection for their slaves. Rev-erend Lee Compere, who ran a mission on the Tallapoosa River, reported that many Indians were opposed to "preaching of the gospel especially to the poor unfortunate blacks." Creeks, in particular, opposed Christian missions, which they demonstrated in an 1828 attack on Compere's home, which doubled as a church. As the Compere family and a group of slaves worshipped, a group of about twenty-five Creek men stormed in "under the pretense of searching for the Black people." The men bound the slaves with cords and belts and took them out into the yard "where they beat them unmercifully."[50] Most Indian masters used less violent means to re-strain their slaves. Planters like Cherokee Joseph Vann and Creek Alex Cornells simply forbade their slaves to attend services, assigning them Sunday work instead. Cornells explained that Christian slaves challenged his authority as well as their own condition, complaining that they "had already been made sullen and crazy by those who had preached to them."[51]

Slaves under Indian masters, like slaves everywhere, protested their con-dition through resistance. A number of African Americans fled their bondage in Indian nations to explore other opportunities. After the Span-ish seized Pensacola in 1781, African Americans from other parts of the South started to trickle in, seeking freedom under the banner of religious sanctuary. In December of that year, a group of four runaway slaves ar-rived in Pensacola, asking for Spanish liberty papers from West Florida governor Arturo O'Neill. Three of the four had come from the Upper Creeks, and they reported that these Indians had taken them from Anglo-American masters some years earlier. O'Neill decided to give the men paying jobs at the town's docks. In part because of African Americans' demand, the Spanish revived their policy of religious sanctuary until 1790, when the royal decree was rescinded as part of the empire's attempt to protect slavery. Even after 1790, however, enslaved African Americans from Indian country continued to see Florida as their land of freedom. In 1795, John Galphin tried to recover his man Jean, whom he believed was living in East Florida under the alias "Simon." Seeking her freedom, Lucy, an enslaved woman belonging to Jack Kinnard, trekked from Kinchafoone on the Lower Chattahoochee to San Marcos de Apalache on the Gulf Coast.[52]

After the Chickamauga warrior White Man Killer and his party stormed John Pettigrew's boat, killing thirteen whites and taking twenty-two slaves captive, White Man Killer did not prove to be a benevolent liberator. On the contrary, according to one of his African American captives, he was a cruel master. In the years that followed the June 1794 attack, White Man Killer moved from the Chickamauga region farther west to the St. Francis River, resisting the federal government's efforts to redeem the black captives he took on the Pettigrew boat. At the St. Francis, Caddos, who resented Cherokee encroachment, killed White Man Killer. Unfortunately for his slaves, this turn of events provided no relief, for White Man Killer's kin, they claimed, also abused them and sold their children away. In June 1800, about six years after their initial capture, a family of six African Americans led by a 45-year-old matriarch arrived at Fort Pickering at Chickasaw Bluffs. They told commanding officer Zebulon Pike their story and appealed to him for protection. Dramatizing their plight, the group claimed that White Man Killer's kin would kill them if they returned. These captives' actions betray their desperation; in turning to the army, they knew that these white men would almost certainly send them to Pettigrew's heirs. Indeed, after some research, Pike placed the group with Jerrard Brandon, who claimed to be John Pettigrew's closest kin. Rather than remain among Indians at St. Francis or flee to parts unknown, this African American family chose to take their chances with a relative of their former white master.[53]

The Pettigrew captives were not the only ones who voluntarily returned to white masters. When Creeks attacked a southern Georgia plantation in May of 1793, they took ten slaves, "one of whom made his escape after killing as he says the Indian who had him in [his] possession." An enslaved boy named John White undertook a long and dangerous journey to return to his former master in Savannah. After being taken by the Creeks in 1797, he escaped and headed west to the Mississippi River, where he found passage on a boat bound for New Orleans. During his meeting there with Spanish officials, White said that he purposely escaped from the Creeks and told the governor the name of his master. Ned and Sam, two young men taken from the Oconee region, became slaves in the Creek Nation. Trader Timothy Barnard related that the men "told him to whom they belonged and were desirous of returning to their master."[54] In 1800, Bartholomew Shaumburgh, commander of Fort Stoddert in Mississippi Territory, wrote that many slaves who lived in the Creek Tensaw region applied to him for help. These African Americans revealed that Creeks had captured them, and many wished to be "restored to their original masters." Perhaps ties of kinship pulled them back to the families they had left behind; perhaps they found Indian country, with relatively fewer African Americans, an isolating place. Some slaves who visited Shaumburgh feared that their masters would sell them to Spanish masters in West Florida or Louisiana. In the Creek Nation or in Georgia, slavery was slavery, dehumanizing and unpredictable, and African Americans in the contested South made the best out of the limited options they had.[55]

By the early nineteenth century, nearly all captives were black, and, in many ways, bondage in Indian country mirrored the slavery practiced by their white Southern neighbors. But the transformation was not complete, nor did it happen overnight. If escalating racism encouraged Indians to distance themselves from those of African descent, kin ties pulled many back. Indian societies, and even individuals, maintained contradictory attitudes about race.

This discrepancy between ideology and practice was not unique to Native Americans. White Southerners, too, sometimes found it difficult to reconcile racial slavery with the intimacy it inevitably created. Whites frequently engaged in sex across the color line, and a small minority acknowledged their mixed-race children. Especially in Caribbean-influenced places like South Carolina and Louisiana, elite mulattos emerged as a distinct group allied by economic interest—and blood—to the white master class. Even when Southern states tightened manumission restrictions after 1800, masters manipulated trust law to give relatives and other favored slaves *de facto* freedom. Among the most notable mixed-race children of privilege was Amanda America Dickson. Born in Georgia in 1849, Dickson was the daughter of planter David Dickson and an enslaved woman named Julia Frances Lewis who belonged to David's mother. Although technically a slave until emancipation, Amanda (called "Miss Mandy" at home) was reared in the Dickson household as her father's favorite. Upon David's death in 1885, Amanda inherited his estate, valued at $500,000, at a time when the average white Georgian owned less than $10 worth of property. The Dickson family's story, though exceptional, points to significant "gaps between the ideals white southerners often projected about themselves and their world and the substance of life on the ground in their society." Among whites, these inconsistencies sprang from the clash between two powerful ideologies—race and the family—as well as judges' reticence to limit masters' power in any way, even if masters used that power to undermine slavery.[56]

In the case of Native people, racial slavery was tempered by more inclusive aspects of captivity—including adoption and marriage. Their ambivalent attitudes toward black captives arose because their captivity continuum had, for centuries, been so broad and allowed for great flexibility in the treatment of the captured. Native women, who had long conferred kin ties through blood and ceremony, provided some of the more memorable rhetorical challenges to the theory of separate creations. During treaty negotiations in 1781, the Cherokee Women's Council addressed U.S. treaty commissioners. The Women's Council, composed of high-ranking members of the seven matrilineages, conferred on political matters and advised the National Council. Their leader, Nancy Ward, offered an alternative to the nativist view on race: "We the women of the Cherokee nation now speak to you. We are mothers, and have many sons, some of them warriors and beloved men. We call you also our sons. We have a right to call you so, because you are the sons of mothers, and all descended from the same woman at first. . . . Why should there be any difference among us? We live on the same land with you, and our people are mixed with white blood."[57] Ward harkened back to kinship as the font of identity, and, in what was perhaps an infusion of these Cherokee ideas with the Christian story of Adam and Eve, argued for monogenesis and universal kinship among all people. Intimacy, whether violent or peaceful, had created kin ties with people of European and African descent through captive adoption and marriage. Ward's acknowledgment of interracial sex and its legacy was echoed by a Creek woman whose son, Davy Cornells or Efau Tustunnuggee, was killed by Americans. Despite the tragedy, Levitia Cornells assured agent Benjamin Hawkins "of her friendship for the white people, being her own blood as well as the red." As the Cherokee National Council consolidated power, Nancy Ward, believing that a strong central government would best protect Cherokee autonomy, voluntarily disbanded the Women's Council around 1819. Ward and thousands of other Indian women ceded clan power for the sake of their people, but many doubtlessly worried about the changes taking place: What were the costs of creating exclusionary Indian nations? What of in-between people? Ward and Cornells realized that race, at the margins, was an unsustainable illusion that required a revolutionary revision of their peoples' past.[58]

Not all blacks in Indian country were slaves. In the early nineteenth century, Moravian missionaries met Suckey Randon, whom they described as a "mulatto." Suckey had likely been taken captive from Georgia some decades earlier. David Randon, the son of Euro-American trader Peter Randon and his Creek wife, was Suckey's master. David's participation in the post-Revolutionary border wars suggests that he also may have been her original captor. David and Suckey became lovers and had five daughters: Lavinia (called "Viney"), Polly, Betsey, Marcy, and Kate. In 1798, David appeared before agent Benjamin Hawkins to give Suckey (whom he called "my Wife") and children their liberty "as fully & completely as if she and they had originally been free." For a lucky few African American captives, marriage remained a path to freedom for themselves and their children. To the visiting missionaries, Suckey Randon certainly seemed free, though she may have missed the company of fellow Christians, who were few and far between in Creek country. According to the missionaries, "She gladly consented [to a service] and added that she would like to hear the Word of God."[59]

Indians grafted ideas about race onto their captivity practices, but the process was slow and uneven, leaving those of African descent in an ambiguous position. The case of an African American woman named Molly illustrates how Cherokees negotiated changing ideas about identity. Just before the Revolution, Sam Dent, a white trader, beat his Cherokee wife to death. Fearing retaliation by her Deer clan kin, Dent fled. In Augusta, Georgia, Dent purchased Molly and offered her to the Deer clan in his wife's stead. Fortunately for Dent, the clan accepted his proposal and adopted Molly, calling her "Chickaw." Chickaw settled into Cherokee society, married, and bore two sons. Several decades later, however, a white American woman brought a legal suit, claiming Chickaw and her sons as slaves. The increasing importance of race and the decreasing power of clans left the family vulnerable. However, Deer clan kin accompanied Chickaw and her sons to the Cherokee Supreme Court, which recognized their membership in the nation and granted them protection. As this case demonstrates, people of African descent drew on more traditional, inclusive elements of Native culture, such as kinship, as they attempted to retain their status in changing Indian societies.[60]

The actions of African Americans also attest to the greater freedom they continued to see in Indian country. While some black captives attempted to flee Indian nations, others refused to return to the United States. Ned, who probably came to the Creek Nation as a runaway, became a slave in the household of Thomas Marshall, a white trader with an Indian family. When Ned's former master John Bard attempted to redeem him, Ned "declared that he would die before he would be brought out of the [Creek] nation." Fearing that Ned would fulfill this threat, Bard sold Ned to the Marshall family for $250. Among the Cherokees, another enslaved man named Ned cut his own throat when he heard that he and his family would be sold to white planters in Natchez, Mississippi Territory. This Ned, though rendered mute by the damage to his vocal cords, survived and the next day was forced to board a Natchez-bound wagon. His three eldest sons, however, managed to run away. It is unclear whether Ned and his family sought to escape bondage under whites or whether, like many other African Americans of their time, they feared the notoriously harsh enslavement of the expanding cotton frontier.[61]

Indian nations were still more inclusive than the Anglo-American South, where African American bondage had been the dominant form of unfree labor since the late seventeenth century. As Southern states further restricted the rights of free people of color in the early nineteenth century, they, too, looked to Native people for protection. William Cooper, a free man who married an enslaved woman, worked hard to earn and preserve his family's freedom, and he chose to do so in Indian country. Cooper called himself "a portugesee," but white contemporaries questioned his racial status, claiming that he looked more like "a Mulato." Cooper worked as an overseer at Big Black, a frontier plantation on the Black Warrior River owned by John Turnbull, a prominent white trader who had fathered a number of children with a Chickasaw woman.[62] During his time at Big Black, William Cooper became involved with an enslaved mulatto woman named Medlong. Cooper saved his wages and, in 1793, purchased Medlong from Turnbull "for the purpose of giving her her freedom." They married and, over the years, produced five children: Kitty, William, John, Abel, and Elizabeth.[63]

When John Turnbull died, his white wife, Catherine, attempted to move all the slaves at Big Black to another of Turnbull's plantations, but William Cooper, explaining that he had purchased Medlong's freedom, refused to release his wife. Catherine Turnbull hired an attorney to look into the matter, and the Cooper family, fearing enslavement, fled. They turned to Turnbull's Chickasaw sons George and William, who had both married Choctaw women and lived in the Chickasaw-Choctaw borderlands, a place where American law could not easily follow and where racial categories were more fluid. In Indian country, a diverse coalition of friends and allies, including George and William Turnbull (who were also heirs to their father's estate), traders James Allen, John Pitchlynn, and Turner Brashears, and federal Indian agent Silas Dinsmoore protected the Coopers and attested to their freedom. Turnbull's sons employed Cooper, probably as an overseer, and Choctaw families hired out several of the Cooper children as wage laborers.[64]

The Coopers were not an isolated case; many other free families of African descent resided in Indian nations. A town in the eastern portion of the Choctaw Nation was home to a diverse community that included free blacks as well as people of mixed African-Choctaw descent. From Creek country in 1832, census-takers commissioned by the U.S. government struggled to categorize the diverse group of people who resided there: How should they count the black wives of Creek men? Where to place people of mixed Indian-African descent? Racial categories, messy throughout the South, were even more fluid among Native Americans. Mixed-race families like the Coopers took advantage of that fluidity, finding the freedom that eluded them elsewhere in the region.[65]

As Native nations incorporated race as a primary category of identity, they confronted their own complicated past. Centuries of color-blind captive adoption and intermarriage resulted in early-nineteenth-century Indian communities that were phenotypically diverse. The complexions of Southern Indians ran the gamut, ranging from fair to coppery to dark. Jane Hill, who taught in a Creek mission school, reported of Creek student Mary Ann Bettis, "her mother is the daughter of a black woman her grandfather was half white & half indian. Mary Ann's father was white & she is the fairest female I have seen in this nation." When Bettis's family came to visit her, Hill was shocked to discover that they were "nearly all of them extremely dark people & her mother has some children who have black fathers."[66] In the early 1840s, hundreds of Choctaws who had

avoided removal and remained in Mississippi sought access to lands allot-
ted to them in their removal treaty, and these claimants first had to establish that they were, in fact, Choctaw citizens. U.S. officials were confounded by the appearances of many of the people they met. A woman
named Hannah Wilson, described by officials as "very fair," told them she
was "a full blood." Another witness, Pah-lubbee, attributed Wilson's fair
complexion to her white father. Sisters Hotemiza and Peggy "to all appearance 3/4 negro" were the daughters of a Choctaw woman named
Bah-pissah and an African American man. Officials also reckoned that
Jim Tom looked very dark, but he, too, was the child of a Choctaw
woman. By rights of matrilineal descent, all these claimants were fully
Choctaw for they were the children of Choctaw women, but the increasing importance of race put their status into question.[67] By the 1820s, Choctaws developed two labels for people like Hannah, Hotemiza, Peggy, and
Jim: *itibapishi toba*, meaning "to become a brother or sister," or the less
sanguine term *issish iklanna*, signifying "half-blood."[68]

As the Choctaw terms suggest, Native attitudes about people of mixed
ancestry varied. In practice, they treated some as brothers and sisters and
others as something less. Although Jim Tom's partial African ancestry was
obvious, he was rather lucky, for his neighbors called him "A Choctaw
citizen." Both Hannah Wilson and Jim Tom married "full bloods" (that is,
people who were recognized as fully Choctaw).[69] Choctaw sisters Molly
and Lucy, born to a Choctaw woman and an enslaved African American
man sometime before 1817, were acknowledged as Choctaws by their
neighbors. According to testimony, "it was the general understanding of
the neighborhood that Molly and Lucy were the children of [Oonnah-
hoka]."[70] In Indian country—and, indeed, throughout the South—local
ties protected free people of African descent. Fellow community members (some of whom were doubtlessly kin) could identify them and vouch
for their freedom. In the Native case, despite the decline of clan power,
matrilineal kinship traditions persisted, and those born to Native mothers
generally fared better than those born to black mothers. Under the Cherokee Constitution of 1827, for example, the children of black women could
not become citizens, but "the posterity of Cherokee women by all free
men" could.[71]

Despite social and sometimes legal prohibitions against interracial sex,
Native people continued to cross the color line. They had ample opportunities to do so, for blacks and Indians mingled in a variety of contexts:

slaves hosted holiday parties in their cabins, inviting Indian friends over for raucous drinking and dancing fetes that sometimes lasted days; a festive atmosphere also accompanied stickball matches, which were well-attended by both Indians and African Americans; Indians who went to Christian churches prayed alongside (and sometimes under the direction of) black congregants; finally, blacks and Indians worked together, and all save the wealthiest masters shared their houses with slaves. Opportunities for intimacy, sexual and otherwise, abounded. Oral histories maintained by Indians' slaves and their ancestors suggest that many Indians, particularly Native men, acted on such opportunities. In W.P.A. interviews, freedpeople revealed that sex between Indian masters and their black slaves was common, and the children of these unions readily acknowledged their multiracial ancestry.[72]

By the 1810s, Indian men who fathered children with black women must have known of the dwindling possibility of inclusion for their descendants. Around 1811, Cherokee Oowanahtekiskee fathered a son with an enslaved woman belonging to the assistant Indian agent Evan Austill, who lived nearby. Eleven years later, Oowanahtekiskee purchased his son Moses from the Austill estate and appeared before the National Council to acknowledge Moses as "my true & begotten son." The council confirmed the boy's freedom, but gave no word on Moses's citizenship.[73]

Another Cherokee, Tarsekayahke or Shoe Boots, followed a similar path. A prolific warrior who participated in the nativist movement and later became, in the words of the Cherokee agent, "a man of very considerable property," Shoe Boots had children with two of his female captives. The first was Clarinda Ellington, a white teen taken by Shoe Boots during an attack on the Kentucky settlement of Morgan's Station in 1793. As a master, Shoe Boots disregarded the line between consensual and coercive sex, arguing that "he saved her life at the time she was taken, & therefore thinks he has a right to keep her as his wife."[74] Over the next ten years, the couple had two sons and a daughter. Clarinda, however, was unhappy and expressed a desire to take the children to visit kin in Kentucky. Though reluctant, Shoe Boots acquiesced. His reservations were well-founded, for Clarinda and the children never returned. After Ellington's departure, Shoe Boots turned to someone who already lived in his household, an enslaved black teen named Doll. Appearing before the National Council in 1824, Shoe Boots pleaded for the Cherokee Nation to recognize his children by Doll as citizens, saying, "knowing what property I have is to be divided Amongst the rest of my friends how can I think of them having boan of my bone and flesh of my flesh to be called their property . . . and for them and their offspring to Suffer for Generations yet unborn is a thought of to[o] great Magnitude for me to remain Silent any longer." The council granted Shoe Boots's eloquent plea but ordered him not to have any more children by Doll, a warning that Shoe Boots did not heed. In all, Doll and Shoe Boots had five children, only three of whom became citizens.[75]

Since the late eighteenth century, Indians had thought of themselves as a race of people separate from whites and blacks. As their economies changed and their polities became centralized, another affiliation became increasingly important to them: national citizenship. Community, once firmly grounded in kinship ties, was now defined by a more complex and exclusionary constellation of factors.

Continuing a process that began in the late eighteenth century, political and economic changes further weakened clan structure. To facilitate their new commercial enterprises, Native people altered an ancient settlement pattern, one that had been in place since the Mississippian era. In the words of Chickasaw agent John McKee, "the indians here are settling out of their old towns, fencing their plantations, and collected round them stocks of hogs & Cattle." All across the region, families moved out of their towns and into the countryside, spreading out along the river valleys. This dispersal reflected—and reinforced—the erosion of clan power. Formerly, matriarchs presided over and nominally owned a complex of houses in which their extended clan kin resided. Matriclans had also controlled the farms that passed from one female generation to next. Once centralized governments assumed control over national territory, clans were no longer the loci of landholding, and having lost their dominion over matters of war and justice, they slowly declined in importance. The civilization policy promulgated by the U.S. government, aided by population dispersal, vaunted the importance of the nuclear, patrilineal family, a shift that happened slowly throughout the course of the nineteenth century. Gradually, national governments stripped the clans of their economic and political power until they were left only religious duties.[76]

Throughout the early nineteenth century, chiefs continued to consolidate power in centralized governments. Cherokee leaders went the furthest. Beginning in 1808, the National Council wrote down and printed the laws they passed, gradually developing a written legal code to replace informal, clan-based justice. In a series of laws passed between 1820 and 1827, the National Council made the Cherokee Nation a constitutional republic, complete with a bicameral legislature, district and superior court system, executive branch, and bureaucracy. In 1818, the Creek National Council wrote down the eleven laws they had passed over the past two decades, and they continued to add more in the years leading up to removal. The Choctaw Nation had long been divided into three districts, each ruled by a hereditary chief. In the early 1820s, district chiefs and their councils began to assume legal prerogatives formerly belonging to clans. Despite this trend, Choctaws were reluctant to invest authority in a centralized state, and Northwestern district chief Greenwood LeFlore's 1826 attempt to unite the Choctaws under a single constitution met with failure. In 1829, the neighboring Chickasaws composed a short list of laws and empowered a body of 100 lighthorse police to enforce it.[77]

The move toward centralization spurred a constitutional revolt among the Choctaws and a civil war in Creek country, but many Indians, even cultural conservatives, willingly acceded certain liberties to their governments. Without centralization, they realized, local leaders and minority factions could cede land. Across Native North America, this scenario played out again and again as self-serving chiefs like Doublehead accepted bribes and sold territory without the knowledge or consent of others. In 1803, leaders of the Cherokee, Creek, Choctaw, and Chickasaw nations signed a pact not to cede any more land, and various principal chiefs renewed the agreement in 1804, 1805, 1807, and 1810. Mohawk John Norton, for one, was impressed: "from the great extent of Territory which I saw yet in the possession of the Southern Nations, I concluded that . . . their Chiefs must have shown more steadiness and unanimity than those to the Northward, or they could not have obtained so well marked a Boundary, nor have retained so extensive a Territory." Yet, those efforts were not enough. Demands for Native land reached a fevered pitch in the post-1812 cotton boom era, when many Americans began to call for Indian removal. According to Cherokee John Ridge, "At length the eyes of our Nation were opened to see their folly." By the 1810s, many Southern Indians committed themselves to preserving their homeland and autonomy, whatever the cost. Refuting the possibility of removal, Creek Cho-chus Miko avowed, "We are free and independent and we shall hold on to our rights as long as we can draw breath."[78]

Answering the crises created by American imperialism, Indians responded by reimagining their nations. Beginning in the seventeenth century, Europeans and Indians alike had referred to Native polities as "nations." The nations that Indians built atop the ashes of Mississippian
chiefdoms were kin-based confederacies, wherein all members were related through blood or ceremony. The bounds of these nations were elas-
tic, allowing for the incorporation of blacks, whites, and Indians. Inclusion was the genius that ensured the growth of the nations during the
eighteenth century, but that model no longer worked in the nineteenth
century when Native people faced an increasingly powerful American
state with a voracious demand for land. Building on indigenous notions of
nationhood, Native leaders also incorporated aspects of republican ideology, redefining their nations as territorially bounded polities populated by
individual citizens. As racial exclusion, in particular, became a component of national identity, people of African descent were no longer welcome members.[79]

In the early nineteenth century, as Native nations developed written
laws, they codified ideas about race that had begun to take shape decades
earlier. The Cherokee, Creek, Chickasaw, and Choctaw nations attempted
to restrict white settlement in their nations to those legitimately married
to Indians, but focused most of their efforts on African Americans. Indian
nations, like Southern states, gradually strengthened slavery through leg-
islation.[80] The Cherokees and Creeks, more affected by encroachment
and therefore under greater pressure to centralize in the pre-removal era,
developed the most elaborate laws. One of the first eleven laws enacted
by the Creek National Council in 1818 stated that "if a Negro kill an Indian, the Negro shall suffer death;" however, "if an Indian kill a Negro he
shall pay the owner the value." The law presumed that every "Negro" was
a slave, and it commodified those of African—but not European or
Indian—descent. A few years later, Creeks also officially outlawed the enslavement of "Prisoners taken in war," making black slaves, whether purchased or born into slavery, the only legitimate chattel. Both nations,
anxious to maintain racial boundaries, attempted to police sexuality:
Cherokees outlawed marriage between Indians and blacks, and Creeks
imposed a fine on those who chose to do so "as it is a disgrace to our Nation for our people to marry a negro." They also prohibited free blacks and
runaways from entering their nations and restricted slaves' ability to trade,
make contracts, and hold property. In 1820, the Cherokees set up a slave

patrol, which operated independently of the lighthorse. On the subject of citizenship, Cherokee law was more explicit than Creek. In a nod to matrilineality, descendants of black women could not become citizens, but "the posterity of Cherokee women by all free men" could. Those visibly of African-Cherokee descent, however, were barred from holding office.[81] The Choctaws did not develop slave codes until after their removal to Indian Territory, and the Chickasaws came under Choctaw law when, in a strange twist of fate, they were forced to incorporate with their old foes after removal. Late 1830s Choctaw laws (which also applied to Chickasaws) barred marriage and even sex with African Americans, restricted black emigration, and prohibited a slave from learning to read or carrying a gun without his owner's permission. The Choctaw constitution of 1838 authorized the General Council "to naturalize and adopt as citizens of this Nation any Indian or descendant of other Indian tribes, except a negro or descendant of a negro."[82]

Originating in the crises of the late eighteenth century, racial slavery as practiced by Indians grew more entrenched in the early nineteenth century as increasingly centralized Native governments protected and promoted the institution. Censuses taken in the 1830s, just prior to removal, reveal a small but growing class of Native slaveholders. The largest concentration of slaves lived in Chickasaw country, where 1,200 African Americans dwelled among some 5,000 Chickasaws. The much larger Choctaw Nation, with a population of about 19,500, owned the fewest slaves, only 521. The 1835 Cherokee census (which did not count thousands of Cherokees who had already removed) recorded nearly 1,600 black slaves and 16,542 Cherokees. The Creeks, numbering around 22,700, held 902 slaves. These Native slaveholders, who included elites and an emerging middle class, had a good deal in common with white masters: larger slaveholders produced staple goods like cotton for the burgeoning trans-Atlantic market, while smallholders used enslaved labor to supplement that of their household; both groups used legal codes and social mores to enforce racial hierarchies; white and Native masters alike worried over runaways, slave resistance, and protection of their private property. By 1809, when Joseph Coleman petitioned other white planters to help Chickasaw George Colbert recover a runaway slave, Coleman called Colbert "Our *Red Friend*," pointing out that slaveholding linked white and Indian elites. Yet, slavery as practiced by Native people was not merely imported from their white neighbors. Rather, two different captivity traditions merged in Indian country, where Native rules of kinship and centuries of captive marriage and adoption confounded racial ideology and, for some, mitigated the severity of bondage.[83]

Whereas once the captivity spectrum had been broad and targeted a wide range of enemy groups, it now focused solely on African Americans and subjected them to a very narrow range of fates, namely transgenerational slavery or sale to another master. Although the process was piecemeal and contested, Indian societies became more closed, largely excluding those of African descent. As Native nations reimagined themselves in the early nineteenth century, they stressed their limited citizenship and territorial sovereignty, simultaneously developing an historical amnesia about the Indian slave trade and distancing themselves from their inclusive past. This reimagination was what led Chickasaw governor Douglas H. Johnston, later in the nineteenth century, to assert, "Our people have no prejudice against the Negro as such and have always treated him, freedman as well as slave, with kindness and forbearance; but we do object to his classification as a member of our tribe . . . keep our rolls pure, so that in the future, as in the past, a Chickasaw can hold his head aloft among the people of the earth and say, 'I am an original American and a Chickasaw.'"[84] By the nineteenth century, membership in the Cherokee, Creek, Choctaw, and Chickasaw nations rested on notions of aboriginal descent, race, and freedom from slavery. Among the five major Southern Indian nations, only the Seminoles retained a wider range of captivity practices and demonstrated a willingness to embrace people of African descent.

8

SEMINOLES AND AFRICAN AMERICANS

As other Southern Indians began to hold black captives in hereditary bondage, the Seminoles chose a unique path. They created a pluralistic society, making room for diverse groups of black and Indian newcomers. Although Seminoles targeted and held African American captives, they did not codify racial slavery. Instead, they looked to the Native past to provide a way to absorb outsiders. Drawing on the chiefly political organization of their ancestors, Seminoles welcomed African Americans as junior members of their chiefdoms, granting them protection in exchange for tribute. The relative freedom that this system afforded African Americans, however, increasingly isolated the Seminoles from the rest of the South, even from other Native Americans, leading outsiders to see them as a major threat to the burgeoning plantation economy.

Most of those who came to be called Seminoles were from Creek country. Following the destruction of the Florida mission system in the first decade of the eighteenth century, some residents of the Flint and Chattahoochee watersheds moved farther south. They did so with the enthusiastic approval of Spanish Florida officials who correctly anticipated that these Indian pioneers could afford the colony military protection from the region's other imperial and Native powers. Creek emigrants began to occupy land vacated by the defeated Apalachees, calling the place *talwa leske* (now Tallahassee), meaning "old fields." They also founded settlements along the Apalachicola and Suwannee rivers, Lake Miccosukee, and the Alachua Prairie. When John Pope traversed the Creek Nation in 1791, he recounted a Creek oral tradition about the settlement of Florida: "the *Creeks* after a long and bloody Contest of 20 Years, exterminated, and repeopled the deserted Villages by slow Emigrations from their own victorious Tribes." Indeed, in 1763, when the British gained Florida from Spain and began to buy tracts of land from surviving mission groups, the Creeks objected, "deny[ing] that these Indians had any right to the lands." By right of conquest, the Creeks claimed the land as their own.

The earliest Creek emigrants to Florida were an ethnic minority within the nation. Residents of what is today southern and central Georgia, most of them spoke the Hitchiti dialect and were derogatorily called *istinko* by Muskogee-proper speakers. Within a few decades, these wayward Hitchitis became increasingly independent. The main body of Creeks began to label them *isti semoli* or "wild men." Just as untamed others could be incorporated into the Creek Nation through adoptive ritual and acculturation, so too could those who refused to participate in Creek government and ceremonies become "wild." Indian agent Benjamin Hawkins explained, "They are called *wild*, because they left their old towns and made irregular settlements in this country to which they were invited by the plenty of game, the mildness of the climate, the richness of the soil, and the abundance of food for cattle and horses." George Stiggins, a Creek of Natchez descent, wrote that a Seminole was "a stray": "Any beast that has strayed from the original flock or fold is called a Seminola."[1]

Chief Cowkeeper was the first to promote Seminole autonomy. A Hitchiti-speaker from the Lower Creek town of Oconee, Cowkeeper moved in the 1750s to the Alachua Prairie near what is now Gainesville. There, the aptly named chief enjoyed the lifestyle of a prosperous cattle rancher, which included the service of both Indian and black slaves. The chief once hosted naturalist William Bartram, treating his guest to "excellently well barbecued" beef ribs. Bartram described Cowkeeper as "a tall well made man, very affable and cheerful . . . his eyes lively and full of fire, his countenance manly and placid, yet ferocious." At the 1765 Treaty of Picolata, Cowkeeper, flush with wealth and success, informed Florida's governor James Grant that the Creeks could not speak for him or his people.[2]

After the initial Hitchiti migrations of the early- to mid-eighteenth century, three major waves of Native groups followed. In the 1780s and 1790s, as citizens of Georgia clamored for Creek land, discontented Creeks sought refuge from their American antagonists in the decidedly more placid land of the Seminoles. The second wave was composed of Red Sticks, who, after defeat, wished to settle beyond the reach of rival Creek leaders who had made the peace with the United States. Finally, the third wave arrived in the 1830s as the Creeks faced forced removal from their homeland. Attempting to find the peace and prosperity that had become increasingly elusive in the Creek Nation, the emigrants formed an ethnically heterogeneous and politically decentralized nation farther south. Each of the latter three emigrant groups had deep grievances with the United States, and they brought to Seminole country a distrust of all things American. These successive waves of new Seminoles renewed their countrymen's commitment to remaining a people apart. By the nineteenth century, Seminoles included the Hitchiti-speaking Mikasukis, Upper Creek refugees, Yuchis, and what Americans called "Spanish Indians." This last group probably included Calusas and Tekestas, the Native people of Florida's southern peninsula. These Spanish Indians had intermarried with Cubans, and many worked on Gulf Coast fishing boats.[3]

Seminole towns and sites. Map by Philip Schwartzberg.

War-weary Creeks were not the only people seeking asylum in Florida. Freedom-seeking slaves from Carolina began to arrive in the late seventeenth century, and in 1693, Spain's King Charles II issued a royal proclamation offering freedom to Catholic converts. Word of the proclamation spread quickly throughout Carolina plantations, and African runaways trickled into the colony, where they established the free black town and militia post Gracia Real de Santa Teresa de Mose. As Georgia governor James Wright saw it, the Spanish protected "run away Slaves, who as soon as they get there throw themselves into the hands & protection of the Priests, and are deem'd by them as Freemen." Although the policy was discontinued when the English took possession of Florida in 1763, the Spaniards revived sanctuary in 1783. Capitalizing on imperial rivalries, enslaved people of Carolina and Georgia looked not northward for their freedom, but farther south.[4]

Under pressure from the United States and attempting to protect the growing plantation economy in East Florida, the Spanish crown rescinded sanctuary in 1790. Thereafter, Florida officials cooperated with American slaveholders by catching and returning fugitive slaves. African Americans continued to arrive in Florida, but in the 1790s, they began to seek their freedom among the Seminoles. East Floridian Jesse Dupont declared that his slaves began to escape around 1791, when two men ran away to Seminole country "and an Indian Negro Stole a wench and Child and since She has been amongst the Indians she has had a Second." In 1808, a resident of St. Augustine petitioned the governor to pressure the Seminoles into giving up his man Ysidoro, whom he felt sure was living among the Alachuas. Slaves from South Carolina and Georgia also attempted to join the Seminoles, though the Creeks sometimes caught the fugitives en route; an enslaved man belonging to Georgian Elijah Walkers was twice apprehended in the Creek Nation.[5]

With Florida's closure of sanctuary, Seminole country became the new locus of black freedom in the region. While the other major Southern Indian nations began to pursue black slavery, political centralization, and a new economy, Seminoles drew on culturally conservative elements of Native culture and incorporated African Americans as valued members of their communities. Together, they created a new society, one that increasingly isolated them from other Southerners, white and Native. But Seminole country was not utopia. Nativism was popular among Seminoles, and the storyteller who provided the most elaborate theory of separate creations was not a Chickasaw or Cherokee planter, but a Mikasuki chief named Neamathla. Though less oppressive than the planter societies emerging in the interior South, Seminole society was hierarchical, composed of allied but unequal groups.

While Seminoles welcomed runaways, they also captured African Americans in warfare, and bought and sold slaves. As chiefs began to accumulate wealth through ranching, they used cattle as a medium of exchange. According to one visitor, Seminoles were "in the habit of purchasing slaves with cattle, when they were rich in the latter species of property."[6] Around 1810 in the town of Picolata, Reading Blunt sold Sarah, an African American woman, to the family of Chief Bowlegs for forty steers, the equivalent of $800. Edward Wanton, longtime trader among the Seminoles, explained, "At that period it was usual for the Indians to rate all negroes on sale at this rate of forty head of beef cattle." If Wanton's recollection of forty steers is accurate, then Seminoles thought that African American women captives were much more valuable than Euro-American ones; just seven years earlier, chiefs Payne and Kinache deemed ten cows an appropriate payment for a teenaged white woman.[7] An 1802 bill of sale records Chief Kinache's purchase of an African American man named Catalina from Bahamian trader Richard Powers "in consideration of the sum of four Hundred Spanish Milld Dollars." After Anglo-Americans planters tried to overthrow the colony of East Florida during the Rebellion of 1795 and the Patriot War of 1812–1813, Spanish officials confiscated much of the dissidents' property, including slaves, and sold it at auction; Seminoles were among the buyers.[8]

Like other Southern Indians, Seminoles accumulated private property, and elites passed down enslaved African Americans and their descendants to relatives. Upon his death around 1790, Falehigee willed his slaves, Sally, Hannah, Tyler, and Tom, to his brother Will. When Will died ten years later, his nephew Econchatta Miko inherited the Africans. By the late 1830s, Econchatta Miko owned twenty-one African Americans, most of whom descended from Falehigee's original four. Harriet Bowlegs, grand-niece of Cowkeeper and daughter of Chief Bowlegs, inherited black captives from her father and from her sister, Sanathlaih-Kee. By the time she moved to Indian Territory in 1838, she owned sixteen African American slaves.[9]

Seminoles maintained traditional captivity practices longer than other Indians, continuing, for example, to capture whites like the Bonnelli family at the turn of the nineteenth century. Such episodes, however, were on the decline. By the early nineteenth century, Seminoles only rarely captured whites, and the First Seminole War (1817–1818) produced the region's last white captives. The war officially commenced on November 21, 1817, when U.S. forces under General Edmund P. Gaines destroyed the Mikasuki village of Fowltown. Just over a week later, as an open boat commanded by R. W. Scott ascended the Apalachicola, Seminoles under Homathle Miko struck back. They killed the boat's fifty passengers and took one soldier's wife, Elizabeth Stewart, as a captive. In December 1817, Seminole forces captured Edmund Doyle and William Hambly as well as Hambly's wife and Hambly's sister-in-law. Doyle and Hambly, merchants from Pensacola-based Panton, Leslie, & Company who had traded among the Seminoles, had been providing Americans with intelligence, including, the Seminoles suspected, the locations of Seminole and Black Seminole towns. Separating them from the Hambly women, Mikasuki warriors took Doyle and William Hambly to several Seminole towns, where chiefs deliberated on the captives' fate. Ultimately, they decided to imprison the traders at the old Spanish fort, San Marcos de Apalache, where Doyle and the Hambly remained until late March 1818, when the U.S. Navy liberated them. The Hambly women, who were redeemed at about the same time, spent their captivity in Seminole villages. As Mrs. Hambly later suggested, the Seminoles may have preserved the women in order to ransom them, although Hambly's sister became the slave of a Black Seminole named Jay Renis, who held her as a "wife." Elizabeth Stewart, held for only five months, was freed when Jackson's troops invaded a village of refugee Red Sticks on Econfina Creek in April 1818. Stewart had been the captive of Yellow Hair, and although she left behind no memoirs, Creeks serving with Jackson's army claimed "that Yellow Hair treated her with great kindness and respect."[10]

Elizabeth Stewart, Edmund Doyle, and the Hamblys were the last white captives held by Southern Indians. Their Seminole captors divided them according to gender, sending the men off to San Marcos and retaining the women at their own villages. The captivity of Mrs. Hambly's unnamed sister, recorded briefly in the diary of a U.S. Army officer who helped redeem her, is particularly intriguing, since she became the sexual partner of a Black Seminole. Stewart and the Hambly women, like generations of female captives before them, crossed cultural boundaries in ways that male captives did not, for their captors saw them as less threatening and

more assimilable. As for Edmund Doyle and William Hambly, their captors spared their lives and forced them to perform tasks such as translating
between the Seminoles and their British collaborators.[11]

The Seminole wars also produced several apocryphal captivity accounts, the most famous of which are attributed to Eunice Barber and
Mary Godfrey. These accounts meshed historical events with fictional-
ized narratives that stressed Seminole savagery. The Barber account, supposedly authored by a captured plantation mistress, was almost certainly
inspired by a real February 1817 Mikasuki attack on Israel Barber's plantation in Camden County, Georgia. The warriors, retaliating for the murder of three of their kinsmen, killed the overseer's wife and children and
took "two hundred dollars worth of negroe Clothing and working tools"
but seized no captives.[12] The Barber attack became infamous, prompting
Andrew Jackson to argue that the Seminoles "visited our frontier settlements with all the horrors of savage massacre; helpless women have been
butchered, and the cradle stained with the blood of innocence." The
Godfrey account, which places Mary Godfrey at the mercy of a Black
Seminole warrior, stressed her sexual vulnerability and presented a dangerous inversion of America's racial hierarchy. Descriptive and lurid, with
just enough historical detail to seem believable, the Barber (1818) and
Godfrey narratives (1836), served as anti-Seminole propaganda during,
respectively, the First and Second Seminole Wars. Although the testimony of Edmund Doyle and William Hambly circulated in American
newspapers, only a few scattered documents reference the captivity of
Elizabeth Stewart and the female Hamblys. The authentic voices of the
region's final white captives remained muted, drowned out by the unam-
biguous fictive accounts that urged Americans to fulfill their imperial
destiny.[13]

Although later to do so than other Southern Indians, Seminoles, too,
narrowed their captivity practices. They grew pessimistic about incorporating non-Indians into their families as adoptees and almost exclusively
targeted people of African descent during their nineteenth-century wars
against American expansion. When General Thomas Jesup enumerated
the origins of African Americans among the Seminoles to the secretary of
war in 1841, he began with "descendants of negroes taken from citizens of
Georgia by the Creek or Muskogee confederacy in former wars."[14] As former residents of the Creek Nation, many Seminoles (or their ancestors)
had fought the Americans during the Revolution and ongoing border wars

with Southern states. When a group of Seminole warriors pledged to join the British in the American Revolution, they stipulated that "Whatever horses or slaves or cattle we take we expect to be our own."[15]

Out of the sixty-eight documented captives in the Mikasuki War (1800–1802), 90 percent were African Americans. Chief Payne, Cowkeeper's nephew and successor, attempted to work with East Florida governor Enrique White to recover black captives taken during the Mikasuki War, but others were not so helpful. William Augustus Bowles, a protagonist of the war, enjoyed the protection of his father-in-law Chief Kinache at Mikasuki. Bowles attempted to capture and retain African Americans who would aid him in his fight to establish an independent "State of Muskogee." African Americans aided Bowles's cause as couriers, soldiers, and sailors. On account of Bowles, according to one Georgian, "many negroes have allredy made an attempt to run from the Overseer." In 1800, a motley group of African Americans, Mikasukis, and renegade whites under Bowles's command succeeded in briefly taking the Spanish fort at San Marcos de Apalache and hoisting the flag of the State of Muskogee. However, when it became obvious that Bowles could not revive a golden age of Muskogee-British trade as he had promised, Creek and Seminole headmen began to tire of the pompous and often delusional fellow. Efau Hadjo, speaker of the Creek National Council, denounced him, saying, "The four Nations have their own kings and Chiefs. We never had a White Chief. This man says he is a chief of our land, he is our director General, he lies." Even Kinache decided that Bowles was more trouble than he was worth. William Augustus Bowles's adventures came to an end when Creek and Seminole warriors captured him in 1803 and turned him over to the Spanish. Attempts by Payne and Lower Creek chief Jack Kinnard to repatriate Florida slaves taken during the Mikasuki War met with limited success. Antonia Bonnelli later testified that most remained among Indians.[16]

In the early to mid-nineteenth century, the Seminoles repeatedly took up arms to defend their land. They fought in three named conflicts—the Patriot War, the First Seminole War, and the Second Seminole War—and in countless other skirmishes against squatters and slavecatchers. By the opening shots of the Second Seminole War in 1835, the young people could not recall a time of peace. At war with the United States much longer than other Southern Indian nations, the Seminoles continued to take black captives, and they encouraged African Americans to join them in their fight against American imperialism.

During the War of 1812, Americans of the South directed their grievances mostly at Native Americans, Spaniards, and the African Americans living among those two groups. Many Southerners, especially those in neighboring Georgia, wished to expel the Spanish from St. Augustine and claim East Florida for themselves. Thus began the Patriot War, an attempt by Georgians and some Florida planters to annex the province to the United States. On March 12, 1812, the Patriots invaded Florida, quickly capturing Fernandina and then heading south toward St. Augustine. They camped two miles outside of the city at Fort Mose, formerly garrisoned by free black troops. From Mose, they looted plantations, using a combination of persuasion and threats to lure planters—many of them of British descent—to their cause. The Patriots laid siege to St. Augustine, prompting the governor to petition the Seminoles for help.[17]

Tony Proctor, an African American translator well-known in the Southern borderlands, warned the Seminoles that the Patriots intended to invade their country. Bowlegs, the younger brother of Chief Payne, prepared his warriors for combat. In addition to the 200 Seminole warriors under Bowlegs were forty African Americans, who lived under Bowlegs' protection at Alachua. Bowlegs' army first attacked Patriot-owned plantations along the St. Johns River, which had the intended effect of cutting off their provisions as well as drawing rebels away from St. Augustine and back to defend their property.[18] During July and August, Bowlegs and his warriors burned houses, took cattle, and captured African American slaves. Near Picolata, they captured some eighty African Americans. Moving north, they took thirty-two more from Francis Fatio's New Switzerland plantation and forty-one from Zephaniah Kingsley's Laurel Grove.[19] Because free black families feared capture, many of them fled from their outlying plantations and homesteads into the relative safety of St. Augustine. More African Americans were either captured by Seminole warriors or voluntarily joined them as white families throughout East Florida abandoned their plantations. Planter Francis Fatio protested that his property was under constant attack "first from Indians, next from negroes—sometime from both."[20]

Aided by Florida's free black militia troops under the command of Lieutenant Juan Bautista Witten, Seminoles and their black captives and runaways turned the tide of the war, lifting the siege of St. Augustine in September 1812. Most of the "Patriots" had left Florida by March 1813, when President Madison recalled them, but they left northern Florida in ruins. According to one resident, "The country was in a very flourishing state when the revolution commenced. . . . It never was so prosperous before or since. It was left by the patriots a perfect desert." In their campaigns against the Seminoles, Patriots had mortally wounded the elderly Chief Payne, nephew of Cowkeeper, and razed the Alachua towns. Payne's successor and brother, Bowlegs, moved his people and the African Americans among them farther west to establish new villages on the Suwannee River.[21]

As the Patriot War concluded, a civil war began in Creek country. Targeting elements of American culture that they considered especially polluting, the rebels were dubbed "Red Sticks" after the traditional war clubs they used in combat. The Red Sticks waged a nativist revolt and scored a resounding—and infamous—victory on August 30, 1813, at Fort Mims, a hastily constructed redoubt that they attacked and burned, killing between 250 and 300 people. Among the dead were Creeks, Americans, and some slaves, but the Red Sticks spared the lives of most African Americans and took additional slaves from the surrounding area, capturing over 200 in total. The Red Sticks' power was finally broken in March 1814 at the Battle of Horseshoe Bend, so-called because the Tallapoosa River bordered the site on three sides. General Andrew Jackson's army of white Americans, Cherokees, Choctaws, and Creeks succeeded in hacking through the Red Sticks' breastwork covering the fourth side, penning the rebels in and slaughtering about 800 of them. Thereafter, Jackson imposed an iniquitous treaty that punished even the friendly Creeks, forcing the nation to give up some 20 million acres and leaving their land scorched and barren, full of broken bodies and bitter hearts.[22]

Contrary to the hopes of Andrew Jackson and other white Southerners, militant resistance against American expansion did not die at Horseshoe Bend. After the war, many Red Sticks—including a teenaged Osceola and the famed warrior Jumper—sought refuge in Florida. Some 2,000 regrouped near the mouth of Apalachicola River, led there, perhaps, by Mikasukis who had aided them during the war. During the spring of 1814, the British launched a southern strategy of attracting enslaved blacks and dissident Indians to fight the Americans. Together, the British and Seminoles constructed a fort at Prospect Bluff, which was then under the command of Jamaican trader and honorary British captain George Woodbine. Alexander Cochrane, recently named commander of the North American squadron, issued a proclamation that circulated among the South's enslaved population beckoning those who "may be disposed to emigrate from the United States" to the British standard: "they will have their choice of either entering into His Majesty's Sea or Land forces or of being sent as FREE settlers to the British possessions in North America or the West Indies where they will meet with all due encouragement."[23] Former Red Stick leaders Josiah Francis and Peter McQueen pledged to support the project, saying, "We will get all the Black Men we can to join your Warriors . . . we will do our best to unite all our Red Brethren [sic] and form a strong Arm, that will be ready to crush the Wicked and rebellious Americans when they shall dare to insult our Father and his Children."[24]

By early 1815, Woodbine estimated that some 300 black families had answered the call. They came from Mississippi Territory, the Creek Nation, East Florida, West Florida, and even from Seminole country. Some had been forcibly taken by Woodbine and his black and Indian troops. Among those at Prospect Bluff were twenty African Americans belonging to Chief Bowlegs and other Seminoles. Woodbine and his army may have captured some of them, but others went voluntarily. An outraged Pensacola trader lamented: "Prospect Bluff & our Lands [are] in possession of the Negroes whom the unspeakable Villains robbed from their Allies the Spaniards of Pensacola & E Florida, & even (astonishing iniquity! ! ! ! ! ! !) from the Indians themselves."[25]

Although Woodbine and Colonel Edward Nicolls succeeded in creating a corps of black and Indian troops, Britain signed the Treaty of Ghent on December 24, 1814, and British troops withdrew a few months thereafter. Owing to a lack of provisions, most Red Sticks went to settle among the Seminoles, but most African Americans remained at Prospect Bluff, where they set up houses and farms along the banks of the Apalachicola and traded with Seminoles at Mikasuki and on the Suwannee. Americans now faced a large, armed maroon population at their doorstep, and General Andrew Jackson, for one, could not brook such a threat. Following ineffective ground attacks, American gunboats ascended the Apalachicola on July 27, 1816 with orders to destroy the "Negro Fort." When a lucky shot, purposely heated red-hot, hit the fort's powder magazine, an explosion destroyed the fort.[26]

Many and probably most of the fort's 300 inhabitants were not inside at the time of the attack, and those who escaped the ensuing slaveraiding sought refuge with Chief Bowlegs on the Suwannee River. Thus, between the Red Stick defeat at Horseshoe Bend in March 1814 and the destruction of the Prospect Bluff fort in July 1816, the Seminoles had absorbed some two thousand Creeks and several hundred African Americans. Under pressure from the United States, Spanish officials pressed Bowlegs to give up the black refugees, but the chief shifted blame to the British: "I know that you think hard of your black people but I did not fetch them here they came here by the persuasion of the British so if you can makeout with the English you are welcome to them."[27] After Prospect Bluff, freedom-seeking slaves of the Deep South had shifted their focus from the British and back to the Seminoles. Just one month later, in April 1816, a Georgia slaveholder living along the St. Marys River reported a recent rash of escapees heading south, presumably to Seminole country.[28]

Following the First Seminole War, Spain transferred control of Florida to the United States, with the province officially changing hands in 1821. In truth, Florida belonged to the Seminoles. For decades, they had held the balance of power, and, as the Patriot War demonstrated, the Spaniards depended on them to defend the colony. During the First Seminole War, there were few confrontations; rather than face Jackson's huge army, the Seminoles opted to flee and endure the loss of their largest settlements. Beyond the war's substantial material costs, the conflict probably served to reinforce anti-American sentiments already prevalent among the nation's African Americans and refugee Red Sticks who, by then, comprised a majority of the population. The razing of the Seminole villages of Fowl-town, Mikasuki, and Bowlegs' Town, like the earlier destruction of Prospect Bluff and the massacre at Horseshoe Bend, were evidence of the Americans' thirst for Native land and the blood they were willing to spill in order the possess the whole of it.[29]

The final captive-taking episodes in the Native South took place during the Second Seminole War. The conflict arose from Seminole opposition to U.S. removal policy, which, over the course of the 1830s and 1840s, sought to force all eastern Indians west of the Mississippi River. On May 9, 1832, Seminole chiefs signed the Treaty of Payne's Landing, which provided for their removal to Indian Territory if they could find suitable lands. After accompanying seven Seminole chiefs to Indian Territory in 1833, U.S. officials produced the Treaty of Fort Gibson, which compelled the Seminoles to remove. Seminole chiefs Holata Emathla, Coa Hadjo, and Jumper claimed that they never signed the document, and others said army officers forced them to do so with threats of violence and imprisonment. While the treaty allowed the Seminoles to remain in Florida until

1837, federal Indian agent Wiley Thompson pushed them to leave as quickly as possible.[30]

In late December 1835, the Seminole resistance effort began with a series of planned attacks. On December 27, as the Seminoles' federal agent Wiley Thompson and army lieutenant Constantine Smith passed a balmy Florida winter afternoon smoking cigars and strolling the grounds of the agency, Osceola and his warriors surprised them, riddling the officials' bodies with musket balls. The following day, the united forces of Micanopy, Jumper, and Alligator launched a devastating surprise attack on Major Francis Dade's two companies as the soldiers marched from Fort Brooke north to Fort King. While Seminole forces suffered only light casualties, only three U.S. troops escaped "Dade's Massacre."[31] At about the same time, Seminoles and African Americans marched together against sugar and cotton plantations that stretched from the St. Johns River to the eastern seaboard. Seminoles sought to destroy Anglo-American property and capture black captives. They also wanted to demonstrate their ability to strike any settlement at will, even those within miles of territorial capital St. Augustine. On December 26 and 27, Seminole and Black Seminole warriors attacked plantations near Volusia. They destroyed Tomoka plantation, including the big house, cotton house, stable, sugar works, tools, clothes, and forty slave cabins. The warriors captured enslaved adult men George, July, Scipio, and Abraham. At nearby Spring Garden plantation, warriors destroyed $130,000 worth of property and captured an additional 130 enslaved African Americans. They also laid waste to the Depeyster and Harriot plantations, taking dozens more black captives. The *St. Augustine Herald* reported, "Some of Depeyster's negroes joined them, and they carried off the rest, about sixty." John Caesar, a Black Seminole, led in the plantation attacks. At the Hunter plantation, John Caesar reportedly attempted to lure John Hunter out of his house by saying that he had cattle and horses to trade. A suspicious Hunter escaped, but his slaves were taken. As John Caesar commanded the Volusia attacks, Chief Philip led his warriors to New Smyrna, where they destroyed a number of sugar plantations and took additional African American captives.[32]

When Seminole warriors attacked white plantations, it is unclear whether enslaved Africans joined them voluntarily or were captured. Some African Americans resisted or evaded Seminole attempts to capture them. In 1836 a free black man, Jim, and an enslaved man named Carlos were out driving cattle when they were surprised and taken by a Seminole war party. Jim,

who had formerly lived among the Seminoles, "practiced considerable du-
plicity with them—representing his willingness to go with them again and
be their slave . . . and joined in their songs and dances." Under cover of
night, however, Jim and Carlos escaped and gave U.S. troops intelligence
concerning Seminole whereabouts.[33] On the other hand, enslaved people
often took advantage of wartime upheaval to seek their freedom. Black
Seminole warriors encouraged enslaved Floridians to desert their masters
and join them. Certainly, Black Seminoles believed an autonomous Seminole Nation was most conducive to their own freedom, and they sought to
rally other people of African descent to their cause. Drawing on the web of
kinship that connected Black Seminoles with other black Floridians,
prominent Black Seminoles Abraham and John Caesar visited St. Augustine and nearby plantations to solicit aid. Enslaved people living in Georgia, Florida, and the Creek Nation attempted to join the Seminoles. Even
free African Americans joined the resistance by contributing ammunition
and supplies at the risk of losing their freedom.[34]

Throughout 1836, Seminole warriors continued to best U.S. troops, but
more alarming to white Americans was the relationship between Seminoles and African Americans. They feared that the alliance grew with each
passing day, as the Seminoles captured slaves and enticed others to escape.
After witnessing unrest among Creeks forced to emigrate, General Thomas
Jesup believed that the Second Seminole War could ignite the entire
South in a general uprising, wherein people of color might destroy the region's plantation economy as well as their white oppressors. Jesup wrote to
the secretary of war, "The two races, the negro and the Indian, are rapidly
approximating; they are identified in interests and feelings." Indeed, white
officers could not help but notice the ferocity and distinction with which
Black Seminoles fought. They also saw African Americans elevated to positions of power within Seminole society, as interpreters, advisers, and military leaders.[35]

Although Americans became most keenly aware of the alliance between
Seminoles and African Americans during the Second Seminole War, this
relationship had been building since 1790 when Florida ended religious
sanctuary. The second decade of the nineteenth century brought the Seminole Nation a generation of war, thousands of Red Stick refugees, and
hundreds of black captives and runaways. Although the Seminoles proved
formidable foes, they did not escape these many wars unscathed: enemies
repeatedly put Seminole fields to the torch, forced families to flee their

villages, and stole stores of food and livestock. Although the Seminoles continued to relocate and rebuild, they found great difficulty in sustaining economic growth, in producing and carrying goods to market. Black and Red Stick newcomers doubtlessly renewed the Seminoles' commitment to cultural and political autonomy, while the exigencies of war made commercial planting and ranching nearly impossible.

As other Indians purposely constructed racially exclusive nations, Seminoles created a distinctive form of social organization that reflected their unique relationship with African Americans. Typically, a detached village or villages of Black Seminoles was affiliated with a particular Seminole chief. In exchange for land and a great deal of liberty, they owed the chief tribute in the form of agricultural produce. In general, the Seminoles maintained a dispersed settlement plan because that form of spatial organization was most conducive to cattle ranching. African American towns lay at a distance of one to three miles from their chiefs' towns, often in less accessible areas such as swamps or high hammocks.

U.S. Army officer George McCall, who visited the black town of Pelahlikaha during the fall of 1826, called it "one of the most prosperous negro towns in the Indian territory." McCall continued, "We found these negroes in possession of large fields of the finest land, producing large crops of corn, beans, melons, pumpkins, and other esculent [sic] vegetables." Horatio Dexter, who traversed Seminole country a few years before McCall, observed that Black Seminoles also grew rice, peanuts, and tropical fruits. Dexter thought Pelahlikaha a rich land: "The hammocks are very numerous and contain from 20 to 300 acres each, all of which are surrounded by Savannahs, which afford coverage and sufficient range for innumeral [sic] cattle." Pelahlikaha was subject to a nephew of Payne, Chief Micanopy, believed by McCall to receive "a tribute of one-third of the produce of the land, and one-third of the horses, cattle, and fowls they may raise." Dexter thought that African Americans owed their chiefs a bit more—"half what the lands produce."[36]

Beyond agricultural produce, Seminole chiefs expected little from their tributaries, leaving them "at liberty to employ themselves as they please."[37] Under such conditions, Black Seminole villages thrived. Experienced agriculturalists, the tributaries produced enough food to feed their own village as well as the chief, his household, and his guests. An 1822 visitor to Seminole country noted that all Black Seminole men owned guns. Like

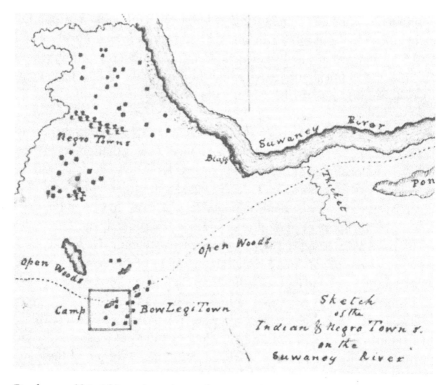

Bowlegs and his African American tributaries. 1818 map by Captain Hugh Young, who served as Andrew Jackson's adjutant-general during the First Seminole War. Courtesy of the National Archives and Records Administration.

Seminole men, they hunted deer, wild turkey, geese, and cranes to supplement their diet. No passes were required to move about the country, and the tributaries were "free to go and come at pleasure."[38] Moreover, many owned "stocks of horses, cows, and hogs, with which the Indian owner never assumes the right to intermeddle." In contrast, free people of color living in the United States faced legal restrictions on their ability to trade, travel, own firearms, and socialize with slaves; sumptuary laws that attempted to regulate behavior and even dress; intrusive monitoring by states through the guardianship and registration systems; and prejudice that made finding jobs and housing difficult. More so than "free" blacks, Black Seminoles enjoyed almost complete autonomy in fashioning separate communities.[39]

Observers thought that the tributaries enjoyed about the same material conditions as their masters. Some whites believed they lived even better, probably because many of the Black Seminoles had picked up recognizable aspects of Euro-American culture from their former masters. One Tennessean, for example, remarked that Pelahlikaha "was laid out like the towns in a *civilized country*, the houses were small and built of pine."[40] Another white traveler was impressed with his quarters—"a new and excellent house, which the Negroes had built to dance in on Christmas."[41] Liberty and economic prosperity seemed to endow the tributaries with good health. One observer noted: "The Indian Negroes are a fine formed athletic race," while another added that they were "the finest looking people I have ever seen."[42]

Few Black Seminoles, however, were actually "free." The emigration rolls of the late 1830s list only 18 free people out of a total of 390 Black Seminoles, about 5 percent of the total. Seminole chiefs freed some, while others had bought their freedom or that of their relatives. For example, when Polly became Chief Bowlegs' sexual partner, he freed her and, later, the children they had together. Plenty, who lived under Chief Micanopy, purchased the freedom of his eldest sons, Juan and Jack, from Halleck Hadjo, while Plenty himself remained a tributary of Micanopy.[43] However, using "slave" and "free" as absolute categories is misleading. Because moving elsewhere would almost certainly result in less freedom, circumstance alone tied Black Seminoles to the land. Some moved during the British occupation of Pensacola, reasoning that the liberty offered by Alexander Cochrane trumped even their tributary status among the Seminoles. In general, however, Black Seminoles found their responsibilities among the Seminoles a light burden. According to traveler William Simmons, "The Negroes uniformly testify to the kind treatment they received from their Indian masters, who are indulgent, and require but little labour from them." When Simmons spoke to Juan, a translator and former adviser to Chief Payne, Juan declared "that his old master, as he called him, had always treated him with the utmost humanity and kindness."[44] Given the autonomy they enjoyed, it is not surprising that Black Seminoles were "violently opposed to leaving the [Seminole] country."[45]

Despite the autonomy that Black Seminoles enjoyed, their labor provided elite Seminoles with a lifestyle similar to that of Native slaveholders. Like other Indian men, Seminole men disdained farming. A rare exception was Friday, a Seminole whose African-derived name suggests that

Black Seminoles also affected their host society in profound ways. When Friday worked his fields, other Seminole men laughed at him, saying that he "works like a negro." According to the Seminole agent, "[w]hen they see this man at work, they exclaim, 'Are we reduced to this degraded state?'"[46] Seminole elites, in contrast, depended on Black Seminoles to supply them with the agricultural surpluses that generated social and political capital. It was chiefly largesse that provided for "the extraordinary & uniform hospitality" that so impressed visitors like Horatio Dexter. According to Dexter, at the behest of every village chief, "I was compelled to spend the night and partake of an entertainment, & was freely furnished with every supply I wanted for my journey." Payne, chief of the Alachua Seminoles, relied on twenty African Americans to tend his fields as well as his considerable livestock, which included 1,500 head of cattle, 400 horses, and some sheep and goats. Chief Opauney of Tolokichopko possessed a peach orchard, potato fields, a stable, a dairy, and a two-story big house. Two miles east of Opauney's residence was a village of some forty African Americans who tended to crops of rice and corn. Horatio Dexter concluded that "in all respect the place resembled the residence of a substantial planter."[47]

In return for tribute, Seminole chiefs offered Black Seminoles, who constantly found their lives, property, and comparative liberty in danger, much-needed protection. Chiefs and warriors protected African Americans from would-be slaveraiders, a common species of criminal in Seminole country. They also dealt with foreign governments on behalf of their tributaries. In 1800, Spanish authorities in St. Augustine accused one of Payne's tributaries of murder. Wrote Governor Enrique White, "Some of your people with a negro in company killed one of my people near town. The Negro is suspected to be the murderer." White demanded that Payne give up the man. Payne expressed a willingness "to keep Peace and a Clean path," but was unable to produce the suspect, explaining "it [is] said by the Negroes that he is dead for the[y] found his gun and where [he] had gone into a Large pond and never Could find where he came out." After offering this excuse, Payne advised Governor White to consider the man dead and drop the matter.[48]

Though ultimately subject to a Seminole chief, each tributary village had an internal political structure complete with its own headmen. Perhaps the most famous of these headmen was Abraham. Born a slave in Pensacola, Abraham fled as a young man to join the British during the War of

1812. He survived the American attack on the fort at Prospect Bluff in 1815, then sought refuge in Seminole country. Settling in Pelahlikaha, Abraham became a community leader and adviser to Chief Micanopy. Abraham owned at least one slave, a man named Charles or Tenebo, and he may have held another. Perhaps black headmen, like their Seminole masters, relied on subaltern labor to provide them with the time and resources they needed to focus on governing their people. With the help of his slave's labor, Abraham eventually managed to accumulate the $300 necessary to purchase and free his son Washington, who had belonged to Chief Micanopy. Colonel William Foster, who met the headman during the Second Seminole War, called Abraham the "Prime Minister of Mickanopy." Greatly impressed by Abraham, Foster likened him to the most skilled politician of his day, writing, "He . . . is compared to Martin Van Buren in our camp." This was not an entirely laudatory description since then, as now, Americans generally believed that such politicians needed a certain duplicitous cunning in order to succeed. Seminoles, however, appreciated Abraham's intelligence and diplomatic skills. Taking a rather different view of Abraham's political acumen, they, like their ancestors, believed that such ability welled from spiritual power. Thus, they sometimes referred to Abraham as a "Prophet."[49]

Linguistic skills and knowledge of Euro-American culture often elevated Black Seminole leaders to positions of power within the Seminole Nation. Because many of these leaders were born outside the nation, they typically knew several European, Indian, and sometimes African tongues. In early America, many people of African descent were renowned translators. Thomas Woodward, a planter in early Alabama, owned some African American slaves who formerly belonged to Yuchi masters. These slaves, Woodward recalled, spoke Yuchi, Muskogee, Hitchiti, passable Shawnee, and some English. Woodward harbored some fear of the power that linguistic skills afforded African Americans reared among Indians: "Nearly all of them, at some time or other, are used as interpreters, which affords them an opportunity to gather information that many of their owners never have, as they speak but one language." Seminole chiefs, few of whom knew English, routinely employed Black Seminole interpreters. Black Seminole headmen also ran errands for their chiefs to St. Augustine and acted as couriers throughout the region. Perhaps most significantly, these headmen also sat on Seminole tribal councils. Captured traders Edmund Doyle and William Hambly reported that black chiefs were among the council members who deliberated on their fate during the First Seminole War.[50]

Some African Americans among the Seminoles could also read and write. In 1820, the Seminoles' agent reported that Black Seminoles encouraged their children to pursue literacy "because, as they believe, it will increase their influence and their comforts." Among the literate of the Seminole Nation was Luis Pacheco, whose white master hired him out as an interpreter for the U.S. Army during the Second Seminole War. One of the few survivors of the Dade Massacre, Pacheco begged for his life, telling Seminole warriors, in Hitchiti, that he was a slave forced to do his master's bidding. Born in 1800, Pacheco grew up on Francis Fatio's New Switzerland plantation, where, along with Fatio's children, he learned to read and write English, Spanish, and French. Pacheco learned some Hitchiti from his brother, who had been taken captive (most likely during the Patriot War), but was later redeemed. After his capture, Pacheco remained among the Seminoles for nearly two years. He later claimed that his education, especially his multilingualism, had preserved his life during his captivity.[51]

Because they commonly saw African Americans in the company of chiefs, many white Americans feared that blacks actually ruled the Seminoles. In 1832, the acting governor of Florida declared, "Those negroes have great influence over them and in fact it is said control their chiefs and councils."[52] Of Joe, Coacoochee's "right hand man," one army officer concluded that he "no doubt exercises great influence, as he possesses considerable shrewdness, and carries in his countenance the marks of a villain."[53] One Charlestonian expressed shock and outrage at the comportment of Black Seminole leaders, who seemed to think themselves equal to white men: "They had none of the servility of our northern blacks, but were constantly offering their dirty paws with as much hauteur, and nonchalance, as if they were conferring a vast deal of honour, of which we should have been proud."[54]

Black Seminoles have been dubbed "maroons,"[55] "partners," "subordinates," "allies,"[56] "half slaves,"[57] and "rather masters than slaves."[58] This difficulty in naming arises from the unique nature of their relationship to the Seminoles. Although the Seminoles' social organization was strikingly similar to vassalage, they drew not on European precedent in crafting their relationship with African Americans, but rather their own past. The relationship between African Americans and Seminole leaders was more accurately that of tributary to chief. The satellite black towns that surrounded chiefs' towns and their payments of agricultural produce are elements strongly reminiscent of the social and political organization that pervaded the region during the Mississippian era. Whereas other Native Americans borrowed aspects of U.S. political organization to construct centralized nations, Seminoles revived and reinvented the chiefdoms of their ancestors. Although the Seminoles' society afforded people of African descent a great deal of freedom, theirs was not an egalitarian one. Whether they came voluntarily, as war captives, or as chattel, all African Americans in Seminole country entered into a similar relationship with a Seminole chief: they were junior members—tributaries—of the chiefdoms that harbored them.

Those closest to the Seminoles were headmen like Abraham. Beyond a few African Americans who married Seminoles, headmen were most integrated into Seminole social networks. Serving as advisers to chiefs, these men spent more time in Seminole villages and excelled as linguists. Some black elites, emphasizing their close ties to Seminole chiefs, adopted surnames such as Payne and Bowlegs. Perhaps most tellingly, Seminole clans temporarily adopted select Black Seminoles so that they, too, could participate in the ceremonies that bound disparate villages together.[59]

Black headmen were the cultural mediators who linked Black Seminoles to their host societies, but, in general, Seminoles and blacks maintained a social distance. According to the Seminoles' agent, Seminoles and Black Seminoles "live[d] in separate families."[60] In an exceptional case, when Chief Bowlegs married a black woman named Polly, he freed Polly and their children, but not Polly's children by other partners. Out of the 390 Black Seminoles captured during the Second Seminole War, only two had Seminole spouses. Toney Barnett, a free man, wed an unnamed Seminole woman, and Pamilla, a slave belonging to Colonel Humphreys, had run away to join an Indian husband. In marriage, Black Seminoles almost exclusively chose other people of African descent. Most had partners living in the same village. John and Flora, for example, lived as tributaries of Micanopy for decades, becoming patriarch and matriarch of a large family. By the time the couple removed to Indian Territory, twelve children and five grandchildren joined them. Others took partners from other Black Seminole villages, and a few, including interpreter John Caesar, had black spouses who labored on white plantations. Kinship thus created a vast web of African connectedness within the Seminole Nation and, significantly, beyond. Traders like free black Felipe Embara, who moved cattle between the Seminole nation and East Florida, helped maintain these connections by carrying news between Florida plantations and Black Seminole villages.[61]

Living at a slight remove from Seminole towns, Black Seminoles constructed a creole culture that distinguished them from their Native hosts. Most significantly, Seminoles reckoned descent matrilineally and maintained a clan system, while Black Seminoles traced their bloodlines through both parents and lacked clans. Unlike many African Americans enslaved under whites, Black Seminoles enjoyed the freedom to name their children, and the names they chose reflect their distinct cultural heritage. Some selected names from classical antiquity like Pompey and Caesar. These names, usually associated with the demeaning nature of slavery under white masters, must have had different connotations for Black Seminoles. Others drew on African naming practices by selecting day names like Monday or Phoebe (meaning Friday), by naming children "Plenty" or "Hard Times" after the circumstances of their birth, or by incorporating a father's first name as a child's surname. Black Seminoles also preserved their African roots in language. Although many spoke Hitchiti or Muskogee with Seminoles and English with white Americans, Black Seminoles spoke a creole language with one another. Surviving evidence indicates that Afro-Seminole Creole, closely related to the Gullah language spoken by African Americans of the Carolina and Georgia Lowcountry, blended English with African languages, including Kikongo, Mandingo, and Efik. One anthropologist has suggested that the village of Pelahlikaha "may derive from the *pakalala*, a challenge stance in the Kongo." During the eighteenth century, many enslaved people came to South Carolina from the Kongo, and a disproportionate number of runaways came from their ranks. For the Kongolese, Spanish Florida may have been particularly alluring since many had converted to Catholicism in Africa. In their spiritual lives, Black Seminoles also borrowed from Native culture—one observer noted that they practiced prophecy and divination in a manner similar to Southern Indians. It is also clear, however, that they incorporated Christian elements, including the celebration of holidays like Christmas, in an era when most Seminoles were hostile to Christianity. Black Seminoles also may have maintained a distinct material culture, for one archaeological study of Pelahlikaha revealed that the black town lacked the large amount of Native pottery usually found in Seminole towns. Like other people of the African diaspora, Black Seminoles fashioned a way of life that blended African, Indian, and European elements, one that drew from and contributed to the society in which they lived.[62]

The inclusive nature of Seminole society contrasted sharply with the racial ideology that shaped communities elsewhere in the South. Throughout the eighteenth century, most Euro-American intellectuals had believed that humans were a unified species and that differences in environment accounted for both physical and cultural variance among people. As early as 1811, however, a North Carolina doctor named Charles Caldwell rejected that theory, proposing instead a natural hierarchy of the races. The developing pseudoscience of phrenology, which supposedly used cranial morphology to measure intelligence, bolstered Caldwell's theory of scientific racism. Philadelphia physician Samuel Morton's influential 1839 study *Crania Americana* used phrenology to formulate an elaborated racial hierarchy—whites at the top, Indians in the middle, and Africans at the bottom. Echoing Indians' earlier theory of polygenesis and the already hardened racial attitudes of white frontierspeople, elite Americans concluded that racial differences were immutable, propelling each group toward its separate destiny: whites would rule the continent, people of African descent would be subservient, Indians would disappear. Or so they believed. In any case, gone were the days when policymakers sought to integrate "civilized" Indians into the republic. By the Jackson era, American expansion showed little regard for nonwhites who stood in the way. The Indian Removal Act, passed in 1830 by a slim margin in Congress, the increasingly harsh slave codes of Southern states, and new restrictions on free people of color in the North were emblematic of the new doctrine of race in America.[63]

Putting these beliefs into practice, many whites sought to enrich themselves and hasten Indian removal by stripping Seminoles of their land and livestock and by kidnapping Black Seminoles. During William Simmons's travels, he found that the Seminoles greatly feared American occupation of Florida: "There was, a general impression among them, that the Americans would seize upon all the Negro property of the Indians; and the latter were also induced to believe . . . that the Americans would rob them and treat them with every degree of injustice and oppression." Such Seminole fears were justified, for unsympathetic white landholders, judges, and politicians often turned a deaf ear to Seminole pleas for redress.[64]

Ever since the Patriot War, slaveholders had sought not only Seminole land, but also Black Seminoles to work that land. Beginning in 1833, a gang of thieves from bordering states began to prey on African Americans living in the Apalachicola River settlements, located less than 100 miles from the borders of Georgia and Alabama. Florida governor James West-cott estimated that the Apalachicola villages contained roughly 1,000 inhabitants led by "[f]ive or six chiefs . . . posess'd of considerable property."[65] One gang hired a slavehunter from Mobile who owned trained bloodhounds to assist them, and they attempted to bribe steamboat captains to transport the captured African Americans. When the Apalachicolas resisted, thieves used physical abuse and threats. A group of slavecatchers headed by Carlton Welborne of Columbus, Georgia, stole twenty-one black slaves from Chief Econchatta Miko, telling the chief that "if he did not fly for safety they should exterminate him and his town."[66] Banding together, Chiefs John Walker, Econchatta Miko, Blount, Davy, and Vacca Pechassie armed their warriors. In addition, they appealed to Indian agents for help. They protested that their stolen African Americans were not runaway slaves, but their own property. Chief John Hicks protested, "I agreed to send away all the black people who had no masters, and I have done it; but still they are sending to me for negroes."[67] Another Apalachicola chief implored, "But is there no *civil law* that will protect me? Are the free negroes and the negroes belonging in this town to be stolen away publicly—in the face of all law and justice?"[68]

The trials of the Factor family and their slaves illustrate the constant danger that phenotypically African people living along the Apalachicola faced after the United States gained Florida. Philatouche, or Black Factor as he was commonly called, was a trader and prominent Lower Creek headman. Likely the son of a black captive, Philatouche was of mixed African-Creek descent. From his village on the Chattahoochee River, Philatouche had launched attacks on American encroachers in the early 1790s. He once explained to the governor of East Florida, "we Expect to loose our land if we dont turn out & fight[.] the virginians has run [out] my people and taken all there hunts & horses." Over the years, Philatouche, possibly through raiding and certainly through his mercantile business, managed to accumulate a number of black captives.[69] On his deathbed in 1816, Philatouche bequeathed to his daughter Nelly Factor a number of enslaved African Americans, including Peggy and her three children, Katy and her three children, Phillis and her child, and a young man named George. To his son Sam Factor, Philatouche gave a woman named Rose who became (or perhaps already was) Sam's lover.[70] Nelly and Sam Factor moved away from their father's village on the Chattahoochee to live among the Seminoles of the Apalachicola River, and Nelly married Chief John Blount. The Factors, being of partial African descent, were perhaps drawn to the Seminole Nation as life in an increasingly intolerant Creek society became uncomfortable. Unfortunately, the Factors did not find peace along the Apalachicola. Like many other Seminole masters, Nelly found herself entangled in a series of lawsuits over her slaves. One army officer observed that so many whites brought suits claiming Black Seminoles that the Seminoles "begin to believe that it is the determination of the United States to take them all." In Nelly's case, a dizzying array of claimants filed suit, including Philatouche's nephew (her cousin) William Kinnard, who claimed the slaves by right of matrilineal inheritance. Although a council of Seminole chiefs ruled that Nelly was the rightful heir to Philatouche's slaves, an attorney for American Margaret Cook kidnapped them anyway.[71]

Also under assault from white slaveholders were Nelly's brother Sam Factor and his family. In 1832, Sam manumitted Rose and their children. Although the Factors lived as free people in the Seminole Nation, they were constant targets for slave-seeking whites. In 1834, Americans Isaac and Levin Brown, who lived in northern Florida, came to the Apalachicola towns and tried to kidnap Sam and Rose's son William Sena Factor. Fortunately, other residents of the town were able to repel the Americans. Soon thereafter, however, slave-seekers did manage to kidnap Rose, her daughter Sarah, and Sarah's children Daniel and Paladore. Rose was sold within the Creek Nation, but sympathetic Creek chiefs recognized her and sent her back to Sam. During the Second Seminole War, in exchange for Rose's service as an interpreter, General Thomas Jesup promised to redeem Rose's daughter and her grandchildren. Rose complied but Jesup did not. Sarah, Daniel, and Paladore remained slaves in Stewart County, Georgia. Encroaching whites made everyday life so unbearable for the Apalachicola Seminoles that most voluntarily removed several years ahead of schedule.[72]

Elsewhere, Seminoles and African Americans alike found themselves besieged by impatient, wealth-seeking whites. Slavetraders attempted to use alcohol and persuasion to purchase African Americans before the scheduled removal west. Seminoles protested such trespass and refused to sell their tributaries. Chief Jumper vented his outrage to Indian agent Gad Humphreys: "It is well known that a great deal of our property, negroes, horses, cattle, &c. is now in the hands of the whites, and yet their laws give us no satisfaction, and will not make them give this property up to us. . . . We were promised *justice*, and we want to see it! These negroes are ours, and we will not consent to surrender them, or say that we are willing to surrender them, or say that we are willing to have them taken."[73] In an attempt to quell rising Seminole ire, Andrew Jackson proclaimed on July 6, 1835, "It is made known to me . . . that the Indians in Florida have no disposition to sell their negroes, and the very idea that any individuals are permitted to come into their country to buy has disturbed them very much, and all say they will neither sell nor leave their negroes."[74]

Whites were not the only slaveholders who menaced the multiracial Seminole Nation. By the early nineteenth century, the South's other major Native nations, the Cherokees, Choctaws, Chickasaws, and Creeks, had abandoned the racial fluidity that formerly characterized their nations and shunned alliances with people of African descent. The only exception came during the Red Stick War, when some Creek warriors welcomed black runaways and captives into their ranks. Even Red Sticks, however, remained ambivalent about the alliance; they killed some African Americans and enslaved others. African Americans must have had similar reservations, for most slaves who escaped from their white masters during the war fled to the British rather than the Red Sticks. During the Seminole Wars, the Seminoles encountered Creeks who attempted to kidnap black tributaries and Cherokees who pressured them to end militant resistance, key episodes that demonstrate the cultural distance that separated Seminoles from other Southern Indians.[75]

During the First Seminole War, General Andrew Jackson invaded Florida with an army of 3,300, including 1,800 Creeks under the command of Coweta headman William McIntosh. Arriving in March 1818, they constructed Fort Gadsden adjacent to the ruins at Prospect Bluff and then marched south to Mikasuki. There, troops killed Kinache and destroyed the town, including "nearly three hundred houses . . . and the greatest abundance of corn, cattle, &c."[76] A soldier reported that the Creeks enthusiastically participated, taking "the greater part" of the plunder.[77]

William McIntosh and his Creek warriors were especially interested in a particular sort of plunder—African American captives. McIntosh, son of a Scottish trader and Wind clan mother, was chief of Coweta and served as speaker for the Lower Creeks at the National Council. A few years earlier, in 1816, McIntosh had joined forces with Americans at Prospect Bluff. McIntosh happened to meet up with them at the mouth of the Apalachicola, where he and 200 Lower Creek warriors had undertaken a slave-hunting expedition. In the 1796 Treaty of Colerain, Creeks agreed to take responsibility for returning African Americans who had run away or been captured during the post-Revolutionary border wars. Thereafter, opportunists like McIntosh used the treaty to claim Black Seminoles as slaves for themselves. Understanding that most survivors of Prospect Bluff had taken refuge with Bowlegs, McIntosh was eager to penetrate their Suwannee River settlements.[78]

On April 16, 1818, Creek and American troops arrived in Bowlegs' territory, where they found a main village flanked to the north by the scattered farms of African American tributaries. Someone had forewarned Bowlegs, however, and only a handful of warriors greeted Jackson's army. The troops managed to kill only nine African American warriors and two Indian men before they razed the towns. Jackson commanded his troops to march back to Pensacola, but William McIntosh made a mental note of the large, prosperous black settlements.[79]

In the years after the First Seminole War, Seminoles and African Americans living along the Suwannee suffered repeated incursions by William McIntosh and his Coweta kin. Although McIntosh claimed that he undertook these expeditions in order to persuade the Seminoles to remove, his true objective was the capture of Black Seminoles. Horatio Dexter, who traversed Seminole country in 1823, saw evidence of the Creeks' depredations everywhere. The Suwannee River, reported Dexter, "was the seat of the most flourishing settlement of the Seminoles Nation not more than two years ago, but since has broken up by the incursion of the Cowetas who carried off or dispersed a band of 60 negroe slaves and a large stock of cattle and horses."[80] William H. Simmons, who traveled through the area one year earlier, gave a similar report: "These people were in the greatest poverty, and had nothing to offer me; having, not long before, fled from a settlement further west, and left their crop ungathered, from an apprehension of being seized on by the Cowetas, who had recently carried off a body of Negroes residing near the Suwaney."[81] As a result of McIntosh's raids, the Seminoles, for the second time in a generation, picked up what was left of their property and relocated deeper into the peninsula. Others moved even farther away. Hitching rides on British ships, some African Americans established a new settlement in the Bahamas, which they dubbed Nicolls' Town after the British colonel who had encouraged all Southern blacks to desert their masters and fight for freedom. Meanwhile, in Florida, the new nucleus of the Seminole Nation became the Withlacoochee River, where Micanopy, nephew of Payne and half-brother of Bowlegs, resided along with his 160 black tributaries.[82]

Creek warriors paid their Seminole kin another unwelcome visit during the Second Seminole War. Promising them ownership of all captured slaves, pay, and an advance on their annuity payment, commanding general Thomas Jesup enlisted the aid of 776 Creek warriors headed by High-headed Jim, Paddy Carr, and Echo Harjo. This time William McIntosh was not among the invading army—the Creek National Council had authorized his execution in 1825 for illegally ceding land to the United States. During their 1837 campaigns with the U.S. Army, the Creeks managed to capture 125 African Americans. Of these prisoners, 90 were Black Seminoles, while the rest had joined the Seminoles only recently as captives or runaways.[83]

Chief Alligator (or Halpatter Tustenuggee) met with a party of these Creeks, who attempted to persuade him to surrender. For years, Creek leaders had argued that they had authority over the Seminoles. A group of chiefs told the secretary of war, "These Indians are a part of our nation, and should possess amongst us no separate and distinct interest. . . . Our great object and wish are, that we may become a united people; already we have been divided too long, and trouble has been the consequence."[84] Seminole chiefs like Alligator, however, feared that the Creeks had the worst of intentions—to kidnap Black Seminoles and spy on behalf of the Americans. A witness recalled Alligator saying, "He does not wish to spill red [meaning Indian] blood but if the Creeks have made up their minds to fight let them come on." At the heart of the differences separating the Creeks and Seminoles was their attitude toward African Americans. Taunting the Creek party, Alligator declared "he understood the Creeks had come for negroes. We have plenty of them said he." Indeed, by that time, many Creek slaveholders practiced only a very particular form of what had once been part of a broad captivity spectrum. Now Creeks were virtually indistinguishable from white slaveholders. Alligator concluded his talk to the Creek party by shaming them for straying so far from their cultural roots; he informed his visitors that the Seminoles' prophets "had said that the Great Spirit was on their side."[85]

Fortunately for Black Seminoles captured by U.S. and Indian troops, commanding officers decided to remove them to Indian Territory as quickly as possible, and they allowed relatively few claims for slaves captured or otherwise "lost" during the war. In 1841, Secretary of War John Bell declared, "No negro should be delivered up under any circumstances unless the claim to him be substantiated by the most satisfactory proof."[86] Of all Southern slaveholders, the Creeks protested the most loudly over this decision. Jesup had promised Creek troops ownership of all slaves they captured during the war, but U.S. officials later retracted this offer. Creeks Opothle Yoholo, Jesse Cornells, Jim Boy, David Barnard, and James Islands appointed an attorney in an attempt to retrieve their lost spoils, and ultimately, they sold their claim to a white slave speculator. U.S. officials declared all Black Seminoles who arrived in Indian Territory "either free, or the property of [Seminole] Indians."[87]

During the fall of 1837, Cherokee chief John Ross sent a delegation to Seminole country at the urging of the federal government. Hoping to secure a more favorable removal treaty for his people, Ross wrote a speech recommending that the Seminoles give up their fight. After reaching Seminole territory, the Cherokee delegation, composed of Hair Conrad, Major Polecat, Richard Fields, Jesse Bushyhead, and interpreter Thomas Woodward, worked tirelessly to gather leading Seminole chiefs and warriors. On November 30 and December 1, 1837, the Cherokee delegation read Ross's talk to a skeptical group of thirty Seminoles at Chickasawatchee Creek.[88]

Ross opened his speech by reminding his Seminole audience of the Native ancestry that bound him to them: "I am of the aboriginal race of the red-man of this great island, and so are you."[89] By the 1830s, however, Cherokees and Seminoles had diverged considerably: The Cherokees maintained a republican form of government with a bicameral legislature, supreme court, and elected officials, as well as mission schools, a national newspaper, and increasingly harsh slave codes. The Seminoles, meanwhile, clung fiercely to their decentralized form of government, purposeful isolation from American culture, and tributary social system. Both nations fought removal, but the Cherokees did so with legal battles and savvy diplomacy, while the Seminoles used armed resistance. Seeking to overcome this difference, Ross revived the language of nativism, appealing to his fellow "red-man." The delegation echoed Ross's argument, "We stated to them that their Nation and the Cherokees, were now the only southern Indians east of the Mississippi river, and as brother Indians, we ought to settle our difficulties together with the United States, in a peaceable and friendly way."[90]

Some Seminoles distrusted the Cherokees from the start. Arpeika, a Mikasuki religious leader, refused to visit them, saying that he "was quite encensed [sic] against the deputation, and charged us with being leagued with the whites to deceive them." Micanopy, Cloud, Nocose Yahola, and others, however, agreed to accompany the Cherokees to Fort Mellon for a talk with Thomas Jesup. Just as the Seminole leaders reached the fort, however, a runner delivered news: Coacoochee, a leading Seminole warrior, had miraculously escaped from a St. Augustine prison. The runner rejoiced that his people "had determined to *fight and die on the land that the Great Spirit had given them.*"[91] In a panic, U.S. officials seized and imprisoned the Seminole leaders, making it appear as though the Cherokees had set a trap for them.[92] With slavehunting Creeks and seemingly conniving Cherokees about them, the Seminoles must have felt truly alienated—all the South's free people, including their fellow Indians, seemed to be conspiring to expel them from the region.

The United States failed in its mission to remove all Seminoles but succeeded in producing a racial faultline that stressed Seminole society to the breaking point. In early 1838, Thomas Jesup spread word that Black Seminoles who surrendered could emigrate west to Indian Territory, where the United States would consider them either free or "slaves" of the Seminoles. By this time, commanding officers pursued the war with desperate brutality, kidnapping Seminole leaders under truce flags, capturing scores of women and children, and burning villages and food stores, all in an attempt to end what would become—and still remains—America's longest and most costly Indian war. In this light, many Black Seminoles found the offer—what they called "Jesup's Proclamation"—alluring. Many must have considered the possibility that they might be sold into slavery in the United States if their fight for Seminole autonomy failed. After his surrender, Abraham explained to Jesup, "We do not live for ourselves only, but for our wives & children who are as dear to us as those of any other men."[93] Hundreds voluntarily came in while others offered no resistance to capture by U.S. troops. By late spring, nearly all Black Seminoles had surrendered or been captured. At the rate of $1.00 per day, the U.S. Army employed many as guides and interpreters. The intelligence and service these Black Seminoles provided proved decisive, for it enabled the army to locate important Seminole leaders and hideouts. Those who worked for the United States contributed to the widening rift between Black Seminoles and their former protectors. After U.S. forces removed over 4,000 Seminoles and nearly 400 Black Seminoles, the groups tried to revive their old tributary system, but the separation between them widened in Indian Territory, leading some to resettle in Texas and, later, Mexico. Back in Florida some 300 Seminoles and a few Black Seminoles successfully evaded removal and stayed in the region, where their descendants remain today.[94]

Together, Seminoles and African Americans developed a unique system of captivity in the American South. Seminole captive-holding differed drastically from that of other Indian nations, which developed plantation economies, centralized governments, and legal codes that equated blackness with enslavement. Instead, the Seminoles reinvented their ancient chiefdoms to create a reciprocal—if unequal—relationship between themselves and the African Americans who lived among them. While Seminoles benefited from the knowledge and labor of Black Seminoles, the tributaries lived in relative freedom, enjoying human rights denied to most other African Americans of their time. Other Indians resisted alliance with people of African descent, but the Seminoles embraced it. In the Second Seminole War, as the United States threatened to usurp their homeland and their autonomy, African Americans and Seminoles found a common enemy in the white Americans who would use racism to disempower them both.

CONCLUSION

In the early nineteenth century, Mrs. William Boyles managed a way-side tavern in Monroe County, Alabama. Among her frequent customers was William Weatherford. Locally regarded as a Southern gentleman, Weatherford owned 300 slaves, managed a large plantation, and bred horses. One day, as Weatherford dined in Mrs. Boyles's tavern, four strangers entered and sat at Weatherford's table. As they ate, these-out-of-towners struck up a conversation. They "wanted to know where that bloody-handed savage, Billy Weatherford, lived."[1]

When the strangers looked at William Weatherford, they thought they saw a white Southern planter—according to a descendant he "was fair, with light brown hair and mild black eyes"—but Weatherford had a more complicated past.[2] William's mother Sehoy III, half-sister to nativist leader Alexander McGillivray, was a Creek who passed on her Wind clan membership to her son. William was born in 1781 at or near the Upper Creek town of Coosada. Most of the town's inhabitants, including his mother Sehoy, were ethnic Koasatis. Originally hailing from the chiefdoms of the Tennessee River valley, the Koasatis fled from their homeland during the late seventeenth century. They were one of the many Native groups that joined the Creek confederacy to protect themselves from Indian slavers. William's father, Charles Weatherford, was of partial Indian descent and had grown up near the trading path linking the Creek Nation to Augusta, Georgia. Both Charles and Sehoy were traders and slaveholders. Ambitious and troublesome, Charles was heavily involved in buying and selling black captives taken during the Revolution and subsequent border wars. He was also accused of selling free blacks and runaways into slavery. Charles's fortunes declined over time, and, in 1798, when the Creek National Council voted to expel troublesome traders, Charles Weatherford was "on the list but reprieved" thanks to the influence of Sehoy's Wind relatives. Despite these efforts, Charles became estranged from the rest of the family within the next year. Sehoy, however, remained a successful businesswoman, and her wealth kept the family living "in some taste." She owned about thirty slaves, although federal Indian agent Benjamin Hawkins called her an "extravagant and heedless" master, suggesting that Sehoy did not conform to white slaveholding standards. William, in his late teens when his parents separated, seems to have coped well. Divorce was fairly common, and young Weatherford, like other Southern Indians, could always turn to his extensive clan kin for support. William excelled at the Creek masculine arts of hunting and stickball, and his reputation as an eloquent speaker may have been what prompted his contemporaries to dub him "Truth Teller."[3]

The course of William Weatherford's life changed dramatically during the summer of 1813 when a civil war erupted in Creek country. Approached by Red Stick leaders, Weatherford agreed to join them. Reportedly, Weatherford decided that "they were his people—he was raised with them, and he would share their fate." Despite his upbringing, William likely believed, as other Red Sticks did, that the Creek Nation's turn toward plantation agriculture, political centralization, and racial slavery was seriously misguided. William Weatherford even persuaded—or perhaps compelled—some of his family's slaves to fight alongside him. A talented equestrian and natural athlete, Weatherford became renowned in battle. In Weatherford's most famous feat, when pursued by American forces during the Battle of the Holy Ground, he mounted his grey horse Arrow and charged off a high bluff into the river some twenty feet below, landing safely. He was also among those Red Sticks who stormed Fort Mims and massacred roughly 300 American and rival Creek inhabitants. It was this episode that prompted the strangers at the tavern—and scores of other white Americans—to call Weatherford a "bloody-handed savage."[4]

Following the Red Sticks' catastrophic loss at the Battle of Horseshoe Bend in March 1814, William Weatherford surrendered to General Andrew Jackson and fought with American troops through the conclusion of the war. Thereafter, with the help of his family, Weatherford established a plantation in southern Alabama near where Fort Mims once stood.[5] The four visitors to the tavern knew this, and they expressed an eagerness to meet Weatherford, "assuring Mrs. Boyles they would kill the red-skinned, bloody-handed savage on sight." Seeing no one in the tavern who fit that description, the men concluded that they would have to look elsewhere. Imagine their surprise, then, when their eating companion volunteered,

"Some of you gentlemen expressed a wish while at dinner to meet Billy Weatherford. Gentlemen, I am Billy Weatherford, at your service!" Eventually, one man sheepishly stepped forward and introduced himself, but the others "quailed under [his] glance." According to Mrs. Boyles, "she never saw men more frightened than were the three belligerently disposed gentlemen."[6]

The story of Billy Weatherford and these four strangers, related by the tavern-keeper to Weatherford's grandson, hints at the South's half-hidden Indian history. To the strangers, Weatherford appeared the quintessential Southern planter. No longer a revolutionary who led Indians and blacks in battle, Weatherford now practiced a form of captivity which mirrored that of his white neighbors. Moreover, the number of African Americans Weatherford owned made him among the interior South's larger slaveholders. Presuming that the Indian whom they sought must possess "red" skin and a savage disposition, the strangers never suspected that the gentleman with brown hair and mild eyes was once the Red Stick called Truth Teller. Nor did Weatherford's dinnertime conversation give anything away, for though he lacked formal schooling, Weatherford "spoke the English language with great propriety," and doubtlessly could hold forth on topics like cotton and slave prices, horse racing, and regional travel. The strangers could not fathom that Weatherford could be an Indian and a planter, a warrior and a slaveholder. Yet, Weatherford answered all those descriptions. The themes that the tavern-keeper's tale highlights— war, slavery, and race—are at the core of both the American past and the Indian past, demonstrating the deep, but often ignored, connections between those histories.[7]

Colonization and the encroachment of the trans-Atlantic economy did not bring inequality to North America. By the time that Europeans arrived in the sixteenth century, many Native Americans already lived in hierarchical societies governed by hereditary chiefs. At the bottom of these societies were captives whom chiefs obtained through war or trade. Native societies maintained a broad continuum that allowed for great flexibility in the treatment of the captured. Chiefs controlled captives, whom they worked, traded, adopted, humiliated, and killed—all to enhance the power of the ruling lineage. In the seventeenth century, most Native chiefdoms fell, dragging theocratic chiefs down with them. Native people, though, continued to wage wars against enemies. Like the chiefs who came before them, captors commodified their enemies, and they seemingly held no moral qualms about selling these spoils to European allies. Hereditary chiefs, however, no longer monopolized captives. Instead, slavers like the Chickasaws used enemies to augment their *group* power by selling captives for trade goods or adopting them to maintain population levels.

In the wake of the Yamasee War, the external market for slaves declined, but Indians continued to capture their enemies. Victors subjected their captured enemies—who by this time included whites, blacks, and Indians—to fates ranging from death to adoption to enslavement. Before the late eighteenth century, Native people did not use skin color to determine a captive's fate; rather, captors focused largely on sex and age when calculating how a captive would best benefit the community. The clan matrons who decided such matters understood that captives possessed diverse forms of power: they quieted crying blood, restored order, performed labor, produced children, and conferred status.

The crises of the late eighteenth century led many to revise their notions about appropriate captives and their treatment. During this period, large numbers of Native people and American settlers moved closer than ever before, but as they exchanged tools, food, ideas, and even people, the two groups developed a language of race that drove them apart. Nativists' message of pan-Indianism and polygenesis spread among Southern Indians, and race gradually eclipsed more localized modes of self-understanding such as kinship. Concurrently, the need for economic diversification following the decline of the deerskin trade led many to embrace commercial planting and ranching. As Native people grew pessimistic about adopting non-Indians and were restrained by headmen from participating in torture, captive-taking became an economic pursuit. Warriors and planters targeted African American captives and subjected them to a narrower range of fates—usually transgenerational bondage or sale. Desperate to retain their homelands and their sovereignty, Native leaders refashioned their kin-based confederacies into centralized nations and attempted to fix categories of "slave" and "free" along racial lines. By the time William Weatherford came of age, racism had transformed Native captivity practices.

Not all Southern Indians complied with the new order. Most notably, Seminoles and their African American tributaries created a unique system of captivity. Periodic infusions of anti-American Creek emigrants contributed to the Seminoles' cultural conservatism, and continual wars throughout the first half of the nineteenth century made commercial planting and ranching impossible. Drawing on their Mississippian roots, the Seminoles developed a more inclusive social model, the tributary system, which afforded African American captives and runaways a great deal of freedom. When U.S. expansion threatened their homeland and their autonomy, the Seminoles and their African American tributaries fought to defend their way of life. Other Indians who visited Seminole country, including Creek soldiers and slavehunters—Weatherford among them—and Cherokee ambassadors in league with the United States, dramatized the cultural chasm that, by the nineteenth century, separated the Seminoles from the rest of the region. Although the United States never truly defeated the Seminoles, decades of war exacerbated racial divisions and ultimately destroyed their tributary system.

William Weatherford was a planter and slaveholder, and by right of matrilineal descent reckoning, he was also unequivocally a Creek Indian who hunted, warred, and traded as his ancestors had for centuries. Without contradiction, he lived as both warrior Truth Teller and gentleman planter Billy Weatherford. Alabama planter J. D. Dreisbach, who married Weatherford's niece Josephine Tate, once boasted, "I hope I may be pardoned for quoting the language of one of the most distinguished ladies of the South, who in speaking of my wife, said, that in her veins runs the very best blood of the South."[8] Dreisbach grew up in an era when the region's Indian past was difficult to ignore: American planters plowed rich Alabama bottomlands only recently abandoned by Creek women; some African American slaves still spoke the Cherokee or Chickasaw of their former masters; traces of Indian ancestry were common in whites and blacks, whether they acknowledged it or not. As Dreisbach implicitly argued, American history and Native history cannot—and should not—be separated, for each is indelibly part of the other. Because of captivity, the histories, cultures, and even the genes of the diverse peoples who inhabit North America are irrevocably intertwined.

NOTES

ACKNOWLEDGMENTS

INDEX

NOTES

Abbreviations

APS   American Philosophical Society, Philadelphia, Pennsylvania

ASP:IA   *American State Papers: Indian Affairs*, 2 vols. (Washington, DC: Gales and Seaton, 1832)

ASP:MA   *American State Papers: Military Affairs*, 7 vols. (Washington, DC: Gales and Seaton, 1832)

BHL   Benjamin Hawkins Letterbook, INHP

DLG   Digital Library of Georgia, dlg.galileo.usg.edu

DMC   Lyman Copeland Draper Manuscript Collection, Microfilm Copy, State Historical Society of Wisconsin, Madison

DRIA   William L. McDowell, ed., *Documents Relating to Indian Affairs, Colonial Records of South Carolina Documents Relating to Indian Affairs*, 2 vols. (Columbia: South Carolina Department of Archives and History, 1992)

DSC   *The De Soto Chronicles: The Expedition of Hernando de Soto to North America in 1539–43*, ed. Lawrence A. Clayton, Vernon James Knight Jr., and Edward C. Moore (Tuscaloosa: University of Alabama Press, 1993)

EFP   East Florida Papers, Microfilm Copy at PKY

FHS   Filson Historical Society, Louisville, Kentucky

FLHS   Florida Historical Society, Cocoa, Florida

GA   Georgia Archives, Morrow

GMA   Gilcrease Museum Archives, Tulsa, Oklahoma

HRB   Hargrett Rare Book and Manuscript Library, University of Georgia Libraries, Athens

INHP   Independence National Historical Park, Philadelphia, Pennsylvania

JBP   Joseph Brown Papers, TSLA

JGP   James Grant of Ballindalloch Papers, Microfilm Copy, LOC

JHPP   John Howard Payne Papers, Microfilm Copy, Ayer MS 689, Edward E. Ayer Manuscript Collection, Newberry Library, Chicago

JRP   James Robertson Papers, TSLA

LC   Joseph Byrne Lockey Collection of Documents Related to the History of Florida, PKY

LOC   Library of Congress, Washington, DC

LR   Letters received

LRSW   Letters received by the Secretary of War

MDAH   Mississippi Department of Archives and History, Jackson

MPA:FD   *Mississippi Provincial Archives: French Dominion*. Vols. 1–3 ed. Dunbar Rowland and A. G. Sanders (Jackson: Press of the Mississippi Department of Archives and History, 1927–1932). Vols. 4–5 ed. Dunbar Rowland, A. G. Sanders, Patricia Galloway (Baton Rouge: Louisiana State University Press, 1984)

MPA:SA   Mississippi Provincial Archives, Spanish Archives Transcripts and Translations, Series 692, MDAH

NA   National Archives, Washington, DC

OIA   Office of Indian Affairs

PC   Papeles Procedentes de Cuba, Microfilm Copy at PKY

PKY   P. K. Yonge Library of Florida History, Department of Special and Area Studies Collections, George A. Smathers Libraries, University of Florida, Gainesville

PPP   Peter Pitchlynn Papers, GMA

SCDAH   South Carolina Department of Archives and History, Columbia

SHC   Southern Historical Collection, Louis Round Wilson Special Collections Library, The University of North Carolina at Chapel Hill

TSLA   Tennessee State Library and Archives, Nashville

WSP   *Winthrop Sargent Papers, 1771–1948*, Microfilm Edition, 7 reels (Boston: Massachusetts Historical Society, 1965)

Introduction

1. Accounts of Le Page Du Pratz and Dumont in John R. Swanton, *Indian Tribes of the Lower Mississippi Valley and Adjacent Coast of the Gulf of Mexico* (Washington, DC: U.S. Government Printing Office, 1911), 143–156; Robert S. Neitzel, *Archeology of the Fatherland Site: The Grand Village of the Natchez*, in *Anthropological Papers of the American Museum of Natural History* 51 (1965), part 1, 83; John T. Penman, "Faunal Remains," in *The Grand Village of the Natchez Revisited: Excavations at the Fatherland Site, Adams County, Mississippi, 1972*, Mississippi Department of Archives and History Archaeological Report 12, 152–154.

2. Randolph J. Widmer, "The Structure of Southeastern Chiefdoms," in *The Forgotten Centuries: Indians and Europeans in the American South, 1521–1704*, ed. Charles Hudson and Carmen Chaves Tesser (Athens: University of Georgia Press, 1994), 125–155. For an examination of fictive kinship in the Old South, see Eugene D. Genovese, *Roll, Jordan, Roll: The World the Slaves Made* (New York: Vintage, 1976), 133–137.

3. Brett Rushforth, "'A Little Flesh We Offer You': The Origins of Indian Slavery in New France," *The William and Mary Quarterly*, 3rd Series, 60 (2003): 806.

4. Orlando Patterson, *Slavery and Social Death: A Comparative Study* (Cambridge, MA: Harvard University Press, 1982), 106–115, 170, 262–273.

5. Quotation from Alan Taylor, "Land and Liberty on the Post-Revolutionary Frontier," in *Devising Liberty: Preserving and Creating Freedom in the New American Republic*, ed. David Thomas Konig (Stanford, CA: Stanford University Press, 1995), 82.

6. Cynthia Cumfur, *Separate Peoples, One Land: The Minds of Cherokees, Blacks, and Whites on the Tennessee Frontier* (Chapel Hill: University of North Carolina Press, 2007), 102.

7. James Mooney, *Myths of the Cherokee* (New York: Johnson, 1970), 15; John R. Swanton, *The Indians of the Southeastern United States* (Washington, DC: U.S. Government Printing Office, 1946), 46; James Axtell, *Imagining the Other: First Encounters in North America* (Washington, DC: American Historical Association, 1991), 6–7.

8. Mooney, *Myths*, 316–317.

9. Governor Johnstone's Report, June 23, 1766, *Mississippi Provincial Archives: English Dominion*, ed. Dunbar Rowland (Nashville, TN: Brandon Printing, 1911), 511; Newton D. Mereness, ed., "Journal of de Beauchamps' Journey to the Choctaws," in *Travels in the American Colonies* (New York: Macmillan, 1916), 262; James Adair, *The History of the American Indians*, ed. Kathryn E. Holland Braund (Tuscaloosa: University of Alabama Press, 2005), 185, 265; James Taylor Carson, *Making an Atlantic World: Circles, Paths, and Stories from the Colonial South* (Knoxville: University of Tennessee Press, 2007), 15–16.

10. W. Fitzhugh Brundage, *The Southern Past: A Clash of Race and Memory* (Cambridge, MA: Harvard University Press, 2005), 2–3.

11. Charles M. Hudson, *The Southeastern Indians* (Knoxville: University of Tennessee Press, 1976), 123–132; George E. Lankford, "World on a String: Some Cosmological Components of the Southeastern Ceremonial Complex," in *Hero, Hawk, and Open Hand: American Indian Art of the Ancient Midwest and South*, ed. Richard F. Townsend and Robert Sharp (New Haven, CT: Yale University Press, 2004), 207–217; F. Kent Reilly, "People of Earth, People of

Sky: Visualizing the Sacred in Native American Art of the Mississippian Period," in Townsend and Sharp, eds., *Hero, Hawk, and Open Hand*, 125–137; John F. Scarry, "The Late Prehistoric Southeast," in Hudson and Tesser, eds., *The Forgotten Centuries*, 17–35.

12. Helen Hornbeck Tanner, "The Land and Water Communication Systems of the Southeastern Indians," in *Powahatan's Mantle: Indians in the Colonial Southeast*, ed. Gregory A. Waselkov, Peter H. Wood, and Tom Hatley (Lincoln: University of Nebraska Press, 2006), 27–42; Hudson, *Southeastern Indians*, 276–277, 313–316.

13. Wilbur R. Jacobs, ed., *Indians of the Southern Colonial Frontier: The Edmond Atkin Report and Plan of 1755* (Columbia: University of South Carolina Press, 1954), xvi, 7, 13, 17, 36, 41–44, quotation on p. 13.

14. First quote from *The Pennsylvania Gazette*, June 26, 1746; second quote from Thomas Gage to William Johnson, August 27, 1769, *The Papers of Sir William Johnson* (Albany: University of the State of New York, 1931), vol. 7, 140–141; Daniel K. Richter, *The Ordeal of the Longhouse: The Peoples of the Iroquois League in the Era of European Colonization* (Chapel Hill: University of North Carolina Press, 1992), Chapter 2 and p. 237.

15. Speech of John Watts, in William Blount to Henry Knox, November 8, 1792, William Blount Letters, FHS; Talk of Mad Dog [Efau Hadjo] to James Burgess and the Seminoles, August 2, 1798, Marie Taylor Greenslade Papers, box 1, PKY, courtesy of FLHS; Talk of the Choctaw Kings, Headmen, and Warriors to Mad Dog, White Lieutenant, Nine Hadjo and Apoyl of the Hickory Ground and all their elder brothers the Creeks in general, June 10, 1795, JRP, reel 801, TSLA.

16. Winthrop Sargent to Timothy Pickering, September 18, 1798, in *The Mississippi Territorial Archives, 1798–1818*, ed. Dunbar Rowland (Nashville, TN: Brandon Printing, 1905), 47. Emphasis in original.

17. Mary Godfrey, *An Authentic Narrative of the Seminole War*, in *The Garland Library of Narratives of North American Indian Captivities* (New York: Garland, 1978), vol. 52, p. 10.

1. Inequality, War, and Captivity

1. Jeffrey P. Brain, "Late Prehistoric Settlement Patterning in the Yazoo Basin and Natchez Bluffs Regions of the Lower Mississippi Valley," in *Mississippian Settlement Patterns*, ed. Bruce D. Smith (New York: Academic Press, 1978), 331–368.

2. Pedro Menéndez de Aviles to Philip II, 1572, in *New American World: A Documentary History of North America to 1612*, ed. David B. Quinn (New York: Arno, 1979), vol. 2, 588–589.

3. John F. Scarry, "The Late Prehistoric Southeast," in *The Forgotten Centuries: Indians and Europeans in the American South, 1521–1704*, ed. Charles Hudson and Carmen Chaves Tesser (Athens: University of Georgia Press, 1994), 17–35; Charles M. Hudson, *Knights of Spain, Warriors of the Sun: Hernando de Soto and the South's Ancient Chiefdoms* (Athens: University of Georgia Press, 1997), 11–30; James B. Griffin, "Comments on the Late Prehistoric Societies in the Southeast," in *Towns and Temples along the Mississippi*, ed. David H. Dye and Cheryl Anne Cox (Tuscaloosa: University of Alabama Press, 1990), 5–15; Vincas P. Steponaitis, "Prehistoric Archaeology in the Southeastern United States, 1970–1985," in *Annual Review of Anthropology* 15 (1986): 363–404.

4. Adam King and Maureen S. Meyers, "Exploring the Edges of the Mississippian World," *Southeastern Archaeology* 21 (2002): 113–114. Chiefdoms in central and southern Florida as well as Cherokee-speakers experienced the Mississippian transformation to a lesser extent. See John Worth, *The Timucuan Chiefdoms of Spanish Florida* (Gainesville: University Press of Florida, 1998), vol. 1, 17–18; Hudson, *Knights of Spain*, 194.

5. Kathleen DuVal, *The Native Ground: Indians and Colonists in the Heart of the Continent* (Philadelphia: University of Pennsylvania Press, 2006), 13–28; Nancy Shoemaker, *A Strange Likeness: Becoming Red and White in Eighteenth-Century North America* (New York: Oxford University Press, 2004), 15–28.

6. Rodrigo Rangel, "Account of the Northern Conquest and Discovery of Hernando de Soto," trans. John E. Worth, *DSC*, vol. 1, 267.

7. Dumont, quoted in John R. Swanton, *Indian Tribes of the Lower Mississippi Valley and Adjacent Coast of the Gulf of Mexico* (Washington, DC: U.S. Government Printing Office, 1911), 51.

8. Philip Phillips and James A. Brown, *Pre-Columbian Shell Engravings from the Craig Mound at Spiro, Oklahoma* (Cambridge, MA: Peabody Museum Press, 1978), vol. 2, plate 17.

9. Letter of Abraham Wood, August 22, 1674, in *Early Travels in the Tennessee Country, 1540–1800*, ed. Samuel Cole Williams (Johnson City, TN: Watauga Press, 1928), 36.

10. Frank G. Speck, "Notes on Chickasaw Ethnology and Folklore," *The Journal of American Folklore* 20 (1907): 50–58.

11. John R. Swanton, *The Indians of the Southeastern United States* (Washington, DC: U.S. Government Printing Office, 1946), 540; James Adair, *The History of the American Indians*, ed. Kathryn E. Holland Braund (Tuscaloosa: University of Alabama Press, 2005), 71; Nathaniel Folsom, Discussion of Choctaw History, 1798, PPP, GMA.

12. John Garrett, "Status, the Warrior Class, and Artificial Cranial Deformation," in *The King Site: Continuity and Contact in Sixteenth-Century Georgia*,

ed. Robert L. Blakely (Athens: University of Georgia Press, 1988), 35–46; Kenneth Parham, "Toqua Skeletal Biology: A Biocultural Approach," in *The Toqua Site—40MR6: A Late Mississippian, Dallas Phase Town*, Tennessee Valley Authority, Publications in Anthropology 44 (1987), vol. 1, 431–451; quotation from Speck, "Notes on Chickasaw Ethnology," 57.

13. John R. Swanton, *Source Material for the Social and Ceremonial Life of the Choctaw Indians* (Washington, DC: U.S. Government Printing Office, 1931), 57, 118; Vincas P. Steponaitis and Vernon J. Knight Jr., "Moundville Art in Historical and Social Context," in *Hero, Hawk, and Open Hand: American Indian Art of the Ancient Midwest and South*, ed. Richard F. Townsend and Robert Sharp (New Haven, CT: Yale University Press, 2004), 180; George E. Lankford, "World on a String: Some Cosmological Components of the Southeastern Ceremonial Complex," *Hero, Hawk, and Open Hand*, 217.

14. Steponaitis, "Prehistoric Archaeology," 372–374; Guy Prentice, "An Analysis of the Symbolism Expressed by the Birger Figurine," *American Antiquity* 51 (1986): 239–266; Susan C. Power, *Early Art of the Southeastern Indians: Feathered Serpents and Winged Beings* (Athens: University of Georgia Press, 2004), 74; R. Douglas Hurt, *Indian Agriculture in America: Prehistory to the Present* (Lawrence: University Press of Kansas, 1987), 11–12.

15. Randolph J. Widmer, "The Structure of Southeastern Chiefdoms," in *The Forgotten Centuries*, 125–155; Cameron B. Wesson, "Chiefly Power and Food Storage in Southeastern North America," *World Archaeology* 31 (1999): 145–164.

16. Vernon James Knight Jr., "Moundville as a Diagrammatic Ceremonial Center," in *Archaeology of the Moundville Chiefdom*, ed. Vernon James Knight Jr. and Vincas P. Steponaitis (Washington, DC: Smithsonian Institution Press, 1998), 44–62.

17. Vernon James Knight Jr., "Social Organization and the Evolution of Hierarchy in Southeastern Chiefdoms," *Journal of Anthropological Research* 46 (1990): 20; Adam King, *Etowah: The Political History of a Chiefdom Capital* (Tuscaloosa: University of Alabama Press, 2003), 115; Le Page Du Pratz in Swanton, *Indian Tribes*, 171.

18. Widmer, "The Structure of Southeastern Chiefdoms," 136.

19. Christopher S. Peebles, "Moundville: Late Prehistoric Sociopolitical Organization in the Southeastern United States," in *The Development of Political Organization in Native North America*, ed. Elisabeth Tooker, *Proceedings of the American Ethnological Society* (1979): 192–193; Swanton, *Indian Tribes*, 39–45, 100–107; Peter H. Wood, "The Changing Population of the Colonial South: An Overview by Race and Region," in *Powhatan's Mantle: Indians in the Colonial Southeast*, ed. Gregory A. Waselkov, Peter H. Wood, and Tom

Hatley (Lincoln: University of Nebraska Press, 2006), 99–106; quotation from Theda Perdue, *Slavery and the Evolution of Cherokee Society, 1540–1866* (Knoxville: University of Tennessee Press, 1979), 12.

20. Antoine Simon Le Page du Pratz, *The History of Louisiana*, ed. and trans. Joseph G. Tregle Jr. (Baton Rouge: Louisiana State University Press, 1975), 352; Le Page Du Pratz in Swanton, *Indian Tribes*, 169–170; St. Cosme in ibid., 172; Juan de Paiva, "Origen y principio del juego de pelota," 1676, in John H. Hann, *Apalachee: The Land between the Rivers* (Gainesville: University Presses of Florida, 1988), 331–353.

21. Paiva, in Hann, *Apalachee*, 343.

22. Mathurin le Petit to Père d'Avaugour, July 12, 1730, in *The Jesuit Relations and Allied Documents, Travels and Explorations of the Jesuit Missionaries in New France: 1610–1791*, ed. Reuben Gold Thwaites (Cleveland: Burrows Brothers, 1900), vol. 68, 127; Le Page Du Pratz in Swanton, *Indian Tribes*, 169; Charles E. Bennett, trans., "The Narrative of Le Moyne," in *Settlement of Florida* (Gainesville: University of Florida Press, 1968), 105.

23. Swanton, *Indian Tribes*, 102–107; Wayne Van Horne, "The Warclub: Weapon and Symbol in Southeastern Indian Societies," (Ph.D. diss, University of Georgia, 1993), 60–74, 119–168; Lewis H. Larson, "Archaeological Implications of Social Stratification at the Etowah Site, Georgia," in *Society for American Archaeology Memoirs* 25 (1971): 58–67; Paiva, in Hann, *Apalachee*, 331–353.

24. Le Petit to D'Avaugour, July 12, 1730, in *The Jesuit Relations*, vol. 68, 127; St. Cosme in Swanton, *Indian Tribes*, 172; Steponaitis, "Prehistoric Archaeology in the Southeastern United States," 389–91; Robert S. Neitzel, *The Grand Village of the Natchez Revisited: Excavations at the Fatherland Site, Adams County, Mississippi*, 1972, Mississippi Department of Archives and History Archaeological Report 12, 126.

25. P. F. X. Charlevoix, December 25, 1721, *Journal of a Voyage to North America*, trans. Louise Phelps Kellogg (London: Dodsley, 1761), 261.

26. Ruth Lapham Butler, trans., *Journal of Paul du Ru, February 1 to May 8, 1700* (Chicago: Caxton Club, 1934), 34.

27. Charlevoix and Le Petit in Swanton, *Indian Tribes*, 102–103.

28. Le Petit to D'Avaugour, July 12, 1730, *The Jesuit Relations*, vol. 68, 131.

29. Le Petit in Swanton, *Indian Tribes*, 103; Hudson, *Knights of Spain*, 164–165, 227, 232, 245; Marvin T. Smith and David J. Hally, "Chiefly Behavior: Evidence from Sixteenth Century Spanish Accounts," *Archeological Papers of the American Anthropological Association*, vol. 3 (1992): 99–109; Timothy Earle, *How Chiefs Come to Power: The Political Economy in Prehistory* (Stanford, CA: Stanford University Press, 1997), 156–157; Smith, "Archaeology of the Southeastern United States," 56.

30. Charlevoix in Swanton, *Indian Tribes*, 102; Richard R. Polhemus, Jefferson Chapman, and Andrea B. Shea, "The Paleoethnobotany of the Toqua Site," in *Toqua*, vol. 2, 1113–1207; Le Page du Pratz, *History of Louisiana*, 338–340; Smith and Hally, "Chiefly Behavior."

31. Mary Lucas Powell, "Of Time and the River: Perspectives on Health during the Moundville Chiefdom," in *Archaeology of the Moundville Chiefdom*, 102; Powell, "Ancient Diseases, Modern Perspectives: Treponematosis and Tuberculosis in the Age of Agriculture," in *Bioarchaeological Studies of Life in the Age of Agriculture: A View from the Southeast*, ed. Patricia M. Lambert (Tuscaloosa: University of Alabama Press, 2000), 25; Clark Spencer Larsen and Leslie E. Sering, "Inferring Iron-Deficiency Anemia from Human Skeletal Remains: The Case of the Georgia Bight," in ibid., 132; Paul Kelton, *Epidemics and Enslavement: Biological Catastrope in the Native Southeast, 1492–1715* (Lincoln: University of Nebraska Press, 2007), 11–28.

32. Alan H. Goodman and George J. Armelagos, "Disease and Death at Dr. Dickson's Mounds," *Natural History* 9 (1985): 12–18.

33. Arthur E. Bogan and Richard R. Polhemus, "Faunal Analysis: A Comparison of Dallas and Overhill Cherokee Subsistence Strategies," in *Toqua*, vol. 2, 971–1111, esp. 986–987; Charles E. Cleland Jr., "Analysis of the Faunal Remains of the Fatherland Site," in *Archaeology of the Fatherland Site*, 97–98; Powell, "Perspectives on Health during the Moundville Chiefdom," 102–119; James W. Hatch and Richard A. Geidel, "Tracing Status and Diet in Prehistoric Tennessee," in *Archaeology* 36 (1983): 56–59; James W. Hatch, Patrick S. Willey, and Edward E. Hunt Jr., "Indicators of Status-Related Stress in Dallas Society: Transverse Lines and Cortical Thickness in Long Bones," *Midcontinental Journal of Archaeology* 8 (1983): 49–71; Hudson, *Knights of Spain*, 230; Rangel, "Account of the Northern Conquest," *DSC*, vol. 1, 291.

34. Mary W. Helms, "Political Lords and Political Ideology in Southeastern Chiefdoms: Comments and Observations," in *Lords of the Southeast*, 188.

35. Larson, "Social Stratification at the Etowah Site," 58–67; Bogan and Polhemus, "Faunal Analysis," in *Toqua*, vol. 2, 988–992; David H. Dye, "Feasting with the Enemy: Mississippian Warfare and Prestige-Goods Circulation," in *Native American Interactions: Multiscalar Analyses and Interpretations in the Eastern Woodlands*, ed. Michael S. Nassaney and Kenneth E. Sassaman (Knoxville: University of Tennessee Press, 1995), 304.

36. George R. Milner, *The Cahokian Chiefdom: The Archaeology of a Mississippian Society* (Washington, DC: Smithsonian Institution Press, 1998), 83–84, 136, 160–161; Thomas E. Emerson, *Cahokia and the Archaeology of Power* (Tuscaloosa: University of Alabama Press, 1997), 228; Melvin L. Fowler, Jerome Rose, Barbara Vander Leest, and Steven R. Ahler, *The Mound 72 Area:*

Dedicated and Sacred Space in Early Cahokia, Illinois State Museum, Reports of Investigations 54 (1999).

37. Stanley H. Ambrose, Jane Buikstra, and Harold W. Krueger, "Status and gender differences in diet at Mound 72, Cahokia, revealed by isotopic analysis of bone," *Journal of Anthropological Archaeology* 22 (2003): 217–226.

38. Christopher S. Peebles and Susan M. Kus, "Some Archaeological Correlates of Ranked Societies," *American Antiquity* 42 (1977): 421–448; Robert S. Neitzel, "Archeology of the Fatherland Site: The Grand Village of the Natchez," in *Anthropological Papers of the American Museum of Natural History* 51, part 1 (1965), 84; Neitzel, *Grand Village of the Natchez Revisited*, 45.

39. Widmer, "The Structure of Southeastern Chiefdoms," 133, 144.

40. Thomas E. Emerson and Eve Hargrave, "Strangers in Paradise? Recognizing Ethnic Mortuary Diversity on the Fringes of Cahokia," *Southeastern Archaeology* 19 (2000): 1–23.

41. Bruce D. Smith, "The Archaeology of the Southeastern United States: From Dalton to de Soto, 10,500–500 B.P.," in *Advances in World Archaeology*, vol. 5, ed. Fred Wendorf and Angela E. Close (Orlando, FL: Academic Press, 1986), 62; Hudson, *Knights of Spain*, 271–303; Patricia S. Bridges, Keith P. Jacobi, and Mary Lucas Powell, "Warfare-Related Trauma in the Late Prehistory of Alabama," in *Bioarcheological Studies of Life in the Age of Agriculture*, 44–58; David H. Dye, "Warfare in the Protohistoric Southeast, 1500–1700, in *Between Contacts and Colonies: Archaeological Perspectives on the Protohistoric Southeast*, ed. Cameron B. Wesson and Mark A. Rees (Tuscaloosa: University of Alabama Press, 2002).

42. Garcilasso de la Vega, "La Florida by the Inca," trans. Charmion Shelby, *DSC*, vol. 2, 439; Hann, *Apalachee*, 181; Rene Laudonniere, *Three Voyages*, trans. Charles E. Bennett (Tuscaloosa: University of Alabama Press, 2001), 81–82.

43. Le Page Du Pratz in Swanton, *Indian Tribes*, 127; Dye, "Feasting with the Enemy"; Peebles, "Moundville," 194; quotation from Laudonniere, *Three Voyages*, 77.

44. Karl T. Steinen, "Ambushes, Raids, and Palisades: Mississippian Warfare in the Interior Southeast," *Southeastern Archaeology* 11 (1992): 132–139; quotation from Garcilasso, "La Florida by the Inca," *DSC*, vol. 2, 439.

45. Ibid., 252; Hudson, *Knights of Spain*, 138–142; Van Horne, "Warclub," 231.

46. Luys Hernandez de Biedma, "Relation of the Island of Florida," trans. John E. Worth, *DSC*, vol. 1, 232–236; James Alexander Robertson, trans., "The Account by a Gentleman from Elvas," *DSC*, vol. 1, 99–104; Rangel, "Account of the Northern Conquest," *DSC*, vol. 1, 292–294; Garcilasso, "La Florida by the Inca," *DSC*, vol. 2, 352–353.

47. Charles M. Hudson, "A Spanish-Coosa Alliance in Sixteenth-Century North Georgia," *The Georgia Historical Quarterly* 62 (1988): 599–626.

48. Bridges, Jacobi, and Powell, "Warfare-Related Trauma," 40–44; Dye, "Warfare in the Protohistoric Southeast," 128.

49. Bennett, trans., "Narrative of Le Moyne," 102, 106; Laudonniere, *Three Voyages,* 83.

50. Ibid., 85–86.

51. Wesson, "Chiefly Power and Food Storage," 145–164.

52. Robertson, trans., "The Account by a Gentleman from Elvas," *DSC,* vol. 1, 60; Garcilasso de la Vega, "La Florida by the Inca," *DSC,* vol. 2, 106, 119; Andrés Reséndez, *A Land So Strange: The Epic Journey of Cabeza de Vaca* (New York: Basic Books, 2007), 91–92, 106–108.

53. Garcilasso, "La Florida by the Inca," *DSC,* vol. 2, 103; quotation from Robertson, trans., "The Account by a Gentleman from Elvas," *DSC,* vol. 1, 60.

54. Garcilasso, "La Florida by the Inca," *DSC,* vol. 2, 103.

55. Menéndez to Philip II, 1572, in *New American World,* vol. 2, 588–589.

56. Du Pratz in Swanton, *Indian Tribes,* 51, 131; Bennett, trans., "Narrative of Le Moyne," 104; Orlando Patterson, *Slavery and Social Death: A Comparative Study* (Cambridge, MA: Harvard University Press, 1982), 60; Raymond Firth, *Symbols: Public and Private* (London: George Allen and Unwin, 1973), 288.

57. Dye, "Feasting with the Enemy," 290–291; Smith and Hally, "Chiefly Behavior," 104–105; Hudson, *Knights of Spain,* 303, 310.

58. Brett Rushforth, " 'A Little Flesh We Offer You': The Origins of Indian Slavery in New France," *William and Mary Quarterly,* 3rd series, 60(2003): 785.

59. Garcilasso, "La Florida by the Inca," *DSC,* vol. 2, 103, 117; Andrés de Barcia, *Barcia's Chronological History of the Continent of Florida,* trans. Anthony Kerrigan (Gainesville: University of Florida Press, 1951), 137, 183–184.

60. Robertson, trans., "The Account by a Gentleman from Elvas," *DSC,* vol. 1, 62; Garcilasso, "La Florida by the Inca," *DSC,* vol. 2, 104–106; Hudson, *Knights of Spain,* 81, 492 n. 53.

61. Robertson, "The Account by a Gentleman from Elvas," *DSC,* vol. 1, 86.

62. Memorial of Hernando Escalante Fontaneda, circa 1575, trans. Buckingham Smith, in *New American World,* vol. 5, 7–14; Pedro Menéndez de Aviles to Philip II, October 20, 1566, in *Spanish Borderlands Sourcebooks,* vol. 24, ed. Eugene Lyon (New York: Garland, 1995), 357–361; Bennett, trans., "Narrative of LeMoyne," 104–105; Menéndez to Philip II, 1572, in *New American World,* vol. 2, 588–589; López de Velasco in John R. Swanton, *Early History of the Creek Indians and their Neighbors* (Gainesville: University Press of Florida, 1998), 389.

63. Garcilasso, "La Florida by the Inca," *DSC,* vol. 2, 312, 400, 439.

64. Reséndez, *Land So Strange*, 112; Álvar Núñez Cabeza de Vaca, *The Narrative of Cabeza de Vaca*, ed. and trans. Rolena Adorno and Patrick Charles Pautz (Lincoln: University of Nebraska Press, 2003), 96, 99, 105–109, quotation on p. 96.

65. Elvas's account seems most plausible here. Robertson, trans., "The Account by a Gentleman of Elvas," *DSC*, vol. 1, 62; quotation from Garcilasso, "La Florida by the Inca," *DSC*, vol. 2, 109.

66. Ibid., vol. 2, 117.

67. Robertson, trans., "The Account by a Gentleman of Elvas," *DSC*, vol. 1, 62; Garcilasso, "La Florida by the Inca," *DSC*, vol. 2, 111–113.

68. Bennett, trans., "Narrative of LeMoyne," 104–105.

69. Charles Hudson, *The Juan Pardo Expeditions: Exploration of the Carolinas and Tennessee, 1566–68* (Tuscaloosa: University of Alabama Press, 2005), 27.

70. Alfred Crosby, "Virgin Soil Epidemics as a Factor in the Aboriginal Depopulation in America," *William and Mary Quarterly*, 3rd series, 33 (1976): 289–299; Hudson, *Knights of Spain*, 422; Wood, "The Changing Population of the Colonial South, 1685–1790," 119–121.

71. Carl F. Klinck and James J. Talman, eds., *The Journal of Major John Norton, 1809–1816* (Toronto: Champlain Society, 1970), 80.

72. Patricia Galloway, *Choctaw Genesis, 1500–1700* (Lincoln: University of Nebraska Press, 1995), 141, 352; Marvin T. Smith, *The Archaeology of Aboriginal Culture Change in the Interior Southeast: Depopulation during the Early Historic Period* (Gainesville: University Presses of Florida, 1987).

73. Dye, "Warfare in the Protohistoric Southeast," 138; quotation from Bossu in Swanton, *Social and Ceremonial Life*, 163.

2. The Indian Slave Trade

1. Benjamin F. French, ed., "An Account of the Discovery of Some New Countries and Nations in North America in 1673, by Pere Marquette and Sieur Joliet," in *Historical Collections of Louisiana* (Philadelphia: Daniels and Smith, 1850), part 2, 279–297.

2. Daniel K. Richter, *The Ordeal of the Longhouse: The Peoples of the Iroquois League in the Era of European Colonization* (Chapel Hill: University of North Carolina Press, 1992), 30–148; French, ed., "Account of . . . Pere Marquette and Sieur Joliet," part 2, 292.

3. Erie Bowne, *The Westo Indians: Slave Traders of the Early Colonial South* (Tuscaloosa: University of Alabama Press, 2005); Verner W. Crane, *The Southern Frontier, 1670–1732* (Tuscaloosa: University of Alabama Press, 2004), Chapter 1; quotation from Maurice Matthews to Lord Ashley, August 30, 1671, *The Shaftesbury Papers*, ed. Langdon Cheves, in *Collections of the South*

Carolina Historical Society, vol. 5 (Charleston, SC: William Ellis Jones, 1897), 334.

4. Bowne, *The Westo Indians*, 86–106; Alan Gallay, *The Indian Slave Trade: The Rise of English Empire in the American South, 1670–1717* (New Haven, CT: Yale University Press, 2002), 40–69; quotations from "Woodward's Westo Discovery," December 31, 1674, in *The Shaftesbury Papers*, ed. Cheves, vol. 5, 456–462.

5. Crane, *Southern Frontier*, 17–80; Gallay, *Indian Slave Trade*, 68–69, 133–149, 294–296; Jerald T. Milanich, *Laboring in the Fields of the Lord: Spanish Missions and Southeastern Indians* (Washington, DC: Smithsonian Institution Press, 1999), 160–166; Governor Francisco Corcoles y Martínez to the King, January 14, 1708, in *Here They Once Stood: The Tragic End of the Apalachee Missions*, trans. and ed. Mark F. Boyd, Hale G. Smith, and John W. Griffin (Gainesville: University of Florida Press, 1951), 90; Bishop Gerónimo Valdés to the King, December 9, 1711, in *Missions to the Calusa*, ed. and trans. John H. Hann (Gainesville: University of Florida Press, 1991), 335–336.

6. James Alexander Robertson, trans., "The Account by a Gentleman from Elvas," *DSC*, vol. 1, 105; Charles M. Hudson, *Knights of Spain, Warriors of the Sun: Hernando de Soto and the South's Ancient Chiefdoms* (Athens: University of Georgia Press, 1997), 262–270; Patricia Galloway, *Choctaw Genesis, 1500–1700* (Lincoln: University of Nebraska Press, 1995), 349; Duane Champagne, *Social Order and Political Change: Constitutional Governments among the Cherokee, the Choctaw, the Chickasaw, and the Creek* (Stanford, CA: Stanford University Press, 1992), 27; Peter H. Wood, "The Changing Population of the Colonial South: An Overview by Race and Region," in *Powhatan's Mantle: Indians in the Colonial Southeast*, ed. Gregory A. Waselkov, Peter H. Wood, and Tom Hatley (Lincoln: University of Nebraska Press, 2006), 60–61, 81, 89, 95–97; Alexander Moore, ed., *Nairne's Muskhogean Journals: The 1708 Expedition to the Mississippi River* (Jackson: University Press of Mississippi, 1988), 36–38.

7. Wendy St. Jean, "Trading Paths: Mapping Chickasaw History in the Eighteenth Century," *American Indian Quarterly* 27 (2003): 758–759.

8. Gallay, *Indian Slave Trade*, 103; Moore, ed., *Nairne's Muskhogean Journals*, 50; John Stewart to William Dunlop, October 20, 1693, in "Letters from John Stewart to William Dunlop," *The South Carolina Historical and Genealogical Magazine* 33 (1931): 172.

9. Crane, *Southern Frontier*, 116–117; James Axtell, *Beyond 1492: Encounters in Colonial North America* (New York: Oxford University Press, 1992), 135–136; Marvin T. Smith, *The Archaeology of Aboriginal Culture Change in the Interior*

Southeast: Depopulation during the Early Historic Period (Gainesville: University Presses of Florida, 1987); quotation from Moore, ed., *Nairne's Muskhogean Journals*, 57.

10. Axtell, *Beyond 1492*, 127–129; Greg O'Brien, *Choctaws in a Revolutionary Age, 1750–1830* (Lincoln: University of Nebraska Press, 2002); Galloway, *Choctaw Genesis*, 314; Smith, *Archaeology of Aboriginal Culture Change*, 26–27, 35, 43, 106–107.

11. Patrick M. Malone, *The Skulking Way of War: Technology and Tactics among the New England Indians* (Lanham, MD: Madison Books, 1991), 32–35; Steven Christopher Hahn, "A Miniature Arms Race: The Role of the Flintlock in Initiating Indian Dependency in the Colonial Southeastern United States, 1656–1730" (M.A. thesis, University of Georgia, 1995), 18–29.

12. Ibid., 33–36; Wayne Van Horne, "The Warclub: Weapon and Symbol in Southeastern Indian Societies" (Ph.D. diss., University of Georgia, 1993), 136, 179; quotation from Moore, ed., *Nairne's Muskhogean Journals*, 37; for northern attacks, see Périer to Maurepas, March 25, 1731, MPA:FD, vol. 4, 74; Périer to Ory, November 15, 1730, MPA:FD, vol. 4, 55.

13. William L. Ramsey, *The Yamasee War: A Study of Culture, Economy, and Conflict in the Colonial South* (Lincoln: University of Nebraska Press, 2008), 61–68; Crane, *Southern Frontier*, 111; Kathryn E. Holland Braund, *Deerskins & Duffels: The Creek Indian Trade with Anglo-America, 1685–1815* (Lincoln: University of Nebraska Press, 1993), 42.

14. William L. McDowell, ed., *Journals of the Commissioners of the Indian Trade, September 20, 1710–August 29, 1718* (Columbia: South Carolina Archives Department, 1955), 53; Bowne, *The Westo Indians*, 65; Braund, *Deerskins & Duffels*, 70–71; Moore, ed., *Nairne's Muskhogean Journals*, 47.

15. Vernon J. Knight and Sheree L. Adams, "A Voyage to the Mobile and Tomeh in 1700, with Notes on the Interior of Alabama," *Ethnohistory* 28 (1981): 182.

16. Moore, ed., *Nairne's Muskhogean Journals*, 48, 76.

17. Ibid., 45, 61.

18. Hubert to the Naval Council, October 26, 1717, MPA:FD, vol. 2, 249.

19. French, ed., "Account of . . . Pere Marquette and Sieur Joliet," 281.

20. From Stephen Bull to Lord Ashley, September 12, 1670, in *The Shaftesbury Papers*, ed. Cheves, vol. 5, 194.

21. Périer to Maurepas, April 1, 1730, MPA:FD, vol. 4, 32, 34 n. 3; Jean-Bernard Bossu, *Travels in the Interior of North America, 1751–1762*, trans. and ed. Seymour Feiler (Norman: University of Oklahoma Press, 1962), 188–190; Louis LeClerc Milfort, *Memoirs, or A quick Glance at my various Travels and my Sojourn in the Creek Nation*, ed. and trans. Ben C. McCary (Kennesaw, GA: Continental, 1959), 59.

22. Told by Benjamin Paul to Morris Swadesh, 1935, Morris Swadesh Collection, part 3, p. 56, APS.

23. Moore, ed., *Nairne's Muskhogean Journals*, 49; Wendy St. Jean, "Trading Paths: Chickasaw Diplomacy in the Greater Southeast, 1690s-1790s" (Ph.D. diss., University of Connecticut, 2004), 61; quotation from "Mr. Carteret's Relation," in *The Shaftesbury Papers*, ed. Cheves, vol. 5, 167-168.

24. Jean-Baptiste Minet, "Voyage Made from Canada Inland Going Southward during the Year 1682," trans. Ann Linda Bell and ed. Patricia Galloway, in *La Salle, the Mississippi, and the Gulf* (College Station: Texas A&M, 1987), 54, 57.

25. Moore, ed., *Muskhogean Journals*, 42-43; Charles M. Hudson, *The Southeastern Indians* (Knoxville: University of Tennessee Press, 1976), 276.

26. John Gilmary Shea, ed., "Letter of J. F. Buisson St. Cosme," in *Early Voyages Up and Down the Mississippi* (Albany: Joel Munsell, 1861), 60-61; Jean-Baptiste Bénard de La Harpe, *The Historical Journal of the Establishment of the French in Louisiana*, trans. Joan Cain and Virginia Koenig and ed. Glen R. Conrad (Lafayette: University of Southwestern Louisiana, 1971), 14; Ruth Lapham Butler, trans., *Journal of Paul du Ru, February 1 to May 8, 1700* (Chicago: Caxton Club, 1934), 66.

27. Moore, ed., *Nairne's Muskhogean Journals*, 37.

28. Wood, "The Changing Population of the Colonial South," 97; Galloway, *Choctaw Genesis*, 2, 340-342, 352-359.

29. Pierre LeMoyne, Sieur d'Iberville, *Iberville's Gulf Journals*, trans. and ed. Richebourg Gailliard McWilliams (Tuscaloosa: University of Alabama Press, 1981), 174; Letter from M. de Tonti to d'Iberville, February 23, 1702, in Patricia Galloway, ed., *LaSalle and His Legacy* (Jackson: University Press of Mississippi, 1982), 168; John R. Swanton, *Source Material for the Social and Ceremonial Life of the Choctaw Indians* (Washington, DC: U.S. Government Printing Office, 1931), 103; Wood, "The Changing Population of the Colonial South," 96-97; quotation from Moore, ed., *Nairne's Muskhogean Journals*, 53.

30. McWilliams, ed., *Iberville's Gulf Journals*, 171-173.

31. Gallay, *Indian Slave Trade*, 149.

32. Bienville to Pontchartrain, October 27, 1711, MPA:FD, vol. 3, 160.

33. McWilliams, ed., *Iberville's Gulf Journals*, 173.

34. Abstract of Letters from Bienville to Ponchartrain, July 28, 1706, MPA:FD, vol. 2, 23; quotation from Minutes of the Naval Council, Speech of De Lamothe, February 7, 1716, MPA:FD, vol. 2, 217.

35. Périer to Ory, December 18, 1730, MPA:FD, vol. 4, 43. For labeling men as "women"—not always derogatorily—see Nancy Shoemaker, *A Strange Likeness: Becoming Red and White in Eighteenth-Century North America* (New York: Oxford University Press, 2004), 101-117.

36. Moore, ed., *Nairne's Muskhogean Journals*, 56.

37. La Harpe, *Historical Journal*, 48.

38. Ibid., 50–52; Crane, *Southern Frontier*, 95–96; Gallay, *Indian Slave Trade*, 291.

39. Minet, "Voyage Made from Canada Inland," 54, 57; Shea, ed., "Letter of J. F. Buisson St. Cosme," 60–61; Butler, trans., *Journal of Paul du Ru*, 66; McWilliams, ed., *Iberville's Gulf Journals*, 172; La Harpe, *Historical Journal*, 48–50, 52; Bienville to Pontchartrain, September 14, 1706, MPA:FD, vol. 3, 34; Crane, *Southern Frontier*, 95–96; Gallay, *Indian Slave Trade*, 291; André Pénicaut, *Fleur de Lys and Calumet, Being the Pénicaut Narrative of French Adventure in Louisiana*, ed. and trans. Richebourg Gailliard McWilliams (Baton Rouge: Louisiana State University Press, 1953), 159.

40. Quotation from Antoine Simon Le Page du Pratz, *The History of Louisiana*, ed. and trans. Joseph G. Tregle Jr. (Baton Rouge: Louisiana State University Press, 1973), 305–306; John Stewart to Queen Anne, March 10, 1711, Archives des Colonies, Archives Nationales, Paris, microfilm copy at LOC, C13C, vol. 2, reel 67, doc. 72; Moore, ed., *Nairne's Muskhogean Journals*, 37; Minet, "Voyage Made from Canada Inland," 47; Bienville to Ponchartrain, September 14, 1706, MPA:FD, vol. 3, 34; Bienville to Pontchartrain, August 20, 1709, MPA:FD, vol. 3, 136.

41. Moore, ed., *Nairne's Muskhogean Journals*, 48–49; quotation from Stewart to Queen Anne, March 10, 1711, LOC; Frank J. Klingberg, ed., *The Carolina Chronicle of Dr. Francis Le Jau, 1706–1717* (Berkeley: University of California Press, 1956), 115–116; Gallay, *Indian Slave Trade*, 185–190.

42. Le Page du Pratz, *The History of Louisiana*, 305–306; Paul Kelton, *Epidemics and Enslavement: Biological Catastrophe in the Native Southeast, 1492–1715* (Lincoln: University of Nebraska Press, 2007), xvii-xx; Wood, "The Changing Population of the Colonial South," 94–95.

43. Robertson, ed., "The Account by a Gentleman of Elvas," DSC, vol. 1, 62; Garcilasso, "La Florida by the Inca," DSC, vol. 2, 109; Memorial of Hernando Escalante Fontaneda, circa 1575, trans. Buckingham Smith, in *New American World: A Documentary History of North America to 1612*, ed. David B. Quinn (New York: Arno, 1979), vol. 5, 7–14; Andrés de Barcia, *Barcia's Chronological History of the Continent of Florida*, trans. Anthony Kerrigan (Gainesville: University of Florida Press, 1951), 103, 109; Charles E. Bennett, trans., "The Narrative of Le Moyne," in *Settlement of Florida* (Gainesville: University of Florida Press, 1968), 104; Rene Laudonniere, *Three Voyages*, trans. Charles E. Bennett (Tuscaloosa: University of Alabama Press, 2001), 11–13.

44. Quotation from David H. Dye, "Warfare in the Protohistoric Southeast, 1500–1700," in *Between Contacts and Colonies: Archaeological Perspectives on the Protohistoric Southeast*, ed. Cameron B. Wesson and Mark A. Rees

(Tuscaloosa: University of Alabama Press, 2002), 138; George R. Milner, "An Osteological Perspective on Prehistoric Warfare," in *Regional Approaches to Mortuary Analysis*, ed. Lane Anderson Beck (New York: Plenum Press, 1995), 221–244.

45. Moore, ed., *Nairne's Muskhogean Journals*, 34, 39, 62.

46. Quotation from Shea, ed., "Journal of the Voyage of Father Gravier," 146; La Harpe, *Historical Journal*, 54; McDowell, ed., *Journals of the Commissioners of the Indian Trade*, 12, 16, 23, 25.

47. Gallay, *Indian Slave Trade*, 116; quotation from Moore, ed., *Nairne's Muskhogean Journals*, 46.

48. Bernard Romans, *A Concise Natural History of East and West Florida*, ed. Kathryn E. Holland Braund (Tuscaloosa: University of Alabama Press, 1999), 125.

49. David I. Bushnell Jr., "The Account of Lamhatty," *American Anthropologist* (1908): 568–574; Gregory A. Waselkov, "Indian Maps of the Colonial Southeast," in *Powhatan's Mantle*, 467–469.

50. McDowell, ed., *Journals of the Commissioners of the Indian Trade*.

51. Crane, *Southern Frontier*, 112–113; William R. Snell, "Indian Slavery in Colonial South Carolina" (Ph.D. diss., University of Alabama, 1972), 96, Appendix I.

52. Gallay, *Indian Slave Trade*, 294–314.

53. Pénicaut, *Fleur de Lys and Calumet*, 159; McWilliams, ed., *Iberville's Gulf Journals*, 119, 171–173; quotation from Le Jau, *Carolina Chronicle*, 39.

54. La Harpe, *Historical Journal*, 53; Pénicaut, *Fleur de Lys and Calumet*, 159; John R. Swanton, *Indian Tribes of the Lower Mississippi Valley and Adjacent Coast of the Gulf of Mexico* (Washington, DC: U.S. Government Printing Office, 1911), 300, 337.

55. Charles M. Hudson, "Introduction," *The Transformation of the Southeastern Indians, 1540–1760*, eds. Robbie Ethridge and Hudson (Jackson: University Press of Mississippi, 2002), xxxvi–xxxviii; Kelton, *Epidemics and Enslavement*, 158.

56. Champagne, *Social Order and Political Change*, 27; Moore, ed., *Nairne's Muskhogean Journals*, 36–37.

57. Rush Nutt, "Nutt's Trip to the Chickasaw Country," ed. Jesse D. Jennings, *The Journal of Mississippi History* 9 (1947): 52.

58. Moore, ed., *Nairne's Muskhogean Journals*, 39–41, quotation on p. 39.

59. Jay K. Johnson, Jenny D. Yearous, and Nancy Ross-Stallings, "Ethnohistory, Archaeology, and Chickasaw Burial Mode during the Eighteenth Century," *Ethnohistory* 41 (1994): 431–446; Moore, ed, *Nairne's Muskhogean Journals*, 43–44; for arrows, see Richard F. Townsend, "American Landscapes: Seen and

Unseen," in *Hero, Hawk, and Open Hand: American Indian Art of the Ancient Midwest and South*, eds. Townsend and Robert V. Sharp (New Haven, CT: Yale University Press, 2004), 33–34.

60. Moore, ed, *Nairne's Muskhogean Journals*, 37–38.

61. Shea, ed., "Letter of J. F. Buisson St. Cosme," 70.

62. Memoir of Bienville, 1726, *MPA:FD*, vol. 3, 538.

63. Wilbur R. Jacobs, ed., *Indians of the Southern Colonial Frontier: The Edmond Atkin Report and Plan of 1755* (Columbia: University of South Carolina Press, 1954), 68.

64. Gibson, *The Chickasaws*, 30; St. Jean, "Trading Paths," 760. The Chickasaw Nation's official website, www.chickasaw.net, explains that "unconquered and unconquerable" is its unofficial motto (accessed 1/28/09).

65. Pénicaut, *Fleur de Lys and Calumet*, 68, 73–76, 79; quotation from Moore, ed., *Nairne's Muskhogean Journals*, 40.

66. Hudson, *Knights of Spain, Warriors of the Sun*, 117–145; John F. Scarry, "The Nature of Mississippian Societies," in *Political Structure and Change in the Prehistoric Southeastern United States* (Gainesville: University Press of Florida, 1996), 21.

67. James Adair, *The History of the American Indians*, ed. Kathryn E. Holland Braund (Tuscaloosa: University of Alabama Press, 2005), 187.

68. John R. Swanton, *Indians of the Southeastern United States* (Washington, DC: Smithsonian Institution Press, 1979), 90–91; Gallay, *Indian Slave Trade*, 145–149, 186; Crane, *Southern Frontier*, 79–80; John H. Hann, *Apalachee: The Land between the Rivers* (Gainsville: University Presses of Florida, 1988), 264.

69. Bienville to Pontchartrain, September 6, 1704, *MPA:FD*, vol. 3, 26–27, quotation on 27; Pénicaut, *Fleur de Lys and Calumet*, 98, 125–126; Diron d'Artaguette to Maurepas, October 17, 1729, *MPA:FD*, vol. 4, 20.

70. Le Jau, *Carolina Chronicle*, 39.

71. Pénicaut, *Fleur de Lys and Calumet*, 133–135, quotation on 135.

72. Father Raphael to Abbé Raguet, May 15, 1725, *MPA:FD*, vol. 2, 484.

73. St. Jean, "Trading Paths," 760.

74. Crane, *The Southern Frontier*, Chapter 7; Gallay, *Indian Slave Trade*, 73–89; Ramsay, *Yamasee War*, Chapter 3.

75. La Harpe, *Historical Journal*, 65–66; Le Jau, *Carolina Chronicle*, 175; Gallay, *Indian Slave Trade*, 334–335; Crane, *Southern Frontier*, 169–170; Ramsey, *Yamasee War*, 147–148; St. Jean, "Trading Paths," 77.

76. Ramsay, *Yamasee War*; Steven J. Oatis, *A Colonial Complex: South Carolina's Frontiers in the Era of the Yamasee War, 1680–1730* (Lincoln: University of Nebraska Press, 2004), 167.

77. Ramsey, *Yamasee War*, 178–179; Crane, *Southern Frontier*, Appendix A; Gallay, *Indian Slave Trade*, 338–346.

78. Snell, "Indian Slavery in Colonial South Carolina," 95, 122–124; Almon Wheeler Lauber, *Indian Slavery in Colonial Times within the Present Limits of the United States in Studies*, in History, Economics, and Public Law 54 (1913): 300–310, 564–568.

79. *South Carolina Gazette*, September 20, 1760.

80. Daniel H. Usner, "American Indians in Colonial New Orleans," in *Powhatan's Mantle*, 163–186; Peter H. Wood, *Black Majority: Negros in Colonial South Carolina from 1670 through the Stono Rebellion* (New York: Knopf, 1974), 261–262, 318; Jacobs, ed. *The Edmond Atkin Report and Plan of 1755*, 45; Isabel M. Calder, ed., "Journals of Sergeant Wright, 1771," in *Colonial Captivities, Marches, and Journeys* (New York: Macmillan, 1935), 239; La Harpe, *Historical Journal*, 126.

3. Crying Blood and Captive Death

1. Red Coat King to Governor Glen, July 26, 1753, in *DRIA*, vol. 1, 380; James Adair, *The History of the American Indians*, ed. Kathryn E. Holland Braund (Tuscaloosa: University of Alabama Press, 2005), 184–186, quotation on 186.

2. Miscellaneous notes, JHPP, reel 1, vol. 2, p. 11; Alexander Moore, ed., *Nairne's Muskhogean Journals: The 1708 Expedition to the Mississippi River* (Jackson: University Press of Mississippi, 1988), 34.

3. Nathaniel Folsom, Discussion of Choctaw History, 1798, PPP, GMA.

4. John R. Swanton, *Social Organization and Social Usages of the Indians of the Creek Confederacy* (New York: Johnson Reprint, 1970), 98.

5. Second Journal of Thomas Bosomworth, in *DRIA*, vol. 1, 310–316; Affidavit of James Geddes, November 6, 1752, in ibid., vol. 1, 342.

6. John Phillip Reid, *A Law of Blood: The Primitive Law of the Cherokee Nation* (New York: New York University Press, 1970); Wayne E. Lee, "Peace Chiefs and Blood Revenge: Patterns of Restraint in Native American Warfare, 1500–1800," *Journal of Military History* 71 (2007): 701–741.

7. John Pope, *A Tour through the Southern and Western Territories of the United States of America* (Gainesville: University of Florida Press, 1979), 63–64.

8. Adair, *History of the American Indians*, 93.

9. Moore, ed., *Nairne's Muskhogean Journals*, 49; Adair, *History of the American Indians*, 183–189, quotation on 185.

10. Caleb Swan, "Position and State of Manners and Arts in the Creek, or Muscogee Nation in 1791," in *Information Respecting the History, Condition and Prospects of the Indian Tribes of the United States*, ed. Henry Rowe

Schoolcraft (Philadelphia: Lippincott and Grambo, 1855), vol. 5, 264; Frank G. Speck, *Ethnology of the Yuchi Indians* (Lincoln: University of Nebraska Press, 2004), 72; George Stiggins, *Creek Indian History: A Historical Narrative of the Geneaology, Traditions and Downfall of the Ispocoga or Creek Indian Tribe of Indians*, ed. Virginia Pounds Brown (Birmingham, AL: Birmingham Public Library Press, 1989), 64–65; Moore, ed., *Nairne's Muskhogean Journals*, 43.

11. David Taitt, "Journal of David Taitt's Travels from Pensacola, West Florida, to and through the Country of the Upper and Lower Creeks, 1772," in *Travels in the American Colonies*, ed. Newton D. Mereness (New York: Macmillan, 1916), 534.

12. Jean-Bernard Bossu, *Travels in the Interior of North America, 1751–1762*, trans. and ed. Seymour Feiler (Norman: University of Oklahoma Press, 1962), 134; Bernard Romans, *A Concise Natural History of East and West Florida*, ed. Kathryn E. Holland Braund (Tuscaloosa: University of Alabama Press, 1999), 146; Richard F. Townsend, "American Landscapes, Seen and Unseen," in *Hero, Hawk, and Open Hand: American Indian Art of the Ancient Midwest and South*, ed. Richard F. Townsend and Robert Sharp (New Haven, CT: Yale University Press, 2004), 33; quotation from Andre Pénicaut, *Fleur de Lys and Calument, Being the Pénicaut Narrative of French Adventure in Louisiana*, ed. and trans. Richebourg Gaillard McWilliams (Baton Rouge: Louisiana State University Press, 1953), 65.

13. Moore, ed., *Nairne's Muskhogean Journals*, 46.

14. Swan, "Position and State," 264–266, 270, 279–280, quotation on 279.

15. Journal of Régis du Roullet's Journey to the Choctaw Nation, 1729, *MPA:FD*, vol. 1, 34.

16. Wayne E. Lee, "Fortify, Fight, or Flee: Tuscarora and Cherokee Defensive Warfare and Military Culture Adaptation," *Journal of Military History* 68 (2004): 713–770.

17. Bienville to the Superior Council of Louisiana, July 23, 1723, *MPA:FD*, vol. 3, 355.

18. Catawba Indians to Governor Glen, 1755, *DRIA*, vol. 2, 48.

19. Bossu, *Travels*, 62.

20. Adair, *History of the American Indians*, 376–380.

21. Stiggins, *Creek Indian History*, 75.

22. Romans, *Concise Natural History*, 150–151; quotation from Adair, *History of the American Indian*, 183.

23. Proceedings of the Council Concerning Indian Affairs, June 18, 1753, *DRIA*, vol. 1, 424; Charles Johnston, "A Narrative of the Incidents Attending the Capture, Detention, and Ransom of Charles Johnston," in *Held Captive by Indians: Selected Narratives, 1642–1836*, ed. Richard VanDerBeets,

(Knoxville: University of Tennessee Press, 1994), 267–269; John McKee to Gov. Blount, August 11, 1794, *Knoxville Gazette*; Antoine Bonnefoy, "Journal of Antoine Bonnefoy," trans. J. Franklin Jameson, in *Travels in the American Colonies*, 241–242; James Robertson to David Henley, October 24, 1795, David Henley Papers, reel 625, TSLA.

24. Bonnefoy, "Journal," 243; Louboey to Maurepas, March 7, 1741, MPA:FD, vol. 4, 177–181; Account of John Stephens, in *South Carolina Gazette*, October 11, 1760.

25. William Martin to Lyman Draper, July 7, 1842, DMC, Tennessee Papers, 3XX4, p. 2.

26. Johnston, "A Narrative," 254, 267.

27. James Axtell, "The White Indians of Colonial America," *The William and Mary Quarterly*, 3rd series 32 (1975): 67–68; Frederick Drimmer, ed., *Scalps and Tomahawks: Narratives of Indian Captivity* (New York: Coward-McCann, 1961), 12; quotation from Journal of Lusser, in *MPA:FD*, vol. 1, 100.

28. Thomas S. Abler provides a discussion in "Scalping, Torture, Cannibalism and Rape: An Ethnohistorical Analysis of Conflicting Cultural Values in War," *Anthropologica* 34 (1992): 14–15.

29. Adair, *History of the American Indians*, 196–197.

30. John R. Swanton, *Indian Tribes of the Lower Mississippi Valley and Adjacent Coast of the Gulf of Mexico* (Washington, DC: U.S. Government Printing Office, 1911), 124.

31. Axtell, "White Indians," 67.

32. John Lawson, *A New Voyage to Carolina*, ed. Hugh Talmage Lefler (Chapel Hill: University of North Carolina Press, 1967), 193.

33. Swanton, *Social Organization and Social Usages*, 355.

34. Tom Hatley, *The Dividing Paths: Cherokees and South Carolinians through the Era of Revolution* (New York: Oxford University Press, 1993), 107; Adair, *History of the American Indians*, 263; John Moultrie to Eleanor Austin, July 10, 1761, Moultrie Family Papers, South Carolina Historical Society, Charleston; William Bull to James Grant, March 28, 1761, JGP, reel 32, box 33, folder 4, frame 82, LOC; John Haywood, *Civil and Political History of the State of Tennessee from Its Earliest Settlement Up to the Year 1796* (New York: Arno Press, 1971), 319; John Haywood Papers, folder 6, doc. 1, TSLA.

35. Bonnefoy, "Journal," 244.

36. Hobert W. Burns, ed., "Memoirs of Mrs. Ann Mathews," in *The Life of Anne Calhoun Mathews: 18 May 1755–19 December 1830* (Palo Alto, CA, 1988), 6; Hatley, *Dividing Paths*, 86, 127–128.

37. Bossu, *Travels*, 64; Mathurin le Petit to Père d'Avaugour, July 12, 1730, in *The Jesuit Relations and Allied Documents, Travels and Explorations of the Jesuit*

Missionaries in New France: 1610–1791, ed. Reuben Gold Thwaites (Cleveland: Burrows Brothers, 1900), vol. 68, 149.

38. Lawson, *New Voyage to Carolina*, 207.

39. John Stuart to James Grant, May 2, 1760, JGP, reel 31, box 31, folder 1, frame 18, LOC; James Mooney, *Myths of the Cherokee* (New York: Johnson Reprint, 1970), 43–44; *South Carolina Gazette*, September 20, 1760; ibid., October 11, 1760; *The Pennsylvania Gazette*, October 30, 1760.

40. *South Carolina Gazette*, September 20, 1760; Affidavit of David Shettroe, *The Philadelphia Evening Post*, August 31, 1776.

41. Alexander Longe, "A Small Postscript on the Ways and Manners of the Indians called Cherokees," ed. David H. Corkran, *Southern Indian Studies* 21 (1969): 45–47, quotation modified from p. 46; Interview with Silversmith, in Daniel S. Butrick to John Howard Payne, December 15, 1835, JHPP, reel 1, vol. 4, p. 31; Swanton, *Indian Tribes*, 125; Adair, *History of the American Indians*, 383; Martin, *Sacred Revolt*, 140–141; Theda Perdue, *Cherokee Women: Gender and Culture Change, 1700–1835* (Lincoln: University of Nebraska Press, 1999), 34–36.

42. Quotations from Mooney, *Myths*, 360, 363; Perdue, *Cherokee Women*, 49.

43. Henry Timberlake, *The Memoirs of Lieut. Henry Timberlake*, ed. Samuel Cole Williams (New York: Arno Press, 1971), 94.

44. Timberlake, *Memoirs*, 82; H. Thomas Foster II, ed., *The Collected Works of Benjamin Hawkins, 1796–1810* (Tuscaloosa: University of Alabama Press, 2003), 63; F. A. Robin and Robert Rea, eds., "Lieutenant Thomas Campbell's Sojourn among the Creeks," *Alabama Historical Quarterly* 36 (1974): 108; Le Page du Pratz, *History of Louisiana*, 374; Bossu, *Travels*, 65; Examination of John Brown, May 27, 1757, DRIA, vol. 2, 380; Ludovic Grant to Governor Glen, July 22, 1754, ibid., 16; Adair, *History of the American Indians*, 383–384, quotation on p. 384.

45. Huspaw King to Charles Craven, 1715, in William L. Ramsey, *The Yamasee War: A Study of Culture, Economy, and Conflict in the Colonial South* (Lincoln: University of Nebraska Press, 2008), 228; Gregory A. Waselkov and Kathryn E. Holland Braund, eds., *William Bartram on the Southeastern Indians*, (Lincoln: University of Nebraska Press, 1995), 58; Journal of Liet. Colonel James Grant of the 40th Regiment, upon an expedition from Fort Prince George against the Cherokees, June 12–16, 1761, JGP, reel 28, box 29, folder 1, frame 6, LOC.

46. "A Fight between the Alabama and the Choctaw" and "The Captive Alabama," in John R. Swanton, *Myths and Tales of the Southeastern Indians* (Norman: University of Oklahoma Press, 1995), 155, 157; Lawrence Keeley, *War before Civilization* (New York: Oxford University Press, 1997), 84.

47. Jack B. Martin and Margaret McKane Mauldin, *A Dictionary of Creek/ Muskogee with Notes on the Florida and Oklahoma Seminole dialects of Creek* (Lincoln: University of Nebraska Press, 2000), 9, 288–289.

48. Foster, ed., *Collected Works of Benjamin Hawkins*, 63; Swanton, *Social Organization and Social Usages*, 437; quotation from Waselkov and Braund, eds., *Bartram on the Southeastern Indians*, 154

49. Kristian Hvidt, ed., *Von Reck's Voyage: Drawings and Journal of Philip Georg Friedrich von Reck* (Savannah: Beehive Press, 1990), 47; quotation from Adair, *History of the American Indians*, 384–385.

50. Le Page du Pratz, *History of Louisiana*, 374; Lawson, *New Voyage to Carolina*, xxxvi, 53, quotation on 207.

51. Adair, *History of the American Indians*, 90.

52. Waselkov and Braund, eds., *Bartram on the Southeastern Indians*, 125.

53. John Stuart to James Grant, May 2, 1760, JGP, reel 31, box 32, folder 1, frame 19, LOC; quotation from Hvidt, ed., *Von Reck's Voyage*, 47.

54. Bossu, *Travels*, 65.

55. Talk of Killa Cunsta to Governor Glen, July 6, 1754, DRIA, vol. 1, 515.

56. Le Page Du Pratz, *History of Louisiana*, 374; quotation from Gregory Evans Dowd, *A Spirited Resistance: The North American Indian Struggle for Unity, 1745–1815* (Baltimore, MD: Johns Hopkins University Press, 1992), 15.

57. Moore, ed., *Nairne's Muskhogean Journals*, 49; Adair, *History of the American Indians*, 390, quotation on 186.

58. Journal of John Buckles, February 22, 1753, DRIA, vol. 1, 384.

59. Quotations from Account of John Stephens, October 11, 1760, *South Carolina Gazette*; Letter from Ft. Prince George, ibid.; *The Pennsylvania Gazette*, May 1, 1760; ibid., July 3, 1760.

60. Maria O. Smith, "Scalping in the Archaic Period: Evidence from the Western Tennessee Valley," *Southeastern Archaeology* 14 (1995): 60–68.

61. James Robertson, "Remarks on the Management of the Scalped-Head" *Philadelphia Medical and Physical Journal* 2 (1805–1806): 27–30.

62. Adair, *History of the American Indians*, 383.

63. Edward Kimber, *A Relation or Journal of a Late Expedition to the Gates of St. Augustine on Florida* (Boston: Charles E. Goodspeed & Co., 1935), 15; Adair, *History of the American Indians*, 183.

64. David H. Dye, "Art, Ritual, and Chiefly Warfare in the Mississippian World," in *Hero, Hawk, and Open Hand*, 203; Adair, *History of the American Indians*, 390; Romans, *Concise Natural History*, 132; Le Petit to D'Avaugour, July 12, 1730, *The Jesuit Relations*, vol. 68, 149; quotation from Report of David Craig to William Blount, March 15, 1792, ASP:IA, vol. 1, 264.

65. "M. Dumont's Memoir," in *Historical Memoirs of Louisiana*, ed. Benjamin F. French (New York: Lamport, Blakeman, & Law, 1853), 88.

66. James Axtell, *The Invasion Within: The Contest of Cultures in Colonial America* (New York: Oxford University Press, 1985); Crémont to Maurepas, February 21, 1737, MPA:FD, vol. 4, 141; quotation from Bienville to Maurepas, December 20, 1737, MPA:FD, vol. 3, 708.

67. Michel Foucault, *Discipline and Punish: The Birth of the Prison*, trans. Alan Sheridan (New York: Pantheon, 1977), quotation on p. 3; Lee, "Peace Chiefs and Blood Revenge"; Abler, "Scalping, Torture, Cannibalism, and Rape."

68. Adair, *History of the American Indians*, 189.

69. Folsom, Choctaw History, 1798, PPP, GMA.

70. Waselkov and Braund, eds., *Bartram on the Southeastern Indians*, 58, 131; Romans, *Concise Natural History*, 147; Joseph Brown, autobiographical sketch, n.d, JBP, folder 1, TSLA.

4. Incorporating Outsiders

1. John R. Swanton, *Source Material for the Social and Ceremonial Life of the Choctaw Indians* (Washington, DC: U.S. Government Printing Office, 1931), 83.

2. John R. Swanton, *Indians of the Southeastern United States* (Washington, DC: Smithsonian Institution Press, 1979), 106, 217; Antoine Simon Le Page Du Pratz, *The History of Louisiana*, ed. and trans. Joseph G. Tregle Jr. (Baton Rouge: Louisiana State University Press, 1975), 300.

3. Charles M. Hudson, *The Southeastern Indians* (Knoxville: University of Tennessee Press, 1976), 161–162.

4. John R. Swanton, *Myths and Tales of the Southeastern Indians* (Norman: University of Oklahoma Press, 1995), 30–34.

5. Talk of Malatchi, June 2, 1753, *DRIA*, vol. 1, 404; Daniel K. Richter, *The Ordeal of the Longhouse: The Peoples of the Iroquois League in the Era of European Colonization* (Chapel Hill: University of North Carolina Press, 1992), 32–33.

6. Alexander Moore, ed., *Nairne's Muskhogean Journals: The 1708 Expedition to the Mississippi River* (Oxford: University Press of Mississippi, 1988), 62.

7. Antoine Bonnefoy, "Journal of Antoine Bonnefoy," trans. J. Franklin Jameson, in *Travels in the American Colonies*, ed. Newton D. Mereness (New York: Macmillan, 1916), 246. For singing, see John Lawson, *A New Voyage to Carolina*, ed. Hugh Talmage Lefler (Chapel Hill: University of North Carolina Press, 1967), 177; Clyde Ellis, *A Dancing People: Powwow Culture on the Southern Plains* (Lawrence: University Press of Kansas, 2003), 173–175.

8. Joseph Brown, autobiographical sketch, n.d, JBP, folder 1, TSLA.

9. Moore, ed., *Nairne's Muskhogean Journals*, 34, 39, 62.

10. William L. Anderson, ed., "Cherokee Clay, from Duché to Wedgwood: The Journal of Thomas Griffiths, 1767–1768," *North Carolina Historical Review* 63 (1986): 501–504.

11. John Marrant, *A Narrative of the Lord's wonderful Dealings, with John Marrant, a Black Now gone to Preach the Gospel in Nova-Scotia) Born in New-York, in North-America, Taken down from his own Relation, arranged, corrected, and published, By the Rev. Mr. Aldridge* in *Held Captive By Indians: Selected Narratives, 1642–1836,* ed. Richard VanDerBeets (Knoxville: University of Tennessee Press, 1994), 177–201.

12. James Seagrove to Jared Irwin, September 18, 1796, "Creek Indian Letters, Talks, and Treaties, 1705–1839," typescript compiled by Louise F. Hays, part 2, 494, GA; *Georgia Gazette*, July 28, 1796; Richard Call to Edward Telfair, July 3, 1791, Telamon Cuyler Collection, HRB, DLG; "A Return of Part of the Property Taken by the Indians from this County [Greene]," 1789, *Georgia Indian Depredation Claims,* ed. Donna B. Thaxton (Americus, Georgia: The Thaxton Company, 1988) 609; E. Merton Coulter, "The Birth of a University, a Town, and a County," *Georgia Historical Quarterly* 46 (1962): 120–121.

13. Deposition of Greenwood LeFlore, February 24, 1843, J. F. H. Claiborne Papers, ms. # 151, box 3, folder 24, SHC.

14. Lawson, *New Voyage to Carolina,* 245; quotation from Miscellaneous notes, JHPP, reel 1, vol. 4, p. 94.

15. Deposition of LeFlore, February 24, 1843, Claiborne Papers, box 3, folder 24, SHC.

16. Henry Timberlake, *The Memoirs of Lieut. Henry Timberlake,* ed. Samuel Cole Williams (New York: Arno Press, 1971), 111, n. 62.

17. "Historical Traditions of Tennessee: The Captivity of Jane Brown and her Family," from *The American Whig Review* 15 (1852), reprinted in *The Garland Library of Narrative of North American Indian Captivities* (New York: Garland, 1978), vol. 64, p. 8; Joseph Brown, autobiographical sketch, n.d, JBP, folder 1, TSLA.

18. Early Life of Margaret Ervin Austill, Jeremiah Austill Papers, ms. #2214-z, SHC; John R. Swanton, *Creek Religion and Medicine* (Lincoln: University of Nebraska Press, 2000), 615.

19. Affidavit of John Eades, October 30, 1793, "Creek Indian Letters," part 1, 349, GA.

20. Thomas S. Woodward, *Woodward's Reminiscences of the Creek, or Muscogee Indians, Contained in Letters to Friends in Georgia and Alabama* (Tuscaloosa and Birmingham: Alabama Book Store and Birmingham Book Exchange, 1939), 41.

21. Tellico Blockhouse Treaty Negotiations, December 28, 1794-January 3, 1795, JRP, reel 801, TSLA.

22. Joseph Martin to Edward Telfair, October 16, 1786, "Cherokee Indian Letters, Talks, and Treaties, 1786–1838," typescript compiled by Louise F. Hays, vol. 1, 5b, GA; H. Thomas Foster, ed., *The Collected Works of Benjamin Hawkins, 1796–1810* (Tuscaloosa: University of Alabama Press, 2003), 169.

23. Mary R. Haas, "Creek Inter-Town Relations," *American Anthropologist* 42 (1940): 483.

24. Relief of George Mayfield, January 13, 1832, 22nd Cong., 1st sess., H.R. 182.

25. Foster, ed., *Collected Works of Benjamin Hawkins*, 321.

26. Relief of George Mayfield, January 13, 1832, 22nd Cong., 1st sess., H.R. 182.

27. Ibid.; Relief of George Mayfield, April 4, 1840, 26th Cong., 1st sess., H.R. 360.

28. Foster, ed., *Collected Works of Benjamin Hawkins, 1796–1810*, 50s; Samuel Alexander to Edward Telfair, 1792, "Creek Indian Letters," part 1, 262, GA; Benjamin Hawkins to Samuel Alexander, January 21, 1799, BHL; Hawkins to Colonel Gaither, January 21, 1799, ibid.

29. Benjamin Hawkins to Samuel Alexander, January 21, 1799, BHL.

30. H. Thomas Foster II, ed., *The Collected Works of Benjamin Hawkins, 1796–1810* (Tuscaloosa: University of Alabama Press, 2003), 50s, 200; Samuel Alexander to Edward Telfair, 1792, "Creek Indian Letters," part 1, 262, GA; Benjamin Hawkins to Samuel Alexander, January 21, 1799, BHL; Hawkins to Colonel Gaither, January 21, 1799, ibid.; James E. Seaver, *A Narrative of the Life of Mrs. Mary Jemison*, ed. June Namias (Norman: University of Oklahoma Press, 1995), 83–84, quotation on p. 84.

31. Judd's Friend quoted in Tom Hatley, *The Dividing Paths: Cherokees and South Carolinians through the Era of Revolution* (New York: Oxford University Press, 1995), 163.

32. Benjamin Hawkins to Thomas Jefferson, July 12, 1800, Vocabularies and Miscellaneous Papers Pertaining to Indian Languages, APS.

33. James Adair, *The History of the American Indians*, ed. Kathryn E. Holland Braund (Tuscaloosa: University of Alabama Press, 2005), 259; quotation from *South Carolina Gazette*, August 15, 1743.

34. Bonnefoy, "Journal," 246–248.

35. Adair, *History of the American Indians*, 259.

36. Gwendolyn Midlo Hall, *Africans in Colonial Louisiana: The Development of Afro-Creole Culture in the Eighteenth Century* (Baton Rouge: Louisiana State University Press, 1992); Foster, ed., *Collected Works of Benjamin Hawkins*, 200.

37. Account of the Swallow Warriour to Capt. Raymond Demere, September 5, 1756, *DRIA*, vol. 2, 197.

38. John Stuart to James Grant, April 3, 1767, JGP, reel 12, box 13, folder 4, frame 206, LOC; Peter H. Wood, "The Changing Population of the Colonial South: An Overview by Race and Region, 1685–1790," in *Powhatan's Mantle: Indians in the Colonial Southeast*, eds. Gregory A. Waselkov, Peter H. Wood, and Tom Hatley (Lincoln: University of Nebraska Press, 2006), 90.

39. Carl F. Klinck and James J. Talman, eds., *The Journal of Major John Norton, 1809–1816* (Toronto: Champlain Society, 1970), introduction, 49, 55; Raymond D. Fogelson, "Major John Norton as Ethno-ethnologist," *Journal of Cherokee Studies* 3 (1978): 250–255.

40. Journal of the Grand Cherokee National Council, June 26, 1792, ASP:IA, vol. 1, 271.

41. Richard Henderson to Governor Martin, December 23, 1782, "Creek Indian Letters," part 1, 42, GA.

42. Greg O'Brien, "The Conqueror Meets the Unconquered: Negotiating Cultural Boundaries on the Post-Revolutionary Southern Frontier," *Journal of Southern History* 67 (2001): 39–72; Marianne Bienvenu to Vaudreuil, August 27, 1743, MPA:FD, vol. 4, 213.

43. Quoted in David H. Corkran, *The Creek Frontier, 1540–1783* (Norman: University of Oklahoma Press, 1967), 323.

44. Hudson, *The Southeastern Indians*, 122.

45. Adair, *History of the American Indians*, 273.

46. James Vernon Knight Jr., "The Formation of the Creeks," in *The Forgotten Centuries: Indians and Europeans in the American South, 1521–1704*, ed. Charles Hudson and Carmen Chaves Tesser (Athens: University of Georgia Press, 1994), 384–386; H. Thomas Foster II, "Evidence of Historic Creek Indian Migration from a Regional and Direct Historic Analysis of Ceramic Types," *Southeastern Archaeology* 23 (2004): 65–84.

47. James Vernon Knight Jr., *Tukabatchee: Archaeological Investigations at an Historic Creek Town, Elmore County, Alabama* (Tuscaloosa: Office of Archaeological Research, Alabama State Museum of Natural History, 1985); John R. Swanton, *Early History of the Creek Indians and Their Neighbors* (Gainesville: University of Florida Press, 1998), 277–282; quotation from Louis LeClerc Milfort, *Memoirs, or A quick Glance at my various Travels and my Sojourn in the Creek Nation*, ed. and trans. Ben C. McCary (Kennesaw, GA: Continental, 1959), 163.

48. George Stiggins, *Creek Indian History: A Historical Narrative of the Genealogy, Traditions, and Downfall of the Ispocoga or Creek Indian Tribe of Indians*, ed. Virginia Pounds Brown (Birmingham: Birmingham Public Library Press, 1989), 44–45; John R. Swanton, *Creek Religion and Medicine* (Lincoln: University of Nebraska Press, 2000), 504–510; John R. Swanton, *Social Organi-*

zation and Social Usages of the Indians of the Creek Confederacy (New York: Johnson Reprint, 1970), 120, 307.

49. Mark F. Boyd, trans., "Expedition of Marcos Delgado from Apalache to the Upper Creek Country in 1686," *Florida Historical Quarterly* 16 (1937): 2–32; Stiggins, *Creek Indian History*, 25; quotation from Talk of the Senecas to the Lower Towns, August 11, 1726, in "Journal of Captain Tobias Fitch's Misson" in *Travels in the American Colonies*, 189.

50. Klinck and Talman, eds., *Journal of Major John Norton*, 47.

51. Alan Gallay, *The Indian Slave Trade: The Rise of English Empire in the American South, 1670–1717* (New Haven, CT: Yale University Press, 2002), 175; quotation from Milfort, *Sojourn in the Creek Nation*, 164.

52. John Stuart to James Grant, August 11, 1766, JGP, reel 10, box 11, folder 2, frame 74, LOC; Anthony Paredes and Kenneth J. Plante, "A Reexamination of Creek Indian Population Trends: 1738–1832," *American Indian Culture and Research Journal* 6 (1983): 3–28; Wood, "Changing Population of the Colonial South," 84–87, quotation on p. 87; Kathryn E. Holland Braund, *Deerskins & Duffels: The Creek Indian Trade with Anglo-America, 1685–1815* (Lincoln: University of Nebraska Press, 1993), 9.

53. J. Leitch Wright Jr., *Creeks & Seminoles: The Destruction and Regeneration of the Muscogulge People* (Lincoln: University of Nebraska Press, 1986), 18; Gregory A. Waselkov and Kathryn E. Holland Braund, eds., *William Bartram on the Southeastern Indians* (Lincoln: University of Nebraska Press, 1995), 108–109; Henry Rowe Schoolcraft, *Notes on the Iroquois; or, Contributions to the Statistics, Aboriginal History, Antiquities, and General Ethnology of Western New York* (New York: Barlett and Welford, 1846), 29.

54. *South Carolina Gazette*, October 21–28, 1732; quotation from Adam Hodgson, *Remarks during a Journey through North America in the Years 1819, 1820, and 1821* (Westport, CT: Negro Universities Press, 1970), 266.

55. Stiggins, *Creek Indian History*, 31–33.

56. Frank G. Speck, *Ethnology of the Yuchi Indians* (Lincoln: University of Nebraska Press, 2004), xii, 7, 68; quotation in Foster, ed., *Collected Works of Benjamin Hawkins*, 39s.

57. Waselkov and Braund, eds., *Bartram on the Southeastern Indians*, 90.

58. Marchand and St. Ange to Périer, September 15, 1732, MPA:FD, vol. 4, 124.

59. Bienville to Maurepas, July 26, 1733, MPA:FD, vol. 1, 211.

60. Miscellaneous notes, JHPP, reel 1, vol. 4, p. 103; John R. Swanton, *Indian Tribes of the Lower Mississippi Valley and Adjacent Coast of the Gulf of Mexico* (Washington, DC: U.S. Government Printing Office, 1911), 334–336, quotation on p. 254.

61. Wendy St. Jean, "Trading Paths: Chickasaw Diplomacy in the Greater Southeast, 1690s-1790s" (Ph.D. diss., University of Connecticut, 2004), 51, 83, 200.

62. James Taylor Carson, *Making an Atlantic World: Circles, Paths, and Stories from the Colonial South* (Knoxville: University of Tennessee Press, 2007), 15–16; Kathleen DuVal, *The Native Ground: Indians and Colonists in the Heart of the Continent* (Philadelphia: University of Pennsylvania Press, 2006), 5.

63. Salmon to Maurepas, February 8, 1733, MPA:FD, vol. 4, 128; Swanton, *Indians of the Southeastern United States*, 663–664; Patricia Galloway, *Choctaw Genesis, 1500–1700* (Lincoln: University of Nebraska Press, 1995), 2, 354–355; Tomatly Mingo quoted in Greg O'Brien, *Choctaws in a Revolutionary Age, 1750–1830* (Lincoln: University of Nebraska Press, 2002), 17.

64. Caleb Swan, "Position and State of Manners and Arts in the Creek, or Muscogee Nation in 1791," in *Information Respecting the History, Condition and Prospects of the Indian Tribes of the United States*, ed. Henry Rowe Schoolcraft (Philadelphia: Lippincott and Grambo, 1855), vol. 5, 260.

65. Swanton, *Social Organization and Social Usages*, 109–111, 269; quotations from Stiggins, *Creek Indian History*, 64–65.

66. Bernard Romans, *A Concise Natural History of East and West Florida*, ed. Kathryn E. Holland Braund (Tuscaloosa: University of Alabama Press, 1999), 139; quotation from Foster, ed., *Collected Works of Benjamin Hawkins*, 74s. For Cherokees, see Klinck and Talman, eds., *Journal of Major John Norton*, 77.

67. Quotation from ibid., 80; Swanton, *Indian Tribes*, 102; Frank G. Speck, "Notes on Chickasaw Ethnology and Folklore," *Journal of American Folklore* 20 (1907): 50–58; Swanton, *Indians of the Southeastern United States*, 664–665; Woodward, *Reminiscences of the Creek*, 19; Swanton, *Social Organization and Social Usages*, 145; Vernon James Knight Jr., "Social Organization and the Evolution of Hierarchy in Southeastern Chiefdoms," *Journal of Anthropological Research* 46 (1990): 17; Speck, *Ethnology of the Yuchi Indians*, 72.

68. Hodgson, *Remarks during a Journey*, 279.

69. Moore, ed., *Nairne's Muskhogean Journals*, 61.

70. St. Jean, "Trading Paths," Chapter 2, 158, 208; Theda Perdue, *"Mixed-Blood" Indians: Racial Construction in the Early South* (Athens: University of Georgia Press, 2003), 23–25.

71. P. M. Hamer, "Fort Loudoun in the Cherokee War, 1758–1761," *North Carolina Historical Review* 2 (1925): 442–458; quotation from *The Pennsylvania Gazette*, October 30, 1760.

72. Duane H. King, ed., *The Memoirs of Lt. Henry Timberlake: The Story of a Soldier, Adventurer, and Emissary to the Cherokees, 1756–65* (Cherokee, NC: Museum of the Cherokee Indian Press, 2007), 35.

73. James Stuart to James Grant, May 2, 1760, JGP, reel 31, box 31, folder 1, frame 18, LOC; John Stuart to James Grant, June 6, 1760, JGP, reel 31, box 32, folder 1, frame 39–40, LOC; "considerable numbers" from Hamer, "Fort Loudoun," 454.

74. Lawson, *New Voyage to Carolina*, 177.

75. Galloway, *Choctaw Genesis, 1500–1700*, 285–303, 359; O'Brien, *Choctaws in a Revolutionary Age*, 12; John Sibley to Samuel Hopkins Sibley, February 28, 1803, in *Louisiana Historical Quarterly* 10 (1927): 499; quotations from Swanton, *Source Material*, 18, 20.

76. James H. Merrell, "The Racial Education of the Catawba Indians," *Journal of Southern History* 50 (1984): 369.

77. Quoted in ibid., 363. For the death and torture of black men, see Peter H. Wood, *Black Majority: Negros in Colonial South Carolina from 1670 through the Stono Rebellion* (New York: Knopf, 1974), 129; Jerald T. Milanich, *Laboring in the Fields of the Lord: Spanish Missions and Southeastern Indians* (Washington, DC: Smithsonian Press, 1999), 187; Letter of Abraham Wood, August 22, 1674, in *Early Travels in the Tennessee Country, 1540–1800*, ed. Samuel Cole Williams (Johnson City, TN: Watauga Press, 1928), 29, 34.

78. Speech of William Christian to Cherokee Mothers, July 1781, DMC, Tennessee Papers, 1XX49.

79. Jean-Bernard Bossu, *Travels in the Interior of North America, 1751–1762*, trans. and ed. Seymour Feiler (Norman: University of Oklahoma Press, 1962), 209. See also Adair, *History of the American Indians*, 67; Kristian Hvidt, ed., *Von Reck's Voyage: Drawings and Journal of Philip Georg Friedrich von Reck* (Savannah, GA: Beehive Press, 1990), 45.

80. Hvidt, ed., *Von Reck's Voyage*, 40.

81. Bossu, *Travels*, 217.

82. Herodotus, *The Histories*, trans. Aubrey de Sélincourt (London: Penguin, 1972), 239. See also Romans, *Concise Natural History*, 111–112.

83. Bossu, *Travels*, p. 65, n. 10; Albert James Pickett, *History of Alabama and Incidentally of Georgia and Mississippi, from the Earliest Period* (New York: Arno Press, 1971), vol. 1, 75.

84. John Rippon, ed., "An Account of the Life of Mr. David George, from Sierra Leone to Africa, given by himself in a conversation with Brother Rippon of London, and Brother Pearce of Birmingham," in *The Baptist Annual Register for 1790, 1791, 1792, & part of 1793, Including Sketches of the State of Religion*

Among Different Denominations of Good Men at Home and Abroad (London, 1793), 474; Bossu, *Travels*, 166.

85. Account of Pierre de Charlevoix, 1721, in *Early Travels in the Tennessee Country, 1540–1800*, ed. Samuel Cole Williams (Johnson City, TN: Watauga Press, 1928), 87.

86. Du Pratz in Swanton, *Indian Tribes*, 92.

87. Adair, *History of the American Indians*, 65.

88. Claudio Saunt, *A New Order of Things: Power, Property, and the Transformation of the Creek Indians, 1733–1816* (New York: Cambridge University Press, 1999), 112. The English were occasionally called "blond" as well. See Bossu, *Travels*, 138.

89. From James Grant's speech at the Picolata Conference, 1767, in *The British Meet the Seminoles: Negotiations between British Authorities in East Florida and the Indians, 1763–68*, ed. James W. Covington (Gainesville: University of Florida Press, 1961), 43.

90. Nathaniel Folsom, Discussion of Choctaw History, 1798, PPP, GMA; Cyrus Byington, *A Dictionary of the Choctaw Language*, eds. John R. Swanton and Henry S. Halbert (Washington, DC: U.S. Government Printing Office, 1915), 266.

91. Speech of Captain Aleck at the Picolata Congress, 1765, in *British Meet the Seminoles*, 29; Journal of Lusser, January 12–23, 1730, in *MPA:FD*, vol. 1, 101; Gagane-huma to Esteban Miró, January 3, 1788, MPA:SA, vol. 3, reel 405, p. 110, MDAH.

92. John Stuart to James Grant, June 1, 1765, JGP, reel 7, box 8, folder 6, frame 233, LOC.

5. *Owned People*

1. Jesse Dupont to Enrique White, January 24, 1802, EFP, section 45, reel 83, doc. 1802–7, PKY; Citizens of St. Augustine to Enrique White, July 1, 1802, PC, legajo 1554B, reel 39, folio 67, PKY; Marguerite M. Mathews, comp., "Bonelly Family Genealogy," Saint Augustine Historical Society, St. Augustine, Florida.

2. Juan Forrester to Enrique White, August 31, 1801, EFP, section 29, reel 43, PKY; White to Someruelos, December 2, 1801, EFP, section 2, reel 10, doc. 1801–394, PKY; Citizens of St. Augustine to White, July 1, 1802, PC, legajo 1554B, reel 39, folio 67, PKY; Petition to Governor Enrique White from Citizens of East Florida, January 27, 1803, EFP, section 29, reel 43, PKY; quotation from Jack Kinnard to Enrique White, October 2, 1801, EFP, section 29, reel 43, PKY.

3. Testimony of [Antonia] Mary Bonelly Leonardy, October 1, 1835, ASP:MA, vol. 6, p. 500.

4. Jack B. Martin and Margaret McKane Mauldin, *A Dictionary of Creek/Muskogee with Notes on the Florida and Oklahoma Seminole Dialects of Creek* (Lincoln: University of Nebraska Press, 2004), 313, 141; Theda Perdue, *Slavery and the Evolution of Cherokee Society, 1540–1866* (Knoxville: University of Tennessee Press, 1979), 4; John Lawson, *A New Voyage to Carolina*, ed. Hugh Talmage Lefler (Chapel Hill: University of North Carolina Press, 1967), 210; John R. Swanton, *Source Material for the Social and Ceremonial Life of the Choctaw Indians* (Washington, DC: U.S. Government Printing Office, 1931), 163; Brett Rushforth, "'A Little Flesh We Offer You': The Origins of Indian Slavery in New France," *William and Mary Quarterly*, 3rd Series, 60 (2003): 783.

5. Charles M. Hudson, *The Southeastern Indians* (Knoxville: University of Tennessee Press, 1976), 184–196; Mathurin le Petit to Père d'Avaugour, July 12, 1730, *The Jesuit Relations and Allied Documents, Travels and Explorations of the Jesuit Missionaries in New France: 1610–1791* (Cleveland: Burrows Brothers, 1900), vol. 68, 127; Talk of the Choctaw Kings, Headmen, and Warriors to the Creeks, June 10, 1795, JRP, reel 801, TSLA; Women's Council quoted in Cynthia Cumfer, *Separate Peoples, One Land: The Minds of Cherokees, Blacks, and Whites on the Tennessee Frontier* (Chapel Hill: University of North Carolina Press, 2007), 38.

6. Patricia Galloway, "'The Chief Who Is Your Father': Choctaw and French Views of the Diplomatic Relation," in *Powhatan's Mantle: Indians in the Colonial Southeast*, eds. Gregory A. Waselkov, Peter H. Wood, and Tom Hatley (Lincoln: University of Nebraska Press, 2006), 345–370, quotation on p. 345.

7. Gregory A. Waselkov and Kathryn E. Holland Braund, eds., *William Bartram on the Southeastern Indians* (Lincoln: University of Nebraska Press, 1995), 58.

8. Antoine Bonnefoy, "Journal of Antoine Bonnefoy," trans. J. Franklin Jameson, in *Travels in the American Colonies*, ed. Newton D. Mereness (New York: Macmillan, 1916), 244–250, first quote p. 274; second quote from John Millar to Arturo O'Neill, September 1, 1788, LC, group 174, box 6, PKY.

9. Deposition of James Ore, June 16, 1792, ASP:IA, vol. 1, 274.

10. Leland Donald, *Aboriginal Slavery on the Northwest Coast of North America* (Berkeley: University of California Press, 1997),137–138; Testimony of Francis Spann, December 10, 1794, printed in *Knoxville Gazette*, March 13, 1795; *Knoxville Gazette*, October 11, 1794; Le Petit to D'Avaugour, July 12, 1730, *Jesuit Relations*, vol. 68, 169; Lawson, *New Voyage to Carolina*, 64, 44, 49; Affidavit of David Shettore, reprinted in *The Philadelphia Evening Post*, August 31, 1776.

11. James Grant to Jeffrey Amherst, October 19, 1760, JGP, reel 31, box 32, folder 2, frame 68–69, LOC; *South Carolina Gazette*, September 20, 1760;

Alexander Hewat, *An historical account of the rise and progress of the colonies of South Carolina and Georgia* (London: Alexander Donaldson, 1779), vol. 2, 239–241; William Byrd III to Capt. James Abercromby, September 16, 1760, in *The Correspondence of the Three William Byrds of Westover, Virginia, 1684–1776* (Charlottesville: University Press of Virginia, 1977), vol. 2, 704.

12. From anonymous letter, quoted in John R. Swanton, *Early History of the Creek Indians and Their Neighbors* (Gainesville: University of Florida Press, 1998), 225; Waselkov and Braund, eds., *William Bartram on the Southeastern Indians*, 51–53, 156.

13. Quotation from H. Thomas Foster II, ed., *Collected Works of Benjamin Hawkins, 1796–1810* (Tuscaloosa: University of Alabama Press, 2003), 30s; James L. Watson, "Slavery as an Institution," in *Asian and African Systems of Slavery*, ed. Watson (Berkeley: University of California Press, 1980), 1–15.

14. Dumont in Swanton, *Indian Tribes of the Lower Mississippi Valley and Adjacent Coast of the Gulf of Mexcio* (Washington, DC: U.S. Government Printing Office, 1911), 71; Waselkov and Braund, eds., *William Bartram on the Southeastern Indians*, 62.

15. James Smith, *An account of the remarkable occurrences in the life and travels of Col. James Smith* (Lexington, KY: John Bradford, 1799), 26.

16. John Rippon, ed., "An Account of the Life of Mr. David George, from Sierra Leone to Africa, given by himself in a conversation with Brother Rippon of London, and Brother Pearce of Birmingham," in *The Baptist Annual Register for 1790, 1791, 1792, & Part of 1793, Including Sketches of the State of Religion Among Different Denominations of Good Men at Home and Abroad* (London, 1793), 474.

17. Lawson, *New Voyage to Carolina*, 59, 208. Emphasis added.

18. Garcilasso de la Vega, "La Florida by the Inca," trans. Charmion Shelby, in *DSC*, vol. 2, 312, 400.

19. Report of Isaac Titsworth to William Blount, August 9, 1795, JRP, reel 801, TSLA; Testimony of Isaac Titsworth, December 20, 1794, printed in *Knoxville Gazette*, January 9, 1795, TSLA.

20. Alexander Moore, ed., *Nairne's Muskhogean Journals: The 1708 Expedition to the Mississippi River* (Jackson: University of Mississippi Press, 1988), 48.

21. Leland Donald, "Was Nuu-chah-nulth-aht Society Based on Slave Labor?" in *The Development of Political Organization in Native North America* (Washington, DC: American Ethnological Society, 1983), 114; Joan B. Townsend, "Pre-contact Political Organization and Slavery in Aleut Societies," in ibid., 125; Brett Rushforth, "Savage Bonds: Indian Slavery and Alliance in New France," (Ph.D. diss., University of California at Davis, 2003), 23; Andrés de

Barcia, *Barcia's Chronological History of the Continent of Florida*, trans. Anthony Kerrigan (Gainesville: University of Florida Press, 1951), 137, 183–184; Andrés Reséndez, *A Land So Strange: The Epic Journey of Cabeza de Vaca* (New York: Basic Books, 2007), 163.

22. Quotation from Foster, ed., *Collected Works of Benjamin Hawkins*, 30s; James Vernon Knight Jr., *Tukabatchee: Archaeological Investigations at an Historic Creek Town, Elmore County, Alabama* (Tuscaloosa: Office of Archaeological Research, Alabama State Museum of Natural History, 1985); Mark Williams and Gary Shapiro, "Paired Towns," in *Lamar Archaeology: Mississippian Chiefdoms in the Deep South*, eds. Williams and Shapiro (Tuscaloosa: University of Alabama Press, 1990), 163–171; R. Douglas Hurt, *Indian Agriculture in America: Prehistory to the Present* (Lawrence: University Press of Kansas, 1987), 15–16, 27–32; Stephen A. Kowalewski and James W. Hatch, "The Sixteenth Century Expansion of Settlement in the Upper Oconee Watershed, Georgia," in *Southeastern Archaeology* 10 (1991): 1–17; Christopher Gadsden, *Some observations on the two campaigns against the Cherokee Indians, in 1760 and 1761* (Charleston, SC: Peter Timothy, 1762), 72.

23. Kathleen M. Brown, *Good Wives, Nasty Wenches, and Anxious Patriarchs: Gender, Race, and Power in Colonial Virginia* (Chapel Hill: University of North Carolina Press, 1996); Rushforth, "Savage Bonds," 23–24; Talk of the Lower Cherokees to Governor Lyttleton, February 11, 1758, *DRIA*, vol. 2, 436; Leland, "Nuu-chah-nulth-aht Society," 112; Nancy E. Levine, "Perspectives on Nyinba Slavery," in *Asian and African Systems of Slavery*, 210; Jack Goody, "Slavery in Time and Space," in ibid., 38–40; Watson, "Slavery as an Institution," in ibid., 4.

24. Journal of John Buckles, April 8, 1754, in *DRIA*, vol. 1, 510; Mereness, ed., "Journal of Colonel George Chicken's Mission from Charleston, South Carolina, to the Cherokees, 1725," in *Travels in the American Colonies*, 116.

25. Bienville to Maurepas, July 26, 1733, *MPA:FD*, vol. 1, 211; John Stuart to Allan Stuart, May 15, 1760, JGP, reel 31, box 32, folder 1, frame 23, LOC.

26. Bonnefoy, "Journal," 245; Tellico Blockhouse Treaty, December 28, 1795–January 3, 1796, JRP, reel 801, TSLA.

27. Bonnefoy, "Journal of Bonnefoy," 245; Louboey to Maurepas, February 8, 1746, *MPA:FD*, vol. 4, 260.

28. William Blount to James Robertson, January 6, 1794, JRP, reel 801, TSLA.

29. James Grant to Jeffrey Amherst, October 19, 1760, JGP, reel 31, box 32, folder 2, frame 70, LOC.

30. James Grant to William Bull, November 19, 1761, JGP, reel 28, box 29, folder 1, frame 44, LOC.

31. James Grant to Jeffrey Amherst, November 19, 1761, JGP, reel 28, box 29, folder 1, frame 45, LOC; Gadsden, *Some observations*, 72.

32. A Talk from the Little Carpenter to Lachlan McIntosh, November 15, 1761, in Gadsden, *Some observations*, 65; Grant to Amherst, October 19, 1760, JGP, reel 31, box 32, folder 2, frame 70, LOC; Grant to Amherst, March 30, 1761, JGP, reel 32, box 33, folder 16, frame 21, LOC; John Stuart to Grant, May 2, 1760, JGP, reel 31, box 31, frame 18, folder 1, LOC; Lachlan McIntosh to James Grant, April 2, 1761, JGP, reel 32, box 33, folder 5, frame 100, LOC; McIntosh to Grant, April 25, 1761, JGP, reel 32, box 33, folder 5, frame 139, LOC; Grant to William Bull, November 19, 1761, JGP, reel 28, box 29, folder 1, frame 44, LOC; Wayne E. Lee, *Crowds and Soldiers in Revolutionary North Carolina: The Culture of Violence in Riot and War* (Gainesville: University Press of Florida, 2001), 128.

33. Matthew Tool to Governor Glen, April 9, 1754, *DRIA*, vol. 1, 488.

34. John Thornton, *Africa and Africans in the Making of the Atlantic World, 1400–1800* (New York: Cambridge University Press, 1998), 74.

35. Petition to Governor White from Citizens of St. Augustine, July 1, 1802, PC, legajo 1554B, reel 39, folio 67, PKY; Mathews, "Bonelly Family Genealogy"; quotation from Petition to Governor White, January 27, 1803, PC, legajo 1555, reel 41, folio 122, PKY.

36. Jacobo Dubreuil to Governor Salcedo, September 4, 1803, PC, legajo 76, reel 250, folio 419, PKY; Enrique White to Jack Kinnard and other chiefs of the Creek Nation, July 14, 1802, EFP, section 29, reel 43, PKY; Enrique White to Carondelet, May 30, 1793, in Lawrence Kinnaird, ed., *Annual Report of the American Historical Association for the Year 1945, Volume 4: Spain in the Mississippi Valley, 1765–1794* (Washington, DC: U.S. Government Printing Office, 1949), 163.

37. Juan Forrester to Enrique White, September 7, 1802, EFP, section 29, reel 43, PKY; Jamie Durouzseaux to Vincente Folch, August 21, 1802, PC, August 21, 1802, legajo 1554B, reel 39, folio 191, PKY; Dubreuil to Salcedo, August 31, 1802, PC, August 31, legajo 2355, reel 381, folio 102, PKY; Forrester to White, September 7, 1802, Heloise H. Cruzat Papers, box 1, PKY, courtesy of FLHS.

38. Waselkov and Braund, eds., *William Bartram on the Southeastern Indians*, 51–53, quotation on 52–53; Lawson, *New Voyage to Carolina*, 240, 187.

39. Rippon, ed., "Account of the Life of David George," 474; Report of Isaac Titsworth to William Blount, August 9, 1795, JRP, reel 801, TSLA; Testimony of Isaac Titsworth, December 20, 1794, in *Knoxville Gazette*, January 9, 1795, TSLA; *Knoxville Gazette*, October 11, 1794, TSLA; Deposition of James Ore, June 16, 1792, *ASP:IA*, vol. 1, 274; Hobert W. Burns, ed., "Memoirs of Mrs. Ann Mathews," in *The Life of Anne Calhoun Mathews: 18 May 1755–19 December 1830* (Palo Alto, CA, 1988), 7.

40. Burns, ed., "Memoirs of Mrs. Ann Mathews," 6–7; *South Carolina Gazette*, September 20, 1760; Tom Hatley, *The Dividing Paths: Cherokees and South Carolinians through the Revolutionary Era* (New York: Oxford University Press, 1995), 136; *The Pennsylvania Gazette*, July 3, 1760.

41. Burns, ed., "Memoirs of Mrs. Anne Mathews," 7; *Knoxville Gazette*, October 11, 1794; ibid., March 13, 1795; William Blount to James Robertson, May 16, 1792, JRP, reel 801, TSLA.

42. Biographical Sketch, JBP, TSLA; Joseph Brown to Judge Grundy, October 7, 1811, Howell Papers, box 2, folder 2, TSLA; Burns, ed., "Memoirs of Mrs. Ann Mathews," 7; Claudio Saunt, *A New Order of Things: Power, Property, and the Transformation of the Creek Indians, 1733–1816* (New York: Cambridge University Press, 1999), 70–73; Hudson, *Southeastern Indians*, 213–218; Donald, *Aboriginal Slavery*, 77.

43. Juan Forrester to Enrique White, September 7, 1802, EFP, section 29, reel 43, PKY; John B. Collins to unknown, May 11, 1802, EFP, section 29, reel 43, PKY; Testimony of [Antonia] Mary Bonelly Leonardy, October 1, 1835, ASP:MA, vol. 6, p. 500; Dubreuil to Salcedo, September 4, 1803, PC, legajo 76, reel 250, folio 419, PKY; Ignacio Balderas to Enrique White, August 12, 1805, EFP, Section 29, reel 43, PKY.

44. Juan Forrester to Enrique White, September 7, 1802, EFP, section 29, reel 43, PKY; Dubreuil to Salcedo, September 4, 1803, PC, legajo 76, reel 250, folio 419, PKY. For "knowers," see John R. Swanton, *Creek Religion and Medicine* (Lincoln: University of Nebraska Press, 2000), 615–616; Hudson, *Southeastern Indians*, 351–365.

45. Mary Rowlandson, *The Sovereignty and Goodness of God*, ed. Neal Salisbury (Boston: Bedford/St. Martin's, 1997), 107.

46. Frederick Drimmer, *Captured by the Indians: Fifteen Firsthand Accounts, 1750–1870* (New York: Dover, 1985), 13.

47. "Mrs. English's Captivity," DMC, Draper's Notes, 30S265–266; Sharon Block, *Rape and Sexual Power in Early America* (Chapel Hill: University of North Carolina Press, 2006), 222–228; June Namias, *White Captives: Gender and Ethnicity on the American Frontier* (Chapel Hill: University of North Carolina Press, 1993), 65–66; Gregory A. Waselkov, *A Conquering Spirit: Fort Mims and the Redstick War of 1813–1814* (Tuscaloosa: University of Alabama Press, 2006), 39–41; quotation from Frederick Drimmer, *Captured by the Indians: Fifteen Firsthand Accounts, 1750–1870* (New York: Dover, 1985), 13.

48. Foster, ed., *Collected Works of Benjamin Hawkins*, 74s; quotations from Adair, *History of the American Indians*, 252, 182, except "if wee doe nott," from Alexander Longe, "A Small Postscript on the ways and manners of the Indians called Cherokees," ed. David H. Corkran, in *Southern Indian Studies* 21 (1969): 37.

49. Bernard Romans, *A Concise Natural History of East and West Florida*, ed. Kathryn E. Holland Braund (Tuscaloosa: University of Alabama Press, 1999), 139.

50. Juan Nepomuceno de Quesada to Juan Forrester, July 4, 1792, EFP, section 32, reel 47, doc. 1792–247, PKY; Juan Forrester to Quesada, September 22, 1792, EFP, section 32, reel 47, doc. 1792–335, PKY; Citizens of St. Marys to Quesada, August 18, 1792, EFP, section 32, reel 47, doc. 1792–291, PKY; Deposition of Alexander Steele, September 12, 1792, EFP, section 32, reel 47, doc. 1792–32, PKY.

51. Romans, *Concise Natural History*, 128.

52. Ibid., 65; Nancy Shoemaker, *A Strange Likeness: Becoming Red and White in Eighteenth-Century North America* (New York: Oxford University Press, 2004), 112.

53. Longe, "A Small Postscript," 31.

54. Theda Perdue, *Cherokee Women: Gender and Culture Change, 1700–1835* (Lincoln: University of Nebraska Press, 1999), 42–44, 56; Kathryn E. Holland Braund, *Deerskins & Duffels: The Creek Trade with Anglo-America, 1685–1815* (Lincoln: University of Nebraska Press, 1993), 12.

55. Block, *Rape and Sexual Power*, 73.

56. White to Someruelos, March 13, 1802, PC, legajo 1553, reel 37, folio 1050, PKY; Forrester to White, September 7, 1802, EFP, section 29, reel 43, PKY; John B. Collins to unknown, May 11, 1802, EFP, Section 29, reel 43, PKY.

57. Waselkov and Braund, eds., *William Bartram on the Southeastern Indians*, 156; Henry Timberlake, *Memoirs of Lieut. Henry Timberlake*, ed. Samuel Cole Williams (New York: Arno Press, 1971), 82; Adam Hodgson, *Remarks during a Journey through North America in the Years 1819, 1820, and 1821* (Westport, CT: Negro Universities Press, 1970), 279.

58. James Wilkinson to Isaac Shelby, June 16, 1796, Isaac Shelby Papers, folder 4, FHS; Timberlake, *Memoirs*, 65; David Taitt, "Journal of David Taitt's Travels from Pensacola, West Florida, to and through the Country of the Upper and Lower Creeks, 1772," in *Travels in the American Colonies*, 558.

59. Ludwick Grant to Governor Glen, February 8, 1753, *DRIA*, vol. 1, 368; Major Andrew Lewis to Captain Raymond Demere, September 11, 1756, *DRIA*, vol. 2, 203; Talk of the Mankiller of Great Tellico to Captain Raymond Demere, February 6, 1757, ibid., 333; Talk of Oxinaa to Raymond Demere, April 8, 1757, ibid., 411; Raymond Demere to Governor Lyttleton, July 30, 1757, ibid., 392; Raymond Demere to Gov. Lyttleton, August 10, 1757, ibid., 397–98.

60. White to Dubreuil, draft, October 8, 1803, EFP, section 29, reel 43, PKY; Dubreuil to Salcedo, September 4, 1803, PC, legajo 76, reel 250, folio 419, PKY; Records of the Cathedral Parish, St. Augustine, White Baptisms, vol. 3, partida

194, PKY; Records of the Cathedral Parish, St. Augustine, White Baptisms, vol. 3, partida 260, PKY; Records of the Cathedral Parish, St. Augustine, White Marriages, partida 106, PKY; Records of the Cathedral Parish, St. Augustine, White and Colored Deaths, partida 313, PKY; Supplemental Affidavit of Antonia Leonardy, October 1, 1835, 25th Congress, 3rd sess., H.D. 225, p. 60; Mathews, comp., "Bonelly Family Geneaology," Saint Augustine Historical Society.

61. Deposition of James Ore, June 16, 1792, *ASP: IA*, vol. 1, 274; Foster, ed., *Collected Works of Benjamin Hawkins*, 321; Caleb Swan, "Position and State of Manners and Arts in the Creek, or Muscogee Nation in 1791," in *Information Respecting the History, Condition and Prospects of the Indian Tribes of the United States*, ed. Henry Rowe Schoolcraft (Philadelphia: Lippincott and Grambo, 1855), vol. 5, 260; John Sevier to Benjamin Hawkins, April 26, 1797, Governor Sevier Collection, TSLA, presented in DLG.

62. Mereness, ed., "Journal of Captain Tobias Fitch's Mission from Charleston to the Creeks, 1726," in *Travels in the American Colonies*, 207.

63. Edmund S. Morgan, *American Slavery, American Freedom: The Ordeal of Colonial Virginia* (New York: Norton, 1975); Brown, *Good Wives*; William Robert Snell, "Indian Slavery in Colonial South Carolina" (Ph.D. diss., University of Alabama, 1972), 53–63; William L. Ramsey, *The Yamasee War: A Study of Culture, Economy, and Conflict in the Colonial South* (Lincoln: University of Nebraska Press, 2008), 171–181.

6. Violent Intimacy

1. Brown dictated his story several times in the 1850s. This reconstruction follows his autobiographical sketch and his letters, both at TSLA. Joseph Brown to Felix Grundy, October 7, 1811, Howell Papers, box 2, folder 2, TSLA; Joseph Brown to the President James Monroe, December 9, 1822, JBP, folder 9, TSLA; all quotations except Timberlake's from Joseph Brown, autobiographical sketch, n.d, JBP, folder 1, TSLA; Henry Timberlake, *The Memoirs of Lieut. Henry Timberlake*, ed. Samuel Cole Williams (New York: Arno, 1971), 82; *Knoxville Gazette*, September 26, 1794.

2. Joseph Brown, "Captivity Narrative," *Journal of Cherokee Studies* 2 (1977): 209.

3. Joseph Brown to the President James Monroe, December 9, 1822, JBP, folder 9, TSLA; Timberlake, *Memoirs*, 82; *Knoxville Gazette*, September 26, 1794.

4. Quotation from Joseph Brown to Felix Grundy, October 7, 1811, Howell Papers, box 2, folder 2, TSLA; Talk of Joseph Brown to Chief Cutteotoy and the Cherokee Chiefs, January 11, 1814, JBP, box 1, folder 5, TSLA; Valuation of the Indian Negroes, December 12, 1814, JBP, box 1, folder 5, TSLA.

5. Duane H. King, "Lessons in Cherokee Ethnology from the Captivity of Joseph Brown, 1788–1789," *Journal of Cherokee Studies* 2 (1977): 223.

6. Lyman Draper, Interview with Joseph Brown, September 20, 1844, DMC, Tennessee Papers, 5XX52.

7. Jennifer Lynn Baszile, "Communities at the Crossroads: Chiefdoms, Colonies, and Empires in Colonial Florida," (Ph.D. diss., Princeton University, 1999), 345.

8. Major Forbes to the Secretary of State, January 29, 1764, *Mississippi Provincial Archives: English Dominion: 1763–1766*, ed. Dunbar Rowland (Nashville, TN: Brandon Printing, 1911), vol. 1, 142–143.

9. Congress at Pensacola between British and Creeks, May 30, 1765, ibid., 208.

10. John Stuart to James Grant, January 20, 1770, JGP, reel 19, box 20, folder 1, frame 29, LOC.

11. Deposition of Joseph Dawes, August 4, 1772, quoted in Joshua Piker, *Okfuskee: A Creek Indian Town in Colonial America* (Cambridge, MA: Harvard University Press, 2004), 190.

12. Deposition of John Reid, April 16, 1777, *Calendar of Virginia State Papers and Other Manuscripts, 1652–1781*, ed. William P. Palmer (New York: Kraus, 1968), vol. 1, 284; quotation from Deposition of Samuel Wilson, April 15, 1777, ibid., 283.

13. Deposition of James Robinson, April 16, 1777, *Calendar of Virginia State Papers*, vol. 1, 286.

14. Nancy Shoemaker, *A Strange Likeness: Becoming Red and White in Eighteenth-Century North America* (New York: Oxford University Press, 2004), 15–29; quotation from James Adair, *The History of the American Indians*, ed. Kathryn E. Holland Braund (Tuscaloosa: University of Alabama Press, 2005), 68.

15. Talk of Tustunnuggee Hopoie and Tuskegee Tustunnuggee (interpreted by Timothy Barnard) to Benjamin Hawkins, March 14, 1809, "Unpublished Letters of Timothy Barnard, 1784–1820," typescript compiled by Louise F. Hays, p. 297, GA.

16. John R. Swanton, *Indians of the Southeastern United States* (Washington, DC: Smithsonian Institution Press, 1979), 122; Frank G. Speck, *Ethnology of the Yuchi Indians* (Lincoln: University of Nebraska Press, 2004), 8, 11; quotation from Talk of Old Tassel to Patrick Henry and Richard Caswell, September 19, 1785, Cherokee Collection, reel 1, box 1, folder 20, TSLA, emphasis added.

17. Colin G. Calloway, *The American Revolution in Indian Country: Crisis and Diversity in Native American Communities* (New York: Cambridge University Press, 1995), quotation on 292–293.

18. *Knoxville Gazette*, May 5, 1792, TSLA; Shoemaker, *Strange Likeness*, 100.

19. Father Raphael to the Abbé Raguet, May 15, 1725, MPA:FD, vol. 2, 486.

20. Alexander Longe, "A Small Postscript on the Ways and Manners of the Indians Called Cherokees," ed. David H. Corkran, *Southern Indian Studies* 21 (1969): 13.

21. Kristian Hvidt, ed., *Von Reck's Voyage: Drawings and Journal of Philip Georg Friedrich von Reck* (Savannah, GA: Beehive Press, 1990), 49.

22. Shoemaker, *Strange Likeness*, 129–140; Gregory Evans Dowd, *A Spirited Resistance: The North American Indian Struggle for Unity, 1745–1815* (Baltimore, MD: Johns Hopkins University Press, 1992), 21, 30.

23. Thomas Loraine McKenney and James Hall, *History of the Indian Tribes of North America, with Biographical Sketches and Anecdotes of the Principal Chiefs* (Philadelphia: E. C. Biddle, 1836), vol. 1, 82–83.

24. Informants Nutsawi and Pinelog, JHPP, reel 1, vol. 3, p. 10.

25. Talk of the Choctaw Kings, Headmen, and Warriors to Mad Dog, White Lieutenant, Nine Hadjo and Apoyl of the Hickory Ground and all their elder brothers the Creeks in general, June 10, 1795, JRP, reel 801, TSLA.

26. Henry Stuart to John Stuart, August 25, 1776, *Colonial and State Records of North Carolina*, vol. 10, 773–779, presented in *Documenting the American South*, docsouth.unc.edu.

27. Ibid., 764.

28. E. F. Rockwell, ed., Journal of Captain Ross, in "Parallel and Combined Expeditions against the Cherokee Indians in South and in North Carolina, in 1776," *Historical Magazine* 2 (1867): 220.

29. James P. Pate, "The Chickamauga: A Forgotten Segment of Indian Resistance on the Southern Frontier" (Ph.D. diss., Mississippi State University, 1969), 54–73; quotation from William Christian to William Harrison, December 16, 1782, Bullitt Family Papers, Oxmoor Collection, folder 412, FHS.

30. Prentice Robinson, *Easy to Use Cherokee Dictionary* (Tulsa, OK: Cherokee Language and Culture, 1996), 22; Pate, "The Chickmauga," 54, 130–138.

31. Alexander McGillivray to unknown, July 5, 1785, MPA:SA, vol. 2, reel 1133, p. 170, MDAH; quotation from McGillivray's speech on behalf of the Chiefs of the Creek, Chickasaw, and Cherokee Nations, July 10, 1785, in *McGillivray of the Creeks*, ed. John W. Caughey (Norman: University of Oklahoma Press, 1938), 92.

32. Esteban Miró to Arturo O'Neill, April 20, 1786, MPA:SA, vol. 2, reel 1133, p. 296, MDAH; Luis de Bertucat to Arturo O'Neill, November 21, 1787, MPA:SA, vol. 3, reel 405, p. 91, MDAH.

33. McGillivray to O'Neill, June 20, 1787, in *McGillivray of the Creeks*, 153; McGillivray to Miró, October 4, 1787, in ibid., 161.

34. Henry Knox to Isaac Shelby, July 29, 1790, Isaac Shelby Papers, folder 2, FHS; William Blount to Henry Knox, November 8, 1792, William Blount Letters, FHS; Timothy Barnard to Edward Telfair, August 14, 1786, "Unpublished Letters of Timothy Barnard," 61, GA; Pate, "The Chickamaugas," 96, 129, 190.

35. Ronald Eugene Craig, "The Colberts in Chickasaw History, 1783–1818: A Study of Internal Tribal Dynamics" (Ph.D. diss., University of New Mexico, 1998), 305; Arturo O'Neill to Baron de Carondelet, April 12, 1793, in *Annual Report of the American Historical Association for the Year 1945, Volume 4: Spain in the Mississippi Valley, 1765–1794*, ed. Lawrence Kinnaird (Washington, DC: U.S. Government Printing Office, 1949), 150; quotation from Juan Delavillebeuvre to Carondelet, September 12, 1792, ibid., vol. 4, 82.

36. Little Turkey to James Robertson, March 28, 1794, JRP, reel 801, TSLA; quotation from John McKee to Winthrop Sargent, August 20, 1800, WSP, reel 5, frame 565.

37. Grand-Pré to Miró, June 1, 1787, *Spain in the Mississippi Valley*, vol. 3, 210–211; quotation from Foucher to Miró, October 20, 1790, ibid., vol. 3, 384.

38. McGillivray to O'Neill, March 28, 1786, in *McGillivray of the Creeks*, 106; Thomas Pinckney to the Senate, January 14, 1788, Governors' Messages, series S165009, message 442, SCDAH; Samuel Cole Williams, ed., "Bro. Martin Schneider's Report of his Journey to the Upper Cherokee Towns, 1783–84," in *Early Travels in the Tennessee Country, 1540–1800* (Johnson City, TN: Watauga Press, 1928), 260; William Davenport to John Sevier, July 28, 1786, "Georgia, East Florida, West Florida, and Yazoo Land Sales: 1764–1850," typescript compiled by Louise F. Hays, 34–35, GA; Philatouche to Enrique White, October 22, 1795, EFP, section 29, reel 43, PKY; William Blount to The Glass, September 13, 1792, JRP, reel 801, TSLA; quotation from John Galphin to unknown, September 18, 1794, EFP, section 29, reel 43, doc. 1794–59, PKY.

39. David H. Corkran, *The Creek Frontier, 1540–1783* (Norman: University of Oklahoma Press, 1967), 324–325; McGillivray to Miró, May 1, 1786, MPA:SA, vol. 2, reel 1133, p. 300; Talk of Part of the Creek Indians to the Georgia Legislature, August 3, 1786, in *McGillivray of the Creeks*, 124; McGillivray to Zéspedes, January 5, 1787, MPA:SA, vol. 3, reel 405, 12, MDAH; Philatouche to Enrique White, October 22, 1795, EFP, section 29, reel 43, PKY.

40. On Blount's nicknames, see H. Thomas Foster II, ed., *The Collected Works of Benjamin Hawkins, 1796–1810* (Tuscaloosa: University of Alabama Press, 2004), 9s–10s; quotation from William Blount to James Seagrove, January 9, 1794, JRP, reel 801, TSLA; William Christian to Sampson Mathews, December 30, 1782, Bullitt Family Papers, Oxmoor Collection, folder 412, FHS; George Stiggins, *Creek Indian History: A Historical Narrative of the Genealogy, Traditions and Downfall of the Ispocoga or Creek Indian Tribe of Indians*, ed. Virginia Pounds Brown (Birmingham, AL: Birmingham Public Library Press, 1989), 77.

41. Conference with Certain Chiefs & Warriors at Philadelphia in June 1794, JHPP, reel 2, vol. 7, part 1, p. 4–5.

42. McGillivray to O'Neill, March 4, 1787, in *McGillivray of the Creeks*, 63.

43. Quotation from Bloody Fellow to Carondelet, August 14, 1793, *Spain in the Mississippi Valley*, vol. 4, 199; McGillivray to Miró, May 1, 1786, MPA:SA, vol. 2, reel 1133, MDAH.

44. Elliott J. Gorn, "'Gouge and Bite, Pull Hair and Scratch': The Social Significance of Fighting in the Southern Backcountry," *American Historical Review* 90 (1985): 18–43; quotation from Prince of Notoly to General Pickens, June 6, 1788, Governors' Messages, series S 165009, message 462, SCDAH, emphasis added.

45. Benjamin Hawkins to Thomas Jefferson, n.d., Vocabulary of Overhill Cherokee and Choctaw, Peter Stephen DuPonceau Collection, Indian Vocabularies, p. 23, APS; Duane Harold King, "A Grammar and Dictionary of the Cherokee Language" (Ph.D. diss., University of Georgia, 1975), 177; Foster, ed., *Collected Works of Benjamin Hawkins*, 250; Claudio Saunt, *A New Order of Things: Power, Property, and the Transformation of the Creek Indians, 1733–1816* (New York: Cambridge University Press, 1999), 115–116; quotation from McGillivray to Vincente Folch, April 22, 1789, in *McGillivray of the Creeks*, 228.

46. McGillivray to Miró, May 1, 1786, MPA:SA, vol. 2, reel 1133, p. 303, MDAH.

47. Population estimate from Bernardo del Campo, June 8, 1783, LC, group 174, box 2, PKY; Zéspedes to McGillivray, June 16, 1786, EFP, section 29, reel 43, PKY; Enrique Grimarest to Arturo O'Neill, March 14, 1783, PC, legajo 36, reel 184, f. 1137, PKY; Francisco Cruzat to Esteban Miró, June 21, 1789, MPA:SA, vol. 3, reel 405, MDAH.

48. Cruzat to Miró, August 23, 1784, *Spain in the Mississippi Valley*, vol. 3, 117.

49. Carlos de Grand Pré to Esteban Miró, n.d., MPA:SA, vol. 3, reel 405, MDAH.

50. Grand-Pré to Miró, October 2, 1790, in *Spain in the Mississippi Valley*, 380; Commandant of the Natchez to Choctaw Chiefs, September 30, 1790, ibid., 382.

51. Tellico Blockhouse Treaty, December 28, 1794–January 3, 1795, JRP, reel 801, TSLA.

52. Affidavit of Thomas Quarterman, August 8, 1789, "Indian Depredations, 1787–1825," typescript complied by Louise F. Hays, vol. 1, part 1, 222, GA; Affidavit of John B. Girardeau, October 26, 1802, "Indian Depredations," vol. 1, part 1, 223–224, GA; U.S. Justices John Stevens, J. S. Bradwell, Thomas Mallard, and Thomas Bacon to the estate of Thomas Quarterman, September 3, 1821, "Indian Depredations," vol. 1, part 1, 245–246, GA; Affidavit of Samuel Spencer, August 2, [year missing], "Indian Depredations," vol. 1, part 1, 224, GA; Affidavit of John Mikal Wagonman and Davis Starrisson, September 30, 1794, Telamon Cuyler Collection, HRB, DLG; Petition of Bennitt Posey, n.d, in *Georgia Indian Depredation Claims*, ed. Donna B. Thaxton (Americus, GA: Thaxton Company, 1988), 595; quotations from Col. Jacob Weed to Gen. James Jackson, May 27, 1788, Telamon Cuyler Collection, HRB, DLG.

53. Isaac Shelby to Henry Knox, January 10, 1794, Miscellaneous Shelby Papers, FHS; The Memorial of William Whitly to the Representatives of the People of Kentucky in General Assembly, n.d., Shelby Family Papers, FHS; Reginald Horsman, *Race and Manifest Destiny: The Origins of American Racial Anglo-Saxonism* (Cambridge, MA: Harvard University Press, 1981).

54. Rockwell, ed., Ross Journal, 219, 215; Robinson, *Cherokee Dictionary*, 88.

55. Memoir of William Lenoir, June 1835, Lenoir Family Papers, ms. # 2262, folder 239, SHC.

56. James Grant to John Stuart, February 5, 1768, JGP, reel 2, box 2, folder 2, frame 172, LOC. Emphasis in original.

57. Enrique White to Baron de Carondelet, October 10, 1793, *Spain in the Mississippi Valley*, vol. 4, 216; James Seagrove to Edward Telfair, October 3, 1793 ASP:IA, vol. 1, 412; William Blount to Henry Knox, May 24, 1793, *The Territorial Papers of the United States: The Territory South of the River Ohio, 1790–1796*, ed. Clarence Edwin Carter (Washington, DC: U.S. Government Printing Office, 1936), vol. 4, 261; William Blount to Henry Knox, May 28, 1793, ibid., 262; quotation from Silas Dinsmoor to David Henley, March 18, 1795, in William G. McLoughlin, *Cherokee Renascence in the New Republic* (Princeton, NJ: Princeton University Press, 1986), 43.

58. Alexander McGillivray to General Andrew Pickens, February 15, 1788, Governors' Messages, series S165009, message 462, SCDAH.

59. Affidavit of William Scarborough, January 9, 1796, "Creek Indian Letters, Talks, and Treaties, 1705–1839," typescript compiled by Louise F. Hays, part 2, 462, GA; Robbie Ethridge, *Creek Country: The Creek Indians and Their World* (Chapel Hill: University of North Carolina Press, 2003), 64, 218–219.

60. Foster, ed., *Collected Works of Benjamin Hawkins*, 102.

61. William C. C. Claiborne to Henry Dearborn, March 4, 1803, in John R. Swanton, *Source Material for the Social and Ceremonial Life of the Choctaw Indians* (Washington, DC: U.S. Government Printing Office, 1931), 105; James Patriot Wilson to Patrick Wilson, April 1803, APS; quotations from Foster, ed., *Collected Works of Benjamin Hawkins*, 62.

62. J. G. M. Ramsey, *The Annals of Tennessee to the End of the Eighteenth Century* (Philadelphia: Lippincott, Grambo, 1853), 622.

63. Elijah Clarke to Edward Telfair, December 4, 1792, C. Mildred Thompson Collection, HRB, DLG; Tom Hatley, *The Dividing Paths: Cherokees and South Carolinians through the Era of Revolution* (New York: Oxford University Press, 1995), 239; Hobert W. Burns, ed., *The Life of Anne Calhoun Mathews: 18 May 1755–19 December 1830* (Palo Alto, CA, 1988); Robert V. Remini, *Andrew Jackson & His Indian Wars* (New York: Viking, 2001), 7–20; first quotation from John Haywood, *Civil and Political History of the State of Tennessee from Its*

Earliest Settlement Up to the Year 1796 (New York: Arno, 1971), 261; James A. Shackford and Stanley J. Folmsbee, eds., *A Narrative of the Life of David Crockett of the State of Tennessee* (Knoxville: University of Tennessee Press, 1973), xv, 15–16, 113, second quotation from p. 206.

64. Adam Hodgson, *Remarks during a Journey through North America in the Years 1819, 1820, and 1821* (Westport, CT: Negro Universities Press, 1970), 263; Arrell M. Gibson, *The Chickasaws* (Norman: University of Oklahoma Press, 1971), 135; quotation from Obediah Lowe to William Panton, May 25, 1797, Heloise H. Cruzat Papers, box 1, PKY, courtesy of FLHS.

65. Benjamin Hawkins to William Panton, June 9, 1798, BHL; Hawkins to Price, May 29, 1798, ibid.

66. Talk of Amahuskasata, Calacusta, and Caatahee, June 27, 1802, "Cherokee Indian Letters, Talks, and Treaties: 1786–1838," typescript compiled by Louise F. Hays, vol. 1, 37, GA.

67. Affidavit of John Eades, October 30, 1793, "Creek Indian Letters," part 1, 349, GA; quotations from Early Life of Margaret Ervin Austill, Austill Papers, SHC.

68. Caleb Swan, "Position and State of Manners and Arts in the Creek, or Muscogee Nation in 1791," in *Information Respecting the History, Condition and Prospects of the Indian Tribes of the United States*, ed. Henry Rowe Schoolcraft (Philadelphia: Lippincott and Grambo, 1855), vol. 5, 280.

69. Allen Gillespie to John Sevier, December 14, 1796, John Sevier Papers, Q-39, TSLA; Haywood, *Civil and Political History of the State of Tennessee*, 264–265; Abstract of Indian Affairs, October 1792, *Territorial Papers*, vol. 4, 185; *Knoxville Gazette*, October 6, 1792; ibid., October 11, 1794; Affidavit of John Pesnell Franklin, October 25, 1802, "Indian Depredations," vol. 2, part 1, 211, GA; "Journal of the Commissioners of the United States," in *ASP: IA*, vol. 1, 681; "A Return of Persons Killed, Wounded, and Taken Prisoners, from Miró District," in ibid., 330.

70. Thomas Perryman to Vincente Folch, n.d., LC, group 174, box 10, PKY.

71. Ibid.

72. Andrew Jackson to Leroy Pope, October 31, 1813, *The Papers of Andrew Jackson*, ed. Harold D. Moser and Sharon MacPherson (Knoxville: University of Tennessee Press, 1984), 443.

73. Brent Gary Bergherm, "The Little Osage Captive: The Tragic Saga of Lydia Carter," *The Arkansas Historical Quarterly* 62 (2003): 123–152; Kathleen DuVal, "Debating Identity, Sovereignty, and Civilization: The Arkansas Valley after the Louisiana Purchase," *Journal of the Early Republic* 26 (2006): 25–58; quotation from Doublehead to Return J. Meigs, November 20, 1802, LR, OIA, Records of the Cherokee Indian Agency in Tennessee, 1801–1835, Microcopy 208, reel 1, NA.

74. Return J. Meigs to William Crawford, May 2, 1815, LR, OIA, Cherokee Agency, Microcopy 208, reel 6, NA; John Pitchlynn to Andrew Jackson, August 18, 1831, LR, OIA, Choctaw Agency, 1824–1876, Microcopy 234, reel 169, frame 927–928, NA.

75. Horatio B. Cushman, *History of the Choctaw, Chickasaw, and Natchez Indians*, ed. Angie Debo (Norman: University of Oklahoma Press, 1999), 401.

76. Michael D. Green, "Alexander McGillivray," in *American Indian Leaders: Studies in Diversity*, ed. R. David Edmunds (Lincoln: University of Nebraska Press, 1980), 41–63.

77. Mad Dog to James Burgess and the Seminoles, August 2, 1798, Marie Taylor Greenslade Papers, box 1, PKY, courtesy of FLHS; James Durouzseaux to Enrique White, January 18, 1794, PC, legajo 208s, reel 286, folio 566, PKY; quotations from Diego de Vegas to Enrique White, January 29, 1795, Elizabeth Howard West Collection, box 5, PKY.

78. Foster, ed., *Collected Works of Benjamin Hawkins*, 136; McLoughlin, *Cherokee Renascence*, 44–46, 53–54, 330; *Laws of the Cherokee Nation: Adopted by the Council at Various Periods* (Wilmington, DE: Scholarly Resources, 1973), 3, 4; Duane Champagne, *Social Order and Political Change: Constitutional Governments among the Cherokee, the Choctaw, the Chickasaw, and the Creek* (Stanford, CA: Stanford University Press, 1992), 94–121; Angie Debo, *The Rise and Fall of the Choctaw Republic* (Norman: University of Oklahoma Press, 1972), 45, 166; quotation from Cushman, *History of the Choctaw, Chickasaw, and Natchez Indians*, 157.

79. Theda Perdue, "Clan and Court: Another Look at the Early Cherokee Republic," *The American Indian Quarterly* 24 (2000): 562–569, quotation on p. 566.

80. Informants Nutsawi and Johnson Pridget, JHPP, reel 1, vol. 3, 53–54, quotation on 53.

81. Richard Lang to Vincente Manual de Zéspedes, July 13, 1789, EFP, section 32, reel 46, doc. 1789–145, PKY.

82. A. W. Putnam, *History of Middle Tennessee; or, Life and Times of Gen. James Robertson* (New York: Arno Press, 1971), 355; quotation from William Kinnear to John Kinnear, 1812, in "Letters from the Invaders of East Florida," ed. Rembert Patrick, in *Florida Historical Quarterly* 28 (1949): 62; Col. Thomas Smith to Gov. Mitchell, August 21, 1812, T. Frederick Davis Collection, box 14, PKY; W. B. Armistead to Edwin Wright Morgan, April 9, 1838, Edwin Wright Morgan Collection, ms. # 3035z, SHC; "Life and Times of Mrs. Jane Murray Sheldon Written at her Dictation in 1889," typescript in PKY.

83. Report of David Craig to William Blount, March 15, 1792, *ASP:IA*, vol. 1, 265; James Robertson to William Blount, October 8, 1794, *Territorial Papers*, vol. 4,

358–359; A Talk from the Hallowing King of the Cowetas and Little Warrior of the Broken Arrow to Enrique White, April 19, 1795, EFP, section 29, reel 43, doc. 1795-20, PKY; A Talk from the Dog Warrior to William Panton, February 25, 1795, PC, legajo 203, reel 282a, folio 1052, PKY; Talk of Alex Cornells to Chickasaw chiefs Billy Colbert, George Colbert, Piolata, Piomingo, and Mylyacabe Mingo, July 27, 1795, JRP, reel 801, TSLA; Benjamin James to Enrique White, September 12, 1795, PC, legajo 31, reel 418, folio 1199, PKY; John Forbes to Enrique White, March 29, 1795, PC, legajo 31, reel 428, folio 1200, PKY; Blount to Robertson, January 20, 1795, JRP, reel 801, TSLA; Blount to Robertson, March 29, 1796, JRP, reel 801, TSLA; Gibson, *The Chickasaws*, 80–90.

84. Blount to Robertson, August 11, 1795, JRP, reel 801, TSLA; Talk of Little Turkey and the Black Fox to Robertson, April 10, 1795, JRP, reel 801, TSLA; Talk of Alex Cornells to Chickasaw chiefs Billy Colbert, George Colbert, Piolata, Piomingo, and Mylyacabe Mingo, July 27, 1795, JRP, reel 801, TSLA; Blount to Robertson, JRP, reel 801, TSLA; Gibson, *The Chickasaws*, 90; quotation from A Talk from Dog Warrior to William Panton, February 25, 1795, PC, legajo 203, reel 282a, folio 1052, PKY.

85. Mary R. Haas, "Creek Inter-Town Relations," *American Anthropologist* 42 (1940): 483; Charles M. Hudson, *The Southeastern Indians* (Knoxville: University of Tennessee Press, 1976), 411.

86. Fray Juan de Paiva, "Origen y principio del juego de pelota," in John H. Hann, *Apalachee: The Land between the Rivers* (Gainesville: University Presses of Florida, 1988), 346.

87. Quotation from Cushman, *History of the Choctaw, Chickasaw, and Natchez*, 130; Hudson, *Southeastern Indians*, 409–410.

88. Carl F. Klink and James J. Talman, eds., *The Journal of Major John Norton, 1809–1816* (Toronto: Champlain Society, 1970), 64; Wayne Van Horne, "The Warclub: Weapon and Symbol in Southeastern Indian Societies" (Ph.D. diss., University of Georgia, 1993), 214–218; Cushman, *History of the Choctaw, Chickasaw, and Natchez*, 124–130.

89. Hudson, *Southeastern Indians*, 235–237, 408–412; quotation from Klinck and Talman, eds., *Journal of Major John Norton*, 57.

90. Cynthia Cumfer, *Separate Peoples, One Land: The Minds of Cherokees, Blacks, and Whites on the Tennessee Frontier* (Chapel Hill: University of North Carolina Press, 2007), 118; quotation from Rowena McClinton, ed., *The Moravian Springplace Mission to the Cherokees* (Lincoln: University of Nebraska Press, 2007), vol. 1, 444.

91. William Blount to Henry Knox, November 8, 1792, *Territorial Papers*, vol. 4, 210.

92. Talk of Efau Hadjo to James Burgess and the Seminoles, August 2, 1798, Greenslade Papers, box 1, PKY. Efau Hadjo, like other Creek leaders, considered the Seminoles as part of the Creek Nation, and thus he referred to four rather than five nations of Southern Indians.

7. Racial Slavery

1. Affidavit of John Lang, October 27, 1802, "Indian Depredations, 1787–1825," typescript compiled by Louise F. Hays, vol. 1, part 1, 25, GA; Affidavit of John McMichael Jr., July 2, 1787, "Indian Depredations," vol. 1, part 1, 104, GA; Affidavit of David McMichael, July 2, 1787, "Indian Depredations," vol. 1, part 1, 104–105, quotation on p. 105, GA; Major Robert Fullwood to General David Adams, January 24, 1833, in *Georgia Indian Depredation Claims*, ed. Donna B. Thaxton (Americus, GA: Thaxton Company, 1988), 198–199; Affidavit of John Lang, October 27, 1802, File II, Record Group 4–2–46, unit 78, doc. 1517, GA.

2. Daniel F. Littlefield Jr., *Africans and Creeks: From the Colonial Period through the Civil War* (Westport, CT: Greenwood Press, 1979), 27; H. Thomas Foster II, ed., *Collected Works of Benjamin Hawkins, 1796–1810* (Tuscaloosa: University of Alabama Press, 2003), 66s.

3. Richard Henderson to Governor John Martin, September 23, 1782, "Creek Indian Letters, Talks, and Treaties, 1705–1839," typescript compiled by Louise F. Hays, part 1, 33, GA.

4. Juan Forrester to Enrique White, July 7, 1801, LC, group 174, box 9, PKY.

5. "Return of Depredations Committed by the Creek Indians," ASP:IA, vol. 1, 77; "Return of Persons Killed, Wounded, and Taken Prisoners," Miscellaneous Creek Indian documents, File II, Record Group 4–2–46, box 76, document 1988, folder 1, GA; "A list of the names of persons killed, murdered, and captured since the 26th of February 1794," *Knoxville Gazette*, October 11, 1794; *Knoxville Gazette*, July 17, 1794; James Bolls to David Henley, June 18, 1801, David Henley Papers, reel 625, TSLA; James Mooney, *Myths of the Cherokee* (New York: Johnson Reprint, 1970), 77.

6. Affidavit of Samuel Parker, October 27, 1821, in *Georgia Indian Depredation Claims*, 445; Affidavit of John Bohun Girardeau, July 30, 1791, "Indian Depredations," vol. 2, part 2, 626, GA; Samuel Cole Williams, ed., "Bro. Martin Schneider's Report of his Journey to the Upper Cherokee Towns, 1783–84," *Early Travels in the Tennessee Country, 1540–1800* (Johnson City, TN: 1928), 262; Testimony of John MacLeod, May 26, 1798, BHL; Testimony of James Moore, June 1, 1798, ibid.; quotation from Affidavit of John Fitzpatrick, October 7, 1791, "Indian Letters, 1782–1839," typescript compiled by Louise F. Hays, 15, GA.

7. Arturo O'Neill to Bernardo de Gálvez, March 24, 1783, PC, legajo 36, reel 183, folio 556, PKY.

8. O'Neill to Gálvez, June 10, 1783, MPA:SA, reel 3311, vol. 2, p. 10, MDAH.

9. Patrick Carr to Governor John Martin, December 13, 1782, "Creek Indian Letters," part 1, 40, GA.

10. Officer corps of Louisiana Companies of Free Blacks and Mulattos to Governor, October 18, 1788, PC, legajo 38, reel 192, folio 1670, PKY; Diego de Vegas to Arturo O'Neill, December 18, 1788, PC, legajo 40, reel 194, folio 1295, PKY; Diego de Vegas to Arturo O'Neill, January 2, 1789, PC, legajo 38, reel 192, folio 1684, PKY; Luis de Bertucat to Arturo O'Neill, November 14, 1791, PC, legajo 40, reel 194, folio 1153. At this time, one peso fetched about 2¼ libras. In the end, Kinache received 200 pesos (452 libras) worth of credit at Panton, Leslie & Co.—plus the kegs of brandy.

11. Lieutenant McClary to Winthrop Sargent, October 8, 1799, WSP, reel 5, frame 212–217; Affidavit of John Whitehead, September 5, 1791, in *Georgia Indian Depredation Claims*, 277; Affidavit of David Garvin, February 4, 1803, "Indian Depredations," vol. 2, part 1, 89, GA; John Whitehead to John Clark, January 26, 1820, OIA, LRSW, reel 2, frame 164–168, NA.

12. Williams, ed., "Bro. Martin Schneider's Report," 262; Tellico Blockhouse Treaty, December 28, 1794–January 3, 1795, JRP, reel 801, TSLA; Affidavit of James F. Foster, September 5, 1821, in *Georgia Indian Depredation Claims*, 107; Affidavit of George W. Foster, June 17, 1822, "Indian Depredations," vol. 2, part 2, 356–357, GA; quotation from Jack Kinnard to Enrique White, October 2, 1801, EFP, section 29, reel 43, PKY.

13. Deposition of Teedoe Brashears, September 1, 1819, PPP, folder 11, GMA; quotation from Daniel Stewart to Governor John Milledge, January 18, 1805, *Georgia Indian Depredation Claims*, 615. For paying debts in slaves, see William Laurence to William Panton, August 15, 1798, Heloise H. Cruzat Papers, box 1, PKY, courtesy of FLHS; Manuel Juan de Salcedo to Vincente Folch, August 18, 1801, PC, legajo 58, reel 388, folio 75, PKY.

14. Dinsmoore quoted in R. Halliburton Jr., *Red over Black: Black Slavery among the Cherokee Indians* (Westport, CT: Greenwood Press, 1977), 15; second quote from Speech of the Creek Representatives, June 25, 1796, APS:IA, vol. 1, 603; The Creek Nation to James Smith, n.d., "Indian Depredations," vol. 2, part 2, 610–611, GA; Affidavit of James Smith, July 21, 1798, "Indian Depredations," vol. 2, part 2, 601, GA; Benjamin Hawkins to John Milledge, July 29, 1806, Telamon Cuyler Collection, HRB, DLG; James Smith to General [Preston?], August 1822, Captain Isaac Vincent Papers, HRB, DLG.

15. Brent Gary Bergherm, "The Little Osage Captive: The Tragic Saga of Lydia Carter," *The Arkansas Historical Quarterly* 62 (2003): 123–152; Thurman

Wilkins, *Cherokee Tragedy: The Ridge Family and the Decimation of a People* (Norman: University of Oklahoma Press, 1986), 69–71.

16. Rowena McClinton, ed., *The Moravian Springplace Mission to the Cherokees* (Lincoln: University of Nebraska Press, 2007), 257; James L. McDonald to John C. Calhoun, November 9, 1824, LR, OIA, Choctaw Agency, Microcopy 234, reel 169, frame 89–91, NA; Will of Young Wolf, March 12, 1814, JHPP, reel 2, vol. 7, part 2, p. 60; Order of the National Committee, May 25, 1824, ibid., p. 60–61; John Pitchlynn to Peter Pitchlynn, July 19, 1824, PPP, file 25, GMA; Bill of Sale, August 18, 1832, ibid.; Daniel F. Littlefield, *The Chickasaw Freedmen: A People without a Country* (Westport, CT: Greenwood Press, 1980), 10; Angie Debo, *The Rise and Fall of the Choctaw Republic* (Norman: University of Oklahoma Press, 1972), 59.

17. Kathryn E. Holland Braund, *Deerskins & Duffels: The Creek Indian Trade with Anglo-America, 1685–1815* (Lincoln: University of Nebraska Press, 1993), 174; Affidavit of John Young, August 8, 1798, BHL; Benjamin Hawkins to James Jackson, July 11, 1799, ibid.; O'Neill to Miró; January 3, 1789, PC, reel 191, legajo 38, folio 681, PKY; John Karnard (Jack Kinnard) to James Seagrove, June 5, 1803, "Creek Indian Letters," part 2, 675, 679, GA, quotation from p. 675; Wiley Thompson to Enrique White, April 20, 1803, EFP, section 32, reel 43, doc. 1803–63, PKY.

18. Caleb Swan, "Position and State of Manners and Arts in the Creek, or Muscogee Nation in 1791," in *Information Respecting the History, Condition and Prospects of the Indian Tribes of the United States*, ed. Henry Rowe Schoolcraft (Philadelphia: Lippincott and Grambo, 1855), vol. 5, 261.

19. Jack Kinnard to Commandant at San Marcos, March 8, 1801, LC, group 174, box 9, PKY; Diego de Vegas to Enrique White, January 29, 1795, Elizabeth Howard West Collection, box 5, PKY; Jack Kinnard to Enrique White, October 2, 1801, EFP, section 29, reel 43, PKY; Salcedo to Someruelos, January 18, 1803, PC, legajo 1555, reel 41, folio 71, PKY.

20. Deposition of Daniel Thornbury, April 10, 1792, *ASP:IA*, vol. 1, 275; James Patriot Wilson to Patrick Wilson, April 1803, APS; quotation from Doublehead to J. D. Chisholm, November 20, 1802, OIA, LR, Records of the Cherokee Indian Agency in Tennessee, 1801–1835, Microcopy 208, reel 1, NA; Theda Perdue, "Women, Men and American Indian Policy: The Cherokee Response to 'Civilization,'" in *Negotiators of Change: Historical Perspectives on Native American Women*, ed. Nancy Shoemaker (New York: Routledge, 1995), 90–114; Halliburton, *Red over Black*, 22; William G. McLoughlin, *Cherokee Renascence in the New Republic* (Princeton, NJ: Princeton University Press, 1986), 83–84; Ronald Eugene Craig, "The Colberts in Chickasaw History, 1783–1818: A Study of Internal Tribal Dynamics" (Ph.D. diss., University of New Mexico, 1998), 232–233.

21. McLoughlin, *Cherokee Renascence*, 92–108; Cynthia Cumfer, *Separate Peoples, One Land: The Minds of Cherokees, Blacks, and Whites on the Tennessee Frontier* (Chapel Hill: University of North Carolina Press, 2007), 111, 122.

22. Benjamin Hawkins to Mr. Steth, December 31, 1798, BHL; McLoughlin, *Cherokee Renascence*, 62; Carl F. Klinck and James J. Talman, eds., *The Journal of Major John Norton, 1809–1816* (Toronto: Champlain Society, 1970), 125; Foster, ed., *Collected Works of Benjamin Hawkins*, 50s; James Durouzeaux to Vincente Folch, April 16, 1804, PC, legajo 2372, reel 436, doc. 17; quotation from Nathaniel Folsom, Discussion of Choctaw History, 1798, PPP, GMA.

23. John Allen, Report of the Chickasaws, February 7, 1830, LR, OIA, Chickasaw Agency, 1824–1870, Microcopy 234, roll 136, frame 18, NA.

24. Quotation from Miscellaneous Notes, JHPP, reel 1, vol. 3, p. 84; Jedidiah Morse, *A Report to the Secretary of War of the United States* (New Haven, CT: Howe and Spalding, 1822), Appendix, 182.

25. Richard A. Sattler, "Cowboys and Indians: Creek and Seminole Stock Raising, 1700–1900," in *American Indian Culture and Research Journal* 22 (1998): 79–100; Joshua Piker, *Okfuskee: A Creek Indian Town in Colonial America* (Cambridge, MA: Harvard University Press, 2004), 119–124; Tom Hatley, *The Dividing Paths: Cherokees and South Carolinians through the Era of Revolution* (New York: Oxford University Press, 1995), 161; Craig, "The Colberts in Chickasaw History," 205; James Taylor Carson, *Searching for the Bright Path: The Mississippi Choctaws from Prehistory to Removal* (Lincoln: University of Nebraska Press, 1999), 71–74, Mushulatubee quote on p. 71.

26. Folsom, Choctaw History, 1798, PPP, GMA.

27. Allen, Report of the Chickasaws, February 7, 1830, LR, OIA, Chickasaw Agency, Microcopy 234, roll 136, frame 18; McLoughlin, *Cherokee Renascence*, 66–67; Dawson A. Phelps, ed., "Excerpts from the Journal of the Reverend Joseph Bullen, 1799 and 1800," *Journal of Mississippi History* 17 (1955): 262; Rush Nutt, "Nutt's Trip to the Chickasaw Country," ed. Jesse D. Jennings, *Journal of Mississippi History* 9 (1947): 46; quotation from Adam Hodgson, *Remarks during a Journey through North America in the Years 1819, 1820, and 1821* (Westport, CT: Negro Universities Press, 1970), 287.

28. Foster, ed., *Collected Works of Benjamin Hawkins*, 66s.

29. Quotation from Cornet of Horse to Major John King, October 16, 1800, "Georgia, East Florida, West Florida, and Yazoo Land Sales," typescript compiled by Louise F. Hays, 134, GA; Hodgson, *Journey through North America*, 269, 278, 282.

30. Peyton Short, "Tour to Mobille, Pensacola, & c," 1809, reprinted in *The Quarterly Publication of the Historical and Philosophical Society of Ohio* 5

(1910): 5–11; Hodgson, *Journey through North America*, 263–272, 284; Nutt, "Trip to the Chickasaw Country," 41–43; Klinck and Talman, ed., *Journal of Major John Norton*, 68; Order of the National Committee, May 25, 1824, JHPP, reel 2, vol. 7, part 2, p. 60–61; John Ridge to Albert Gallatin, February 27, 1826, JHPP, reel 3, vol. 8, p. 105–106; Arrell M. Gibson, *The Chickasaws* (Norman: University of Oklahoma Press, 1971), 122–133; Jack Goody, "Slavery in Time and Space," in *Asian and African Systems of Slavery*, ed. James L. Watson (Berkeley: University of California Press, 1980), 25–26; Carson, *Searching for the Bright Path*, 81; bacon quote from James Patriot Wilson to Patrick Wilson, April 1803, APS; inns quote from Morse, *Report to the Secretary of War*, Appendix, 183; "house" quote from Mechal Sobel, *The World They Made Together: Black and White Values in Eighteenth-Century Virginia* (Princeton, NJ: Princeton University Press, 1989), 127.

31. John Pope, *A Tour through the Southern and Western Territories of the United State of America* (Gainesville: University of Florida Press, 1979), 66; Jack B. Martin and Margaret McKane Mauldin, *A Dictionary of Creek/Muskogee with Notes on the Florida and Oklahoma Seminole dialects of Creek* (Lincoln: University of Nebraska Press, 2004), 33–34; Benjamin Hawkins, A comparative vocabulary of the Muskogee or Creek, Chickasaw, Choctaw, and Cherokee Languages, July 12, 1800, Peter Stephen DuPonceau Collection, Indian Vocabularies, p. 36–37, APS; Judge Campbell to Thomas Jefferson, August 5, 1800, DuPonceau Collection, APS; Vocabulary of the Chickasaw Language, General D. Smith, July 6, 1800, DuPonceau Collection, APS.

32. John McKee to Winthrop Sargent, October 26, 1799, WSP, reel 5, frame 245–247; McKee to Sargent, February 20, 1800, WSP, reel 5, frame 371–371a; McKee to Sargent, August 20, 1800, WSP, reel 5, frame 564–566.

33. Affidavit of Stephen Corker, November 5, 1820, "Indian Depredations," vol. 2, part 1, 58–59, GA. For the sisters, see John Whitehead to John Clark, January 26, 1820, OIA, LRSW, reel 2, frame 164–168, NA.

34. Affidavit of John Lang, October 27, 1802, "Indian Depredations," vol. 1, part 1, 25, GA; Affidavit of John McMichael Jr., July 2, 1787, "Indian Depredations," vol. 1, part 1, 104, GA; Affidavit of David McMichael, July 2, 1787, "Indian Depredations," vol. 1, part 1, 104–105, quotation on 105, GA; Major Robert Fullwood to General David Adams, January 24, 1833, in *Georgia Indian Depredation Claims*, 198–199; Affidavit of John Lang, October 27, 1802, File II, Record Group 4-2-46, unit 78, doc. 1517, GA; Affidavit of Joseph Heard, September 1821, in *Georgia Indian Depredations*, 453–454; Affidavit of John Fitzpatrick, October 7, 1791, "Indian Letters," 15–16, GA; Foster, ed., *Collected Works of Benjamin Hawkins*, 126; Testimony of David Hay, June 5, 1798, BHL.

35. Edmund Gray to John Fallowfield, May 15, 1751, *DRIA*, vol. 1, 83; quotation from Deposition of Richard Smith, July 12, 1751, *DRIA*, vol. 1, 103.

36. Quoted in Hatley, *The Dividing Paths*, 111–112.

37. Affidavit of John Elliott, August 1789, "Indian Depredations," vol. 1, part 1, 234, GA.

38. Jack Kinnard to James Seagrove, June 5, 1803, "Creek Indian Letters," part 2, 675, GA.

39. Wiley Thompson to Enrique White, April 20, 1803, EFP, section 32, reel 57, doc. 1803–63, PKY.

40. Affidavit of Thomas Flournoy, September 3, 1831, "Indian Depredations," vol. 1, part 2, 290, GA; Affidavit of George Reeds, February 4, 1796, "Indian Depredations," vol. 2, part 1, GA; Robert Flournoy, November 11, 1802, "Indian Depredations," vol. 4, 200, GA; quotations from Affidavit of Robert Flournoy, September 3, 1821, "Indian Depredations," vol. 2, part 2, 434, GA.

41. William Ward to John C. Calhoun, December 24, 1824, LR, OIA, Choctaw Agency, Microcopy 234, reel 169, frame 142–144. See also Petition of Martin Palao and José Monroy, November 3, 1788, PC, legajo 38, reel 191, folio 600, PKY; Affidavit of Isaac Bush, October 16, 1824, "Creek Indian Letters," part 3, 976, GA; James Jackson to the Chehaw King, March 5, 1799, ibid., part 2, 522, GA; Benjamin Hawkins to Captain Cook, Telamon Cuyler Collection, HRB, DLG.

42. Manuel de Lanzos to Enrique White, February 19, 1795, PC, legajo 31, reel 418, folio 1163, PKY.

43. Manuel de Lanzos to Arturo O'Neill, March 21, 1793, PC, legajo 64, reel 440, folio 50, PKY.

44. George P. Rawick, ed., *The American Slave: A Composite Autobiography*, Supplement, Series 1 (Westport, CT: Greenwood Press, 1977), vol. 12, 128.

45. Patrick Minges, ed., *Black Indian Slave Narratives* (Winston-Salem, NC: Blair, 2004), 38.

46. Michael P. Johnson and James L. Roark, *Black Masters: A Free Family of Color in the Old South* (New York: Norton, 1984).

47. Eugene D. Genovese, *Roll, Jordan, Roll: The World the Slaves Made* (New York: Vintage, 1976), 133–137; Peter Kolchin, *American Slavery, 1619–1877* (New York: Hill and Wang, 1993), 63–70; Halliburton, *Red over Black*, 38; quotation from McClinton, ed., *Moravian Springplace Mission*, vol. 1, 227.

48. Carl Mauelshagen and Gerald H. Davis, eds., *Partners in the Lord's Work: The Diary of Two Moravian Missionaries in the Creek Indian Country, 1807–1813* (Atlanta: Georgia State College Press, 1969), 30, 40, 52.

49. Gibson, *The Chickasaws*, 116–125; Littlefield, *The Chickasaw Freedmen*, 7–8; Clara Sue Kidwell, *Choctaws and Missionaries in Mississippi, 1818–1918*

(Norman: University of Oklahoma Press, 1995), 71–72; Barbara Krauthamer, "Blacks on the Borders: African-Americans' Transition from Slavery to Freedom in Texas and the Indian Territory, 1836–1907" (Ph.D. diss., Princeton University, 2000), 185; quotation from Phelps, ed., "Journal of the Reverend Joseph Bullen," 271.

50. Sylvia R. Frey and Betty Wood, *Come Shouting to Zion: African American Protestantism in the American South and British Caribbean to 1830* (Chapel Hill: University of North Carolina Press, 1998); Lee Compere to Thomas McKenney, May 20, 1828, LR, OIA, Creek Agency, 1824–1876, Microcopy 234, reel 221, frame 704–707. On Creek opposition to missionaries, see Duane Champagne, *Social Order and Political Change: Constitutional Governments among the Cherokee, the Choctaw, the Chickasaw, and the Creek* (Stanford, CA: Stanford University Press, 1992), 166.

51. McClinton, ed., *Moravian Springplace Mission*, vol. 2, 204, 259; Kidwell, *Choctaws and Missionaires*, 96; quotation from Mauelshagen and Davis, eds., *Partners in the Lord's Work*, 73.

52. O'Neill to Gálvez, December 11, 1781, PC, legajo 36, reel 183, folio 373, PKY; O'Neill to Josef de Ezpeleta, July 31, 1783, PC, legajo 36, reel 185, folio 1244, PKY; O'Neill to Navarro, August 8, 1783, PC, legajo 614A, reel 211, doc. 88; John Galphin to Enrique White, November 14, 1795, EFP, section 29, reel 43, PKY; Jack Kinnard to James Seagrove, June 5, 1803, "Creek Indian Letters," part 2, 675, GA.

53. Zebulon Pike to David Henley, June 3, 1800, Zebulon M. Pike Papers, APS; Pike to Winthrop Sargent, July 6, 1800, WSP, reel 5, frame 509–510.

54. James Jackson to James Seagrove, May 9, 1793, in *The Papers of James Jackson*, ed. Lilla M. Hawes (Savannah: Georgia Historical Society, 1955), 61; William E. Hulings to James Jackson, Telamon Cuyler Collection, HRB, DLG; Deposition of Nathaniel Howell and Ann Howell, C. Mildred Thompson Collection, HRB, DLG.

55. Bartholomew Shaumburgh to Sargent, January 1, 1800, WSP, reel 5, frame 311.

56. Jennifer M. Spear, "Race Matters in the Colonial South," *Journal of Southern History* 73 (2007): 579–588; Johnson and Roark, *Black Masters*, 45–46; Joel Williamson, *New People: Miscegenation and Mulattoes in the United States* (New York: The Free Press, 1980), 2–24; Ira Berlin, *Slaves without Masters: The Free Negro in the Antebellum South* (New York: Pantheon, 1974), 101–104; Kent Leslie Anderson, *Woman of Color, Daughter of Privilege: Amanda America Dickson, 1846–1893* (Athens: University of Georgia Press, 1995); Joshua D. Rothman, *Notorious in the Neighborhood: Sex and Families across the Color Line in Virginia, 1787–1861* (Chapel Hill: University of North Carolina Press, 2003), quotation on p. 6.

57. Talk by Cherokee women, July 31, 1781, Nathanael Greene Papers, quoted in Cumfer, *Separate Peoples*, 38.

58. Foster, ed., *Collected Works of Benjamin Hawkins*, 39.

59. Mauelshagen and Davis, eds., *Partners in the Lord's Work*, 71–72; Affidavit of Thomas Duffel, July 4, 1835, "Indian Depredations," vol. 4, 289, GA; Declaration of David Randon, May 19, 1798, BHL; Frey and Wood, *Come Shouting to Zion*, 80–117.

60. Theda Perdue, "Clan and Court: Another Look at the Early Cherokee Republic," *American Indian Quarterly* 24 (2000): 562–569.

61. Foster, ed., *Collected Works of Benjamin Hawkins*, 268, 313, quotation on 268; McClinton, ed., *Moravian Springplace Mission*, vol. 1, 393.

62. William Dunbar to Winthrop Sargent, August 30, 1800, WSP, reel 5, frame 570–571.

63. Quotation from Deposition of John Pitchlynn, September 25, 1819, PPP, folder 11, GMA; List of the names and discription of Medlong, a Mulatto woman & her children & grandchildren, September 25, 1819, PPP, folder 15, GMA.

64. Dunbar to Sargent, August 30, 1800, WSP, reel 5, frame 570–571; Dunbar to Sargent, September 11, 1800, WSP, reel 5, frame 590–591; Deposition of Teedoe Brashears, September 1, 1819, PPP, GMA; Certificate of James Allen, October 2, 1817, ibid.; Deposition of James Allen, April 16, 1819, ibid.; Deposition of Silas Dinsmoore, September 25, 1819, ibid.; Deposition of John Pitchlynn, September 25, 1819, ibid.

65. Carson, *Searching for the Bright Path*, 80; B. S. Parson and Thomas J. Abbott to Lewis Cass, September 7, 1832, LR, OIA, Creek Agency, Microcopy 234, reel 223, frame 308, NA.

66. Jane Hill to Thomas McKenney, May 29, 1828, LR, OIA, Creek Agency, Microcopy 234, reel 221, frame 821–825, NA.

67. Case 127, February 1, 1843, J.F.H. Claiborne Papers, ms. #151, box 3, folder 41, SHC; Case 89, January 25, 1843, ibid.; Case 90, January 26, 1843, ibid.; Testimony on Case 90, January 25, 1843, ibid.; Testimony on Case 90, March 27, 1843, Claiborne Papers, box 3, folder 42, SHC.

68. Greg O'Brien, *Choctaws in a Revolutionary Age, 1750–1830* (Lincoln: University of Nebraska Press, 2002), 103; Cyrus Byington, *A Dictionary of the Choctaw Language*, eds. John R. Swanton and Henry S. Halbert (Washington, DC: U.S. Government Printing Office, 1915), 180, 197, 214, 352, 465.

69. Case 90, January 26, 1843, Claiborne Papers, box 3, folder 41, SHC; Testimony on Case 90, March 27, 1843, ibid., folder 42, SHC; Case 127, February 1, 1843, ibid., folder 41, SHC.

70. Case 87, January 25, 1843, Claiborne Papers, box 3, folder 41, SHC.

71. Johnson and Roark, *Black Masters*, 35–36, 45–46; quotation from Constitution of the Cherokee Nation, July 1827, in *Laws of the Cherokee Nation: Adopted by the Council at Various Periods* (Wilmington, DE: Scholarly Resources, 1973), 120.

72. McClinton, ed., *Moravian Springplace Mission*, vol. 1, 29; ibid., vol. 2, 48–49, 62, 143, 397; Krauthamer, "Blacks on the Borders," 200; Celia E. Naylor, *African Cherokees in Indian Territory: From Chattel to Citizens* (Chapel Hill: University of North Carolina Press, 2008), 78–90; Fay A. Yarbrough, *Race and the Cherokee Nation: Sovereignty in the Nineteenth Century* (Philadelphia: University of Pennsylvania Press, 2008), Chapter 6.

73. Testimony of George or Oowanahtekiskee, November 6, 1822, JHPP, reel 2, vol. 7, part 2, 48–49; Testimony of Samuel Dale, October 9, 1822, ibid., 47–48; Declaration of the National Council, November 6, 1822, ibid., 49; Jeremiah Austill, "An Autobiography," *Alabama Historical Quarterly* 6 (1944): 81.

74. R. J. Meigs, Interview with Shoe Boots and Clarinda Ellington, October 19, 1803, LR, OIA, Cherokee Agency, Microcopy 208, roll 2.

75. Tiya Miles, *Ties that Bind: The Story of an Afro-Cherokee Family in Slavery and Freedom* (Berkeley: University of California Press, 2005); Miscellaneous notes, JHPP, reel 1, vol. 2, 31–39, quotation on 35–36.

76. Quotation from John McKee to Winthrop Sargent, March 21, 1801, WSP, reel 5, frame 794–795; John Ridge to Albert Gallatin, Sketch of the Cherokee Nation, February 27, 1826, JHPP, reel 3, vol. 8, 104; McLoughlin, *Cherokee Renascence*, 169, 337; Fred Eggan, "Historical Changes in the Choctaw Kinship System," *American Anthropologist* 39 (1937): 34–52.

77. Champagne, *Social Order and Political Change*, 114–121, 149–154; Gibson, *The Chickasaws*, 137; McLoughlin, *Cherokee Renascence*, 284–285.

78. Champagne, *Social Order and Political Change*, 113, 131, 140, 160, 172; Joel W. Martin, *Sacred Revolt: The Muskogees' Struggle for a New World* (Boston: Beacon Press, 1991), 118–119; Craig, "The Colberts in Chickasaw History," 269; first quotation from Klinck and Talman, eds., *Journal of Major John Norton*, 59; second quotation from John Ridge to Albert Gallatin, February 27, 1826, JHPP, reel 3, vol. 8, 106; third from Cho-chus-micco to Richard M. Johnson, 1828, LR, OIA, Choctaw Agency, Microcopy 234, reel 169, frame 470–471, NA.

79. McLoughlin, *Cherokee Renascence*; Eggan, "Historical Changes in the Choctaw Kinship System," 41–42; Benedict Anderson, *Imagined Communities: Reflections on the Origin and Spread of Nationalism* (London: Verso, 2006), 6–7.

80. On Southern states, see Kolchin, *American Slavery*, 127–129.

81. All Creek quotations from Laws of the Creek Nation, January 7, 1825, Keith Read Collection, HRB, DLG; *Laws of the Cherokee Nation*, 9, 24–25, 37–39, 120–121, quotation from 120; McLoughlin, *Cherokee Renascence*, 340–341.

82. *The Constitution and Laws of the Choctaw Nation* (Park Hill, Cherokee Nation: John Candy, 1840), 11, 12, 19, 20–21, 28, quotation on p. 12.

83. 1832 Census of Creek Indians taken by Parsons and Abbott, OIA, Microcopy T-275, roll 1, frame 112, 194, NA; David W. Baird, *Peter Pitchlynn: Chief of the Choctaws* (Norman: University of Oklahoma Press, 1972), 45–46; Carson, *Searching for the Bright Path*, 80; Littlefield, *Chickasaw Freedmen*, 10; Gibson, *The Chickasaws*, 163; Christine Bolt, *American Indian Policy and American Reform: Case Studies of the Campaign to Assimilate the American Indians* (London: Allen & Unwin, 1987), 152; Klinck and Talman, eds., *Journal of Major John Norton*, 68; John Ridge to Albert Gallatin, February 27, 1826, JHPP, reel 3, vol. 8; McLoughlin, *Cherokee Renascence*, 71, 170; quotation from Joseph Coleman to Samuel Goodwin, December 24, 1809, Cameron Family Papers, ms. #133, Records of Ante-Bellum Southern Plantations from the Revolution through the Civil War, series J, part 1, reel 10. For emerging Indian middle class, see Miles, *Ties that Bind*, 38.

84. Anderson, *Imagined Communities*, 204; Johnston quoted in Wyatt Jeltz, "The Relations of Negroes and Choctaw and Chickasaw Indians," *The Journal of Negro History* 33 (1948): 37.

8. Seminoles and African Americans

1. Brent Richards Weisman, *Unconquered People: Florida's Seminole and Miccosukee Indians* (Gainesville: University Press of Florida, 1999), 14; John R. Swanton, *Early History of the Creek Indians and Their Neighbors* (Gainesville: University Press of Florida, 1998), 398–399; William C. Sturtevant, "Creek into Seminole," in *North American Indians in Historical Perspective*, ed. Eleanor Leacock and Nancy Oestreich Lurie (New York: Random House), 105; quotes from H. Thomas Foster II, ed., *The Collected Works of Benjamin Hawkins, 1796–1810* (Tuscaloosa: University of Alabama Press, 2003), 26s, and George Stiggins, *Creek Indian History: A Historical Narrative of the Genealogy, Traditions, and Downfall of the Ispocoga or Creek Indian Tribe of Indians*, ed. Virginia Pounds Brown (Birmingham, AL: Birmingham Public Library Press, 1989), 46.

2. Patrick Riordan, "Seminole Genesis: Native Americans, African Americans, and Colonists on the Southern Frontier from Prehistory through the Colonial Era" (Ph.D. diss., Florida State University, 1996), 195–198; Gregory A. Waselkov and Kathryn E. Holland Braund, *William Bartram on the Southeastern Indians* (Lincoln: University of Nebraska Press, 1995), 50–53, quotation on p. 51; Weisman, *Unconquered People*, 14.

3. William H. Simmons, *Notices of East Florida, with an account of the Seminole Nation of Indians* (Charleston, SC: A. E. Miller, 1822), 59; Timothy Barnard to the Georgia House, October 17, 1786, "Unpublished Letters of Timothy Barnard," typescript compiled by Louise F. Hays, 66–69, GA; Archibald Clark to William Schley, September 4, 1836, Telamon Cuyler Collection, HRB, DLG; Weisman, *Unconquered People*, 24–27; Kenneth W. Porter, *The Black Seminoles: History of a Freedom-Seeking People*, ed. Alcione M. Amos and Thomas P. Senter (Gainesville: University Press of Florida, 1996), 36; John T. Ellisor, "The Second Creek War: The Unexplored Conflict" (Ph.D. diss, University of Tennessee, 1996), 196–201.

4. Jane Landers, "Gracia Real de Santa Teresa de Mose: A Free Black Town in Spanish Colonial Florida," *American Historical Review* 95 (1990): 9–30; Jane Landers, *Black Society in Spanish Florida* (Urbana: University of Illinois Press, 1999), 3; quotation from James Wright, Answers to queries sent by the Lords of Trade [in] 1761, 1762, James Wright Collection, HRB, DLG.

5. Enrique White to Jared Irwin, April 26, 1797, "Georgia, East Florida, West Florida, and Yazoo Land Sales: 1764–1850," typescript compiled by Louise F. Hays, 104, GA; quotation from Jesse [Josiah] Dupont to Enrique White, January 24, 1802, EFP, section 45, reel 83, doc. 1802–7, PKY; Juan Luis Martineau Florienter to Enrique White, May 9, 1808, EFP, section 44, reel 80, doc. 1808–13, PKY; Benjamin Hawkins to David Mitchell, December 7, 1812, Telamon Cuyler Collection, HRB, DLG.

6. Simmons, *Notices of East Florida*, 75.

7. Quotation from Affidavit of Edward M. Wanton, January 14, 1835, ASP: MA, vol. 6, 461; Dubreuil to Salcedo, September 4, 1803, PC, reel 250, legajo 76, folio 419, PKY.

8. Affidavit of James Hall, June 11, 1818, "Land Sales," 221, GA; Jesup to J. C. Spencer, December 28, 1841, 27th Cong., 2nd sess., H.D. 55, p. 2–3; James Cusick, *The Other War of 1812: The Patriot War and the American Invasion of Spanish East Florida* (Athens: University of Georgia Press, 2003), 49–51; quotation from Bill of Sale, Richard Powers to Kinegee [Kinache], September 20, 1802, PC, legajo 219, folio 599, PKY.

9. *John Milton v. Econchattamicco, District of West Florida*, April 12, 1831, ASP:MA, vol. 6, 467–468; Petition of Econchattamicco, April 2, 1836, ASP: MA, vol. 6, 462; John Casey to Isaac Clark, July 11, 1838, 25th Cong., 3rd sess., H.D. 225, 119–121; "Negroes, &c., Captured from Indians in Florida," 25th Cong. 3rd sess., H.D. No. 225; Affidavit of Edward M. Wanton, January 14, 1835, ASP: MA, vol. 6, 461; Mark F. Boyd and Gerald M. Ponton, ed., "A Topographical Memoir on East and West Florida with Itineraries by Captain Hugh Young," *Florida Historical Quarterly* 13 (1934): 92.

10. Boyd and Ponton, eds., "A Topographical Memoir . . . by Captain Hugh Young," 144; Gaines to Calhoun, December 2, 1817, *ASP:MA*, vol. 1, 687; Edward Brett Randolph Diary, January–May 1818, ms. #619-z, SHC; Thomas S. Woodward, *Woodward's Reminiscences of the Creek, or Muscogee Indians, Contained in Letters to Friends in Georgia and Alabama* (Tuscaloosa: Alabama Book Store and Birmingham Book Exchange, 1939), 45, quotation on p. 54.

11. Testimony of Edmund Doyle and William Hambly, May 2, 1818, *ASP:MA*, vol. 1, 715. For torture allegations, see William Kinnear to John Kinnear, [1812], in "Letters from the Invaders of East Florida," ed. Rembert Patrick, in *Florida Historical Quarterly* 28 (1949): 62; Col. Thomas Smith to Gov. David Mitchell, August 21, 1812, T. Frederick Davis Collection, box 14, PKY; W. B. Armistead to Edwin Wright Morgan, April 9, 1838, Edwin Wright Morgan Collection, ms. # 3035z, SHC; "Life and Times of Mrs. Jane Murray Sheldon Written at her Dictation in 1889," typescript in PKY.

12. William Gibson to David Mitchell, February 26, 1817, "Creek Indian Letters, Talks, and Treaties, 1705–1839," typescript by Louise F. Hays, 885–886, GA; quotation from affidavit of Israel Barber, May 5, 1817, "Indian Depredations, 1787–1825," typescript by Louise F. Hays, vol. 2, part 1, 94, GA.

13. Quotation from Statement of Andrew Jackson, May 29, 1818, *The Debates and Proceedings in the Congress of the United States*, 15th Cong., 2nd sess. (Washington, DC: Gales and Seaton, 1855), 2242; *Narrative of the Tragical Death of Mr. Darius Barber, and His Seven Children* (Boston: David Hazen, 1818); *An Authentic Narrative of the Seminole War; and of the Miraculous Escape of Mrs. Mary Godfrey, and Her Four Female Children* (New York: D. F. Blanchard, 1836). For newspaper accounts of Doyle and Hambly, see, for example, *Alexandria Gazette*, December 22, 1818; *The Centinel of Freedom*, December 22, 1818; *Boston Daily Advertiser*, December 26, 1818.

14. Jesup to J. C. Spencer, December 28, 1841, 27th Cong., 2nd sess., H.D. 55, p. 2–3.

15. Copy of a Talk from the Seminolle Indians, September 3, 1777, quoted in Riordan, "Seminole Genesis," 198; Talk of James Grant to Lower Creek Headmen, September 8, 1769, JGP, reel 2, box 2, folder 2, frame 208, LOC.

16. Petition to Governor White, January 27, 1803, PC, legajo 1555, reel 41, folio 122, PKY; Citizens of St. Augustine to White, July 1, 1802, PC, legajo 1554B, reel 39, folio 67, PKY; Richard Lang to James Jackson, June 26, 1800, "Land Sales," 119, GA; White to Someruelos, May 29, 1802, PC, legajo 1553, reel 37, folio 1274, PKY; Forrester to White, September 16, 1801, EFP, section 29, reel 43, PKY; White to Chief Payne, July 18, 1800, EFP, section 29, reel 43, PKY; J. Leitch Wright, *William Augustus Bowles: Director General of the Creek Nation* (Athens: University of Georgia Press, 1967), 124–125, 140–149; Affidavit of

Antonia Leonardy, March 31, 1835, 25th Cong., 3rd sess., H.D. 225, p. 59;
Georgian quotation from John King to James Jackson, July 12, 1800, "Land
Sales," 127, GA; Second quote from Talk of Efau Hadjo to Benjamin Hawkins,
November 25, 1799, Marie Taylor Greenslade Papers, box 1, PKY, courtesy of
FLHS.

17. Cusick, *The Other War of 1812*; Petition of Zephaniah Kingsley, n.d., Philip
May Collection of Zephaniah Kingsley, folder 4, PKY.

18. Tuskegee Tustunneggee to Benjamin Hawkins, September 20, 1812, LC, group
174, box 11, PKY; Alexander Cornells to Benjamin Hawkins, September 19,
1812, LC, group 174, box 11, PKY; Petition of Zephaniah Kingsley, n.d., Phillip
May Collection of Zephaniah Kingsley, folder 4, PKY.

19. F. S. Fatio to Peter Early, December 11, 1813, "Creek Indian Letters," part 3,
843, GA; Abraham Befsent to David Mitchell, August 15, 1812, "Creek Indian
Letters," part 3, 757, GA; Thomas Smith to Thomas Pickney, July 30, 1812,
Davis Collection, box 14, PKY.

20. Landers, *Black Society in Spanish Florida*, 96–102; Cusick, *The Other War of
1812*, 205; quotation from F. S. Fatio to Peter Early, December 11, 1813, "Creek
Indian Letters," part 3, 843, GA.

21. Tuskgee Tustunneggee to Benjamin Hawkins, September 20, 1812, LC, group
172, box 11, PKY; Kindelán to Manuel Lopez, September 9, 1812, EFP, section
15, reel 27, PKY; Kindelán to Ignacio Salens, October 2, 1812, EFP, section 37,
reel 72, PKY; Smith to Flournoy, February 24, 1813, Davis Collection, box 14,
PKY; Cusick, *The Other War of 1812*, 231–257; quotation from Testimony of
Zephaniah Kingsley, November 1846, Phillip May Collection of Zephaniah
Kingsley, folder 7, PKY.

22. H. S. Halbert and T. H. Ball, *The Creek War of 1813 and 1814*, ed. Frank L.
Owsley Jr. (Tuscaloosa: University of Alabama Press, 1969); Gregory A.
Waselkov, *A Conquering Spirit: Fort Mims and the Redstick War of 1813–1814*
(Tuscaloosa: University of Alabama Press, 2006), 137, 146–147.

23. Waselkov, *A Conquering Spirit*, Appendix 1, 241; Hawkins to John Armstrong,
October 11, 1813, ASP:IA, vol. 1, 852; Weisman, *Unconquered People*, 48;
Nathaniel Millett, "Britain's Occupation of Pensacola and America's Response: An Episode of the War of 1812 in the Southeastern Borderlands,"
Florida Historical Quarterly 84 (2005): 232–233; quotation from Proclamation
of Alexander Cochrane, April 2, 1814, Papers of Vincente Sebastian Pintado,
reel 3, PKY.

24. Talk of Josiah Francis and Peter McQueen to Alexander Cochrane, September
1, 1814, LC, box 21, PKY.

25. Pintado to José de Soto, April 29, 1815, Pintado Papers, reel 3, PKY; Unknown
to John Forbes, November 2, 1814, Heloise H. Cruzat Papers, box 2, PKY,
courtesy of FLHS; A File of Witnesses that may be examined by Commis-

sioners in Pensacola in the suit vs. Woodbine, 1815, Cruzat Papers, box 3, PKY; Millett, "Britain's Occupation of Pensacola," 245, 249–50; quotation from James Innerarity to John Forbes, August 12, 1815, Greenslade Papers, box 2, PKY.

26. Claudio Saunt, A New Order of Things: Power, Property, and the Transformation of the Creek Indians, 1733–1816 (New York: Cambridge University Press, 1998), 273–288; José de Soto to Carlos Reggio, February 20, 1816, Cruzat Papers, box 2, PKY.

27. Saunt, New Order, 288; Coppinger to Bowlegs, September 26, 1816, LC, group 174, box 12, PKY; quotation from Bowlegs to Coppinger, September 10, 1816, EFP, section 29, reel 43, PKY. The previous year Bowlegs had returned some 27 East Florida slaves headed for Prospect Bluff. See Juan Ruiz de Apodaca to Miguel de Lardizábal y Uribe, August 19, 1815, LC, group 174, box 12, PKY. An additional 63 runaway East Florida slaves remained unaccounted for.

28. John Floyd to David Mitchell, April 12, 1816, Telamon Cuyler Collection, HRB, DLG.

29. Jackson to Calhoun, March 27, 1818, ASP:MA, vol. 1, 700; John K. Mahon, "The First Seminole War, November 21, 1817–May 24, 1818," Florida Historical Quarterly 77 (1998): 62–67; John Missall and Mary Lou Missall, The Seminole Wars: America's Longest Indian Conflict (Gainesville: University Press of Florida, 2004), 41–43.

30. John K. Mahon, History of the Second Seminole War, 1835–1842 (Gainesville: University of Florida Press, 1985), 81–83.

31. J. T. Sprague, The Origin, Progress, and Conclusions of the Florida War (Philadelphia: G. S. Appleton, 1848), 87–92; Mahon, Second Seminole War, 101–107.

32. Claim of J. Bulow Jr., 25th Cong., 2nd sess., S.D. 36, p. 2; Affidavit of Francis Pellicer Jr., 25th Cong., 2nd sess., S.D. 36 , p. 9–10; "Life and Times of Mrs. Jane Murray Sheldon," PKY; quotation from St. Augustine Herald, January 13, 1836, reprinted in ASP:MA, vol. 6, 21–22.

33. The Pennsylvanian, March 17, 1836, Goza Historical Newspaper Collection, PKY.

34. Samuel Blair, Marshal of East Florida District, to Asbury Dickins, August 25, 1836, in The Territorial Papers of the United States: The Territory of Florida, ed. Clarence Edwin Carter (Washington, DC: National Archives, 1959), vol. 25, 328–331; Affidavit of John Winslett, December 21, 1838, ASP:MA, vol. 6, p. 453; Winfield Scott to Brig. Gen. Jones, July 6, 1836, ASP:MA, vol. 7, p. 353; Kenneth W. Porter, "John Caesar: Seminole Negro Partisan" The Journal of Negro History 31 (1946): 207; Porter, "Negroes and the Seminole War, 1835–1842," Journal of Southern History 30 (1964): 427–450; Porter, "Florida Slaves and Free Negroes in the Seminole War, 1835–1842," The Journal of Negro History 28 (1943): 390–421.

35. Jesup to Poinsett, June 16, 1837, *ASP:MA*, vol. 7, 876.
36. McCall quotes from George A. McCall, *Letters from the Frontiers: Written during a Thirty Years' Service in the Army of the United States* (Philadelphia: Lippincott, 1868), 160; Dexter quotes from Report of Horatio Dexter to William DuVal, Observations on the Seminole Indians, submitted August 26, ,1823, typescript in Edward T. Keenan Collection, box 3, PKY; James Durouzeaux to Vincente Folch, April 16, 1804, PC, legajo 2372, reel 426, doc. 17, PKY; Jordan Thomas Herron, "The Black Seminole Settlement Pattern, 1813–1842" (M.A. Thesis, University of South Carolina, 1994), 41–42; Wiley Thompson to Lewis Cass, April 27, 1835, *ASP:MA*, vol. 6, 533–534; Testimony of Lieutenant Mitchell, February 2, 1837, *ASP:MA*, vol. 7, 387.
37. Report of Dexter, Keenan Collection, PKY.
38. Simmons, *Notices of East Florida*, 75, 76, 48; Jedidiah Morse, *Report to the Secretary of War of the United States on Indian Affairs* (New Haven, CT: Converse, 1822), appendix, 309; quotation from McCall, *Letters from the Frontiers*, 160.
39. Ira Berlin, *Slaves without Masters: The Free Negro in the Antebellum South* (New York: Pantheon, 1974), 60–65, 92–97, 110, 122; quotation from Wiley Thompson to Lewis Cass, April 27, 1835, *ASP:MA*, vol. 6, 533–534.
40. John Erwin Memoir, 1836, reel 1002, TSLA. Emphasis added.
41. Simmons, *Notices of East Florida*, 44.
42. Report of Dexter, Keenan Collection, PKY; Simmons, *Notices of East Florida*, 76.
43. "Negroes, &c., Captured from Indians in Florida," 25th Cong., 3rd sess., H.D. 225, p. 66–69, 74–80, 83–89, 95–96, 122–123.
44. Simmons, *Notices of East Florida*, 76–77.
45. R. K. Call to Andrew Jackson, March 22, 1835, reprinted in *The Philanthropist*, July 15, 1836, Goza Collection, PKY.
46. Both quotes from Morse, *Report to the Secretary of War*, Appendix, 309.
47. James Covington, *The Seminoles of Florida* (Gainesville: University Press of Florida, 1993), 29; quotes from Report of Dexter, Keenan Collection, PKY.
48. Enrique White to Chief Payne, July 18, 1800, EFP, section 29, reel 43, PKY; Chief Payne to Enrique White, July 29, 1800, EFP, section 29, reel 43, PKY.
49. Jacob Rhett Motte, *Journey into Wilderness: An Army Surgeon's Account of Life in Camp and Field during the Creek and Seminole Wars, 1836–38*, ed. James F. Sunderman (Gainesville: University of Florida Press, 1953), 211; "List of slaves and free negroes," 27th Cong., 2nd sess., H.D. 55, p. 5; "Negroes, &c., Captured from Indians in Florida," 25th Cong., 3rd sess., H.D. 225, p. 77; Deed of Sale, Micanopy to Abraham, April 17, 1841, Records of the Southern Superintendency of Indian Affairs, 1832–1870, Letters Received by the Western Superintendency, Microcopy 640, roll 3, frame 857,

NA; Manumission of Washington by Abraham, September 14, 1841, ibid., frame 858, NA; Kenneth Wiggins Porter, "The Negro Abraham," *Florida Historical Quarterly* 25 (1946): 1–43; quotation from John and Mary Lou Missall, eds., *This Miserable Pride of a Soldier: The Letters and Journals of Col. William S. Foster in the Second Seminole War* (Tampa: University of Tampa Press, 2005), 118.

50. Woodward, *Reminiscences of the Creek*, 41, quotation on p. 108; Simmons, *Notices of East Florida*, 76; James Gadsden to Lewis Cass, July 6, 1833, *Territorial Papers*, vol. 24, 858–861; White to Someruelos, March 13, 1802, PC, legajo 1553, reel 37, folio 1050, PKY; White to Someruelos, May 29, 1802, PC, ibid., folio 1274, PKY; Bowlegs to José Coppinger, September 18, 1816, EFP, section 29, reel 43, PKY; "Trial of Arbuthnot and Ambrister," *Alexandria Gazette*, December 22, 1818.

51. Quotation from Morse, *Report to the Secretary of War*, Appendix, 310; John C. Casey to Major Isaac Clark, July 11, 1838, 25th Cong., 3rd sess., H.D. 225, p. 120; Alcione M. Amos, "The Life of Luis Fatio Pacheco: Last Survivor of Dade's Battle," *Seminole Wars Historic Foundation Pamphlet Series* 1 (2006): 1–6; D. B. McKay, ed., *Pioneer Florida* (Tampa: Southern Publishing, 1959), vol. 2, 481.

52. Acting Governor Westcott to Abraham Bellamy, February 2, 1832, *Territorial Papers*, vol. 24, 669. See also J. A. Peniere to Andrew Jackson, July 15, 1821, in Morse, *Report to the Secretary of War*, Appendix, 311.

53. Letter from anonymous army officer, May 1, 1841, printed in *The Globe*, May 24, 1841, Goza Collection, PKY.

54. Motte, *Journey into Wilderness*, 210. In this case, I assume that Motte's use of "northern" refers to "north of Florida."

55. Joshua R. Giddings, *The Exiles of Florida* (Baltimore, MD: Black Classic Press, 1997).

56. Weisman, *Unconquered People*, 47.

57. Morse, *Report to the Secretary of War*, Appendix 311.

58. George Brooke to Gad Humphreys, May 6, 1828, Keenan Collection, box 4, PKY.

59. Porter, "The Negro Abraham"; Rebecca Bateman, "'We're Still Here': History, Kinship, and Group Identity among the Seminole Freedmen of Oklahoma" (Ph.D. diss., Johns Hopkins University, 1990), 23; Rebecca Bateman, "Naming Patterns in Black Seminole Ethnogenesis," *Ethnohistory* 49 (2002): 243.

60. Morse, *Report to the Secretary of War*, Appendix, 309.

61. "Negroes, &c., Captured from Indians in Florida," 25th Cong., 3rd sess., H.D. 225, p. 66–69, 74–80, 83–89, 95–96, 122–23; John Casey to Isaac Clark, July 11, 1838, 25th Cong., 3rd sess., H.D. 225, 119–121; Enrique White to Damaso Yglesias, August 24, 1808, EFP, section 32, reel 59, PKY.

62. Bateman, "Black Seminole Ethnogenesis," 227–257, quotation from p. 230; Bateman, "History, Kinship, and Group Identity," 254–255; Boyd and Ponton, eds., "A Topographical Memoir. by Captain Hugh Young," 94; Herron, "The Black Seminole Settlement Pattern," 47, 52–72.

63. Reginald Horsman, *Race and Manifest Destiny: The Origins of American Racial Anglo-Saxonism* (Cambridge, MA: Harvard University Press, 1981), especially 116–128; Claudio Saunt, *Black, White, and Indian: Race and the Unmaking of an American Family* (New York: Oxford University Press, 2005), 55–61.

64. Wiley Thompson to Lewis Cass, December 12, 1834, ASP:MA, vol. 6, 520–522; quotation from Simmons, *Notices of East Florida*, 41.

65. Acting Governor Westcott to Abraham Bellamy, February 2, 1832, *Territorial Papers*, vol. 24, 668–670, quotation on p. 668.

66. Superior Court decision, District of West Florida, March 1836, ASP:MA, vol. 6, 469; Grant Foreman, *Indian Removal: The Emigration of the Five Civilized Tribes of Indians* (Norman: University of Oklahoma Press, 1972), 324–325; for quotation, see Archibald Smith to Commissioner of Indian Affairs, February 19, 1837, 25th Cong., 2nd sess., S.D. 393, p. 12.

67. Talk of John Hicks, January 14, 1829, Keenan Collection, box 4, PKY.

68. John Walker to Wiley Thompson, July 28, 1835, ASP:MA, vol. 6, 463.

69. Lord Dunmore to Philatouche, February 5, 1793, EFP, section 29, reel 43, PKY; quotation from Philatouche to Juan Nepomuceno de Quesada, October 22, 1795, EFP, Section 29, reel 43, PKY; Saunt, *New Order of Things*, 131.

70. Testimony of James Hardage, Case of *William Everett vs. Margaret Cook*, Superior Court of East Florida, June 22, 1829, LR, OIA, Microcopy 234, Florida Superintendency, 1824–1853, reel 287, p. 233–234, NA; Testimony of Noah Harrod, ibid., p. 234–235; DuVal to Worth, December 22, 1842, LR, OIA, Florida Superintendency, Microcopy 234, r. 289, p. 346–347, NA.

71. Wiley Thompson to Lewis Cass, December 12, 1834, ASP:MA, vol. 6, 520–522; Testimony of James Hardage, Everett vs. Cook, June 22, 1829, LR, OIA, Florida Superintendency, Microcopy 234, reel 289, p. 233–234, NA; Oren Marsh to William DuVal, May 29, 1829, *Territorial Papers*, vol. 24, 232–234; Talk of John Hicks to Gad Humphreys, August 15, 1828, Keenan Collection, box 4, PKY; quotation from George M. Brooke to Gad Humphreys, May 6, 1828, ibid.

72. R. C. Gatlin to William Worth, January 10, 1843, OIA, LR, Florida Superintendency, Microcopy 234, reel 289, p. 346, NA; George Walker to Archibald Smith, December 22, 1842, ibid., p. 346–48; William Worth to J. S. Brown, December 19, 1842, ibid., p. 348; Case of Matthew Solana, October 19, 1843, LR, OIA, Seminole Agency, 1824–1881, Microcopy 234, reel 806, frame 266–270, NA; Memorial of William Sena Factor to Senate Committee on

Indian Affairs, May 1, 1852, LR, OIA, Microcopy 234, Seminole Agency, reel 801, frame 603–605, NA; Case of William Sena Factor, M. Thompson to Jacob Thompson, December 6, 1858, LR, OIA, Seminole Agency, Microcopy 234, reel 802, frame 472–475, NA; Wiley Thompson to George Walker, November 24, 1834, ASP:MA, vol. 6, p. 463–464; Archibald Smith to C. A. Harris, May 14, 1837, 25th Cong., 2nd sess., S.D. 393, p. 15; George Gibson to Lewis Cass, August 19, 1836, Territorial Papers, vol. 25, 327.

73. Wiley Thompson to Lewis Cass, July 19, 1835, ASP:MA, vol. 6, 460; quotation from Speech of Jumper, Talk of Seminole Chiefs to Humphreys, April 17, 1828, Keenan Collection, box 4, PKY.

74. Endorsement by Andrew Jackson, July 6, 1835, ASP:MA, vol. 6, 478.

75. Chiefs of Coweta to Benjamin Hawkins, September 16, 1813, ASP:IA, vol. 1, 853; Waselkov, A Conquering Spirit, 146–149, 192.

76. Gaines to Calhoun, December 2, 1817, ASP:MA, vol. 1, 687; quotation from Jackson to Calhoun, March 27, 1818, ibid., 700.

77. Edward Brett Randolph Diary, April 1, 1818, SHC.

78. Jackson to Calhoun, April 20, 1818, ASP:MA, vol. 1, 700–701; Felipe Fatio to José Cienfuegos, November 26, 1817, LC, group 174, box 13, PKY; Grant, Indian Removal, 316; J. Leitch Wright, Creeks & Seminoles: The Destruction and Regeneration of the Muscogulge People (Lincoln: University of Nebraska Press, 1986), 198–199, 210; Porter, Black Seminoles, 17; Kevin Mulroy, Freedom on the Border: The Seminole Maroons in Florida, the Indian Territory, Coahuila, and Texas (Lubbock: Texas Tech University Press, 1993); 11; Mahon, History of the Second Seminole War, 20.

79. Alan K. Craig and Christopher S. Peebles, "Captain Young's Sketch Map, 1818," Florida Historical Quarterly 48 (1969): 176–179; John K. Mahon, "The First Seminole War, November 21, 1817-May 24, 1818," Florida Historical Quarterly 77 (1998): 62–67; Missall and Missall, Seminole Wars, 41–43.

80. David B. Mitchell to John C. Calhoun, December 7, 1819, LRSW, OIA, Microcopy 271, frame 1516, NA; quotation from Report of Dexter, Keenan Collection, PKY.

81. Simmons, Notices of East Florida, 41.

82. Kenneth Wiggins Porter, "Notes on Seminole Negroes in the Bahamas," Florida Historical Quarterly 24 (1945): 56–60; John M. Goggin, "An Anthropological Reconnaissance of Andros Island, Bahamas," American Antiquity 5 (1939): 21–26; Report of Dexter, Keenan Collection, PKY.

83. Ellisor, "The Second Creek War," 255–257; [Roll of] Negroes [captured and returned to] citizens in the Indian country [for] reward to the Indian captors, 1837, HRB, DLG; The Broome Republican, February 2, 1837, Mickler Historic Florida Newspaper Collection, PKY; Foreman, Indian Removal, 179, 347; Littlefield, Africans and Seminoles, 17–18, 36–59.

84. Roly McIntosh, Foshutchee Micco, Chilly McIntosh, and K. Lewis to Lewis Cass, June 5, 1834, *ASP:MA*, vol. 6, 471.

85. Frank Laumer, ed., *Amidst a Storm of Bullets: The Diary of Lt. Henry Prince in Florida, 1836–1842* (Tampa: University of Tampa Press, 1998), 59–60.

86. John Bell to Walker K. Armistead, March 12, 1841, *Territorial Papers*, vol. 26, 283.

87. Creek Chiefs to C. A. Harris, May 8, 1838, 25th Cong., 3rd sess., H.D. 225, 91–92; Littlefield, *Africans and Seminoles*, 36–59, 71–74; quotation from W. G. Freeman to Major R. A. Zantzinger, April 7, 1838, 25th Cong., 3rd sess., H.D. 225, p. 27.

88. John Ross to the Chiefs, Headmen, and Warriors of the Seminoles, October 18, 1837, 25th Cong., 2nd sess., H.D. 285, p. 6; Gary E. Moulton, "Cherokees and the Second Seminole War," *Florida Historical Quarterly* 53 (1975): 296–298.

89. Ross to Seminoles, 25th Cong., 2nd sess., H.D. 285, p. 6.

90. Richard Fields et al to John Ross, February 17, 1838, in Grant Foreman, "Report of the Cherokee Deputation into Florida," *Chronicles of Oklahoma* 9 (1931): 431.

91. Ibid., 433, 435.

92. John Ross to Joel Poinsett, March 8, 1838, 25th Cong., 2nd sess., H.D. 285, 15–19.

93. Littlefield, *Africans and Seminoles*, 18–19, 28; Missall and Missall, *Seminole Wars*, xv; Mahon, *Second Seminole War*, 326; Abraham to Jesup, April 25, 1838, quoted in Porter, "The Negro Abraham," 38–39.

94. Mahon, *Second Seminole War*, 206; Motte, *Journey into Wilderness*, 210; W. G. Freeman to C. A. Harris, March 15, 1838, 25th Cong., 3rd sess., H.D. 225, p. 80; J. A. Chamber, Field Order 14, November 8, 1837, 25th Cong., 3rd sess., H.D. 225, p. 5; *Daily National Intelligencer*, October 19, 1841, Goza Collection, PKY; Mahon, *Second Seminole War*, 232, 283. For relations in Indian Territory, see Littlefield, *Africans and Seminoles*, 68–203; Mulroy, *Freedom on the Border*, 33, 61–182; Porter, *The Black Seminoles*, 111–225. For Florida, see Clay MacCauley, *The Seminole Indians of Florida* (Gainesville: University Press of Florida, 2000), xlii, xlvii–xlviii, li, 477, 490, 526; Charles Howe to Gustavious Loomis, March 8, 1858, LR, OIA, Seminole Agency, Microcopy 234, roll 802, frame 399–400, NA; Affidavit of Charles Howe, March 8, 1858, ibid., frame 400.

Conclusion

1. Extract from a letter from Charles Weatherford to authors, October 17, 1890, in H. S. Halbert and T. H. Ball, *The Creek War of 1813 and 1814*, ed. Frank L. Owsley Jr. (Tuscaloosa: University of Alabama Press, 1969), 175–176, quotation on p. 176.

2. Ibid., 176.

3. Gregory A. Waselkov, *A Conquering Spirit: Fort Mims and the Redstick War of 1813–1814* (Tuscaloosa: University of Alabama Press, 2006), 34, 43–47; Benjamin Hawkins to William Panton, June 9, 1798, BHL; Testimony of James Moore, June 1, 1798, ibid.; Declaration of John MacLeod, May 26, 1798, ibid.; James Durouzeaux to Timothy Barnard, January 12, 1789, "Unpublished Letters of Timothy Barnard, 1784–1820," comp. Louise F. Hays, p. 88, GA; Affidavit of Daniel McNeil, December 16, 1802, "Indian Depredations, 1787–1825," comp. Louise F. Hays, vol. 2, part 1, p. 167, GA; first quotation from Hawkins to Price, May 29, 1798, BHL; second and third quotations from H. Thomas Foster II, ed., *The Collected Works of Benjamin Hawkins, 1796–1810* (Tuscaloosa: University of Alabama Press, 2003), 43, 40s.

4. Benjamin W. Griffith Jr., *McIntosh and Weatherford, Creek Indian Leaders* (Tuscaloosa: University of Alabama Press, 1988), 3–4, 77–78, 129–131, 252–254; quotation from Thomas S. Woodward, *Woodward's Reminiscences of the Creek, or Muscogee Indians, Contained in Letters to Friends in Georgia and Alabama* (Tuscaloosa and Birmingham: Alabama Book Store and Birmingham Book Exchange, 1939), 96.

5. Waselkov, *Conquering Spirit*, 175, 206.

6. Weatherford to Halbert and Ball, October 17, 1890, in *Creek War*, 176.

7. J. D. Dreisbach to Lyman Draper, July 1874, DMC, Georgia, Alabama, and South Carolina Papers, 1V62, p. 1–4, 13.

8. Ibid., p. 24; Thomas McAdory Owen and Marie Bankhead Owen, *History of Alabama and Dictionary of Alabama Biography* (Chicago: S. J. Clarke, 1921), vol. 3, 508.

ACKNOWLEDGMENTS

My road to this book began many years ago when I was an undergraduate at the University of Georgia. Before then, I'd been an eager student of Southern history—of Oglethorpe and colonization, of slavery and the Civil War. At Georgia, I learned of an older South, one dominated by Native people. But I also learned that these two Souths were never really separate, that the region was and is diverse and contested. Since then, I've been fascinated by the region's Native history, and, fortunately, I've had extraordinary teachers to guide me. My undergraduate mentors Charles Hudson, David Hally, and Claudio Saunt continue to inspire me.

Along with my family, this book is dedicated to my advisors, Mike Green and Theda Perdue. They have offered encouragement, criticisms, and advice, as well as the occasional bourbon. Mike and Theda are as generous as they are brilliant, and I am grateful to them for all they've done for me and for the field of Native American history. Kathleen DuVal read this manuscript more than once, listened to several conference papers, and offered invaluable advice every step of the way. Thanks also to Harry Watson and Vin Steponaitis, for their guidance in the fields of Southern history and Southeastern archaeology, respectively. This project benefited from conversations with my fellow graduate students at UNC, including Willoughby Anderson, Megan Devlin O'Sullivan, Malinda Maynor Lowery, Rose Stremlau, Tim Williams, and Katy Smith.

I completed this manuscript at the end of a two-year postdoctoral fellowship at the McNeil Center for Early American Studies. Dan Richter's hard work and generous spirit make the McNeil Center the truly extraordinary place that it is. My exchanges with fellows, visiting scholars, and seminar-goers has certainly enhanced the quality of this project, and I thank everyone for their support and encouragement. I am grateful to the many people who offered feedback after I presented the first chapter at a

MCEAS Friday seminar in December 2007. Special thanks to fellows Brian Murphy, Zara Anishanslin, Michele Currie Navakas, Hunt Howell, Adam Jortner, Julie Kim, Robb Haberman, Laura Keenan Spero, Matthew Garrett, and Joanna Cohen. I could not ask for better colleagues or better friends.

My new colleagues at Indiana University have given me a warm welcome, and I appreciate their enthusiasm for this project. Talking with Sarah Knott, Kirsten Sword, and Amrita Chakrabarti Myers has helped me think through issues of slavery and freedom.

As a scholar interested in Native history, early American history, Southern history, and women's history, I've attended a wide range of conferences over the years, and I'm grateful to all those who have offered their comments and suggestions, especially Kathryn H. Braund, Brett Rushforth, Celia Naylor, and Faye Yarborough. Tyler Boulware's research recommendations proved very helpful. John Boles, four anonymous readers, and Wayne Lee offered feedback on an earlier essay on Creek captivity practices. My thanks to the *Journal of Southern History* for allowing me to include portions of that essay in this book.

I am deeply grateful to my editor Joyce Seltzer, who has been an enthusiastic supporter of this book since we met. She challenged me to think about this project in new ways, and our conversations have always energized me. Thanks also to Jeannette Estruth and all the staff at Harvard University Press. Two anonymous readers offered very insightful and stimulating comments on the manuscript, and I thank them for their thoughtful suggestions. Thanks also to Philip Schwartzberg for creating the maps and to Danille Christensen and Gene Navakas for editorial help.

The Barra Foundation, the Andrew W. Mellon Foundation, UNC's Royster Society, the Center for the Study of the American South, the Filson Historical Institute, the Tennessee Historical Society, and the American Philosophical Society have generously supported this project. For their help with research, I thank all the staff at the American Philosophical Society, the Independence National Historical Park Archives, the Gilcrease Museum Archives, the Southern Historical Collection, the Georgia Archives, the Filson Historical Society, the Tennessee State Library and Archives, the Mississippi Department of Archives and History, the South Carolina Department of Archives and History, the South Carolina Historical Society, the St. Augustine Historical Society, and Special Collections at the University of Florida Libraries, and especially Bruce Chappell, Jim Cusick, Laura Clark Brown, Matthew Turi, and Glenn Crothers.

During this project, I have meditated often on the life-sustaining power of kinship, and, in that spirit, I'd like to thank my family. My brothers, Danny and Matthew, have always been great friends and great listeners. My grandparents Nachel and Jeanie Wilkins and my friend Christie Cabe put me up during research trips. My parents, Dan and Janice, have offered me an abundance of love and support over the years, and I owe everything to them.

INDEX

CPSIA information can be obtained
at www.ICGtesting.com
Printed in the USA
BVHW031108040921
615953BV00004B/4

9 780674 064232